WOMEN, PREACHERS, METHODISTS

WOMEN, PREACHERS, METHODISTS

Papers from two conferences held in 2019,
the 350th anniversary of
Susanna Wesley's birth

edited by John Lenton, Clive Murray Norris,
and Linda A. Ryan

Oxford Centre for Methodism and Church History
2020

First published 2020 in the United Kingdom

Oxford Centre for Methodism and Church History, Oxford Brookes University, Harcourt Hill Campus, Oxford, OX2 9AT

admin.ocmch@brookes.ac.uk

British Library Cataloguing in Publication Data

A CIP catalogue record for this book is available from the British Library

Library of Congress Cataloguing in Publication Data
Lenton, John, Norris, Clive Murray & Ryan, Linda
Women, Preachers, Methodists

ISBN 9798489688987 hardback

This book is dedicated to Dorothy Graham, preacher,
pioneer historian of women preachers,
and friend

Contents

Contributors

JILL BARBER is a former Vice President of the Methodist Conference, and Director of the Museum of Primitive Methodism at Englesea Brook. Jill has enjoyed working in libraries, archives and museums for over forty years. Previous roles include Education and Publications Officer at Westminster City Archives, and Head of Heritage Services for Hertfordshire. Jill has recently retired to Aberystwyth, where she studied for her first degree, and gained her PhD, based on research at the National Library of Wales into Sources for Welsh Family and Local History. She has a passion for women's history and has published articles on 'The Sexual Harassment of Female Servants in 19th Century West Wales', and the 'Hidden Histories' of Primitive Methodist women.

DAVID BUNDY is Associate Director of the Manchester Wesley Research Centre and Research Professor of World Christian Studies at New York Theological Seminary. He is a scholar of Holiness and Pentecostal Movements and has also published widely in Early Asian and African Christian Studies. He is the author of *Visions of Apostolic Mission: Scandinavian Pentecostal mission to 1935* (2009).

WILLIAM GIBSON: Professor Gibson is Director of the Oxford Centre for Methodism and Church History and has written widely on religion and society in the eighteenth century. He is a fellow of the Royal Historical Society and of the Society of Antiquaries. His book *Samuel Wesley and the Crisis of Tory Piety, 1685-1720* will be published by Oxford University Press in 2021.

CHRISTINA LE MOIGNAN: After reading Classics at Oxford, Christina spent five years in Nigeria as a postgraduate student/lecturer, and then worked briefly for MIND (then the National Association for Mental Health). She was one of the first women to offer for the Methodist presbyteral ministry when it became open to women, and after training at Wesley House Cambridge was ordained in 1976. She served in the Hunts Mission, Southampton and Gosport and Fareham circuits before moving to Birmingham, where she taught ethics at Queen's (an ecumenical theological training college for Anglican, Methodist and URC students), and then served as Chair of the Birmingham district, during which time she was President of the Methodist Conference (in 2001-2).

JOHN LENTON is the Honorary Librarian of the Wesley Historical Society Library and an active Methodist local preacher. He has written much on Methodist history, notably *John Wesley's Preachers* (2009) with many articles on women preachers where he was the first to upset the view that women preachers mostly gave up in Wesleyanism after 1802.

TIM MACQUIBAN is presently Research Director of the Englesea Brook Chapel and Museum of Primitive Methodism. He was the founder Director of the Wesley and Methodist Studies Centre at Oxford Brookes University and has links to Brookes's partner institutions in Manchester and Cambridge as a historian of eighteenth and nineteenth century Methodist history, worship and spirituality. He has taught in Oxford as well as latterly, before so-called retirement to Chester, in Salisbury, Cambridge and Rome. He is President of the Wesley Historical Society.

JUDITH MAIZEL-LONG comes from Whitwell, Derbyshire. Baptized and confirmed aged twenty-one, and an accepted presbyteral candidate in 1978 at twenty-six, Judith has served in circuits in Yorkshire, Kent, Sussex and Essex, and has contributed to Methodist and ecumenical publications. Judith has also taught mission and pastoral theology and been a staff member of Churches Together in Britain and Ireland. Judith's interests include language, worship, Christian doctrine, and the mission of the church.

CLIVE MURRAY NORRIS researches and writes on early Methodist history, especially its finances and organization. He is presently a Research Fellow at the Oxford Centre for Methodism and Church History, Oxford Brookes University. His *Thomas Wride and Wesley's Methodist Connexion* was published by Routledge earlier this year.

PRISCILLA POPE-LEVISON is Associate Dean for External Programs and Professor of Ministerial Studies at Perkins School of Theology, Southern Methodist University, Dallas, Texas. Her published areas of research—seven books and numerous articles, dictionary entries, and chapters—include women's religious history, Methodist history and theology, contextual theology, missiology, evangelism, and ecumenism. Her most recent historical book, *Building the Old Time Religion: women evangelists in the Progressive Era* (2014) earned the Smith/Wynkoop Book Award from the Wesleyan Theological Society and was listed in *Choice* as an Outstanding Academic Title.

LINDA A. RYAN is a mature researcher with an interest in early Methodism, and more specifically eighteenth-century attitudes to children, education and gender. Her book, *John Wesley and the Education of Children; gender, class and piety*, was published in 2018. Her research locates Wesley's philosophy of education, informed as it was by contemporary notions of social class and gender roles, in the context of revolutionary changes in the understanding of childhood in eighteenth-century England. She has also contributed a chapter to *Teleology and Modernity* (2019), and published articles in *Wesley and Methodist Studies* and the *Journal of Religious History, Literature and Culture*.

COLIN C. SHORT is a supernumerary Methodist minister living in St Austell, Cornwall, who has served as a circuit minister in five circuits from County Durham to Cornwall. Family associations mean his engagement with the Bible Christians goes back over fifty years, and he has published several books and many articles about them. He is Chairman of the Cornish Methodist Historical Association, and in 2019 was made a Bard of the Cornish Gorsedh for his services to Cornwall and proficiency in the Cornish language.

CHARLIE WALLACE, the son and grandson of United Methodist ministers, did postgraduate work with church historian Frank Baker at Duke University, living for two years in Bromley, Kent, while researching his dissertation. After ten years of parish and campus ministry and seminary teaching in Maryland, he became Chaplain at Willamette University in Salem, Oregon, and has been fully retired since 2015. He has published articles on John, Charles, and Susanna Wesley and edited the latter's 'complete writings'.

ERYN WHITE is a Reader in the Department of History and Welsh History at Aberystwyth University. She works on early modern Welsh history in general but has special research interests in various aspects of the Methodist revival in Wales, including the role of women and questions of identity, as well as the relationship with the Welsh language and with education. Her latest work on the history of the early Methodist societies in south west Wales was published by the University of Wales Press in June 2020.

TIM WOOLLEY is superintendent minister of the Hinckley Methodist circuit in Leicestershire. He is a Research Associate of Wesley House, Cambridge, an adjunct lecturer in Wesleyan Theology and Spirituality at Cliff College, and a part-time tutor for Spurgeon's College and for Oxford University Department of Continuing Education. He has published articles in *Wesley and Methodist Studies* and his research interests are in the fields of nineteenth-century British Methodism, revivalism and evangelical nonconformity.

MICHAELA YOUNGSON is a Methodist presbyter and was President of the Methodist Conference in 2018-19. She trained at Queen's College, Birmingham, and has served in circuit ministry as well as at Methodist Church House. She has an MA in Spirituality, and is the author of two books, *Making the Colours Sing* (2005) and *The Weaver, the Word and Wisdom: worshipping the triune God* (2007). Michaela is currently Chair of the London district of the Methodist Church, the only district in the Connexion to have three Chairs—sharing strategic leadership across the diverse, complex and exciting context of London. She is a regular contributor to Radio 4's *Daily Service* and to Radio 2's *Pause for Thought* and, in her spare time, works as an artist, fusing glass to very high temperatures.

Illustrations

Abbreviations

AM	*Arminian Magazine.*
BCMag	*Bible Christian Magazine.*
BCMin	*Bible Christian Minutes.*
BC	Bible Christian.
b.	Born.
Chilcote, 1991	Paul W. Chilcote, *John Wesley and the Women Preachers of Early Methodism* (Metuchen, NJ, 1991).
Clarke, 1823	Adam Clarke, *Memoirs of the Wesley Family collected principally from original documents* (London, 1823).
Clarke, 1832	Adam Clarke, *Memoirs of the Wesley Family collected principally from original documents* (London, 1832).
Digest	*A Digest of the Rules, Regulations and Usages of the Bible Christian Connexion.*
DMBI	John Vickers (ed.), *A Dictionary of Methodism in Britain and Ireland* (Peterborough, 2000).
e.m.	Entered ministry.
Field-Bibb	Jacqueline Field-Bibb, *Women Towards Priesthood: ministerial politics and feminist praxis* (Cambridge, 1991).

Graham, 2010	E. Dorothy Graham, *Chosen by God: a list of the female travelling preachers of early Primitive Methodism* second edition, enlarged (Evesham, 2010).
JRL	Methodist Archives and Research Centre at John Rylands Library, University of Manchester.
JWL	John Telford (ed.), *The Letters of John Wesley* 8 vols (London, 1931).
JWP	John Lenton, *John Wesley's Preachers: a social and statistical analysis of the British and Irish preachers who entered the Methodist itinerancy before 1791* (Milton Keynes, 2009).
KJV	King James Version.
Lloyd	Jennifer M. Lloyd, *Women and the Shaping of British Methodism: persistent preachers 1807-1907* (Manchester, 2009).
LPL	Lambeth Palace Library.
Mack	Phyllis Mack, *Heart Religion in the British Enlightenment: gender and emotion in early Methodism* (Cambridge, 2008).
Mills	Joan Mills, *What are our Thoughts on Women Preachers? The female itinerant preachers of the Bible Christian Church.*

	Access https://dcx0k27cd6yp9.clo udfront.net/wp- content/uploads/2015/04/The- Female-Itinerant-Preachers-of- the-Bible-Christian-Church.pdf.
Minutes	*Minutes of Conference/Minutes of Several Conversations at the . . . yearly conference of the people called Methodists . . .* (London) with date. Wesleyan to 1932. Methodist from 1932.
MNC	Methodist New Connexion.
Ms Journal	*Manuscript Journal of the Bible Christian Conference.*
Palmer, *Four Years*	Phoebe Palmer, *Four Years in the Old World; comprising the travels . . . and evangelistic labours of Dr and Mrs Palmer in England, Ireland, Scotland, and Wales* (New York, 1866).
PM	Primitive Methodist.
PMM	*Primitive Methodist Magazine.*
PWHS	*Proceedings of the Wesley Historical Society.*
Ryan	Linda A. Ryan, *John Wesley and the Education of Children: gender, class and piety* (London, 2018).
Scotland	Nigel Scotland, *Apostles of the Spirit and Fire: American revivalists and Victorian Britain* (Milton Keynes, 2009).

Shaw and Short	Thomas Shaw and Colin C. Short, *Feet of Clay: the life and ministry of William O'Bryan, founder of the Bible Christians* (Porthleven, 2007).
Shorney	David M. Shorney, '"Women may preach but men must govern": Gender Roles in the Growth of the Development of the Bible Christian Denomination' in *Gender and Christian Religion: Studies in Church History 8* (Woodbridge, 1998), pp. 309-22.
Smith	Thornley Smith, *A Christian Mother: memoirs of Mrs Thornley Smith with extracts from her letters* (London, 1885).
Taft Memoirs	Mary Taft, *Memoirs of Mrs Mary Taft formerly Miss Barritt written by herself* pts 1 and 2 (London, 1827), pt 3 (Shebbear, Devon, 1831).
Wallace	Charles Wallace jr (ed.), *Susanna Wesley: the complete writings* (Oxford, 1997).
WHS	Wesley Historical Society.
WJW	Frank Baker (ed.) et al., *The Works of John Wesley: bicentennial edition* (Oxford and Nashville) with volume number.
WM	Wesleyan Methodist.
WMM	*Wesleyan Methodist Magazine.*

WMS	*Wesley and Methodist Studies.*
Z. Taft	Zechariah Taft, *Biographical Studies of the Lives and Ministries of Various Holy Women* 2 vols Leeds, 1825, 1828; reprinted Peterborough, 1992).

Foreword

When I first experienced my call to ministry while a student in university in the late 1970s, I had never seen a woman in the pulpit. As I have contemplated that lacuna over the years, it strikes me as particularly strange given my deep heritage in an ecclesial tradition, Methodism, in which women were robustly active from Susanna Wesley onwards. I was baptized in the sanctuary of a United Methodist church and remained active in that church through my childhood and teenage years. Every summer, our youth group went on a mission trip through the auspices of the Appalachian Service Project, a service ministry founded by a United Methodist minister. In high school, my best friend's father served as the superintendent for the Cincinnati district, where I grew up. I enrolled in a United Methodist university, DePauw University, and attended the college church, Gobin Memorial United Methodist Church. Yet, despite being immersed in so much Methodism over two decades, I had no female role models—none at all.

Since the mid-1990s, I have devoted my research and writing to the recovery of women's religious experiences and activities, scouring archives for women's writings and source material from Cape Breton, Nova Scotia to Seattle, Washington, from the Oxford Centre for Methodism and Church History at Oxford Brookes University to the Diakoniewerk Martha-Maria e.V. in Nuremberg, where German Methodist deaconesses flourished in the late nineteenth century. In the lives and ministries of many of these women, I observe and document their courage, tenacity, and faith in the God who called them to religious work and who sustained them in the face of opposition, ridicule and outright condemnation.

A volume like *Women, Preachers, Methodists,* which undertakes the superlative recovery and interpretative work to bring to life a host of Methodist women engaged in religious work is as

1

needed now in the twenty-first century as it was when women's studies first emerged as an academic discipline in the 1960s. The task remains daunting, yet a multi-authored volume like this one reaches across a broad spectrum of centuries, approaches, topics, and of course, women themselves. Looking back at my own call story, I wish I had known about these Methodist foremothers, pioneers in ministry.

Priscilla Pope-Levison

Introduction

In 2019 the Methodist Church in Great Britain celebrated the 350th anniversary of Susanna Wesley's birth in 1669. Two commemorative conferences were held that year. The first in July, entitled 'The Bright Succession: after Susanna Wesley, gender, heritage and faith' was held under the auspices of the Methodist Heritage Committee at the University of Lincoln. It included a visit to Epworth Old Rectory, where Communion was celebrated in Susanna Wesley's kitchen by the British Methodist President, Barbara Glasson.[1] Many of the papers given at the Lincoln conference, which looked at Susanna herself, her influence on John Wesley and on Methodism in general, appear in the first part of *Women, Preachers, Methodists*. The second conference, called '"An Extraordinary Call": Methodist women preachers in Britain 1740 to the present', was organized in November by the first two editors of this book, with the help of the staff of the Oxford Centre for Methodism and Church History at the Oxford Brookes University campus at Harcourt Hill. Almost all of the papers from this second conference on Methodist women preachers in Britain have been included in the book's second and third parts.[2]

Women, Preachers, Methodists' editors wish to acknowledge the financial and other support which they have received. First, they are grateful to the Susanna Wesley Foundation at Southlands College, University of Roehampton, for providing a

---

[1] The President of the Conference is the minister elected by the Conference to follow John Wesley. He/she presides over it and travels round the Connexion, preaching and speaking for the following year.

[2] Most can also be listened to on the Centre's YouTube channel, https://www.youtube.com/channel/UCplXKBopIZBtsrj02WUSZJw/videos (accessed 8 November 2020).

generous grant which not only supported the November 2019 conference in Oxford but also made this publication possible. Second, the editors express their gratitude for the significant monetary support from the World Methodist Historical Society, headquartered at Drew University, New Jersey and from the (British) Wesley Historical Society. Third, the editors wish to record their warm appreciation of the efforts and achievement of Christine Jones in compiling the list of biblical references and the index, both indispensable tools to scholars and casual readers alike. Finally, they also wish to thank Daniel Reed and the staff of the Oxford Centre for Methodism and Church History for much help, in the first place in hosting the conference, and in the second place in facilitating the production and publication of the book. We hope that the planned new series of publications, of which this is the first, will be as successful as the conference.

It has been said there are many 'Methodisms',[3] and Methodism has since the eighteenth century taken many forms, not all of which reunited with the Deed of Union in 1932. Included are chapters on Calvinistic Methodism in Wales in the early period and aspects of the Holiness movement in Britain in the nineteenth century. One of the most important, though earlier not much written about, has always been the Methodism of women and women's leadership within it.[4] *Women, Preachers, Methodists* is about women in Methodism and their efforts, sometimes successful, sometimes less so, to express their views and play a part in leading worship, despite living in a patriarchal society. In the first part it concentrates on one woman, Susanna Wesley, her struggles with her husband Samuel, and her legacy to Methodism. The second and largest part deals with women preachers in Britain from *c*.1740 to 1932.

---

[3] D. Hempton, *Methodism and Politics in British Society 1750-1850* (London, 1984), p. 11, quoting Raphael Samuel.

[4] D. Hempton, *Methodism: empire of the Spirit* (New Haven, 2005), p. 5; 'Methodism was predominantly a women's movement and needed to be treated as such'.

The final part comprises three reflections by modern women ministers on their call to ministry and preaching. With each part the scope becomes wider, bringing the story of women's leadership in Methodism to the present day.

The importance of gender in Methodist history

Much of the writing about gender has been to see it in terms of oppression and the struggle women have in seeking equality with men. This is to look at history as though our ancestors were living today and should be judged in today's terms. Women were often silenced, interpreted and misinterpreted, and their words usually edited by men. Mary Taft's Ms (manuscript) Journal has notes on it by her husband Zechariah, asking her to add more dates for eventual publication (by him).[5] However, it is too easy to see examples of this and forget that women wanted to have their work approved, improved and edited, because that was the norm in the society in which they lived, and one which they accepted. Nor were masculine/feminine roles necessarily as we might at first think. At the beginning of our period it was Susanna Wesley who was the successful manager of the family, where Samuel was more 'feeling' for the welfare of the poor of his parish.[6] Field, in a key article in 1999, analysed Methodist records to show the importance of women within it at all periods.[7] Where Malmgreen had said that 'the most basic facts about sex ratios in church membership and participation are unknown',[8] Field showed that women were

---

[5] Library of Birmingham, Wolfson Centre for Archival Research, Autobiographical preaching diary of Mary Taft, Ms 977.

[6] J. Gregory, 'Gender and the Clerical Profession 1660-1850' in R. N. Swanson (ed.), *Studies in Church History*, vol 34, (Bury St Edmunds, 1998), 261-2. For Mary Taft see J. Lenton, 'Mary Barritt Taft (1773-1851): A Successful Revivalist?' in *PWHS*, vol 62, no 1, (2019), 15-34.

[7] C. D. Field, 'Adam and Eve: gender in the English Free Church constituency' in *Journal of Ecclesiastical History*, vol 44, no 1, (1993), 63-79.

[8] G. Malmgreen (ed.), *Religion in the Lives of English Women 1760-1930* (London and Bloomington, IN, 1986), p. 2.

always in a majority. And it was not just numbers that made women important. Methodism was sympathetic to women and to what were seen as women's concerns and temperament. The ideas behind Methodism, and the intellectual independence of women like Susanna Wesley or Mary Bosanquet Fletcher, gave Methodist women strength to seek ways of leading, encouraging and opening the way for spiritual growth, similar to those they could see laymen pursuing.[9]

The two sons of Susanna, having watched their mother lead worship within the family home and attract large numbers to join her, were not about to disapprove of women exerting similar leadership roles. Within the Methodist system, as class-leaders, visitors, and prayer leaders, there were many opportunities for women to help in the great enterprise of 'spreading scriptural religion' across the country. Skills learnt were then applied to exhort, to preach and teach. Some became evangelists.

The historiography of women in Methodism has always been mixed. Under Wesley women were able to write and be published, at least in the *Arminian Magazine* which Wesley himself controlled.[10] After his death, in the main Wesleyan Connexion, women preachers were gradually written out. Though most continued to preach, their obituaries never mentioned it. Even the Primitive Methodist (PM) and Bible Christian (BC) movements, with early leaders who actively defended women's preaching and had women itinerants, gradually restricted women's activities and eventually prevented women from becoming itinerants. Towards the end of the nineteenth century this process began to reverse. Women

---

[9] J. Field-Bibb, 'The worst of heresies' in *Modern Churchman*, vol 33, no 4, (1992), 13.

[10] Margaret Jones, '"Her Claim to Public Notice": reflections on the historiography of women in British Methodism' in R. Sykes (ed.), *God's Own Story: some trends in Methodist historiography* (Oxford, 2003), pp. 22-9.

preachers were encouraged once more, especially as semi-professional evangelists in the Wesleyan and some other Methodist churches. Kendall's history encouraged a romantic view of the heroic early PM itinerant women.[11] Church did the same for the Wesleyans in the mid-twentieth century.[12] At the grass roots in rural areas especially, women preachers were always popular and invited to lead evangelical meetings and Sunday School Anniversaries. Perhaps it was partly the curiosity factor noted in several chapters. For missioning new areas women preachers were often placed in the vanguard.

Part 1: Susanna Wesley; 'A bright succession'

This part consists of four very different chapters. The first, by Charles Wallace, the doyen of experts on Susanna Wesley, begins by looking at the importance of the methodology of history with particular reference to Susanna as women's history. He also explains the significance of seeing Susanna Wesley not just as the mother of the Wesley brothers (though she was, as Clarke and Kirk portrayed her),[13] but as an educated woman of her time, the trusted daughter of the celebrated Nonconformist divine who was charged with his literary work. She was also the wife and mother of clergy, the household manager, the educator of children, the thinker (not always logically in her husband's view!), letter-writer and author. Wallace identifies the new developments in Susanna historiography which have happened since he published the collected writings.

The second chapter features William Gibson, the acknowledged expert on Samuel Wesley, writing about several aspects of Susanna's marriage, all linked to politics. Church historians have been known to concentrate on religion and miss the way

---

[11] H. B. Kendall, *The Origin and History of the Primitive Methodist Church* 2 vols (London, 1905). See chapter eleven in this volume.

[12] L. F. Church, *More about the Early Methodist People* (London, 1949).

[13] *Clarke, 1823*; J. Kirk, *The Mother of the Wesleys: a biography* (London, 1866).

7

politics and religion interact. Gibson skilfully explains the importance of political events in influencing how the marriage between Susanna and Samuel developed. He shows the importance of why the marriage happened when it did. He explains its breakdown in 1702-3, making it clear that Samuel was not in London for Convocation, as earlier historians had surmised. He looks also at the political complexities of the prayer meeting Susanna held in the Rectory and the question of her 'Presbyterian' baptism. Finally, he examines the well-known stories of the ghost ('Old Jeffrey') and links all these together to the legitimacy of religious authority and its political importance in this period. The marriage is examined from Samuel's point of view.

Next Linda Ryan discusses concepts of childhood and gender in the long eighteenth century. With particular regard to the thinking of John Locke, Ryan examines attitudes towards female education during this period. As well as examining Susanna's education system at Epworth, Ryan discusses her influence through John on the education of girls and young women. Ryan argues that although her practice was striking for its time, it still conformed to the gender constraints of the period. While Susanna believed it important that her daughters should be heard and understood and given an education equal to their brothers at home, this was not without its problems. Ryan points out that Susanna's educational model was not as austere as some earlier authors have suggested. She then explains Susanna's legacy through her influence on her son John and his thinking on girls' education and how that worked out in practice.

Like the third chapter, the fourth deals with Susanna's legacy for those of her gender. John Lenton takes up John Walsh's passage about John Wesley's use of the idea of the extraordinary call, justifying the use of laymen. The well-known story of Susanna in later life in London and Thomas Maxfield is examined in detail. He then looks at the legacy for the whole cadre of Methodist itinerant preachers. The same principle is then applied to the correspondence between John Wesley and Mary Bosanquet which justified lay women preaching as well as laymen, as 'extraordinary' as Methodism itself. This links with the second part of the book.

Part 2: Methodist women preachers; 'An extraordinary call'

This second part is the largest, representing the number of papers given at the 'Extraordinary Call' conference. There were more papers on the nineteenth century than any other period, partly reflecting recent scholarship and the questions around women preachers in Methodism. In the eighteenth century Chilcote's book still holds the field.[14] Little has been added apart from work on Sarah Perrin. In the nineteenth century though Lloyd's book summarises much of the scholarship and has many insights, yet the research presented here shows that there are many issues raised by her which can profitably be revisited.[15] For the twentieth century we wait for more scholars to venture into the period. Field-Bibb, one of the earliest, remains one of the best, but much has happened since she wrote both to add and to change views.[16]

There is little specifically on Scotland, but the first chapter of this part features Methodism in Wales, since it was in Wales that the British evangelical revival began, and the earliest Methodist woman who can be claimed to be a preacher was the Calvinistic Methodist Elizabeth Thomas in a remote village in Ceredigion. Eryn White paints the setting for her in chapter five, showing how the definition of exhorters was different in Welsh society. She explains the difficulties for women in conservative Wales, looks at Jane Owens who also preached and why, and the part played by Welsh women in the religious revival, particularly through hymn-writing. White shows how Calvinistic Methodist

---

[14] *Chilcote, 1991.*

[15] *Lloyd.* See particularly notes in chapter eight of this volume.

[16] *Field-Bibb.*

women preachers partly because they were very few have been overlooked by earlier historians.

Chapters five and six deal with early Methodist women preachers. In the latter John Lenton looks at their call and their calling, what they did as preachers. The process of becoming preachers is examined. In each case the absence of male preachers meant women being pressed, often unwillingly, into service by the waiting congregation who would not allow them to leave until they had spoken. Lenton identifies three types of these women preachers in the period up to 1820, including local preachers on the preaching plans of the circuit.[17] The fact of their continuance after the official ban by the Wesleyan Conference in 1803 is emphasized.

John Wesley's longevity and patronage of women preachers meant the Wesleyan Conference did not codify its opposition to women preachers until 1803. This long protected period allowed women preachers to maintain their preaching in practice to beyond 1820. In contrast the founders of the Primitive Methodists and Bible Christians who encouraged women to preach and enter the itinerant ministry, Hugh Bourne and William O'Bryan, lost power in their connexions relatively early, 1842 in Bourne's case,[18] and 1829 for O'Bryan.[19] Women itinerant preachers within these two denominations had less time to flourish. We move to the Primitive Methodists in chapter seven. Tim Macquiban finds new evidence in the reports from the early itinerant women preachers, showing how they were used for the missionary work. The evidence allows the women to speak their own words rather than those of their male colleagues or later historians. Their role was missionary and evangelistic, telling of their own conversion and encouraging

---

[17] Circuits are sub-regional groupings of local Methodist congregations, which in turn form part of districts. See *DMBI* for a fuller definition.
[18] See S. Calder, *The Origins of Primitive Methodism* (Woodbridge, 2016), pp. 101-5.
[19] See pp. 103-4 below.

their hearers to embark on the same road. Their careers as itinerants were typically brief. In this, as in the next chapter, there is clear evidence of women itinerants standing up for their rights despite the official record attempting to hide such disagreements.

Chapter eight deals with the Bible Christians. Using largely their own documents, including the Ms BC Conference Journal, Colin Short shows they were similar in many ways to the Primitive Methodists. Both had women itinerants, but in each women had different status from the men. Short suggests their status should be seen as equivocal; for example women BC ministers did not baptize. Short shows how many modern commentators have missed the point that defence of women's preaching (both Primitive Methodists and Bible Christians) differs from defence of women as itinerants (Bible Christians only). Bible Christians also differed from the Primitive Methodists in having what Short calls a 'final cohort' of women candidates in the 1890s, including at least one woman coming from outside the church who entered their ministry. Their time was brief, however, with the last one being forced out by the church's formation with others of the United Methodist Church in 1907.[20]

The holiness movement and evangelists, a recurring theme for women preachers in Methodism throughout this period, are discussed in the next two chapters. First, David Bundy rescues from oblivion a fascinating and virtually unknown figure, a Wesleyan minister's wife who became a holiness preacher. He argues that it was within the burgeoning radical holiness networks after 1870 that Catherine Smith found her voice, and that the networks were important for supporting her transition

---

[20] Lillie Edwards continued her service as pastor in the same circuit till she chose to retire. The events of 1907 could be taken as a warning of the dangers of ecumenism for women of the 1950s and 60s who were kept from being able to candidate for the ministry by the prospect of Anglican-Methodist Union; see *Field-Bibb*, pp. 49-67.

into various forms of public ministry. Catherine Smith moved from more 'separate spheres' to less 'separate spheres'.[21] Bundy argues that she was preaching to women only and this was doubtless true much of the time, but there were also instances when the official Wesleyan rules were breached (her husband heard her, for example) and though she had misgivings, she continued to speak. Second, Tim Woolley considers the British visit of Phoebe Palmer, a much better-known woman preacher. Palmer was a mass communicator who is representative of several other female American evangelists who visited Britain in this period, including the little-known black preacher Zilpha Elaw (*c.*1790-1873).[22] Woolley links Palmer to the emergence of another great woman preacher, Catherine Booth. He also looks at the complex relations of nineteenth-century Methodism with revivalism, how Palmer presented the idea of sanctification, assessing her legacy. Woolley also emphasizes how role models were significant for Palmer; both Mary Bosanquet Fletcher and Mary Taft appear in Palmer's writings. Madeley was a point of pilgrimage for her.

Completing this part of the book Jill Barber looks at the extinction of female itinerant ministry in the PM Connexion and identifies many different causes. Johnson noted an interesting similar decline in the actual numbers of Quaker female ministers, from the early 1800s when two-thirds of Quaker ministers were female to two-fifths by the early 1900s.[23] The editors have encouraged more writing on the Primitive Methodists and the Bible Christians because they were the Methodists who included women in their itinerant ministry,

---

[21] See A. Vickery, 'Golden Age to Separate Spheres? A Review of the Categories and Chronology of English women's history' in *The Historical Journal*, vol 36, no 2, (1993), 383-414.

[22] *Scotland*, chapters three, six and nine.

[23] D. A. Johnson, 'Gender and the Construction of Models of Christian Activity: A Case Study in Church History' in *Studies in Christianity and Culture*, vol 73, no 3, (2004), 247-72.

and yet it was there that the worst loss of women's earlier gains occurred. Barber shows how men decided what the women's position should be. She links the process to Darwin's 'survival of the fittest' hypothesis and discusses similar changes happening elsewhere in Methodism. Barber points out lessons for modern Methodists today, such as the need to encourage leaders from all groups, including all ethnicities, which are represented within the Church.

Part 3: Women Methodist ministers reflect

The final part is composed of three personal accounts of how women ministers have answered their call and then been received by the Methodist Church in the late twentieth century. Two (Christina Le Moignan and Michaela Youngson) were elected President of the Conference. Two (Le Moignan and Judith Maizel-Long) were among the earliest entrants to the ministry, at a time where there were few other women ministers. The first of these chapters by Christina Le Moignan suggests that most women ministers were accepted by most of the Church, that the rarity of women ministers gave her at least advantages and that Methodists are (and were) a kindly and accepting community.

The second and rather longer chapter by Judith Maizel-Long suggests that male domination and patriarchy remained and that women were in some situations discriminated against. She describes her call from a Jewish background, the influences upon her which led her to candidate for the ministry, and what happened next. This paper was offered to the 'Extraordinary Call' conference but was reluctantly side-lined by the organizers due to time constraints. However, they were delighted to be able to add it to the final part of this volume, as a feminist and enriching contribution. The final chapter by Michaela Youngson, both inspiring and witty, takes the view that discrimination should be fought, but that the future and mission of the Church is what is important and that has to include all women and all others previously excluded in leadership roles.

She makes the interesting point that when opinion in Conference and other church gatherings changed, then the 'laughter changed sides'. As with some other chapters she includes some poetry and ends with Charles Wesley. All three link their call and ministry back to the Wesleys and specifically to Susanna and John Wesley.

Inevitably there are major topics of women's ministry in Methodism not covered in this volume. The professionalization of women evangelists and the rise of deaconesses in the late nineteenth century in most of the British Methodist churches are not discussed. The Wesley Deaconess Order's progress in the twentieth century has been covered by Dorothy Graham.[24] Women local preachers are hardly mentioned after the early period.[25] The existence of women of many different races in Methodism, symbolised recently by the election of the first black woman minister as President, is almost completely overlooked.[26] However, by signalling these gaps, the editors hope to encourage future research on such areas. We hope you will find a feast within the pages following—or perhaps more precisely, 'an antepast of heaven'.[27]

---

[24] E. D. Graham, *Saved to Serve: the story of the Wesley Deaconess Order 1880-1978* (Peterborough, 2002); E. D. Graham, 'The Wesley Deaconess Order 1890-1978':
https://www.primitivemethodistwomen.org/the-wesley-deaconess-order/ (accessed 2 September 2020).

[25] The records of the Local Preachers Mutual Aid Association could be studied to examine their changing attitudes, exemplified by women being elected as national officials.

[26] Sonia Hicks, e.m. 1986, was designated as President for the 2021 Conference. Chapter ten below quoting *Scotland* shows that Zilpha Elaw, previously thought of as an American woman evangelist who preached in Britain among other places, married and settled down in British Methodism, being reported more than twenty years later as a class leader in an East End circuit.

[27] Hymn 454, verse 2 in Methodist Church of Great Britain, *Singing the Faith* (London, 2011).

1: Susanna Wesley: history, her story and our heritage

Charles Wallace

My chapter's title is a somewhat awkward attempt to pay respect to three sub-communities of interest that converge in our celebration of Susanna Wesley in the 350th year of her birth. I wanted to use the occasion to weave together history, the testimony of a particular woman, and the Christian/Wesleyan tradition, all three of which contribute to what we might call 'Susanna Studies', investigating the woman herself as well as the 'bright succession' that follows in her train. Thus, I do not wish to present a radically revisionist, hot-off-the-press analysis of Susanna Wesley, though I will allude to some new documentary discoveries and gratefully acknowledge the new findings and perspectives which my co-contributors have brought to the conversation.

So my primary aim is to contextualize our 'Susanna 350' discussion by reflecting on the collaborative enterprise of history, on her story (emphasizing its gendered elements), and on that special freighted version of history we call tradition or (in the British Methodist Church's designation) heritage.

Even in a post-modern world an aspiring church historian needs to join a pre-modern guild. On our side of the water, the mysteries of that profession are guarded and dispensed by the American Society of Church History. It meets annually, usually in the same major city that also welcomes the American Historical Association (and various other smaller-focused satellite societies). At one of my first such gatherings after completing postgraduate study, I do not remember any of the papers or presentations, or even the food and drink of the unofficial afterhours sessions. Instead, what stuck with me was the inscription on a little button that one of the publisher's tables was dispensing to anyone who would take it. It read: 'Want to make history? Become an historian'!

There is a message here for our consideration of Susanna Wesley and the tradition which in many ways formed her life and issues from it down to the present day: that message in one word is *agency*. Historians are trained (and duly initiated) as *agents* (maybe in a country that loves murder mysteries, we should say *detective* agents!). It is not some vague spirit called 'history' that mindlessly records the past sometime in the future, but a flesh-and-blood historian, a whole flock of them, actually, who actively ferret out details and make sense of a past era or some slice of it — in the language (and the cultural context) of their own time.

As the popular American historian Jill Lepore tells her students at Harvard, 'To write history is to make an argument by telling a story about dead people'. And according to one of her reviewers, making that argument involves actively employing 'conceptual imagination, persuasive logic, deep research, and compelling evidence'.[1] *Making* history in this sense is an art and a craft, as well as a sort of forensic science, and it must be energetically, thoughtfully and collegially practised with all the awareness one can muster.

---

[1] Lepore's engaging assignment for her new undergraduates is 'How to write a paper for this class' and her second sentence is a point well taken by all historians, young and otherwise: 'You'll be dead one day, too, so please play fair, and remember: never condescend. It's probably bad enough being dead without some smart aleck using your life and times to make a specious claim'. It is available at: https://scholar.harvard.edu/files/jlepore/files/lepore_how_to_write_a _paper_2009_0_1.pdf (accessed 2 September 2020). The historian Robert Westbrook's comments on her work are in a book review of 8 April 2019 in *The Christian Century*, vol 24, (2019), 23, https://www.christiancentury.org/review/books/jill-lepore-s-book-civics-course-americans-need (accessed 2 October 2020).

The historians among us can all come up with favourite examples who model Lepore's class-room description. Among Methodist historian-detective agents, I would nominate two from this part of the world to whom I personally owe debts. The first, brought up in Hull in the old East Riding of Yorkshire, was my dissertation supervisor Frank Baker, who was already well-ensconced at Duke University and the Wesley Works Project by the time I began studies there in 1968. Not only did he support my unwieldy attempts at quantitative social history (I wrote a ponderous dissertation that attempted to count and classify Methodists and Dissenters in the West Riding), but he inspired me back into documentary history with a magisterial paper on Susanna Wesley he delivered in 1980 just as the second wave of feminism was cresting. The occasion was a huge denominational conference in Cincinnati called 'Women in New Worlds: Historical perspectives on the Wesleyan tradition'. It was a great harvest of then recent work on women's history, and it inspired more work (for instance Paul Chilcote's *John Wesley and the Women Preachers of Early Methodism*),[2] as well as my own attempt to let Susanna speak in her own voice so that others might discover (and argue over) her influence. I always secretly regarded my publication of *Susanna Wesley: the complete writings*[3] as a kind of 'prequel' to the thirty-odd volumes of *The Works of John Wesley*. But few of us can match Baker's dogged search for evidence and accuracy, both in writing history and establishing and editing a text.

My second example grew up in Boston (Lincolnshire, not Massachusetts). Before I could even begin my project, Frank Baker suggested I immerse myself in *Susanna Wesley and the Puritan Tradition in Methodism* and interview its author, John

---

[2] *Chilcote, 1991.*

[3] (New York, 1997). This 502-page Oxford University Press edition continues to sell, albeit in small numbers, to this day.

Newton.[4] He graciously welcomed me to his office for over an hour one afternoon at the West London Methodist Mission and provided me with leads about where to find her letters and papers, and how to gain access to them. I could not have pulled Susanna's writings together without his whole-hearted support and encouragement. His commitment to social holiness and ecumenism actively reinforced his careful historical scholarship and his churchmanship, and continues to inspire us.[5]

One more feature of practising historians: their 'social location' determines what subjects they might be drawn to, and how they will engage them. As grateful as I am to these two departed Methodist historians, they and I, and most of the history profession, are still male. In the US, only about twenty percent of history doctoral degrees went to women when I was in graduate school; by 2014 they had doubled to forty percent, but it still feels like *men* are 'making' more history than women. Here I was in the 1980s, a male scholar trained by one male historian and 'resourced' by another, trying to represent a person who was surely one of church history's eminent women. Yes, over the years Susanna has had her female biographers, notably Eliza Clarke, Mabel Brailsford, and Rebecca Lamar Harmon.[6] Let me also acknowledge one other woman scholar of my own generation, Elizabeth Hart, who grew up in the British

---

[4] J. A. Newton, *Susanna Wesley and the Puritan Tradition in Methodism* (London, 1968). It was a delight to have John's wife Rachel as an active participant at the conference at Lincoln.

[5] It confirms my nod in the direction of these two 'historical' figures that John Lenton's chapter four in this volume also leans on Baker and Newton. Lenton finds them in important agreement with his own careful scholarship that Susanna inspired her son John to support Thomas Maxfield as a bona fide preacher. Near the first, if not *the* first, of Wesley's lay preachers, Maxfield turns out to be one of the most important members of Susanna's 'bright succession'.

[6] E. Clarke, *Susanna Wesley* (London, 1886); M. R. Brailsford, *Susanna Wesley: the Mother of Methodism* (London, 1938); R. Lamar Harmon, *Susanna: mother of the Wesleys* (Nashville, 1968).

Methodist Church, head librarian at Vancouver School of Theology. Before her untimely death, she was working on Susanna Wesley, briefly collaborating with me, and starting to investigate the Susanna portraiture that Peter Forsaith has brought to fruition in his work.[7]

In any case, since this occasion, too, seems to feature several male historians, I am happy a woman President of the Conference (Barbara Glasson) and two other participants (Judith Rossall and Linda Ryan) played key roles in our conference offering us analysis and a balanced gender perspective. Women's history is indeed everyone's history, and the social location of female historians obviously contributes to an enriched understanding of the subject in front of us (and many others).

Her story

Thus we turn to 'her story'—not just a bad pun for women's history, but an indication that the particulars of Susanna Wesley's life, work, and heritage deserve continuing analysis and still profit from a gender studies perspective. Long before Baker and Newton took up the task, earlier editors, biographers, and historians had recorded the basic details from her own writings (and from oral traditions, some more reliable than others).

Her life: daughter of a notable London Dissenter, well-educated enough to read and argue her way into the Church of England while not yet thirteen; her marriage to another convert from

---

[7] 'Susanna Annesley Wesley—An able divine' in *Touchstone* (1988), 4-12; 'Susanna Wesley and her Editors' in *PWHS*, vol 48, no 6, (1992), 202-9, and vol 49, no 1, (1993), 1-10; 'A Tinge of the Ideal: Trans-Atlantic interpretation in portraits of Susanna Wesley' in N. Semple (ed.), *Canadian Methodist Historical Society Papers* vol 8, (1991, for 1988 and 1990), 137-57. P. Forsaith, 'The Curious Incident of Susanna Wesley's Rosebud Lips' in N. Virgoe (ed.), *Angels and Impudent Women: women in Methodism—papers given at the 2005 Conference of the Wesley Historical Society* (Loughborough, 2007), pp. 31-51.

Dissent, who became a priest and an aspiring poet; their long sojourn in two Lincolnshire parishes (two and a half, counting Wroot) in which ten children grew to adulthood and eight or nine others died either in infancy or early childhood.

Her work: bearing those children (and bearing *with* that husband), raising and teaching those who survived, running a rectory; tending her own spiritual and intellectual life (and ministry!) in the midst of it all; advising and teaching growing daughters and advising her sons (usually by letter) in their own theological, pastoral and evangelistic work—sometimes critiquing it, but by the end of her days wholeheartedly supporting it.

However, we have learned more as new sources have come to light since the middle of the twentieth century, and as others have been noticed (even though already present in archives), and still others have been more effectively mined.[8] Not surprisingly, many of the Susanna Wesley materials that have surfaced outside of the usual collections do not lend themselves to hagiography. I will mention just two instances.

First, the discovery and publication of her letters to Dean George Hickes (styled as 'Bishop of Thetford' by the Non-jurors) and Lady Henrietta Yarbrough, a resident of Snaith, close to Epworth, gives further evidence of difficulties in Susanna and Samuel's marriage. Moreover, this incident begs comparison with the other example of marital and ecclesiastical tensions evident a decade later, when Susanna was accused by her husband of irregular worship in the Rectory during his absence in London. Bill Gibson has recently connected the two incidents, linking them with his further discovery that Samuel

---

[8] A notable example of such effective mining has been Linda Ryan's recent work on educating children in early Methodism. Her book (originally an Oxford Brookes doctoral thesis) is *John Wesley and the Education of Children: gender, class and piety* (London, 2018), and her contribution to our conference, chapter three in this volume, focuses on female education, Susanna Wesley and her familial legacy.

called out her irregular 'Presbyterian' baptism in episcopal visitation returns. While this might have been a shot at the more liberal Bishop Wake of Lincoln, it might also have been a dig at his wife, who by this calculation was not quite the conservative churchwoman she claimed to be. Add this story to other hints in her letters and diaries, and we need to admit that Susanna's situation was not always a happy one.[9]

Second, another Susanna letter, this one not included in *The Complete Writings*, has turned up in a book of transcribed Wesley family writings at the John Rylands Library. It is unclear who copied it out in 1864, but it is dated 2 August 1725, addressed to John Wesley and details Susanna's anxiety and exasperation with her high-spirited daughter Hetty, whose love interest, an attorney named Green, asked for her hand, but was refused by her father. Nevertheless, Green, three associates, and a man in black that the family assumed was a clergyman, swooped down unannounced, took Hetty off from Wroot and kept her out all night. No one knew whether Green had married or would marry her, but the closing sentences from Susanna's brief letter to John indicate that things would not end well:

> We should be easy to part with her, being quite tired out with her very licentious and scandalous adventures of which we fear the worst, though if she should be kept as a miss[tress?], it will be no great surprise. I need not tell you that this is an

---

[9] See 'Susanna Wesley's Political Marriage,' Gibson's stimulating chapter two in this volume, which details the *continuing* difficulties of her relationship to Samuel, using previously unexploited archival material such as a fuller set of the Hickes correspondence, which recently surfaced in Lambeth Palace. The earlier version of the documents is R. Walmsley, 'John Wesley's Parents: Quarrel and Reconciliation' in *PWHS*, vol 29, no 3, (1953-4), 50-7. Information on Susanna's non-episcopal baptism is also in Gibson's recent article '"None but Presbyterian Baptism": Samuel and Susanna Wesley, monarchy and marriage' in *PWHS*, vol 61, no 5, (2018), 179-86.

adventure that ought to be mentioned to no one till we be certain whether she be wife or not.

She did not marry Green, but she became pregnant, and quickly married at her father's order the first 'suitable' suitor he could find, a local plumber and glazier named Wright. And *that* did not turn out well. This newly found letter, though, does support what the novelist Arthur Quiller-Couch understood in his 1903 novel *Hetty Wesley*, namely that neither Samuel nor Susanna handled the situation well.[10] That, of course, is easy for him/us to say, but it is another humanizing illustration of the Wesley family, Susanna in particular, and another incident that foregrounds early eighteenth-century gender issues.

There are already several letters in the John Rylands which show Susanna taking issue with her sons at about the time of their evangelical conversions. In addition, though, Joseph Priestley, Unitarian minister and discoverer of oxygen, was provided with a trove of such correspondence by his disciple, Samuel Badcock, who had been given them by Samuel Wesley jr's family in Tiverton. Priestley published them, including one from Susanna, in 1791, but they were already circulating a decade and a half earlier, and Randy Maddox at Duke has found this 'new' one in the *St James's Chronicle* for 21-4 September 1776. I hope to give it a proper editing later, but here is a sample. It is dated 12 January 1738/39 and in it Susanna is making common cause with her *eldest* son Samuel in trying to restrain what she felt at the time were her *youngest* son Charles's emotional excesses:

> These 'Brethren in the Faith' (as they call their Society) put a
> Fallacy on themselves, and allow nothing to be true Faith but

---

[10] A. Quiller-Couch, *Hetty Wesley* (New York and London, 1903). See E. Knights, 'A 'Licensuous' Daughter: Mehetabel Wesley, 1697-1750' in *Women's Writing: the Elizabethan to Victorian period*, vol 4, no 1, (1997), 15-39. Knights places Hetty Wesley in her literary context and publishes the 'new' letter as an example of the pressures on the family regarding her spirited behaviour. See JRL, DD Wes 8/21.

Assurance of their Salvation, which in Reality is no Faith at all. I intend to write to Charles once more on this subject, and then leave off (for I am too old for Controversy). If you will give me Leave I will transmit my Letter to you first, and if you approve of it let it be sent immediately from Tiverton; and if I should err in any Thing be so kind as to set me right. I shall gladly stand corrected by you. I abhor that leading Question among them, viz. 'What [do] they feel?' — What can open a wider Door to Enthusiasm than such a Question?

Obviously, such family conversation reinforced anti-Wesleyan prejudices, even four decades later after Methodism's fervour had settled somewhat. Perhaps its publication at the time of the American Revolution was a way of critiquing Wesley's case against the colonies. Joseph Priestley certainly used similar letters that way in his published collection in 1791. And there is no reason to assume that either he or Badcock is forging a Susanna letter. The point here, however, is not to debunk early Methodism, so much as it is to account for the perspective then and there of the founders' mother. It turns out, she underestimated herself in her assertion that she was 'too old for controversy'; nor could she foresee a time when she might still become a champion of her sons' movement.

However, Frank Baker (who else?) worked out that the year just prior to her death she had authored an unattributed pamphlet (which John saw through publication) arguing against George Whitefield, of all people. As is often usual, an eighteenth-century pamphlet title just about says it all: *Some Remarks on a Letter from the Reverend Mr. Whitefield to the Reverend Mr. Wesley, in a Letter from a Gentlewoman to her Friend.*[11] She has taken on the evangelical revival's rock star in an early skirmish of the Calvinist-Arminian conflict. Too bad her one actual publication is anonymous, but this 'gentlewoman' had done her theological

---

[11] London [n.p.], 1741. For an annotated version of the letter see *Wallace*, pp. 462-84.

homework, reviewed the controversy and pointedly and effectively represented her son's side.

These newer discoveries, I believe, support my *agency* argument. Historians make history, but so, too, in the popular sense, do the actors that historians study. In a patriarchal era, young Susanna Annesley so thoroughly learned the lessons of Nonconformity (the importance of God and a 'conscience void of offence toward God and toward man') that she dissented against her father's Dissent, actively resisted her husband for conscience's sake on at least two notable occasions; critically addressed her sons' revival; and finally supported them against the era's most famous preacher. All that Methodist scholars have discovered (and historians of women as well) in the last half century complicates, augments, calls for reassessment of what we have always known about this remarkable active woman. My hope as Susanna's editor and abettor is that these sorts of debate will continue.

We have touched on 'history' and 'her story'. What about my final category?

Our heritage

I need to admit that 'Methodist heritage' has a homey, friendly feel to it, much more so than our equivalent office in the United Methodist Church in the States, 'The General Commission on Archives and History,' which has more of a bureaucratic ring to it, even though the folks in Madison, New Jersey, are *almost* as sprightly and user-friendly in their publications and outreach.[12] *Heritage* is a legacy, an inheritance, something that is passed on as part of one's birthright. It is tradition. But *tradition* sounds more useful in light of my earlier mantra about making history, which is *agency*, because it involves actively receiving it from past generations, actively using it and recasting it in our own

---

[12] Methodist Heritage is the part of the British Methodist Church which organized the 'Bright Succession' conference at which this paper was first given.

lives and times, and actively passing it on to subsequent generations. This is what conferences like 'A Bright Succession: after Susanna Wesley . . .' and 'An Extraordinary Call . . .' invite us to do, whether we are professionals (in such roles as historian, biographer, social critic, theologian, editor) or interested lay-people who identify as insiders of the Methodist heritage. Let me offer general reflections on the practice of tradition from two still-important American religious scholars of the past: H. Richard Niebuhr and Jaroslav Pelikan.[13]

Consider first this insight from Niebuhr's classic *The Meaning of Revelation*. In it he takes *history* seriously, but simultaneously gives *heritage* or *tradition* a special place as a legitimate kind of history. In a section entitled 'History as lived and seen' he begins to develop exactly what that distinction might be by quoting two sources describing America's origin as an independent nation. One version of 'history as contemplated from the outside' he takes from the then current *Cambridge Modern History*, which abstractly describes the beginnings of the American nation in 1776. In this version the focus is on Congress passing a resolution 'which made the colonies independent communities'. It then analyses the Declaration of Independence as a political document, concluding 'The doctrine of the equality of men, unless it be qualified and conditioned by reference to special circumstance, is either a barren truism or a delusion'.[14]

---

[13] Both were intellectual giants during my seminary training at Yale Divinity School. Niebuhr, who had died three years before I arrived, still dominated conversation in the areas of history, sociology, ethics and theology. Of his many writings, his most famous is the classic *Christ and Culture* (New York, 1951), still in print. Pelikan, who had just joined the faculty, became the pre-eminent historian of doctrine of the twentieth century, eclipsing even Adolf von Harnack's three-volume *History of Dogma* with his own five-volume *The Christian Tradition: a history of the development of doctrine* (Chicago, 1971-91).
[14] *The Meaning of Revelation* (New York, 1941; pb. 1960), pp. 44-5. I have reversed the order of Niebuhr's two literary examples for effect.

Contrast that with the familiar words of Lincoln's Gettysburg Address, which re-presents the same occasion in terms of 'our history' or 'history as lived': 'Four-score and seven years ago our fathers brought forth upon this continent a new nation, conceived in liberty and dedicated to the proposition that all men are created free and equal.' Both accounts are true (or at least can be justified by the 'facts'), both are critical (in one sense), but one is a specially meaningful history that speaks to Americans of 'our' foreparents and of what has formed us and what we still aspire to (particularly in the context of a Civil War that tested the nation's principles and threatened its existence). Niebuhr regards the *Cambridge Modern History* account as 'outer history,' seen from a distance, a critical history of things. Lincoln's brief oration he views as 'inner history,' a lived identity, a critical history of persons, detailing what they are and ought to be about. This latter view gives us a clue to heritage and tradition.

My second authority is the late Jaroslav Pelikan, whose 1983 Jefferson Lectures at the Library of Congress were entitled *The Vindication of Tradition*. The final lecture 'Tradition as Heritage' is particularly helpful for our purposes, especially his memorable opening sentence: 'Tradition is the living faith of the dead, traditionalism is the dead faith of the living'.[15] He further notes that 'tradition*ism*' is probably what gives *tradition* a bad name. It is easy to understand why reformers protest against the tyranny of the past and yearn for revolutionary new insight and creativity. The traditionalism in which letter obscures spirit will not provide a useable past to a contemporary community. Neither will creativity and new insight come to us by the sloughing off of tradition. Rather, Pelikan argues that tradition rightly done (a community in dialogue with the living faith of the dead) is precisely where we will find insight and creativity. From Pelikan's point of view that is not just telling a story or

---

[15] J. Pelikan, *The Vindication of Tradition* (New Haven, 1986), p. 65.

making an argument *about* dead people (as Jill Lepore puts it) but including some of them in our conversation!

And that also calls on our *agency*. Tradition is not *our* heritage until we receive it and work out how to believe and practise it (to make it!) in and for our own era, and then hand it on. As Bishop Elaine Stanofsky said during last year's session of our Oregon-Idaho Conference (just a month before our Susanna celebration and in the midst of all the brokenness in the US version of the Wesleyan tradition), 'We make tradition by the practice of our faith.'

Let me conclude by suggesting some illustrative examples of our practice in and around the 'Susanna Wesley 350 Methodist Heritage Conference 2019'.

Before I was even called in to pick and introduce passages from Susanna's pen in a small gift anthology (and subsequently invited to address the conference), some faithful British Methodists were already 'practising tradition'. You took *note* of the Susanna 350th anniversary and took *authority* not just to recount her life and witness, but also to set it in the context of an ongoing tradition, 'A Bright Succession', in fact . . . in which strands of gender, heritage and faith, which began long before Susanna and which she enriched in her life and handed on, continue to the present day.

Prayer and liturgy is part of tradition. For instance, Jenny Carpenter, Vice Chair of Trustees at Epworth Old Rectory, wrote a wonderful saint's-day-style collect focusing on Susanna. It was used in choral evensong at Lincoln Cathedral, the evening our conference began! Another developing tradition relating to Susanna is the exciting pedagogy Siggy Parratt-Halbert is discovering and perfecting in her artistic work in Sheffield. Her engaging cartoons will be one of the strong visual memories of our conference. And what a wonderful practice of tradition took place at the Old Rectory at Epworth on a beautiful Saturday afternoon, when the Conference President, Barbara Glasson, celebrated Eucharist in the back garden and all came forward to partake of it in Susanna's kitchen—the very place where she was bold enough to lead worship in the winter of 1712 during her husband's absence (and without his permission).

And, then, there is creative use of sacred text. The Church's representatives and I were also practising tradition around the creation of that aforementioned 'gift book' of Susanna's spirituality.[16] From the Methodist Church's point of view, it needed to be a 'devotional', about a hundred pages long and broken up into short selections (short selections being the only way to keep Susanna brief!) It should include a number of her prayers. And maybe it could *exclude* words that might contribute to any stereotype we are not happy about in the twenty-first century . . . such as a child should 'fear the rod and cry softly'! These are all *active choices* that denominational heritage folk might appropriately make, and they will to a certain extent constitute the heritage, at least as regards Susanna Wesley, that gets handed on.

And, of course, the same was true of my editorial activity. What is in the 'canon'? That involves my 'social location' and 'world view' as a retired university chaplain and Methodist historian who has some warm-hearted and neo-orthodox tendencies, but also ones that drink deeply of critical scholarship, social gospel and liberation theology. What sort of choices did *I* make? First, I suggested sections that would emphasize what I believe to be underrated sides of her work.

An opening section sought her own reflections on 'Turning Points' in her life, indicating that her spirituality was honed not *just* in a prayer closet, but in the midst of important crises, opportunities and perplexities. Her faith was a 'lived religion' as we soon learn, getting her view on her marriage, her

---

[16] C. Wallace, *From a Mother's Pen: selections from the spiritual writing of Susanna Wesley* (London, 2019).

theological politics, her children, her financial difficulties, her illnesses, her widowhood.

The two sections that follow indicate one of my major discoveries in collecting all of her writings together: the breadth and intensity of her intellectual life and the way it overlapped with her spirituality. In the 'lifelong learning' section I selected a range of her ruminations on the work of the 'public intellectuals' of her age, many of whom also influenced her son John (no doubt in part from her conversations with him) and appeared in his *Christian Library*. Who knew she read Pascal's *Pensées* (in English translation), George Herbert's poetry, and one of the main sources of Wesleyan Christian perfection, Richard Lucas? Baker and Newton did, but I thought others deserved to know, as well. In reading, commenting on and recommending such work, after all, *she* too was practising tradition.

And a special part of that practice is highlighted in the third section, celebrating her role as teacher, not only of reading, writing, and religion to her youngest children, but the ongoing tutorials she supplied her family as they grew older (particularly the daughters who would not otherwise continue their education the way her sons were privileged to do). Thus 'lifelong teaching' covers some of the same territory as the previous chapter, but with a special focus on what she felt the young women in her family needed to know. Among other Susanna gems, this section includes my nomination of her best slogan, good instruction for both teachers and learners: 'Reverence yourself and do nothing unworthy the reason God has given you'. Her specific writings on the Creed, the Ten Commandments and her 'Religious Conference' all reveal considerable sophistication and wide reading; that last composition even includes sophisticated examples of then-current scientific knowledge. Here is a practical theologian at work in a teaching ministry, perhaps anticipating the later popular publishing work that John Wesley would employ.

The final section, 'Prayerful Wisdom', permitted me to mine some of the best bits from her spiritual diaries. Though hard to date and otherwise place in context, these entries do offer insight into her soul: what she has been reading or otherwise wrestling with. A good example is her struggle to overcome self-doubts about her ability actually to educate her children. In it, she 'writes through' her uncertainties, finally convincing herself to carry on with her project. Another covers three modes she frequently returns to: nurturing her children, her regular discipline of meditation, and her vow to practise moderate drinking. One entry even records her rather boldly taking a vow in imitation of the *patriarch* Jacob: basically, if God will give you food and other necessaries of life, 'then the Lord should be your God'. Another dwells on the advice 'Love God and love your neighbour' which she sees as helpful for any Christian over-sensitive about what her or his duty should be.

To sum up, 'my' and maybe 'our' Susanna, the one we might want to hand on to a new generation, is a strong woman, much edgier than the sweet caricature of mother-cum-primary-teacher. She is a capable woman, finding in *her* tradition of belief and practice a strong calling to journey actively and successfully through changes in the ecclesiastical landscape; to take authority in resisting patriarchy; and always to read, write, think, pray and connect with God and those around her. There is much to learn in our dialogue with her, whether we are women trying to follow a call to ministry in the midst of a busy family life, or people trying to find a balance between an active and a contemplative life; or anyone needing to be liberated from forces that seek to hold us down.

Finally, some questions to ponder: what sort of arguments do we historians and/or bearers of tradition make in our conversation with a woman long-dead, but in many ways very much with us? What has her story contributed to history and heritage, and thus to *our* understanding and our *very identity* here and now and in the days ahead? What of her story do we wish to fashion and hand on?[17]

---

[17] One of my greatest academic satisfactions has been watching others use my editorial work in *The Complete Writings* to make new arguments in their dialogue with Susanna. Evangelical home schoolers in the US have expressed gratitude (though I am sometimes nervous that they may be reading Susanna from a rather 'originalist' perspective). A theologically-literate psychiatrist, Pauline Watson, has not only looked at Susanna's influence on her sons, but actually quoted her in her recent book's title '*Two Scrubby Travellers':* *a psychoanalytic view of flourishing and constraint in religion through the lives of John and Charles Wesley* (Abingdon, 2018). There are all sorts of 'agents' (historians and practitioners of tradition) who are asking new questions about and dialoguing with Susanna. May they continue to discover and express new truths from the past and create new resources for facing the future!

2: Susanna Wesley's Political Marriage

William Gibson

The anniversary of the birth of Susanna Wesley in 2019 focused on her role in the story of Methodism; but it perhaps did so at the expense of her husband, Samuel. In many ways, Samuel and Susanna were well-matched. Both were children of Protestant Dissenting families who conformed to the Church of England. Both were convinced Tories and High Church in their principles. And, arguably, both were stubborn and unbending in their religious views. This paper takes some episodes in their marriage to explore its character. The first of these suggests that Susanna and Samuel Wesley's marriage was, like many at the time, essentially a political as well as a religious one. Legitimacy in marriage could only be conferred by a lawful ruler. The second episode examines the breakdown of the Wesleys' marriage in 1702-3, during which Samuel left Susanna. The third episode is the best known, the occasions when Susanna held prayer meetings in the rectory at Epworth; the fourth is the matter of Susanna's baptism, which became an issue in 1712. And finally, there is consideration of 'Old Jeffrey' the Epworth rectory ghost. In all cases the contemporary issue of the legitimacy of religious authority was to the fore. The episodes, taken together, demonstrate that Susanna and Samuel's marriage was deeply political.

Samuel and Susanna Wesley married on 12 November 1688, at St Mary-le-Bow Church, London; Samuel was twenty-six, and Susanna was nineteen. Over a decade earlier, in *Maggotts*, the collection of poems he published as an Oxford undergraduate, Samuel Wesley had referred to marriage as a 'noose', so he was not at that stage entirely convinced of its benefits. When they married, Samuel was without permanent employment; he was only a deacon and not yet a priest in the Church of England. The decision to marry at such a stage of life when he was without clear financial prospects, or a place to live, was unusual. The customary motives for a hasty marriage did not apply. It is clear that their first child was not on its way, and it was not that Susanna wanted to escape her parents' home since Samuel and Susanna lived with the Annesleys in the first years of their marriage. So why did they marry in November 1688?

On 5 November 1688, William of Orange landed at Torbay. His planned invasion had been widely expected since the spring. Word reached London by 8 November that William had landed, and it was assumed that the Church, aristocracy and people would favour William and the Protestant cause. Whether Samuel and Susanna knew, or expected, that William had a good chance of toppling James is unclear. They might have anticipated a protracted civil war. However, their marriage four days later on 12 November 1688, at a climactic moment of James's reign, might not be coincidental. It seems possible that Susanna and Samuel wanted to be married under the legitimacy of James, or at least before the possibility of any military conflict between William of Orange and James II. Samuel's commitment to James II was profound: he had contributed a poem to the official University of Oxford's volume of verse celebrating the birth of the King's son, James Edward in June 1688.[1] Susanna, as will be seen, never accepted the lawfulness of the overthrow of James II (Susanna went to her grave believing that James and his descendants were the rightful kings, and denying the validity of the kingship of William III, George I and George II). So a desire to be married under a rightful king, or before a period of political upheaval, probably determined the marriage date. As will be seen, the issue of the legitimacy of the Protestant succession dogged their marriage.

The Wesleys' marriage was famously fertile. By 1715, they had eleven sons, of whom only three survived to adulthood, and

---

[1] W. Gibson, '*Strenæ Natalitiæ*: Ambivalence and Equivocation in Oxford in 1688' in *History of Universities*, vol 31, no 1, (2018).

seven daughters surviving.[2] So Susanna had nineteen pregnancies, and possibly more. The only hint of tension early in their marriage is in an entry in the *Athenian Mercury* in 1697, in which Wesley wrote a regular column dealing with religious questions. When asked by a correspondent, whether a man should marry 'a woman of good temper but no religion; or a woman who was religious but ill-tempered', his response was the former, because 'if they [women] bridle not their tongue, all religion is in vain.'[3]

In 1702, the couple experienced a serious split. It may have been prompted by the death of James II, the exiled Stuart king, in September 1701.[4] The account of the split has hitherto been dependent on Robert Walmsley's discovery in 1953 of some correspondence between Susanna Wesley and the Rev. George Hickes in Hickes's letterbook. Hickes had been dean of Worcester but had refused the oaths to William and Mary and had been ejected as a Non-juror.[5] But Walmsley did not quote all the letters; Hickes's letters have now been located at Lambeth Palace and can be cited in full.[6]

---

[2] Christ Church, Oxford, Wake Letters 5, no 233, 20 November 1715.

[3] G. D. McEwen, *The Oracle of the Coffee House: John Dunton's Athenian Mercury* (San Marino, CA, 1972), pp. 149-50.

[4] This is the opinion of G. Hammond, *John Wesley in America: restoring primitive Christianity* (Oxford, 2014), p. 16.

[5] Non-jurors claimed to be the continuing Church of England and regarded the vast majority of Anglican clergy who had accepted William and Mary to be schismatic. J. H. Overton, *The Nonjurors, their Lives, Principles and Writings*, (London, 1902); R. D. Cornwall, *Visible and Apostolic: the constitution of the Church in High Church Anglican and non-juror thought* (Delaware, 1993).

[6] Walmsley, 'John Wesley's Parents'. The Hickes letters are in LPL, Ms 3171. The transcriber of the letters clearly got some of the letters in the wrong order, one marginal note says 'this was ye occasion of the Dean's letter and should have come before it' Ms 3171, f. 240. Moreover there is some confusion arising from the transcription since in some places Susanna refers to Hickes as his 'lordship' — since

In March 1702, Samuel noticed that Susanna did not say 'Amen' at the end of prayers for the King, William III. Despite his earlier attachment to James, Samuel Wesley had accepted the legitimacy of the Revolution of 1688 and sworn the oaths to William and Mary as the new King and Queen. Samuel asked to see Susanna privately and enquired why she did not pray for the King. When she told him that she did not regard William III as the rightful king, Samuel 'Immediately kneeled down and imprecated the Divine Vengeance upon himself and all his posterity if ever he touched me more or come into a bed with me before I had begged God's pardon and his, for not saying Amen to the prayer for the King.'[7]

That night, Samuel acted on his oath and refused to share a bed with Susanna. She told Samuel that his refusal to sleep with her was wrong. What troubled Susanna in general was that the episode demonstrated that men had more power over their bodies than women; and that Samuel had a freedom of conscience that he did not permit to her.[8] In some respects this was disingenuous, Susanna <u>had</u> told Samuel that his oath was unlawful and unreasonable, so she had the freedom to comment on his actions. Susanna's principal concern was religious, she was terrified that her soul was in peril, she wrote "'tis a fearful thing to fall into the hands of the living God or to trifle with Divine Vengeance'.[9] But in anger at her, Samuel left Epworth and went to London.

Samuel's departure from Epworth, which John Wesley later claimed was for a whole year, has been represented by Methodist historians as a departure to enable him to attend Convocation, rather than as a consequence of his breach with

---

in 1694 he had been consecrated as the Non-juring Bishop of Thetford—but the transcriber refers to him as dean.

[7] *Wallace*, p. 35.

[8] Ibid., p. 35.

[9] LPL, Ms 3171, f. 239.

Susanna.[10] The historian George Stevenson hinted that the records were incomplete, but claimed that Wesley was in Convocation.[11] In 1823 Adam Clarke noted that he had heard directly from John Wesley 'that his father was Convocation man that year.'[12] In 1886, Luke Tyerman, Samuel Wesley's biographer, seems to have accepted the accounts of Clarke and Stevenson.[13] But Tyerman was a precise historian, and recognized that there was a problem with the historical record. Tyerman wrote 'It is impossible to say what part Samuel Wesley took in these convocation debates; and, in the absence of information, the reader is left to guess.'[14]

In fact, it is now clear from Gerald Bray's work on the history of Convocation, that Samuel Wesley was not elected to Convocation in 1701, or 1705. He was only elected to Convocation in 1710 and did not stand for election again in 1714.[15] Confirmation that Samuel was not in London at Convocation came from Susanna herself, who wrote that Samuel was in London 'where he designs to try if he can [to] get

---

[10] Stevenson commented: 'The question of Mr. Wesley's attending Convocation in the year 1701, and twice afterwards, is one of considerable importance for two reasons: first, his three attendances cost him £150, money which he could ill spare, seeing it was all required for the expenses of his family; secondly, he has been by some writers much blamed for accepting such an appointment at all, and thus absenting himself from home and parish.' G. J. Stevenson, *Memorials of the Wesley Family: including biographical and historical sketches of all the members of the family for two hundred and fifty years* (London, 1876), p. 72.

[11] Ibid., pp. 82-3.

[12] *Clarke, 1823*, p. 95.

[13] L. Tyerman, *The Life and Times of the Rev. Samuel Wesley MA, Rector of Epworth and Father of the Revs John and Charles Wesley* (London, 1866), pp. 249-50.

[14] Ibid., p. 258.

[15] G. Bray (ed.), *Records of Convocation vol 9 (1701-8), vol 10 (1710-13), vol 11 (1714-60), Canterbury* (Woodbridge, 2006).

a chaplain's place in a man of war.'[16] Clearly Samuel could not be both attending Convocation and seeking a post as a naval chaplain. The sanitised version was to give an acceptable reason for Samuel's departure other than his breach with Susanna.

Samuel tried to keep the quarrel private, but was not entirely successful. His brother-in-law, John Dunton, with whom Samuel had fallen out, had just survived his own scandal—in which he was thought to be womanizing too soon after his wife's death. When this happened, Dunton wrote cryptically: 'Sam Wesley . . . may find enough in his own life to damp his censuring of me.'[17]

The unexpected death of William III on 8 March 1702 brought Queen Anne to the throne. Anne could claim a direct descent from James II. Therefore the issue of Samuel's prior oath to James would have lapsed and Queen Anne as his daughter could be regarded as Queen by hereditary descent. This had the potential to ease the tensions between Samuel and Susanna, but it did not.

In March 1702, Susanna wrote, 'we are not likely to live happily together.' Nevertheless, Samuel sent money to Epworth for her maintenance as she had six small children to care for. In an attempt to resolve their differences over the oath, Susanna wrote to her friend and neighbour Lady Yarborough that:

> I've offered since I last wrote . . . to put this business to a reference, provided I might choose one referee and my Master another, but I fancy he'll never agree to it. He is fearful of my communicating it to any person which makes me somewhat more confin'd than usually.[18]

A month later, Susanna began writing to George Hickes. Susanna presented her case to Hickes, stating: 'My Master will

---

[16] *Wallace*, p. 37.
[17] J. Dunton, *The life and errors of John Dunton, late citizen of London . . .* (London, 1705), pp. 408-9.
[18] LPL, Ms 3171, f. 239.

not be persuaded he has no power over the conscience of his wife . . .' She went on that Samuel 'will do anything rather than live with a person that is a declared enemy of his country, which he believes himself obliged to love before all in the world.' But Susanna said she could not ask a pardon for something which she did not believe was a sin; and in response Samuel had charged her with pride and obstinacy.[19]

Hickes's response is of considerable interest. Although Susanna thought of herself as a Non-juror, the fact that she continued to receive Communion in the Church of England indicated to Hickes that she was not. Hickes even referred to her as such, mentioning that she might refer the issue to 'any able divines of your Communion.'[20] Hickes was also careful to separate the issue of Susanna's failure to say 'amen' at prayers for the King from that of Samuel's oath not to live with her. Of her refusal to say 'Amen', he wrote, it was an 'Error of yours in which the Faith is not concerned, . . . an error, in which (if it be an error) as learned and pious men as any are of ye Communion of the Church of England have been and still are deceiv'd as well as yourself . . .'[21]

---

[19] LPL, Ms 3171, f. 249. Susanna added 'My Master is in London'.

[20] LPL, Ms 3171, f. 240; the emphasis is mine.

[21] LPL, Ms 3171, f. 240. Later on in the letter, Hickes also wrote: 'To say Amen to an unrighteous prayer is to blaspheme the God of righteousness & in the most solemn manner to curse the wronged person against whom that unrighteous prayer is put up; and therefore to ask God or him pardon for not ratifying such a prayer, or a prayer which you believe to be such, with your own mouth would be to act against the sacred nature of truth and justice, to mock and affront the God of truth & justice and to bely and prostitute your own conscience in a most shameful manner, which is not only the noblest faculty that belongs to your soul but God's vicegerent therein. Wherefore good Madam, stick to God and your conscience which are your best friends whatever you may suffer for adhering to them. This is your critical time of trial; God calls you to take up the cross & do not decline it & he that calls you to it will enable you to

Of Samuel's oath, Hickes said it was an 'unjust oath contrary to his conjugal duty, and so much to your injury for an erroneous opinion & practice . . .'.[22] Hickes suggested writing to Bishop James Gardiner of Lincoln, Samuel's diocesan bishop and a former rector of Epworth, and if that failed at least Susanna would have the comfort that she had used 'unfeigned endeavours in having used all means for his conversion & reconciliation to you.'[23] Nevertheless, Hickes pointed out to Susanna: 'Husbands & fathers and masters may be tyrants as well as kings and princes & persecute their domestick subjects for truth and righteousness sake & when that happens the persecuted wife and children & servants are truly Xian confessors.'[24] In other words, for Hickes, the duty of a woman in an unhappy marriage was to endure it and hope for redemption as Christian martyrs did.

Samuel returned to Epworth from London intent on ensuring that Susanna submitted to him and 'implicitly obey him in all matters of conscience'. She refused, even though she 'foresaw many great evils would inevitably befall me if I refused to satisfy his desires.'[25] Consequently, Samuel again left her, refusing to allow the Archbishop of York or Bishop of Lincoln to act as arbitrators. Susanna related that Samuel had met an unnamed clergyman soon after to whom he told his marital woes. His advice was that Susanna was to be condemned but Samuel should nevertheless return to her, which he did. In July 1702 the rectory in Epworth was burnt in a fire and two thirds of it were destroyed. Susanna referred to the accident as 'the finger of God' and concluded 'May heaven avert all evil from

---

bear it & give you comfort in bearing of it, till he shall some way or other lawfully discharge you from it. He will be an husband to you if your husband cast you off; he can raise up your friends to help you whom you do not yet know.'
22 LPL, Ms 3171, f. 240.
23 LPL, Ms 3171, f. 240.
24 LPL, Ms 3171, f. 240.
25 LPL, Ms 3171, f. 240.

my children and grant that the heavy curse my Master has wished upon himself and his family may terminate in this life.'[26] Walmsley's comment on this crisis was that the fire 'brought Samuel to his senses' and that he returned to the house. In fact, Samuel had returned before the fire. The assumption in many biographies of Susanna and Samuel Wesley is that their breach was healed in 1702, since, as Charles Wallace put it, 'the fruits of their reconciliation arrived on June 17 1703, a baby boy christened John.'[27] Certainly Samuel's comment to Susanna at the start of their dispute, 'you and I must part: for if we have two kings we must have two beds', seemed to have been resolved.[28]

Susanna's views of marriage were at stark variance with orthodox Tory views of the institution. One writer, whose views of marriage George Hickes strongly endorsed, was Mary Astell. She made a direct analogy between the authority of kings, and that of a man over his wife. A woman, Astell claimed, 'elects a monarch for life' in the form of a husband 'and gives him authority which she cannot recall however he might misapply it . . . , the will of the sovereign is all in all.' Husbands were 'absolute sovereigns' over their wives.[29] There is no doubt that Hickes, as a firm Tory and Non-juror, believed in non-resistance in the state and by analogy in the household also.[30]

---

[26] LPL, Ms 3171, f. 241.

[27] *Wallace*, p. 13.

[28] Ibid., p. 13.

[29] M. Astell, *Some Reflections upon Marriage* (London, 1700), p. 115.

[30] Evidence of Hickes's views on passive obedience and non-resistance are abundant; see for example, G. M. Yould, 'The origins and transformation of the Non-juror schism, 1670-1715: illustrated by special reference to the career, writings and activities of Dr. George Hickes, 1642-1715', University of Hull, PhD thesis, 1979; W. Gibson, *The Church of England 1688-1832: unity and accord* (London, 2001), p. 36; W. B. Gardner, 'George Hickes and the Origins of the Bangorian Controversy' in *Studies in Philology*, vol 39, no 1, (1942), 65-78.

John Kent's print 'The Happy Marriage and the Unhappy Marriage' of about 1690 graphically depicted the political character of authority in marriage. The 'unhappy marriage' print was one in which a wife usurped her husband's role— including wearing his wig and snatching his keys and the devil sat on their yoke with fighting cocks by their side. In contrast, the 'happy marriage' was marked by a compliant wife and 'the pleasures of a marriage bed.'[31] This print seemed to capture exactly the issue at stake in the Wesleys' marriage.

John Kent, 'The Happy Marriage and the Unhappy Marriage' 1690.
British Museum print no 1906,0823.4

It seems likely that Susanna submitted to Samuel, they certainly resumed the physical side of their relationship since they were to have a number of other children, including Charles. But Susanna did not abandon her political opinions. In 1709 she wrote:

---

[31] This image is discussed in more detail in M. Knights's *Devil in Disguise: deception, delusion, and fanaticism in the early English Enlightenment* (Oxford, 2011), pp. 117-19.

> Whether they [the British people] did well in driving a Prince from his hereditary throne, I leave to their consciences to determine; though I cannot tell how to think that a King of England can ever be accountable to his subjects for any maladministrations or abuse of power, but as he derives his power from God, so to Him only must he answer for using it . . .[32]

Susanna's political and religious principles appear to have been erratic. She veered between Tory Jacobitism and more Whiggish opinions. For example, in a letter to her son, Samuel, on 11 March 1704, Susanna wrote her opinions of the issue of self-preservation: 'The first thing that seems dictated by nature's law is self-preservation . . . But forasmuch as a virtuous life presupposes life, I think the first thing nature teaches us is care of life and to preserve it.'[33]

This was a classic *Whig* account of the right of people to defend themselves. Self-defence lay behind the Puritan rationale for the Civil War and the Whig justification for resisting James II. In each case tyrants appeared to be willing to kill or persecute people and self-defence was the basis in which Charles I was executed and James II ejected. It was a principle formally denounced by the University of Oxford and the Church in 1683 which denied that there was a right of self-defence. In contrast, Mary Astell was more representative of Toryism in arguing that subjects had no right of self-defence, their obedience to God and King meant that they should give their lives for both.

The third episode in the Wesleys' marriage came in 1710, when Samuel *was* elected to Convocation and had to spend six months each year in London. He appointed Daniel Inman as curate of Epworth in his absence. At the end of 1711, Inman wrote to Samuel that people in the parish were abandoning worship in

---

[32] Walmsley, 'John Wesley's Parents', 57. Wallace suggests that the blank refers to William III and this seems likely given the context. *Wallace*, p. 204.

[33] *Wallace*, p. 42.

the parish church and were instead attending prayer meetings that Susanna was holding in the rectory kitchen. Samuel wrote to Susanna expressing his concern, but Susanna held her ground and defended the meetings. Gradually they grew to more than two hundred attenders and took up the whole ground floor of the rectory.

When Samuel mentioned to Susanna that Inman referred to the meetings as a 'conventicle'—an illegal Dissenter meeting— Susanna naively replied: 'I suppose [Inman] thinks the sermons I read better than his own.' She went on: 'what does this calling it [a conventicle] signify? Does it alter the nature of the thing?'[34] She also claimed that, if Samuel insisted on shutting the meetings, the parishioners would not return to the parish church. She wrote: 'I can now keep them to the Church, but if it is laid aside, I doubt they'll ever go to hear him [Inman] more . . .'.[35] Samuel's concern was that in Convocation he was attacking Dissenters, like Presbyterians, Quakers and Baptists, for holding meetings separate from the parish worship, but in his own parish his wife was holding just such a meeting.

In reply to another request from Samuel to stop the meetings, Susanna replied with a heavily laden warning:

> If you do after all think fit to dissolve this assembly, do not tell me any more that you desire me to do it, for that will not satisfy my conscience; but send me your positive command in such full and express terms as may absolve me from all guilt and punishment for neglecting this opportunity of doing good to souls, when you and I shall appear before the great and awful tribunal of our Lord Jesus Christ.[36]

Faced with Susanna's words, Samuel relented and the meetings continued until his return to the parish. But to find his wife usurping his curate's role, and in such a politically

---

[34] Ibid., p. 81.
[35] Ibid., p. 82.
[36] Ibid., p. 13.

embarrassing fashion, must have been vexing and problematic to Samuel. Here too, Susanna seems to have been inconsistent; as a Tory she ought to have held a high view of the authority of the Church and the priesthood, but at the same time she usurped them.

The bruising matter of the prayer meeting may lie behind the fourth episode in the marriage.[37] In 1712, Samuel Wesley made his reply to Bishop Wake of Lincoln's visitation queries.[38] Wesley's response to the question about whether all the parishioners in Epworth were baptized was astonishing: he wrote that the only possible unbaptized adult was Susanna, who—and here the record quoted Wesley directly—'has none but Presbyterian Baptism'.[39] This was a pretty startling matter: the rector naming his wife, Susanna, as the only unbaptized person in the parish.[40]

Samuel Wesley was pointing out the inconsistency of Susanna's position. If, as seems likely from the dispute on the prayer meeting, their relationship was not entirely patched up, the visitation return enabled Samuel to make a point to Susanna. Her irregular conventicle in the rectory was a public embarrassment to him. Samuel's work in Convocation risked being undermined because Susanna was holding an irregular meeting in his own parish. Worse still, Susanna could not even lay claim to valid episcopal baptism in the Church of England.

---

[37] This episode is discussed in more detail in W. Gibson, '"None but Presbyterian Baptism"'.

[38] The visitation returns have been published in J. Broad (ed.), *Bishop Wake's Summary of Visitation Returns for the Diocese of Lincoln 1706-15* 2 vols (Oxford, 2012).

[39] Oxford, Christ Church, Oxford, Wake Ms, 279. Visitation of Lincoln, 1712, Epworth entry. Presumably Susanna was baptized by her Dissenting father, Samuel Annesley.

[40] It is not clear whether the word 'possible' was used by Samuel Wesley or by the transcriber of the visitation return. It is likely that it was the latter, since the return was addressed to a bishop who did not accept that lay baptism was invalid.

Samuel also saw some of the inconsistency of his wife's views. If she was a Jacobite in politics and a Non-juror in theology, she should have held as high a view of the need for episcopal baptism as Samuel himself. But Susanna, presumably, did not feel a need to be episcopally baptized, having been baptized by her Presbyterian father.[41]

Susanna's political and theological views may have confused Samuel. Her commitment to the Jacobite cause ought to have excluded Whiggish principles, yet she recommended Whig theorists, like John Locke for her sons to read. High Churchmen rejected Dissenting baptism (which Susanna had received) as non-existent since, in their view, Dissenting clergy were mere laymen. Hence Samuel's dismissive comment that 'Presbyterian baptism' was really not a valid baptism at all. Susanna's claim to hold High Church principles seemed incongruous as she did not seem to recognize the necessity of baptism from an Anglican clergyman.

In 1717, another episode occurred that sheds some intriguing light on Samuel and Susanna's marriage. Their home was the scene of three months of a haunting or poltergeist phenomenon. The family nicknamed the spirit 'Old Jeffrey'. It knocked and rattled the house and scared the children and servants. There were also apparitions of animals.[42] The family considered all sorts of explanations for the phenomenon. The one intriguing possibility is that it was associated with Susanna's dogged attachment to the Stuart cause.[43] When Samuel, during family

---

[41] Samuel Annesley had received Presbyterian orders in 1644.

[42] The 'Old Jeffrey' episode is complex and fascinating and is discussed in considerable detail in my forthcoming book on Samuel Wesley: W. Gibson, *Samuel Wesley and the Crisis of Tory Piety, 1685-1720* (Oxford, 2021).

[43] The most recent treatment of the issue is in K. D. Yates, 'Jeffrey the Jacobite Poltergeist: the politics of the ghost that haunted the Epworth rectory in 1716-17' in *Wesleyan Theological Journal* (2015), p. 71.

worship, prayed for the new Hanoverian King, George I, 'Old Jeffrey' knocked; whereas when he omitted the prayers, he remained silent. Like Susanna, 'Old Jeffrey' seems to have been a Jacobite.

John Wesley was fascinated by the episode, though he had been at school in London when it had happened. In 1784, he wrote a description of the events for the *Arminian Magazine* in which gave details of the haunting.[44] His comments on the knocking during prayers for the King were that,

> At six in the evening he had family prayers as usual. When he began the prayer for the king, a knocking began all round the room, and a thundering knock attended the 'Amen.' The same was heard from this time every morning and evening while the prayer for the king was repeated.[45]

Significantly, Wesley wrote that, as both his parents were dead 'and incapable of being pained thereby', he provided the reader with what he called 'a key to this circumstance.' He then gave an account of the dispute between Samuel and Susanna in 1702 over prayers for William III. John Wesley recorded that his father had 'vowed he would never cohabit with her till she did . . . [say] Amen'. But he returned without Susanna's agreement to do so. Wesley's conclusion was that 'I fear his vow was not forgotten before God.' In other words, John Wesley associated the events with the political disputes between Samuel and Susanna.

Samuel and Susanna's marriage gradually became less fraught. In January 1722, Susanna wrote to her brother, Samuel Annesley, about his breach with her husband. Samuel Annesley believed that his brother in law had poorly managed the funds he sent him from the East Indies to safeguard. Susanna wrote to her brother that it was 'a very hard part' to be caught between

---

[44] John Wesley called the article 'An Account of the Disturbances in my Father's House', in *AM*, vol 7, (1784), 548-50, 606-8, 654-6.
[45] Ibid., 550.

her brother and her husband, for both of whom she was 'full of tenderness' and who she regarded with 'the utmost kindness and respect.'[46] Yet even in this, she wrote with an element of regret. Speaking of Samuel Annesley's threats to sue her husband, Susanna replied frankly that it would do her brother no good. And she wrote of her husband: 'since I have taken my husband for better or worse, I'll make my residence with him. Where he lives I will live and where he dies will I die and there will I be buried.'[47] In fact, Susanna was not buried with Samuel, but with her parents at Bunhill Fields, the cemetery of the London Dissenting community. This was extremely rare in the Church of England, clerical wives were almost without exception buried with their husbands. Admittedly Susanna outlived Samuel by seven years most of which were spent with her various children, so she had severed ties with Epworth for some time. But the choice to be buried at Bunhill Fields among Dissenters from the Church cannot be overlooked.

On one, undated, occasion Susanna wrote in her journal about her expectations for her life. She wrote of the years of 'care, frugality and industry' and the hope of being amply rewarded in an 'ensuing summer'; and she wrote of being 'greatly disappointed . . . that all [her] prospects of ease and plenty was but a dream.' Yet she reproved herself for the pride and 'idolatry' of these expectations.[48]

Susanna's marriage to Samuel was one of personal incompatibility, despite the claims of their religious and political agreement. Samuel expected his wife to conform to the role of an obedient Tory wife who deferred to him in matters of politics and religion. But Susanna could not do this, and here lay their problems. It was not a marriage that had been breached but healed in 1701-2, it was probably one marked by repeated breakdowns and disagreements. In part this was due to

---

[46] *Wallace*, p. 93.
[47] Ibid., p. 95.
[48] Ibid., pp. 272-3.

Susanna's failure to observe the contemporary norms for a Tory wife, and equally due to Samuel's spikiness and difficult character. The Wesleys' marriage is testimony to the profoundly political and religious character of marriage in the period in general, and their marriage in particular.

3: Female Education: Susanna Wesley, Epworth and familial legacy

Linda A. Ryan

This chapter examines the way Susanna Wesley instructed her children at Epworth, and will demonstrate that although her attitude to the education of her daughters was striking for the time, it nonetheless conformed to the gender constraints of the period. Indeed, this chapter demonstrates that although Susanna Wesley believed that it was important for her daughters to be heard and understood, and she gave them an education equal to their brothers at home, the male and female children in the Wesley household were not educational equals. Evidence presented in this chapter also argues that Susanna Wesley's education system was not as austere and puritanical as some earlier scholars have contended.[1]

While Susanna's own upbringing, and the period in which she undertook the education of her children, may be viewed as confined to the end of the seventeenth and beginning of the eighteenth centuries, as John Lenton states in chapter four of this volume, 'all historians agree that Susanna Wesley was a major influence on her son John'. Indeed, there is little doubt that John's thinking on child-rearing and education was profoundly influenced by his mother. The second part of this chapter discusses the familial legacy of Susanna and Samuel

---

[1] Marjorie Bowen claimed that 'There was not a child who came into contact with eighteenth-century Methodism who must not have been the worse for it. A terrible heritage had Mrs Susanna Wesley left behind her; her ideas of education were wielded in the hands of her son into an evil thing that did unrecorded harm to thousands of children.' M. Bowen, *Wrestling Jacob* (London, 1937), p. 317 cited in R. F. Wearmouth, *Methodism and the Common People of the Eighteenth Century* (London, 1945), p. 207.

Wesley, including the influence it had on John Wesley's thinking regarding the education of girls and young women; an influence and legacy that may therefore be considered relevant across the long eighteenth century.[2]

Concepts of childhood and gender in the long eighteenth century

In 1684 a Somerset landowner, Edward Clarke, asked his friend John Locke, a tutor to a gentleman's son, for guidance on the education of his own son. In response, Locke produced the first of what became a series of letters, published under the title *Some Thoughts Concerning Education*, in 1693.[3] Although his treatise appears to demonstrate a marked gender bias, Locke himself stated:

> I have said *he* here, because the principal aim of my discourse is how a young gentleman should be brought up from his infancy, which, in all things will not so perfectly suit the education of daughters, though where the difference of sex requires different treatment, it will be no hard matter to distinguish.[4]

In his letter to Edward Clarke, dated 1 January 1685, Locke suggested: 'There will be some though no great difference, for making a little allowance for beauty and some few other considerations of the sex, the manner of breeding of boys and

---

[2] For a detailed examination of the influences on John Wesley's thinking and practice concerning child-rearing and education see *Ryan*. The 'long eighteenth century' is often used of the period 1688-1832.

[3] For a detailed examination of Locke's *Some Thoughts Concerning Education*, together with the also influential work by Jean-Jacques Rousseau on the education of children (*Emile*, published in 1762) see *Ryan*, pp. 13-18.

[4] J. Locke, *Some Thoughts Concerning Education* (London, 1693), pp. 1-8, 16, 67.

girls, especially in their younger years, I imagine should be the same.'[5]

In an earlier letter to Mary Clarke, Locke advised that 'meat, drink, lodging and clothing should be ordered after the same manner for the girls as for the boys'. While a dancing master would give boys 'graceful motions, manliness, and a becoming confidence', girls would learn 'fashion and easy comely motion'. He did concede one difference in the treatment of daughters, arguing that their governing and disciplining belonged to mothers; a father ought 'to strike very seldom, if at all to chide his daughters', he wrote.[6] Indeed, far from advocating a special, separate and distinct form of education for girls, what Locke proposed for a girl's education closely resembled that of young gentlemen. Both were to be home educated by a tutor, and learn modern languages through conversation, rather than by the rote memorization method used in grammar schools.[7]

Locke's treatise argued that in terms of thought and reason children should be considered as a *tabula rasa*. He insisted that as no two children were alike, they were not be instructed by exactly the same method. Indeed, it was in Locke's recognition of the individuality of the child that his work was to have a profound effect on how children were raised and educated. They were to be treated as rational creatures, and great care was to be taken in forming their minds.[8] Locke also contended that:

> The child ought very early to have imprinted on his mind a true notion of God as the independent Supreme Being, author and maker of all things, from whom we receive all our good,

---

[5] B. Rand (ed.), *The Correspondence of John Locke and Edward Clarke* (London, 1927), p. 121.

[6] Ibid., pp. 234-9, 103-4.

[7] M. A. Butler, 'Early Liberal Roots of Feminism: John Locke's attack on patriarchy' in N. J. Hirschmann and K. M. McClure (eds), *Feminist Interpretations of John Locke* (Pennsylvania, 2007), p. 116.

[8] Locke, *Some Thoughts Concerning Education*, pp. 33, 261.

that loves us, and gives us all things, and consequent to it a love and reverence of him.

He contended that children should be taught to pray and to read scripture-history, and to learn by heart the Lord's Prayer, Creed and Ten Commandments. The bible, he suggested, provided children with easy and plain moral rules for reading and instruction in the whole conduct of life.[9]

Following the publication of *Some Thoughts Concerning Education* a gradual change in attitude led many parents to acknowledge that childhood was no longer solely a preparation for adulthood or heaven but was to be valued in its own right. Parents were no longer bound by Puritan teaching on discipline and original sin. Parental authoritarianism increasingly gave way to a desire among parents to set a 'good example'.[10] By the mid-eighteenth century the older patriarchal family authority was giving way to a new parental ideal characterized by a more affectionate and equalitarian relationship with children. Nevertheless, throughout the century the role of both parents in the child's upbringing remained clearly defined.[11] As James Buchanan declared in 1770, the belief remained that:

> The father ought to lay out and superintend their education; the mother to execute and manage the detail of which she is capable. The father should direct the manly exertions of the intellectual and moral powers of his child: his imagination and the manner of these exertions are the peculiar province of the mother.[12]

---

[9] Ibid., pp. 157-8.

[10] D. B. Paxman, 'Imaging the Child: bad parents in the mid-eighteenth-century English novel' in *Journal for Eighteenth-Century Studies*, vol 38, no 1, (2015), 135-51.

[11] G. J. Barker-Benfield, *The Culture of Sensibility: sex and society in eighteenth-century* (London, 1992), p. 102.

[12] J. Buchanan, *Plan of an English Grammar School Education* (London, 1770), p. 33.

The thinking of Locke, which argued against sending children to public schools, raised for many the question of whether a child flourished under authority or liberty. Adam Smith stated in his *Theory of Moral Sentiments* that 'Domestic education is the institution of nature; public education the contrivance of man. It is surely unnecessary to say which is likely to be the wisest'.[13] Regarding the family as the main wellspring of national morality, virtue, in the view of religious authors like Sarah Trimmer, could only be nurtured within the home through the devoted vigilance of parents, who would supervise the early education and reading of their children with constant attention to the inculcation of religious principles.[14] Despite the expansion of establishments for girls' education throughout the eighteenth century, the commonly held view was that the home was the most suitable place for girls to be educated. John Bennett declared in 1787: 'Whatever elegant or high-standing schools may be sought out for a girl, a mother seems the only governess intended by nature'.[15] This did little to change existing assumptions that girls belonged at home under the supervision of their mothers, where their virtue could be protected. Girls were expected to be devout, to provide spiritual support in the household, and to know how to conduct themselves in a moral fashion.[16]

---

[13] A. Smith, *The Theory of Moral Sentiments . . .* vol 2, sixth edition (London, 1790), p. 79.

[14] S. Woodley, "'Oh Miserable and Most Ruinous Measure': the debate between private and public education in Britain, 1760-1800' in M. Hilton and J. Shefrin (eds), *Educating the Child in Enlightenment Britain: beliefs, cultures, practices* (Farnham, 2009), pp. 35-7.

[15] J. Bennett, *Strictures on Female Education, Chiefly as it Relates to the Culture of the Heart, in Four Essays, By a Clergyman of the Church of England* (London, 1787), p. 138.

[16] John Gregory defined religion as a peculiarly feminine province, arguing that it was 'rather a matter of sentiment than reasoning', and suggested that women were 'peculiarly susceptible to the feelings of

The writer and philosopher Mary Astell (whose views on marriage are referred to by Bill Gibson in chapter two of this volume),[17] a contemporary of Locke, argued that if all children were 'blank slates' at birth, with no innate ideas, and girls were taught embroidery, music, and household management rather than mathematics and Greek, then it should not be surprising that women did not fully develop rationality.[18] Astell's *A Serious Proposal to the Ladies* published between 1694 and 1697, and *The Education of Girls,* published in 1687, were both widely read and discussed in relation to the education of élite girls during the first half of the eighteenth century.[19] Astell condemned those who taught young ladies to value themselves 'on nothing but their clothes', and advised girls that 'it will not be near so advantageous to consult with your dancing-master as with your own thoughts'. She encouraged them to use their own enquiry to search out the 'hidden beauties' of religion; and advised them to become Christians by choice, rather than by conformity with those among whom they lived.[20] Girls were encouraged to read edifying texts such as religious and moral treatises; but although reading was generally approved of when associated with piety and chastity, girls were warned against reading that might have a pernicious effect on the female mind. The reading

---

devotion'. J. Gregory, *A Father's Legacy to his Daughters; by the late Dr Gregory of Edinburgh* (Edinburgh, 1774), pp. 10-13.

[17] Mary Astell is referred to as 'the first English feminist' by J. Batchelor, 'Mary Astell', in *The Literary Encyclopedia,* https://www.litencyc.com/php/speople.php?UID=168&rec=true (accessed 29 August 2020).

[18] N. J. Hirschmann, 'Intersectionality Before Intersectionality was Cool: the importance of class to feminist interpretations of Locke' in Hirschmann, *Feminist Interpretations of John Locke* (2007), p. 174.

[19] M. Hilton, *Women and the Shaping of the Nation's Young: education and public doctrine in Britain 1750-1850* (Aldershot, 2007), p. 45.

[20] M. Astell, *A Serious Proposal to the Ladies for the Advancement of their True and Greatest Interest* (London, 1697), pp. 7-36.

of fiction, it was suggested, softened young women up for seduction.[21]

That is not to suggest that all female education was trivial or superficial. There were many women who possessed intellectual abilities, including a knowledge of mathematics or classical languages, having acquired these skills because they were either daughters of learned men who instructed them at home, or of wealthy men who employed tutors. Indeed, by the end of eighteenth century, Hester Chapone's *Letters on the Improvement of the Mind: addressed to a young lady*, published in 1773, was widely read. Addressed to her fifteen-year-old niece, the *Letters* incorporated a course of self-education which included a systematic study of the bible, training in accountancy and domestic management, translations of the classics, and a range of modern literature in French and English, as well as botany, geology, astrology, geography and ancient and modern history.[22] Despite this, Dr John Gregory's *A Father's Legacy to his Daughters*, published a year after Chapone's *Letters*, advised young women: 'But if you happen to have any learning, keep it a profound secret, especially from the men, who generally look with a jealous and malignant eye on a woman of great parts and a cultivated understanding.'[23]

Not all girls were educated at home. Over the course of the century a great number of schools for girls were established. Although these varied widely in their quality and scope, most combined writing and arithmetic with social 'accomplishments' designed to equip girls for marriage. By 1759 an anonymous writer in the *Annual Register* noted that: 'Every village in the neighbourhood . . . has one or two little boarding schools . . . the

---

[21] S. Bygrave, *Uses of Education: readings in enlightenment in England* (Lewisburg, 2009), p. 83.
[22] J. Goodman, 'Class and Religion' in J. C. Albisetti (ed.) et al., *Girls' Secondary Education in the Western World* (New York, 2010), pp. 54-60, 165-7.
[23] Gregory, *A Father's Legacy*, pp. 31-2.

expense is small and hither the blacksmith, the alehouse-keeper, the shoemaker, etc., sends his daughter, who, from the moment she enters these walls becomes a "young lady"'.[24]

Even in charity schools, boys were taught separately from girls. As soon as they could read competently, boys learned to write in 'a fair legible hand' and were taught 'the grounds of arithmetic to fit them for services or apprentices'. Girls were taught to read, and although 'several learned to write', generally they were instructed in how to 'knit their stockings and gloves, and to mark, sew, make and mend their clothes'.[25] Thomas Coram, who in 1741 opened the Foundling Hospital in London, wrote in March 1737:

> It is an evil amongst us here in England to think girls having learning given them is not so material as for boys to have it. I think and say it is more material, for girls when they come to be mothers will have the forming of their children's lives and if mothers be good or bad the children generally take after them, so giving girls a virtuous education is a vast advantage to their posterity as well as to the public.[26]

The provision of a basic education was not only divided along gender lines. Hymn writer Isaac Watts declared that 'The poor who are bred in towns and cities should enjoy some small advantages in their education, beyond those who are born in far distant fields and villages'. He added:

> I will by no means contend for writing as a matter or equal necessity or advantage with that of reading . . . and there may also be some of the poor who dwell in very obscure villages, and are confined to rural labours, and others in towns or cities, and especially girls, whose business is most within doors at home, who may have but very little occasion, and as little

---

[24] Hilton, *Women and the Shaping of the Nation's Young*, p. 45.

[25] Anon., *An Account of Charity-schools Lately Erected in England, Wales, and Ireland* (London, 1706), p. 4.

[26] L. Picard, *Dr. Johnson's London: coffee-houses and climbing boys . . .* (London, 2000), p. 176.

inclination to use a pen. I would not therefore by any means have it made a necessary part of a charity-school that the children should be taught to write.[27]

Susanna Wesley's educational practice at Epworth

Despite prevailing sentiments, in the predominantly feminine atmosphere at Epworth, it is evident from Adam Clarke's *Memoirs of the Wesley Family*, published in 1832, that the Wesley daughters were both lively and literate.[28] Indeed, Susanna Wesley's attitude towards her daughters' education was striking for the time since she argued that:

> No girl be taught to work till she can read very well, and then that she be kept to her work with the same application, and for the same time, that she was held to in reading. This rule also is much to be observed; for the putting of children to learn sewing before they can read perfectly is the very reason why so few women can read fit to be heard, and never to be well understood.[29]

Susanna Wesley had been instructed by her father Samuel Annesley to a level far beyond that which was customary for her time and sex. Referring to the Wesley family, Adam Clarke noted that as 'their circumstances were narrow and confined, the education of their progeny fell particularly upon themselves, and especially Mrs Wesley, who seems to have possessed every qualification requisite for either a public or private teacher.'[30] While much has been written about Susanna's hand in the education of her children, it is important to note that Samuel Wesley instructed his sons in Latin, Greek and classical

---

[27] I. Watts, *An Essay Towards the Encouragement of Charity Schools . . .* (London, 1728), pp. 15, 30.
[28] Adam Clarke referred to John Wesley's sisters as Emilia (Emily), Mary, Anne, Susanna (Sukey), Mehetabel (Hetty, and sometimes Kitty), Martha (Patty, or Pat) and Kezzia (Kezze, or Kez in family chapters). *Clarke, 1832,* pp. 466-540.
[29] *Wallace,* p. 373.
[30] *Clarke, 1832,* p. 256.

literature, laying the foundation for their future learning at Westminster, Charterhouse and Oxford.[31] He was also happy for his daughters to use his extensive library.[32] Indeed, it was in Samuel's library that Emilia Wesley found, in 1712, a letter concerning the work of the Danish missionaries in India. Although Susanna Wesley's education method had begun in earnest after the Epworth fire in 1709, and she did not read the letter until later, Claire Potter argues that 'the missionaries' work relating to the education of children did not so much change Susanna's own methods, as confirm them and inspire her to develop them further'.[33]

It was through their mother that all the Wesley children, both sons and daughters, were instructed in a strong and rational foundation of religious education and raised in an atmosphere of piety and learning. While Susanna Wesley's educational method resonated with Lockean influences, the Puritan virtues of industry, sobriety, frugality and temperance were combined with a recognition of the individuality of the child.[34] 'There is nothing I now desire to live for', Susanna Wesley stated in a letter to her son Samuel on 11 October 1709, 'but to do some small service to my children; that as I have brought them into the world, I may, if it please God, be an instrument of doing good to their souls'.[35]

The male and female children in the Wesley household were not educational equals. While the expectation was that the boys would go on to receive a public school education designed to

---

[31] A. A. Dallimore, *Susanna: the mother of John and Charles Wesley* (Darlington, 1992), p. 89.
[32] G. M. Best, *Seven Sisters* (Weston-super-Mare, 2012), p. 2.
[33] C. Potter, 'The Influence of Danish Missionaries to India on Susanna Wesley's Methods of Education and Inspiration, and the Subsequent Influence on John Wesley', unpublished paper given at the Oxford Institute of Methodist Theological Studies, August 2013, pp. 3-15.
[34] *Ryan*, pp. 50-1.
[35] *Clarke, 1832*, p. 281.

prepare them for university, for the Wesley girls, their mother's tuition was the only schooling they received. Although she believed that it was important for her daughters to be heard and understood, and she gave them an education equal to their brothers at home, a public school and university education was available to males only. That we know so much about the way Susanna Wesley instructed her children arises from the details she herself set out in 1732. John Wesley's growing interest in child-rearing and education prompted him to write to his mother asking for an account of her Epworth system. Her reply, dated 24 July 1732, has come to be regarded as one of her most important pieces of writing.

Unfortunately, the precise text of this 'Education Letter' is uncertain since the original letter has been lost, and there is no convincing evidence that any Wesley family biographer beyond Adam Clarke had access to it.[36] However, the 'Education Letter' was reproduced by John Wesley in two published forms; the earliest and longer version in the 1749 instalment of his *Journal*, and the second, published thirty-five years later, in the *Arminian Magazine* of 1784.[37] A problem arises when comparing the two versions. The shorter version, reproduced in 1784, includes the section from Susanna's original letter with her insistence on conquering the will of children from an early age. However, the most striking difference is an additional paragraph that appears in this later version, but which is neither in the earlier version, nor in Clarke's *Memoirs of the Wesley Family*.[38] It states:

---

[36] E. Kurtz Lynch, 'John Wesley's Editorial Hand' in Jeremy Gregory (ed.), *John Wesley: tercentenary essays: proceedings of a conference held at the University of Manchester, June 2003*, Special Issue of the *Bulletin of the John Rylands University Library*, vol 85, (Manchester, 2005), pp. 176, 196.

[37] Susanna's letter is in *WJW*, vol 19, pp. 286-8; The letter is part of John Wesley's 'Sermon on Colossians 3:20 —Children, Obey your Parents in all things': *AM*, vol 4, (1784), 457-64.

[38] *Clarke, 1832*, pp. 261-7.

> At all events, from the age, make him do as he is bid, if you whip him ten times running to effect it: let none persuade you, it is cruelty to do this: it is cruelty not to do it. Break his will now, and his soul will live, and he will probably bless you to all eternity.[39]

It is likely that this additional paragraph was added by John Wesley to reinforce his message on parental authority.[40] Although his upbringing at Epworth had convinced him that Christian education had to begin in the home, Wesley's sermon *On Family Religion*, delivered on 25 May 1783, asserted that the wickedness of children was generally due to the fault or neglect of their parents in taking too soft and tender a line with their children. This, he suggested, would be like 'offering up their sons and their daughters unto the devil'.[41]

By removing from Susanna Wesley's authorship the paragraph exhorting: 'if you whip him ten times running to effect it let none persuade you it is cruelty to do this . . .', her practices appear rather more compassionate than some commentators have hitherto argued. That is not to suggest that Susanna Wesley dismissed the use of the birch rod; indeed, she taught all her children 'to fear the rod, and cry softly'. However, it should be borne in mind that the use of the rod was an accepted method of punishment for wrong-doing in eighteenth-century England; but instead of turning first and frequently to the rod, Susanna's methods were primarily directed toward minimizing the need for punishment.[42] She wrote that although 'the education of so many children must create abundance of trouble'; it was 'no small honour . . . to be entrusted with the care of so many souls'.[43] John Wesley was to record in 1766: 'I remember to have heard my father asking my mother "How could you have the

---

[39] *AM*, vol 4, (1784), 463-4.
[40] *Ryan*, p. 43.
[41] *WJW*, vol 3, pp. 335-7.
[42] Lynch, 'John Wesley's Editorial Hand', pp. 197-206.
[43] *Wallace*, p. 210.

patience to tell that blockhead the same thing twenty times over?" She answered "Why, if I had told him but nineteen times, I should have lost all my labour'". John's conclusion: 'What patience indeed, what love, what knowledge is requisite for this!'[44]

In stating that children: 'should be always commended and frequently rewarded' for obedience, Susanna Wesley's practices appear to show affection and respect for their efforts.[45] Samuel Wesley, writing to his eldest son Samuel, stated 'You know what you owe to one of the best mothers . . . [I have] often reflected on the tender and peculiar love which your mother has always expressed towards you . . . the particular care she took of your education'.[46] Susanna Wesley treated her children as individuals; writing to her husband in February 1712, she stated 'I take such a proportion of time as I can best spare every night to discourse with each child by itself on something that relates to its principal concerns'.[47] The time the children spent individually with her was not intended for teaching or instruction, but advice, and listening to the issues that were of concern to each of them. When the Epworth fire split the household to different locations, Susanna wrote to her daughter Sukey stating:

> Since our misfortunes have separated us from each other, and we can no longer enjoy the opportunities we once had of conversing together, I can no other way discharge the duty of a parent, or comply with my inclination of doing you all the good I can, but by writing. You know very well how I love you.[48]

Anxious to instil habits of virtue and piety, Susanna Wesley insisted that an important part of the upbringing for the Wesley

---

[44] *WJW*, vol 10, p. 341.
[45] Lynch, 'John Wesley's Editorial Hand', p. 206.
[46] Dallimore, *Susanna*, p. 95.
[47] *Clarke, 1832*, p. 330.
[48] Ibid., p. 283.

children was that they learned self-discipline and self-control. Regulation in eating and sleeping was a feature of the Epworth household and Susanna stated that her children 'might have nothing they cry'd for'. Drinking or eating between meals was forbidden. She did not supply toys for her family, but they did play cards, and a dancing master came to Epworth.[49] Nevertheless, the Wesley children grew up in an environment where they were deliberately deprived of contact with other boys and girls of their own age who might encourage frivolity in them.[50]

Susanna Wesley insisted on 'a regular method of living'. She taught her children to read at the age of five, and expected them to learn prayers, catechism, and portions of scripture 'as their memories could bear'.[51] Classes were conducted six days a week, from nine to twelve and from two until five.[52] Pairs of older and younger siblings read one another a chapter of each testament and the 'Psalms for the day' as appointed in the Book of Common Prayer.[53] Writing to John in a letter dated 21 February 1732, Susanna declared 'There are few, if any, that would entirely devote above twenty years of the prime of life in hopes to save the souls of their children . . . for that was my principal intention, however unskilfully or unsuccessfully managed'.[54]

---

[49] Dallimore, *Susanna*, p. 65. Wesley was subsequently to reflect that the use of a dancing master might teach his preachers courtesy and grace of movement. R. F. Snowden, *Such a Woman: the story of Susanna Wesley* (London, 1963), p. 22.

[50] G. Lloyd, *Charles Wesley and the Struggle for Methodist Identity* (Oxford, 2007), p. 8.

[51] *WJW*, vol 19, p. 288.

[52] Dallimore, *Susanna*, p. 57.

[53] C. Wallace, 'Charles Wesley and Susanna' in K. G. C. Newport and T. A. Campbell (eds), *Charles Wesley Life, Literature and Legacy* (Peterborough, 2007), p. 73.

[54] *Wallace*, p. 150.

Adam Clarke suggested in his *Memoirs of the Wesley Family* that both Samuel and Susanna Wesley intended their daughters to become governesses.[55] He described Emilia as having a 'strong sense, much wit, prodigious memory and a talent for poetry', adding that she was a 'classical scholar who wrote in a beautiful hand'. Kezzia was described by Clarke as 'capable of high cultivation', but 'prevented from improving her mind' by ill health throughout her life; and Martha as 'distinguished for deep thoughtfulness'. A particular accolade was pronounced on Hetty:

> The pains taken with her education were crowned with success, for at the early age of eight years she had made such proficiency in the learned languages that she could read the Greek text. She has naturally a fine poetic genius, which, though common to the whole family, shone forth in her with peculiar splendour and was heightened by her knowledge of the fine models of antiquity.[56]

The adult lives of the Wesley girls were far from happy. Although it would be unfair to apportion blame, their education eventually proved a curse rather than a blessing because most of the men with whom they came into contact were intellectually far inferior to them. Indeed, Clarke recorded of Hetty: 'She appears to have had many suitors, but they were generally of the airy and thoughtless class, and ill-suited to make her either happy or useful in a matrimonial life';[57] and Charles Wallace alludes to Susanna's 'anxiety and exasperation with her high-spirited daughter Hetty', in the opening chapter of this volume. Both Emilia and Kezzia became teachers for limited periods at boarding schools in Lincoln, although in neither case does it appear to have been an enjoyable or rewarding experience. Clarke recorded that Emilia, 'though she

---

[55] NB not all the Wesley daughters are included here, only those referred to by Clarke in connection with the scope of this chapter.

[56] *Clarke, 1832*, pp. 466, 539, 511, 487.

[57] Ibid., p. 487.

had the whole care of the school, was not well used and was worse paid'. Writing to her brother John in July 1731, Kezzia responded to the letter in which he had sent her a suggested reading list by complaining:

> I am entirely of your opinion, that the pursuit of knowledge and virtue will most improve the mind: but how to pursue these is the question. Cut off indeed I am from all means which most men, and many women, have of acquiring them. I could like to read all the books you mention, if it were in my power to buy them, but as it is not at present, nor have any of my acquaintances I can borrow them off . . . I had rather you had not told me of them, because it always occasions me some uneasiness that I have not books and opportunity to improve my mind.[58]

Charles Wesley, undoubtedly influenced by the level of education his sisters received at Epworth, ensured that his daughter Sally had an education beyond that expected of most girls, including a strong grasp of Latin.[59] In a letter to his eighteen-year-old daughter in 1777, Charles reminded Sally:

> I think you may avail yourself of my small knowledge of books and poetry. I am not yet too old to assist you a little in your reading, and perhaps improve your taste in versifying . . . Witness your brothers; who I do not love a jot better than you. O be you as ready to show me your verses, as they their music.[60]

Susanna's legacy: John Wesley and female education

Undoubtedly influenced by his own upbringing, John Wesley argued that the most suitable place where a daughter's piety and virtue could be nurtured and protected was in the family home. Girls, Wesley contended, should be instructed at home

---

[58] Ibid., pp. 466, 487, 540-1.
[59] G. M. Best, *Charles Wesley: a biography* (Peterborough, 2006), pp. 314-20.
[60] F. Baker, *Charles Wesley As Revealed by His Letters*, The WHS Lecture no 14, (London, 1948), p. 115.

'as my mother did, who bred up seven daughters to years of maturity'.[61] Even though girls were frequently educated at home, their education was seldom as rigorous as Susanna Wesley's for her daughters. While it is evident from John's correspondence with his sisters that he was keen that they continue to improve their minds by advancing their knowledge into adulthood, his thinking on female education was rather ambivalent. Indeed, the evidence demonstrates that although he undoubtedly encouraged female education, the primary purpose of instruction was not academic, but to ensure girls were pious and virtuous. He argued that girls should receive an education in order to read and understand the bible, and thus be fit 'for the enjoyment of God in eternity'.[62] On a visit to Dublin, in April 1785, he noted with joy the conversion of a number of girls who were 'as serious and staid in their whole behaviour as if they were thirty or forty years old'.[63] Wesley informed Philothea Briggs, the teenage daughter of his book steward at the Foundery, that 'all the knowledge you want is comprised in one book — the Bible. When you understand this, you will know enough.'[64]

That is not to suggest that Wesley was opposed to young women acquiring an education. Indeed, he wrote in correspondence between himself, Ann Granville and Nancy Griffiths in June 1731 of Mary Astell's *A Serious Proposal to the Ladies* (1697): 'surely her plan of female life must have pleased all the thinking part of her sex'.[65] However, it was not until 1780 that Wesley himself published in the *Arminian Magazine* 'A Female Course of Study'.[66] Reiterating that the bible contained all the knowledge they needed, he reminded young women that 'all you learn is to be referred to this, as either directly, or

---

[61] *WJW*, vol 3, p. 343.
[62] Ibid., vol 3, pp. 335-7.
[63] Ibid., vol 23, p. 349.
[64] *JWL*, vol 5, p. 221.
[65] *WJW*, vol 25, p. 285-9.
[66] J. Wesley, 'A Female Course of Study' in *AM*, vol 3, (1780), 602-4.

remotely conducive to it'. Although not opposed to young women acquiring an education, Wesley contended that they should 'begin and end [their study] with divinity'. Although he argued that boys, no matter what their station, were 'to be trained 'in every branch of useful learning', Wesley's female course of study conformed to eighteenth-century thinking in that it was intended only for those 'females who had a good understanding and much leisure'.[67]

It is evident from Wesley's writings that the place of the family in instructing children was, for him, paramount. He asked his listeners and readers to consider what the consequence would be if family religion was neglected and suggested that if they did not take care of the rising generation, 'the present revival of religion would in a short time die away'. He warned parents that it was their responsibility to watch over their children with utmost care, 'that when you are called to give account of each to the Father of Spirits you may give your accounts with joy and not with grief'. He asserted that the wickedness of children was generally due to the fault or neglect of their parents; and that taking too soft and tender a line with their children would be like 'offering up their sons and their daughters unto the devil'.[68]

Perhaps unsurprisingly, some parents reacted to this by pointing out that Wesley had no children of his own.[69] Adam

---

[67] Ibid., p. 602. This was probably from a letter to Ann Loxdale. See I. Rivers, *Vanity Fair and the Celestial City: Dissenting, Methodist, and evangelical literary culture in England 1720-1800* (Oxford, 2018), p. 83 n. 37. The information comes courtesy of Randy Maddox.

[68] *WJW*, vol 3, pp. 335-7. Wesley was not alone in this view; Bernard Mandeville claimed that 'No pity does more mischief in the world, than is excited by the tenderness of parents, and hinders them from managing their children'. B. Mandeville, 'An Essay on Charity and Charity Schools' in *The Fable of the Bees* second edition (London, 1723), p. 294.

[69] *WJW*, vol 22, p. 63.

Clarke responded to such criticism by stressing the significant influence on Wesley of his mother Susanna:

> It has been wondered at that a man who had no children of his own could have known so well how they should be managed and educated; but that wonder will at once cease, when it is recollected by whom he was himself educated; and who was his instructress in all things, during his infancy and youth.[70]

Despite the importance he placed on family, Wesley's views on the parent/child relationship appear to be ambivalent. Whilst the salvation of the child's soul depended on piety and virtue learned in relationship with, and by example of parents, this does not appear to have necessitated, in Wesley's view, the sort of deep emotional attachment brought about by parenthood. Wesley was very fond of the two daughters of his wife Mary Vazeille as step-daughters, and later delighted in seeing his step-grandchildren, about whom he showed concern, and for whom he felt much love.[71] However, Wesley's love for children was always subordinate to his primary concern to save their souls. John Wesley's seemingly underdeveloped sense of the impact of parenthood was evident in his reaction to his sister Martha, whose children died of fever.[72] Though he expressed fondness for Martha, Wesley told her that the death of her children was 'a great instance of the goodness of God toward you'; he reasoned that she was always complaining about them, and would now have more time to devote to her own religious

---

[70] *Clarke, 1832*, p. 174.

[71] *JWP*, p. 111. Wesley left the coins and the contents of the drawer in his bureau 'to his grand-daughters Mary and Jane Smith'; T. Hurst, 'Biographies in Church Monuments: William Smith and Jane Vazeille of Newcastle upon Tyne' in D. J. Hart and D. J. Jeremy (eds), *Brands Plucked from the Burning: essays on Methodist memorialisation and remembering* (Evesham, 2013), pp. 202-3.

[72] The correspondence between members of the Wesley family, Potter suggests, gives the impression of very close-knit relationships, with each taking a keen interest in the lives and thoughts of the others; Potter, 'The Influence of Danish Missionaries to India', p. 2.

concerns.[73] Although Wesley's remarks appear to demonstrate a lack of feeling, they were spoken in affection; and Henry Rack suggests that this sort of sentiment was commonplace at the time.[74] With child mortality high, avoiding excessive attachment to one's offspring may have served as an emotional defence mechanism.[75] Indeed, as Bill Gibson states in chapter two of this volume, Samuel and Susanna Wesley had had eleven sons, of whom only three survived to adulthood. Puritan religious conviction had led parents to regard children as having been temporarily entrusted to them by God, and Christian doctrine offered consolation on a child's death that he or she had moved to a better place.[76]

Perhaps for this reason, Wesley rarely discussed parental relationships in his writings, and when he referred to them regarding the death of a child, he focused on the triumph of faith rather than the emotion of bereavement.[77] A letter written by Charles Wesley to Selina, Countess of Huntingdon after the death of his infant daughter on 28 July 1755 revealed that his brother's lack of emotional empathy had its consequences:

> He cannot feel my reasons for staying with my wife. I sent him word, as soon as she was delivered. He has never since taken the least notice of her, or her child. I did not particularly mention the child because I would not give him, or his wife, pain. I do not inform him of her death, because I would not give them pleasure.[78]

Indeed, Phyllis Mack suggests that Charles Wesley's experience of bereavement gave him greater empathy and compassion than

---

[73] *WJW*, vol 26, pp. 90-1.

[74] H. D. Rack, *Reasonable Enthusiast: John Wesley and the rise of Methodism* (London, 1989), p. 354.

[75] R. Porter, *England in the Eighteenth Century* (London, 1998), p. 30.

[76] J. Bailey, *Parenting in England c.1760-1830: emotion, identity and generation* (Oxford, 2012), p. 40.

[77] *Mack*, p. 91.

[78] Lloyd, *Charles Wesley and the Struggle for Methodist Identity*, p. 138.

his brother and enabled him to enter other people's suffering more than John. Writing to Mrs Jones on 13 January 1750, Charles stated: 'He that shall come will come and wipe away all tears from your eyes. I bear your burthen till then, as your brother and companion in tribulation'.[79] John Wesley's emotional detachment appears not to have changed over his lifetime. In 1791 he wrote to Adam Clarke following the death of Clarke's eldest daughter, stating 'You startle me when you talk of grieving so much for the death of an infant . . . if you love them thus all your children will die'.[80]

Beyond the home, John Wesley contended that parents should ensure that their daughters were sent to a 'mistress who truly fears God, one whose life is a pattern to her scholars, and who has only so many that she can watch over each as one that must give account to God'.[81] His criticism of existing educational establishments, for failing to safeguard the physical and spiritual lives of children in their care, led him to establish in 1746 a fee paying boarding school in Kingswood, near Bristol. Not only did he implement strict rules governing the school, but he demanded that masters be selected for their piety above their educational credentials, a condition not without its difficulties. It was intended that the school accommodate fifty boys aged between six and twelve, but perhaps under pressure from his friends for places for their daughters as well as their sons, some girls were admitted to Kingswood in its early years.[82]

Wesley drew up rules specifically for girls but, unlike those for the boys, these were never published. There were notable and significant differences between the rules for girls and boys. Despite a comprehensive curriculum for boys at the school, in keeping with eighteenth-century thinking on female education,

---

[79] *Mack*, p. 210.
[80] John Wesley letter to Adam Clarke dated 3 January 1791 in *JWL*, vol 8, p. 253.
[81] *WJW*, vol 3, pp. 341-3.
[82] *Ryan*, pp. 60-1.

girls were instructed only in 'such things as are needful for them'; i.e. reading, writing, English grammar, arithmetic, sewing, and needlework.[83] Although a small number of girls were admitted to Kingswood in the early years, and women were among the staff, the demand for places appears to have been limited and short-lived. The register of names, though not complete, only included boys enrolled at the school, although it is known that Samuel Lloyd sent his niece Molly to Kingswood for a short time.[84] Wesley's friend and fellow evangelical, William Grimshaw, not only sent his son John, but his thirteen-year-old daughter Jane. Sadly, Grimshaw, who was by then twice widowed, was to face further tragedy when Jane became ill and died at the school in January 1750.[85] It would seem that Molly Lloyd's experience of Kingswood was far from satisfactory and she was withdrawn from the school.[86]

At the Methodist Conference in 1774 it was agreed that the Connexion would pay for at least some of the daughters of Wesley's preachers to attend school. Among Wesley's preachers there were those who had lost wives, often in childbirth, leaving them with a young family. Recognizing the need to support the families of preachers, Wesley stated in 1779: 'The daughters of travelling preachers from the time that they are nine years of age, shall receive from the said Collection eight guineas a year for four years.'[87] What is unclear is whether the decision by the Connexion to support the girls was based on a desire to see

---

[83] W. T. Graham, *Wesley's Early Experiments in Education* (Ilkeston, 1990), pp. 11-12.

[84] A. H. L. Hastling, *The History of Kingswood School: together with register of Kingswood School and Woodhouse Grove School, and a list of masters* (London, 1898), pp. 1-127.

[85] A. G. Ives, *Kingswood School in Wesley's Day and Since* (London, 1970), p. 39.

[86] *Ryan*, pp. 60-1.

[87] *WJW*, vol 10, p. 432, nn. 522 and 523.

them educated, or a commitment to offer financial support to preachers and their families.[88]

Despite his undoubted sympathy for the poor, there is much in Wesley's writing that suggests his attitude accorded with conventional thinking. Alongside religious instruction, teaching in Methodist schools was to be gender defined, with boys 'instructed in reading, writing and arithmetic', while girls were 'taught reading, writing and needlework'.[89] The provision of an education was not intended to give children aspirations above their station; nor did literacy, and even higher-order skills such as casting accounts, change traditional social hierarchies.

Although Wesley advised parents against sending their daughters to large boarding schools, he supported several smaller boarding establishments run by governesses. He declared of Mary Bosanquet's school in 1765: 'I rode to Leytonstone and found one truly Christian family . . . what that at Kingswood should be, and would be if it had such governors'.[90] He wrote in 1782 that he had 'spent an agreeable hour at the boarding school in Sheriffhales', adding that 'the Misses Yeomans are well qualified in their office', and that 'several of the children are under strong drawings'.[91] Mrs Edwards, who Wesley described as 'a person of no extraordinary natural abilities' taught 'near a hundred children' in her school in Lambeth, keeping them 'in as good, if not better, order than most school mistresses in the kingdom'.[92]

---

[88] Perhaps the fact that support was offered during formative years, rather than from birth, suggests that there was some desire to support education.
[89] W. W. Stamp, *The Orphan-house of Wesley, with notices of Early Methodism in Newcastle-upon-Tyne, and its vicinity* (London, 1863), p. 269.
[90] *WJW*, vol 22, p. 17.
[91] 'Drawings' assumed to mean drawn to piety. *WJW*, vol 23, p. 233 and n. 72. Sheriffhales is near Madeley, in Shropshire.
[92] *WJW*, vol 24, p. 66.

The school run by Mrs Owen and her daughters in Publow, Somerset, six miles south of Kingswood, was described by Wesley as 'perhaps the best boarding school for girls in Great Britain'.[93] He commended Frances Owen for limiting her boarders to twenty so that she could look after them properly. Nevertheless, in a letter dated 6 September 1772, published in the *Arminian Magazine* for 1785, Owen suggested that, as several of the children's parents were not spiritual and were consequently 'pleased with trifles', they had begun to teach the children 'to make artificial flowers, network, and little pieces of embroidery'.[94] Unhappy with the inclusion of such 'worldly' accomplishments, Wesley's early support for the school appears to have declined, since he suggested that the school had lost its 'original simplicity'.[95]

Wesley frequently corresponded with Mary Bishop; and a letter from her dated 4 March 1777 appeared in the *Arminian Magazine* for 1788. Bishop confirmed that she was able to keep 'all eye and all ear' on her charges, and save them from the 'contagion of bad example'.[96] Wesley advised Bishop: 'Let it be said of the young women you educate: Grace was in all her steps, heaven in her eye; In all her gestures sanctity and love.[97] Wesley condemned as unwise and unkind those parents who desired to make their daughters 'finer than themselves'. Threatening to 'make their ears tingle', he warned Bishop on 17 July 1781 not to be influenced by the 'fashions of the world', but to set an example herself, and thereby train her pupils by 'all mildness and firmness' to a Christian life of primitive simplicity.[98] In a further letter to Wesley, Bishop once again complained about parents who were threatening to remove their daughters

---

[93] Ibid., vol 10, p. 432.
[94] *AM*, vol 11, (1785), 551-2.
[95] *JWL*, vol 7, p. 74.
[96] *AM*, vol 11, (1788), 103. Bishop ran a school in Keynsham, near Bristol. Ives, *Kingswood School*, p. 39.
[97] *JWL*, vol 7, p. 63.
[98] Ibid., vol 7, p. 74.

because they were not being instructed in dancing. Wesley responded: 'If dancing be not evil in itself, it leads young women to numberless evils . . .'[99]

Among Wesley's wealthy followers was Lady Darcy Maxwell, who in July 1770 opened a day school for children of the poor in Edinburgh.[100] In June 1782, Wesley noted that the forty children in the school were 'swiftly brought forward in reading and writing, and learn the principles of religion'. It seems, however, that the involvement of an aristocratic patron in the education of the poor was not without its complications. Wesley lamented: 'I observe in them all the *ambitiosa paupertas* [ambitious poverty]. Be they ever so poor, they must have a scrap of finery. Many of them have not a shoe to their foot; but the girl in rags is not without her ruffles'.[101]

Wesley encouraged the opening of schools in his preaching-houses.[102] The account by Silas Told of his time at the Foundery school between 1744 and 1751 gives an insight into how Wesley's schools for pauper children were run. It also provides evidence of the disparity between the numbers of boys and girls receiving an education and suggests that only the achievements of boys were worthy of mention. Told's account, published in 1786, stated:

> I was established in the Foundery School and in the space of a few weeks, collected three score boys and six girls; but the society being poor, could not grant me more than ten shillings per week. This, however, was sufficient for me, as they boarded and clothed my daughter. Having children under my care from five in the morning till five in the evening, both winter and summer, sparing no pains, with the assistance of an usher and four monitors. I continued in the school seven

---

[99] Ibid., vol 7, p. 228.
[100] Ibid., vol 5, pp. 181-2.
[101] *WJW*, vol 23, p. 241.
[102] For an explanation of the pattern of Wesley's preaching-houses see *Ryan*, pp. 89-95.

years and three months, and discharged two hundred and seventy five boys; most of them were fit for any trade.[103]

Along with religious instruction, boys were taught reading, writing, and arithmetic, whereas girls (largely outnumbered by boys) received instruction in reading, writing, and needlework. Wesley's own judgement on the work of the Foundery school was that 'an happy change was soon observed in the children, both with regard to their tempers and behaviour'; adding 'they learned reading, writing and arithmetic swiftly and at the same time they were diligently instructed in the sound principles of religion.'[104]

Conclusion

Evidence presented in this chapter demonstrates that the provision of an education in eighteenth-century Britain was not only dependent on social status; it was also divided along gender lines. Although Susanna Wesley had been instructed to a level far beyond that which was customary for her time and sex, and her attitude towards her daughters' education was striking for the time, female education was nonetheless restricted by the gender constraints of the period. Not only were her daughters unable to attend public school or university, but their education, while enabling them to advance their learning to a level beyond that of many of their peers, was not always a blessing.

Contemporary scholarship surrounding the education system adopted by Susanna Wesley at Epworth refutes previous claims that her system was austere and puritanical. Undoubtedly, she was, as Wallace states in the opening chapter of this volume, a 'strong woman, much edgier than the sweet caricature of mother-cum-primary-teacher'. But, as this chapter argues, it is evident that her methods were governed by respect and

---

[103] S. Told, *An Account of the life, and dealings of God with Silas Told, late preacher of the Gospel* . . . (London, 1786), pp. 95-6.
[104] *WJW*, vol 9, pp. 278-9.

affection for her children. While her assertion that her children should 'fear the rod, and cry softly' might appear harsh when taken out of context, her insistence on a regular method in all things was designed to instil habits of self-discipline and self-control among her offspring. These were important aspects of piety and virtue, to be learned alongside academic advancement, and designed to safeguard her children from frivolity and sin; for as Susanna herself stated, it was 'no small honour . . . to be entrusted with the care of so many souls'.

John Wesley's thinking on female education was undoubtedly influenced by his upbringing at Epworth. His mother's education system demonstrated that education was important not only for learning but as an aid to piety. Wesley encouraged women and girls to be educated, but the evidence demonstrates that the significance of this education lay in how it might enhance their piety, that their souls might be saved, rather than advancing their intellect. Wesley may have been more ready to instruct the poor in writing and accounts than many of his contemporaries. Nevertheless, his thinking was of its day. Educating children of the poor was regarded as a means by which they might be inculcated in religion, obedience, and industriousness, while ensuring they remained 'in their station'.[105]

That Wesley's educational programme was more evangelical than academic is hardly surprising. Raised himself in an atmosphere of piety and learning, Wesley was in adulthood a prominent figure at the heart of the spiritual revival in the British Isles in the eighteenth century. He regarded scholarship

---

[105] For example, Isaac Watts concluded: 'The masters and mistresses of these schools among us teach the children of the poor which are under their care to know what their station in life is, how mean their circumstances are, how necessary 'tis for them to be diligent, laborious, honest and faithful, humble and submissive, what duties they owe the rest of mankind and particularly their superiors.' Watts, *An Essay Towards the Encouragement of Charity Schools*, p. 26.

as a Christian virtue, and championed education as an aid to piety.[106] His Arminian theology argued that salvation through faith was available to all; hence education should be available to all. He argued that the sole end of life, and consequently of education, was to prepare for eternity; 'for this and no other purpose is our life either given or continued', he stated.[107] Yet salvation through faith required not only a change of 'mind', but a change of 'heart'; therefore, education represented, just as it had done for his mother, just one aspect of what Wesley considered necessary for an individual to live a Christian life of holiness.

Thus education and literacy, combined with Wesley's Arminian doctrine of self-advancement for all, often led to upward social mobility, and gave the adult poor within Methodist societies, particularly women, opportunities to become involved, either within the society, or as preachers and teachers of the young. Although Wesley encouraged learning which conformed to Christian values of virtue, morality and piety, by exposing followers to the practice of frequent reading, Methodism ignited an urge for self-improvement, which was supported through association with preachers and fellow Methodists.[108] John Lenton, in chapter four of this volume, refers to the 'accounts of Susanna's time each week with each child individually and her advice to her sons as seen in her letters to them . . . [and] the prayer meetings she held in her kitchen' as highly significant. They were the beginnings of a familial legacy, the influence of which was far-reaching. That Susanna's sons recognized and acknowledged the spiritual importance of women's actions indeed laid the foundation for the 'bright succession, and the extraordinary call' to which this volume rightly pays homage.

---

[106] L. A. Ryan, 'John Wesley and the Teleology of Education' in W. Gibson, D. O'Brien, and M. Turda (eds), *Teleology and Modernity* (Abingdon, 2019), pp. 56-68.

[107] *WJW*, vol 3, p. 25.

[108] *Ryan*, p. 172.

4: Susanna Wesley, John Wesley and 'the Extraordinary Call' [to preach]

John Lenton

This chapter began as a paper at the Lincoln conference in summer 2019 to celebrate Susanna's 350th birthday. In November 2019 there was a second conference with the title of 'An Extraordinary Call' about Methodist women preachers in Britain from the beginnings of Methodism to the present. The influential historian John Walsh has an important passage about John Wesley's phrase 'the Extraordinary Call': Wesley:

> Had a simple criterion for the evaluation of each providential call to a new, irregular 'prudential help'. Did it win souls and build them up? . . . A conviction, buoyed up by *frissons* of pre-millennial hope, that this was an 'extraordinary', almost Pentecostal outpouring of the Spirit, enabled him to justify the use of [male] lay preachers ('*extraordinary* messengers, raised up by God to provoke the *ordinary* ones to jealousy') and to sanction women preachers on the same grounds, assuring one of these, Mary Bosanquet, that since Methodism was 'an extraordinary dispensation of his providence, therefore I do not wonder if several things occur therein which do not fall under the ordinary rules of discipline'.[1]

This chapter attempts to explain and discuss that statement and link Wesley's ideas in it to the influence of Susanna Wesley. It also links the first section of this book about Susanna Wesley based on the papers given at the Lincoln conference to the

---

[1] J. Walsh, 'Religious Societies; Methodist and Evangelical' in W. J. Shiels and D. Wood (eds), *Voluntary Religion* (Oxford, 1986), pp. 279-302; the quotation is on p. 291. Walsh wrote relatively little, but his pupils are still rewriting Methodist history.

second section on women preachers composed of papers from the second conference held at Oxford.

There are three important ideas which can be found in Walsh's quotation. The first is the contrast between the ordinary and the extraordinary and that the extraordinary messenger whether male or female was the instrument of God's work.[2] The second is the idea of providence as the dispenser of these extraordinary calls and indeed of the whole Methodist phenomenon. The third is the idea that the extraordinary dispensations of providence could be justified by the preachers' success.[3]

All historians agree that Susanna Wesley was a major influence on her son John.[4] Chilcote suggests that 'It is difficult to exaggerate the influence that Susanna Wesley exerted on her sons and consequently on the religious movement which they founded'.[5] More recently, as Charles Wallace noted, Pauline Watson has married history and psychology to show how important Susanna's influence was on both John and Charles.[6] The accounts of Susanna's time each week with each child individually and her advice to her sons as seen in her letters to them are well known. However, the prayer meetings she held in her kitchen, which we should assume both John and Charles would have joined occasionally and would certainly be aware of, with more than two hundred attenders in the building, are worth emphasizing for their influence on the brothers and their

---

[2] After the lecture was delivered at the Lincoln conference Bill Gibson made the point that for eighteenth-century English clergymen 'ordinary' was an adjective of 'ordinal', i.e. rule or rubric. An 'extraordinary' event could be outside the rule but was not therefore invalid.

[3] Definition of success, and providence included later in this chapter and in the conclusion.

[4] John, Charles and Samuel agreed that their father Samuel Wesley also had a large influence on them. On John Wesley the literature is vast. Rack's *Reasonable Enthusiast* remains the best biography.

[5] *Chilcote, 1991,* p. 17.

[6] Watson, *'Two Scrubby Travellers'*.

belief in the spiritual importance of women's actions.[7] The story of John's escape from the fire is another episode which Susanna and others told and retold. This event, later immortalised for Methodists in the painting by Henry Perlee Parker, and the story told by the family, especially Susanna,[8] influenced the young John to believe that God had preserved him for a purpose. He was the child rescued in extraordinary circumstances for a special and providential destiny.[9]

What that destiny was to be was not at first clear. In the 1730s he thought he was called to convert the native Americans. When he returned from what appeared to be his failure in Georgia and followed Charles through a conversion experience, becoming one of the leaders of the revival, the purpose was from then on to 'spread scriptural holiness' throughout the country.[10] It is unsurprising that John looked for similar extraordinary methods and ways in which God's purposes could be worked out to help that revival and commend them to others. To his mind the extraordinary events were always justified by their

---

[7] Rack, *Reasonable Enthusiast*, pp. 53-4, 58. Susanna held the meetings in 1712. John did not go to the Charterhouse until January 1714. Baker pointed out that Susanna referred to these meetings as 'our society'; F. Baker, The People Called Methodists: Polity' in R. E. Davies, A. R. George and E. G. Rupp (eds), *History of Methodism in Great Britain* 4 vols (London, 1965), vol 1, p. 216; *Wallace*, pp. 78-9.
[8] *Wallace*, p. 235, cf. I. J. Maddock, 'The Whole World is now my parish' in I. J. Maddock (ed.), *Wesley and Whitefield? Wesley versus Whitefield?* (Eugene, OR, 2019) pp. 44-5. For an assessment of the 'scene painting' of the fire at Epworth see P. Forsaith, *Image, Identity and John Wesley: a study in portraiture* (Abingdon, 2018), pp. 56-61.
[9] Walsh described this as 'regarding himself as a man guided as with pillars of cloud and fire by clear leadings of Providence'; Walsh, 'Religious Societies: Methodist and Evangelical', p. 191.
[10] Modern historians would say he did not fail completely; see the revisionist study by Hammond, *John Wesley in America*. For the Aldersgate conversion experience see R. Maddox (ed.), *Aldersgate Reconsidered* (Nashville, 1990). For spreading scriptural holiness see pp. 551-4.

success.[11] To Susanna, her success in her 1712 kitchen meetings, when over two hundred came and the whole ground floor was taken over, was such that she was prepared to stand up for them to her husband and anyone else who chose to condemn her as a mere woman.[12] The fact that it was the handiwork of the Lord was proved to her by the success of her actions in that the behaviour of people of the parish had improved. More came to church.[13] The failure in Georgia showed that Wesley had not found his divine purpose and he never went back to America, in contrast to Whitefield who returned again and again and has even been described as an 'American Patriot'.[14] Success in terms of numbers of converts was to be used to justify Wesley's preaching outside, his preaching in other clergy's parishes when they protested, then lay preaching, class meetings and eventually, in the 1760s and '70s, preaching by women. John Wesley acknowledged the debt to his mother when he described her as 'in her measure and degree, a preacher of righteousness'.[15]

The phrase 'extraordinary' was used by Wesley to relate what happened at the beginning of the revival. By 1739 it had spread first in London and then in Bristol. The chief leader was George Whitefield, who was the first to preach outside in Bristol in February 1739 and also in London. Thousands gathered to

---

[11] See n. 14 below.

[12] *Wallace,* pp. 78-83 and see chapter two in this book especially section three.

[13] Ibid. pp. 13, 81-2. See also for a new description of the whole affair the forthcoming W. Gibson, *Samuel Wesley and the Crisis of Tory Piety,* chapter seven and especially pp. 308-12. I am grateful to Bill Gibson for letting me look at a draft copy.

[14] See for example the discussion in C. G. Pestana, 'Whitefield and Empire' in G. Hammond and D. Ceri Jones (eds), *George Whitefield: life, context and legacy* (Oxford, 2016), p. 96.

[15] *WJW,* vol 19, p. 284.

listen.[16] Whitefield wanted others to follow his example and persuaded his friends the Wesley brothers to preach outside in those two cities.[17] Societies were founded in each. The preachers were invited further afield, particularly near Bristol, and societies were founded close by in both Wiltshire and Somerset. John Wesley used the metaphor of an extraordinary call in a letter to his anxious younger brother in June 1739: 'And to do this I have both an ordinary call and an extraordinary . . . perhaps this might be better expressed in another way. God bears witness in an extraordinary manner that my thus exercising my ordinary call is well-pleasing in his sight.'[18]

While his ordinary call was his ordination as a priest, the extraordinary call to preach outside was supported by the testimony of the Spirit as seen in the success in making converts and growth of spiritual life in their membership of the societies.[19]

Lay preachers

It is fascinating to discover that Susanna was at the heart of the change to the 'irregular prudential help', i.e. laymen preaching, which Wesley introduced early in the rise of Methodism.[20] In the revival there were not enough clergymen to preach and lead worship to meet the demand. In August 1739 Whitefield went to America again. The Wesleys and their clerical friends (few of whom were prepared to preach in the open air) began to look

---

[16] R. P. Heitzenrater, *Wesley and the People Called Methodists* (Nashville, 1995), p. 99 'the numbers ranged from one to seven thousand'.
[17] Maddock, 'The Whole World is now my parish', pp. 51-61.
[18] John Wesley to Charles Wesley, 23 June 1739, *WJW*, vol 25, p. 660.
[19] F. Baker, *John Wesley and the Church of England* (London, 1970), p. 137, cf. John Wesley's letter in *WJW*, vol 26, p. 206 where Wesley decries 'order'.
[20] See the most thorough investigation of the story, F. Baker, 'Thomas Maxfield's First Sermon' in *PWHS*, vol 27, (1949-50), 7-15. See also Newton, *Susanna Wesley*, pp. 180-1 and *JWP*, pp. 32-3.

for laymen in both cities to take more responsibility in leading the societies. It is at this point that the story is told about Susanna Wesley in London. She was living at the Wesleys' London headquarters, the Foundery on City Road, from late 1739.[21] This was an old building which had been altered to become a place for them to ride out from and return to. It was where their publications could be stored and sold, and where the early Methodists met for society and class meetings and also preaching, the important part of early Methodist worship. There are two versions of the story. In the first telling by Thomas Coke and Henry Moore in 1792, Wesley being:

> About to leave London for a season, he appointed one whom he judged to be strong in faith . . . to meet the Society at the usual times, to pray with them, and give them such advice as might be needful. This was Mr Maxfield . . . This young man, being fervent in spirit and *mighty in the Scriptures*, greatly profited the people: they crowded to hear him; and by the increase of their number, as well as by their earnest and deep attention, they insensibly led him to go further . . . He began to preach and the Lord so blessed the word, that many were not only deeply awakened and brought to repentance but were also made happy in a consciousness of pardon. The Scripture marks of true conversion, inward peace and power to walk in all holiness, evinced the work to be of God.

> Some however were offended at this *irregularity*, as it was termed: a complaint was made in form to Mr Wesley, and he hastened to London to put a stop to it. His mother then lived in his house adjoining to the Foundery. When he arrived, she perceived that his countenance was expressive of dissatisfaction and enquired the cause. 'Thomas Maxfield', said he abruptly, 'has turned preacher, I find.' She looked attentively at him, and replied 'John, you know what my sentiments have been: you cannot suspect me of favouring readily any thing of this kind; but take care what you do with

---

[21] *Wallace*, xiv; G. J. Stevenson, *City Road Chapel London and its Associations, Historical, Biographical and Memorial* (London, 1872).

respect to that young man, for he is as surely called of God to preach as you are. Examine what have been the fruits of his preaching, and hear him also yourself.' He did so: his prejudice bowed before the force of truth; and he could only say *'It is the Lord: let him do what seemeth him good'*.[22]

In the second, later (and shorter) version by Adam Clarke, Clarke says Wesley told him this story. Susanna:

Repeatedly sat under the ministry of the first [lay] man Mr Thomas Maxfield[23] who attempted to officiate among the Methodists [in London] in this hitherto unprecedented way . . . Being informed of this new and extraordinary thing, [Wesley] hastened back to London to put a stop to it. Before he took any decisive step, he spoke to his mother on the subject and informed her of his intention. She said, (I have had the account from Mr Wesley himself) 'My son, I charge you before God, beware what you do; for Thomas Maxfield is as much called to preach the Gospel as ever you were'![24]

Few others would at that point have dared to stop John Wesley doing what he wanted. Susanna did. John listened to Maxfield and changed his mind. Maxfield had persuaded his hearers, bringing about conversions. This success in preaching proved to both Susanna (who had heard him 'repeatedly') and John Wesley that God had given Maxfield, in John's later words, 'an extraordinary call'.[25] The result was the beginnings of the preaching cadre known as 'John Wesley's preachers' and the

---

[22] T. Coke and H. Moore, *The Life of the Rev John Wesley A.M.* (London, 1792), pp. 231-2. Italics as in the original. Coke and Moore were the Conference's choice as the first official biographers of Wesley after his death. The biblical quotation is 1 Samuel 3:18 (KJV).

[23] Thomas Maxfield (native of Bristol and died 1784) was an itinerant preacher in Methodism 1741-1763. Later ordained (1758), in 1763 he set up a separate chapel in Little Moorfields.

[24] *Clarke, 1823*, pp. 353-4 was, admittedly, emphasizing the importance of Wesley's family.

[25] Compare Wesley arguing 'his blessing my work is abundant proof'; *WJW*, vol 26, p. 237.

itinerant Methodist ministry that continues to this day. It is a good story, much retold, not least from the Methodist pulpit by those preachers. For as Clarke said 'the great body of the Methodist Preachers [will not] forget that Mrs Wesley, the mother of their Founder, was the patroness and first encourager of the Lay Preachers'.[26]

The second version has three new points. Susanna had been listening to Maxfield's preaching for some time. This was not a sudden judgement, but a considered one. Secondly Clarke quotes Wesley as the authority for the story. It would seem likely that Wesley was also the source for Coke and Moore, though they as usual give no source. Finally, Susanna becomes the 'patroness and first encourager' of the lay preachers. Kirk, her nineteenth-century biographer, extended this by describing her 'an instrument in the Divine hand', to whom we are 'indebted for an institution which has developed into a regular ministry, second to none' and an 'order of lay preachers by whose Sunday labours the kingdom of Christ is largely extended'.[27]

When Wesley looked back on the event in later life, he realised the importance of the call to lay men to preach. He saw the key nature of the decision. If the *ordinary* clergy would not preach, then *extraordinary* lay men must. Their preaching led to an outpouring of the Spirit which under any criteria must be judged to be extraordinary. Wesley's belief was that the extraordinary dispensations of providence in using laymen was justified by the preachers' success.[28]

The story about Susanna Wesley and Thomas Maxfield is significant. But questions have to be asked about it. First,

---

[26] *Clarke, 1823*, p. 354. The phrase 'patroness' meant advocate or supporter, which is what Susanna was. There was no financial implication here.

[27] J. Kirk, *The Mother of the Wesleys: a biography* fourth edition (London, 1866), p. 216.

[28] *JWP* especially chapter twenty-one.

Wesley himself never wrote it down. The earliest account only appears in 1792 with Coke and Moore's biography. I am not doubting them or Adam Clarke. However, Wesley could not tell Moore or Clarke before 1778 or Coke before 1776.[29] Wesley's memory was less good in old age. Did it actually happen like that or was Wesley putting together several different occasions? Another reason for questioning the story is that it is difficult to date and some historians think Maxfield was not the first lay preacher.[30] Best and others argue against Maxfield being the first lay preacher and London the place where he preached in favour of John Cennick and Bristol.[31] And of course, if it were Bristol, then Susanna was not there.

Baker pointed out that both stories could be correct and that the best date for the story was early 1741.[32] He suggested John Cennick could have been first, but was already linked to Whitefield rather than Wesley. Maxfield would still be the first lay preacher authorized only by Wesley. It remains very interesting that the anecdote was told about Susanna. It was a sign she had already been adopted by Methodism in the period after Wesley as the original Methodist heroine, the 'Mother of the Founder' in Clarke's words, and so her blessing as 'patroness and first encourager' was useful both for the itinerant ministry and for the role of lay preaching. One argument in favour of the story, and Susanna's importance as the patron of lay preaching in Methodism, is that it was accepted both by Frank Baker who did the most detailed investigation and by

---

[29] Wesley first met Coke in July 1776, Moore in 1778 and Clarke in 1782. It is unlikely he told any of them the story immediately as the story comes from no other source. The earliest it is likely to have been told is therefore the 1780s when Wesley himself was in his eighties and the events were at least forty years earlier.

[30] M. Noll, *The Rise of Evangelicalism* (Manchester, 2004), p. 95 states that Cennick was the first lay preacher.

[31] G. M. Best, *The Cradle of Methodism 1739-2017* (Bristol, 2017), and Best, *John Cennick* (Bristol, 2016).

[32] Baker, 'Thomas Maxfield's first sermon'.

John A. Newton, Susanna's modern biographer.[33] Vicki Tolar Burton has an important passage about Susanna's influence on her son: 'could women lead classes and bands? Of course. His early education was led by a woman'.[34]

One more appearance of this word 'extraordinary' in connection with lay preaching is in the unpublished manuscripts of Charles Wesley's poetry in the John Rylands Library: a series of verses headed by Charles 'Hymns for Preachers extraordinary'. These undated verses are not particularly significant but clearly refer to the laymen who became itinerant preachers employed by the two brothers to spread the gospel. They show that <u>both</u> brothers, the acknowledged leaders of early Methodism, employed the word 'extraordinary' regularly to describe their preachers who were to be so important.[35]

Women preachers

We turn to John Wesley and his attitude to women preachers. From the early days of the Methodist movement, women had a prominent part. To quote Chilcote: 'Women invited and hosted the preachers, founded prayer meetings and societies on . . . their own initiative, and propagated and maintained the faith'.[36] Because women did this, and were encouraged to do so by both Wesleys, they were leading classes which sometimes, especially in smaller societies, were mixed, and they might easily move on to exhortation and even preaching. In the first period of Methodism (up to 1760) such women were few and might often be frowned on by the leadership. Charles Wesley recorded in May 1743, when he examined the society at Evesham, that 'one

---

[33] Another point in favour of accepting the story is that it was one told by Wesley against himself. Such stories rarely reached his writings, but might well be recounted to his associates in old age.
[34] V. Tolar Burton, *Spiritual Literacy in John Wesley's Methodism* (Waco, TX, 2008), p. 193.
[35] JRL, Ms, MA 1977/583/8.
[36] *Chilcote, 1991*, p. 49.

only person I reproved; not suffering her any longer, notwithstanding her great gifts, to speak in the church or usurp authority over the men'.[37] In addition, from the earliest days women were in the majority among band members, society members and attenders. They were also the vast majority of the early class leaders. There is a list in April 1742 of the Foundery Society's sixty-six leaders, forty-seven women and nineteen men.[38] John Wesley was concerned at this point that women should not be seen to preach in the Methodist societies. Attacked for a multitude of his actions by contemporaries in print, by letter and verbally, he sought to reduce obloquy by denying that Methodist women preached.[39]

However, women were encouraged to be class leaders, to speak in the class meeting, prayer meeting and later the love feast. They were encouraged to visit the sick and prisons, to read scripture aloud in various meetings, to teach and to exhort their fellows, both male and female, all actions Susanna had done.[40] Grace Murray and Sarah Perrin are both good examples of this. The Wesleys appointed both of them housekeeper of one of the three main Methodist centres (Grace at Newcastle, Sarah at Bristol). They sent them separately to different societies where they and the itinerants were unable to go and expected them to report on the itinerants. John took both Grace and Sarah at different times with him on long journeys to meet the women in

---

[37] S. T. Kimbrough jr and K. G. C. Newport (eds), *The Manuscript Journal of Charles Wesley MA* (Nashville, 2007), vol 2, p. 342 and n. This was the Charles Wesley who received many letters in the early 1740s from Sarah Perrin about her witnessing in different societies. He wrote frequently to her in reply and he does not seem to have reproved her.

[38] Stevenson, *City Road Chapel London*, pp. 28-39.

[39] *Chilcote, 1991*, pp. 54-8.

[40] *Ryan*, pp. 61-2, 97, 153-4. Burton, *Spiritual Literacy*, pp. 158-61.

the societies, to expound scripture and exhort. John described Grace as a 'fellow labourer in the Gospel'.[41]

In the 1760s this began to change further. Both Sarah Crosby and Mary Bosanquet were encouraged to preach; they also taught.[42] Others followed them. Sarah Crosby in 1761 moved to Derby, a place at the time not in any circuit. A Methodist member and Sarah's convert Mrs Dobinson had rented a large house in Derby in order to form a Methodist society.[43] Sarah was invited to stay where she led a class of about thirty. One day two hundred people turned up to it, so she preached to them.[44] She wrote to the nearest preacher to come and visit and also wrote to Wesley to inquire as to what more she should do. Wesley replied three days later, telling her in one breath 'The Methodists do not allow women preachers' and in the next 'I do not see that you have broken any law. Go on calmly and steadily'. He did not tell her not to preach.[45]

In the summer of 1771 there was an important exchange of letters between John Wesley and Mary Bosanquet.[46] Mary wrote first a lengthy letter in which she recounted her history in Leytonstone and Cross Hall. She explained her practice, the fact that one of the circuit's itinerant preachers had objected, but that others had invited her to go with them and to speak after them,

---

[41] G. M. Best, *A Tragedy of Errors: the story of Grace Murray, the woman whom John Wesley loved and lost* (Bristol, 2016), pp. 49ff, and quotation p. 87. G. Lloyd, 'Sarah Perrin (1721-1787): Early Methodist Exhorter' in *Methodist History*, vol 41, no 3, (2003), 79-88. J. Lenton, 'Surviving Letters Received by Charles Wesley' in *Proceedings of the Charles Wesley Society*, vol 19, (2015), 47-50.

[42] *DMBI*. For Bosanquet see also D. R. Wilson, '"Thou shal[t] walk with me in white": Afterlife and Vocation in the Ministry of Mary Bosanquet Fletcher' in *WMS*, vol 1, (2009), 71-85.

[43] *Chilcote, 1991*, p. 120.

[44] *AM*, vol 29, (1806), 518.

[45] *JWJ*, vol 27, Letters 3, pp. 241-2 and nn. 24 and 25. This volume of the letters, published in 2015, replaces *JWL* for the period 1756-65.

[46] *Chilcote, 1991*, pp. 126-7.

and that there had been occasions when she had been invited to speak by herself.[47] She listed objections to her preaching and then answered them. Among her answers was the quoting of biblical, including prophetic, calls to women.[48] She then continued:

> Objection: But all these were extraordinary calls; sure you will not say that yours is an extraordinary call?
>
> Answer: If I did not believe so, I would not act in an extraordinary manner. I do not believe every woman is called to speak publicly, no more than every man is called to be a Methodist preacher. Yet some have an extraordinary call to it, and woe to them if they obey it not.[49]

Mary Bosanquet was arguing for the extraordinary call of women to preach on the same grounds as for men, that it led to an outpouring of the Spirit and new converts and so was successful. More people would come to hear her than would come for the male preacher and so she was enabled to save souls that would otherwise remain in darkness, what Chilcote refers to as the practical argument of 'uncontested fruit'.[50] The last sentence of Bosanquet's answer, as Wilson points out, links what Mary was doing to the prophetic tradition and to the arguments used by Susanna Wesley to defend her teaching ministry in the parish of Epworth to her absent husband, Samuel.[51] Mary's arguments, so carefully presented, and her

---

[47] The preacher who objected to her was almost certainly John Atlay, who is referred to as 'Mr A' in a letter to Sarah Crosby of the same date. *JWL*, vol 5, pp. 257-8. Ironically Atlay had been converted by a woman preacher, Hannah Harrison.

[48] Wilson, 'Afterlife and Vocation', 81-4 focuses on the prophetic emphasis in Bosanquet's arguments.

[49] *Chilcote, 1991*, pp. 299-304. *Lloyd*, pp. 34-5 mistakenly argues that this was Bosanquet introducing the idea of an extraordinary call, twice mentioning it.

[50] P. W. Chilcote, *The Methodist Defense of Women in Ministry: a documentary history* (Eugene, OR, 2017), p. 11.

[51] Wilson, 'Afterlife and Vocation', 81-2.

obvious success swayed Wesley. In a much shorter letter he replied on 13 June 1771:

> My dear sister
> I think the strength of that cause rests there, on your having an *Extraordinary* Call. So, I am persuaded has every one of our Lay Preachers: otherwise I could not countenance his preaching at all. It is plain to me that the whole work of God is a wonderful dispensation of His Providence. Therefore I do not wonder if several things incur therein which do not fall under ordinary rules of discipline. St Paul's ordinary rule was 'I permit not a woman to speak in the congregation' yet in extraordinary cases he made a few exceptions; at Corinth in particular. I am my dear sister,
> Your affectionate brother
> J. Wesley [52]

Note Wesley's reference to 'Providence'.[53] To him all his preachers were lay, whether men or women, and possessed an extraordinary call, otherwise he could not justify them. He even adopted Paul, so often seen as the misogynist bane of women preachers, for the idea of the extraordinary call for women.[54] From then on there were a number of women preachers, whom Wesley encouraged and who, in different ways, were licensed to preach. Often our knowledge of this is dependent on oral testimony, such as when John Wesley is supposed to have said to the Cornish preacher Ann Gilbert 'Do all the good you can'.[55]

---

[52] *JWL*, vol 5, 257. In the original Ms, *extraordinary* is underlined for emphasis. Eryn White (chapter five) and Jill Barber (chapter eleven) also discuss this Pauline injunction.

[53] For Wesley on providence see R. E. Richey, 'Methodism and Providence' in K. Robbins (ed.), *Studies in Church History Subsidia 7: Protestant evangelicalism: Britain, Ireland, Germany and America c.1750-c.1950* (Oxford, 1990), pp. 51-77 esp. p. 61 and n. 29.

[54] 1 Corinthians 14:34-5, 1 Timothy 2:11-13. It is only fair to Paul to say that most modern commentators doubt the authenticity of both passages.

[55] *Chilcote, 1991*, p. 145 quoting Z. *Taft*, 1:49.

However, there are a few examples, mostly towards the end of Wesley's life, when he went further, including one where he mentions providence. One example of this was with Sarah Mallet, to whom Wesley sent an authorization to preach from the Conference in 1787.[56] The note in question read: 'We give the right hand of fellowship to Sarah Mallet and have no objection to her being a preacher in our connection, so long as she preaches the Methodist doctrine and attends to our discipline'.[57] Sarah's modern biographer, David East, pointed out this was an extraordinary act by Wesley, that it happened to nobody else, man or woman, and that she, Sarah, certainly took it as a command to preach and travel.[58] East speculated that Wesley, who at the same time had begun to ordain male itinerant preachers, was preparing a new status for women preachers as well. He even suggested that 'Wesley was moving towards the idea of appointing Sarah as one of his itinerant preachers'.[59] This is conjecture, but the fact remains that the note to preach for a woman from Conference was unique, and therefore was definitely 'extraordinary'. Later in 1789, while defending Sarah Mallet, Wesley wrote about her preaching 'Perhaps there was some end of Divine Providence (not known unto us) to be answered thereby'.[60]

Another Wesley letter to another woman preacher, the Lancashire Ann Cutler, is worth mentioning for its opening sentence:

---

[56] D. East, *My Dear Sally: the life of Sarah Mallet, one of John Wesley's preachers* (Loughborough, 2003).
[57] Z. *Taft*, 1:84. There is a slightly different version in the *Methodist Recorder*, see J. Conder Nattrass, 'Great Yarmouth' in *PWHS*, vol 3, no 3, (1901), 74. The main difference in the *Recorder* version is that the conditional clause becomes 'continues to preach the Methodist doctrine' which implies she had already been doing it.
[58] East, *My Dear Sally*, pp. 50-60.
[59] Ibid., p. 57.
[60] *Chilcote, 1991*, p. 197.

My Dear Sister[61]

There is something of the dealings of God with your soul, which is out of the common way. But I have known several whom he has been pleased to lead in exactly the same way;[62]

After a little more Wesley concludes: 'Go on, in the name of God and in the power of his might'. The phrase 'out of the common way' is another method of expressing the idea of 'extraordinary'.

At the end of his life, in January 1791,[63] Wesley received a letter from an Irish Methodist, Alice Cambridge, asking for advice about her preaching. Wesley immediately replied that conscience 'will not permit you to be silent when God commands you to speak'.[64]

Conclusion

John Wesley was encouraged by his mother Susanna, both by her earlier actions, and by her own advice, to adopt the 'extraordinary' idea of allowing laymen to preach. It had been 'extraordinary' for John and Charles Wesley to preach outside in other men's parishes, but it was justified by their 'providential success'. The same logic was used by Whitefield and the Wesleys to allow laymen to preach. It was successful, it showed God's providence was at work; it was 'extraordinary' and Wesley, after his conversation with Susanna, was prepared to justify it. It had, after all, been happening in other places, in

---

[61] JRL, MA/2009/001/2, given this century by its owner Mrs Anne Brown.

[62] Compare *JWL*, vol 8, pp. 214-15 where Telford has 'exactly in'.

[63] Only sixteen later letters written by Wesley have survived.

[64] *JWL*, vol 8, pp. 28-9. J. J. McGregor, *Memoir of Miss Alice Cambridge* (Dublin, 1832), pp. 39-40. In the letter Wesley says he had received her letter an hour previously.

Wales, for example, and in America and in Germany.[65] Why should it not happen here as well?

As the Methodist movement developed under Wesley's control, so its needs grew, and the numbers of women of sufficient ability and experience grew with it. David Hempton has famously called Methodism 'a religion of female preponderance'.[66] He added:

> But in the context of undeniable female successes, Wesley adopted an increasingly pragmatic view of women's public role, culminating in his characteristic invention of the device of 'the extraordinary call' which was a way of allowing him to hold on to a conventional Pauline hermeneutic, while acknowledging that women's abilities could be successfully harnessed to the mission of the church.

The successes of many women such as Elizabeth Hurrell[67] and Sarah Crosby, and the logic of Mary Bosanquet, led him to see that the device of 'an extraordinary call' which he had already used for laymen could be used in the case of women as well. It was providence which led Sarah Crosby to Mrs Dobinson's house in Derby. It was providence which took the well-educated southerner Mary Bosanquet to Methodist Yorkshire, where she was to preach to thousands in a quarry at Golcar in 1776, and later took her to Madeley to marry John Fletcher and settle to preach there.[68] It was providence which led poor country girls such as Ann Cutler and Sarah Mallet to begin preaching successfully in Lancashire and Norfolk.

Finally Wesley used the idea of providence again when in 1784 he wanted to ordain preachers for America. He began his

---

[65] J. Walsh, 'Origins of the Evangelical Revival' in G. V. Bennett and J. Walsh (eds), *Essays in Modern Church History in Memory of Norman Sykes* (London, 1966). For Wales see also Eryn White's chapter, which follows.

[66] Hempton, *Methodism: empire of the Spirit*, p. 137.

[67] For Elizabeth Hurrell see *Chilcote, 1991*, pp. 270-1.

[68] Ibid., pp. 166-8.

justification for that step as follows: 'By a very uncommon train of providences',[69] the jurisdiction of the Bishop of London in America had been ended by the 1783 peace. This enabled Wesley to claim that there was a need for him to ordain preachers for the Americans. The example highlights Wesley's unanswerable logic. As with laymen preaching in 1741 and women preaching in 1771, Wesley's use of God's providence was justified by events. The American Methodist Episcopal Church, which he created in 1784, became more successful than its British mother and grew faster than any other religious group in America for the next century. The preachers in British Methodism today, male and female, who claim to be 'Mr Wesley's preachers' are still examined about their call, which reminds each of us of the device of the 'extraordinary call', that product of John Wesley's fertile mind, influenced in several ways by his mother Susanna, which he used to encourage and justify lay men and women preaching.

---

[69] A claim described by Ward as the 'understatement of the century'. W. R. Ward, 'The legacy of John Wesley: the pastoral office in Britain and America' in A. Whiteman, J. S. Bromley and P. G. M. Dickson (eds), *Statesmen, Scholars and Merchants: essays in eighteenth-century history presented to Dame Lucy Sutherland* (Oxford, 1973), reprinted in A. Chandler (ed.), *The Selected Writings of W. R. Ward* (Farnham, 2014), p. 154.

5: 'A Woman is stir'd up to speak':[1] pioneer women preachers of eighteenth-century Welsh Methodism

Eryn White

This chapter looks at the potential for activism and agency among the eighteenth-century female recruits of the Methodist movement in Wales, focusing on the extent to which they were able to take on preaching roles. The evangelical revival had a significant effect on the country during this period, but it was only in the nineteenth century that formal Methodist denominations came into being as a result. The revival also had the effect of revitalizing existing Dissenting groups, leading to a striking growth in Nonconformist causes by the early nineteenth century. The aim of this chapter is to discuss the implications that this had for women, for whom there were increased, but limited, opportunities to contribute during the fervour of revival and its aftermath. By assessing the limited evidence available, this chapter looks at how these women analysed and described their spiritual condition, and how they expressed their faith through letters, hymns, and in a few cases, by exhorting in their local Methodist societies.

The evangelical revival had a substantial impact in Wales, transforming the religious adherence of the population within the space of a century. By the time of the 1851 religious census, worshippers with the four largest Nonconformist denominations, including both strands of Methodism, Calvinistic and Wesleyan, together outnumbered Anglican worshippers in Wales.[2] The Wesleyan Methodists gained a

---

[1] National Library of Wales, Aberystwyth (NLW), Calvinistic Methodist Archive (CMA), Diaries of Howel Harris 72, 29 April 1741.

[2] I. Gwynedd Jones, *Explorations and Explanation: essays in the social history of Victorian Wales* (Llandysul, 1981), pp. 178-9.

substantial following during the nineteenth century, but in the eighteenth century it was the Calvinist branch which led the way, and which would emerge as the single largest denomination in Wales by the mid-nineteenth century.[3] The progress of the Wesleyan movement was initially slow, hampered by problems of communication, without many Welsh-speaking preachers and without the ready assistance with translation provided by the Welsh movement to its Calvinistic allies. George Whitefield, for instance, was generally accompanied by Welsh-speaking companions on his preaching tours in Wales.[4]

As a result, the Wesleyan cause was largely confined during the eighteenth century to areas where there was greater knowledge of English, such as Cardiff, Breconshire and south Pembrokeshire. Even by 1790, membership of Wesleyan Methodism had reached just 566.[5] By contrast the decision in 1800 to embark on a Welsh-medium mission in Wales led to a rapid growth in north-east Wales in the early years of the nineteenth century, spreading swiftly to the rest of the country to establish Wesleyan Methodism as the fourth major Nonconformist denomination by the middle of the century, following after the Calvinistic Methodists, Congregationalists

---

[3] While Arminians, including John Wesley, maintained that salvation was conditional on faith, Calvinists such as George Whitefield maintained that salvation was predestined by God, and could not be 'earned'. See L. Madden (ed.), *Methodism in Wales: a short history of the Wesley tradition* (Llandudno, 2003).

[4] For instance, Howel Harris accompanied him to speak in Welsh after Whitefield's preaching in English in areas of south Carmarthenshire in April 1743. CMA, Trevecka Ms 856, Howel Harris to John Lewis, 18 April 1743. E. M. White, 'Whitefield, Wesley and Wales', *PWHS*, vol 58, no 3, (2011), 136-50.

[5] D. G. Knighton, 'English-speaking Methodism' in Madden (ed.), *Methodism in Wales*, p. 5.

and Baptists in terms of numbers of worshippers.[6] Yet the relative scarcity of Wesleyan causes in the eighteenth century means that this chapter will inevitably concentrate on the role of women in the Calvinistic branch of Methodism.[7]

The influence of the evangelical revival began to be felt in Wales from the mid-1730s, with the two main leaders, Daniel Rowland and Howel Harris,[8] agreeing in 1737 to pool their efforts, marking the real commencement of the Methodist movement in the country. Their followers were quickly organized into societies, mostly located in south Wales within the diocese of St Davids, the largest of the four Welsh dioceses, covering much of mid and south-west Wales. Growth was gradual and Methodism remained an essentially south Walian phenomenon until around the 1780s. From then on, the movement gained ground substantially in the North as well as the South, making Methodism a truly national religious movement, with a major influence on society and culture.[9]

The Welsh language was an important element in these developments since it was the sole language of the overwhelming majority of the population.[10] Seventeenth-century Puritanism had struggled to overcome the hurdle of language, with only a limited number of Welsh-speaking

---

[6] G. T. Hughes, 'Welsh-speaking Methodism' in Madden (ed.), *Methodism in Wales*, pp. 25-32.

[7] See also Diana Thomas *passim* in chapter six and n. 71 below. She presumably preached only in English.

[8] 'Howel' in Welsh: generally spelt 'Howell' in English.

[9] For a fuller account, see G. Williams, W. Jacob, N. Yates and F. Knight, *The Welsh Church from Reformation to Disestablishment, 1603– 1920* (Cardiff, 2007); D. Ceri Jones, B. S. Schlenther and E. M. White, *The Elect Methodists: Calvinistic Methodism in England and Wales 1735– 1811* (Cardiff, 2012); E. M. White, *The Welsh Methodist Society: the early societies in south-west Wales 1737–1750* (Cardiff, 2020).

[10] G. H. Jenkins, R. Suggett and E. M. White, 'The Welsh Language in Early Modern Wales' in G. H. Jenkins (ed.), *The Welsh Language before the Industrial Revolution* (Cardiff, 1997), pp. 45-50.

followers to provide information and guidance in a medium that would be understood by most of the people.[11] The great historian of Welsh religion, Glanmor Williams, consistently argued from the 1960s to the 1990s that the Protestant Reformation truly came of age in Wales during the eighteenth century.[12] It is difficult not to agree with that assessment, as the growth of literacy through the medium of Welsh and the development of a homegrown brand of the Protestant faith led to a more wholehearted acceptance of Protestantism than had been seen previously.

The success of Calvinistic Methodism in Wales meant that the movement's attitude towards women became increasingly influential in terms of religion and society. However, it was an attitude which was in many aspects consistently very conservative, certainly on the question of women preachers. Most members of early societies were women, a fact acknowledged by William Williams in one of his prose works in 1777.[13] Yet, leadership roles at every level were filled almost exclusively by men. This may explain why so few accounts of women and Methodism, or indeed of women and religion in Wales in general, have been written.[14] A few prominent women,

---

[11] See G. H. Jenkins, *Protestant Dissenters in Wales 1639–1689* (Cardiff, 1992).

[12] G. Williams, *Welsh Reformation Essays* (Cardiff, 1967), p. 30; G. Williams, *The Welsh and their Religion: historical essays* (Cardiff, 1991), p. 54.

[13] '*mae mwy o fenywaid yn proffesu nag sydd o wrywiaid*' ('there are more women professing than there are men'), G. H. Hughes (ed.), *Gweithiau William Williams Pantycelyn, Cyfrol II: Rhyddiaith* (Cardiff, 1967), p. 298.

[14] Religion features in some chapters in S. Clarke and M. Roberts (eds), *Women and Gender in Early Modern Wales* (Cardiff, 2000), and a volume of the *Journal of Welsh Religious History* was dedicated to papers produced by a conference on women and religion: J. R. Guy, K. Jenkins and F. Knight (eds), *Journal of Welsh Religious History*, vol 7, 'Wales, Women and Religion in Historical Perspective', (1999).

such as Ann Griffiths (1776–1805) and Sarah Jane Rees (or Cranogwen, 1839–1916) have received individual attention, but often with a focus on their literary contribution.[15] Indeed, beyond Wales, although the prevalence of women in emerging or minority religious movements is evident, there has been little written on the subject by either historians of religion or those concerned with women's history.[16]

On the question of women preachers, the perceived need for 'an extraordinary call' to justify women's activity was the same in Wales as in England.[17] The same concept of a 'call' to preach was in fact what gave authority to all the Methodist lay preachers, who in Wales were normally referred to as exhorters, and who were said to 'exhort' or 'discourse' rather than to preach. Care was taken over terminology to avoid seeming to encroach on the jurisdiction of the church and its ordained ministers. There was a particular need to tread carefully because one of the main leaders, Howel Harris, remained a layman and had been refused ordination in the Church because of his Methodist activities, which were regarded as highly irregular by the Bishop of St Davids.[18]

For similar reasons, caution was certainly exercised over the role allowed to women, so as not to stray too far from what was acceptable to the Established Church. Despite this, in 1741

---

[15] A. M. Allchin, *Ann Griffiths* (1976); A. M. Allchin, *Ann Griffiths: the furnace and the fountain* (Cardiff, 1987); D. G. Jones, *Cofiant Cranogwen* (1932); G. Jones, *Cranogwen: Portread Newydd* (Llandysul, 1981); C. Lloyd-Morgan, 'From temperance to suffrage?' in A. John (ed.), *Our Mother's Land: chapters in Welsh women's history, 1830–1939* (Cardiff, 1991), pp. 135-58; H. A. Hodges, *Flame in the Mountains: Williams Pantycelyn, Ann Griffiths and the Welsh hymn*, ed. E. Wyn James (Tal-y-bont, 2017).

[16] Malmgreen (ed.), *Religion in the Lives of English Women*, p. 1.

[17] Walsh, 'Religious Societies; Methodist and Evangelical'.

[18] CMA, Diaries of Howel Harris 48, 18 August 1739; G. Tudur, *Howell Harris: from conversion to separation 1735–1750* (Cardiff, 2000), pp. 27-30.

Harris granted permission to one woman to speak in her local society. This was Elizabeth Thomas of Blaen-porth, near Aberporth, in south Cardiganshire, one of the earliest recorded Methodist women preachers anywhere. Since she was still alive over fifty years later in 1792, she was obviously a young woman at this point, very likely still in her twenties, as were many of the early society members.[19] Harris visited the society there on 29 April 1741, staying the night at Cwmhowni, the farmhouse where the local society met regularly. The name Cwmhowni means 'valley of the Howni' and the farm was situated in a steeply wooded valley through which the river Howni runs down to the sea in Aberporth. The location is typical of early Welsh rural societies, which often met in fairly remote farmhouses, outside of villages, but close enough to centres of population for sufficient numbers to be able to gather together. Harris recorded in his diary that night:

> I find some do meet but ye men being not gifted a poor humble experienced Loving broken soul a Woman is stir'd up to speak a little & finds great Effect & had Scruples on her mind about it—I said she may I thought when ye Lord gave her Power, Love and success discourse a little in a Society private till ye Lord should send some body fitter—I could not discourage her when I saw her spirit.[20]

It was, therefore, only partial approval to 'discourse a little', with the proviso, 'till ye Lord should send some body fitter', yet this constituted approval, nonetheless. Significantly, it was granted on the basis of the belief that 'ye Lord gave her Power', so that Elizabeth Thomas was perceived to have a call to preach, thirty years before John Wesley sanctioned Mary Bosanquet because of her 'extraordinary call'.[21] The same test seems to have been applied in both cases before coming to the decision that a

---

[19] NLW, St Davids Probate, SD/1792/9: Morgan Hughes, Blaen-porth, Cardigan, 1792; White, *The Welsh Methodist Society*, pp. 144-5.
[20] CMA, Diaries of Howel Harris 72, 29 April 1741.
[21] *JWL*, vol 5, p. 257.

woman might be allowed to preach. It is also significant that she was said to be 'stir'd up to speak', suggesting an external force beyond her own will. Another factor may be the fact that Elizabeth Thomas was described as having a 'great Effect', despite her own scruples. She was confined to the private society, since a very clear distinction was drawn in the early Methodist movement between private and public roles, with some exhorters only allowed to speak in the societies, as their talents were judged not suited to more public preaching.[22] A woman discoursing in a private society would not draw public attention and would not technically flout either canon law or St Paul's injunction that women should be silent in the churches, so this situation avoided any major controversy.[23]

However, this did indeed prove to be a temporary measure, possibly because of a more stringent system of approving would-be preachers. In the first few years of revival, a number of individuals began to take on roles as lay preachers, but by the early months of 1743 the Association,[24] the new governing body of the movement, had taken responsibility for overseeing the activities of the exhorters. Once the Association was set up, there was a rigorous procedure to make sure that only approved candidates would be allowed to speak at Methodist meetings. Part of the rationale was a desire to make sure that nobody spoke out of turn or acted in a way which brought the movement into disrepute, as Howel Harris explained, to 'prevent Confusion & least wicked Persons should go out in our Names & do mischief'.[25]

---

[22] White, *The Welsh Methodist Society*, pp. 76-8.
[23] John Lenton (chapter four) and Jill Barber (chapter eleven) also discuss how St Paul's words were interpreted in respect of women preaching.
[24] The Association was the governing body of Welsh Calvinistic Methodism.
[25] CMA, Trevecka College/1 2945, p. 50, 4 January 1744.

It may well be that giving official sanction to a woman preacher would have been considered too controversial since the name of Elizabeth Thomas does not appear on any list of approved exhorters. William Richard was appointed to oversee the society of Blaen-porth, amongst others in south Cardiganshire and north Pembrokeshire, in February 1743, with private exhorters including John Lloyd, John Gibbon and John Griffith later appointed to assist him in his circuit.[26] If Elizabeth Thomas was at this point side-lined by the Association, she would not have been the only exhorter to be rejected for various failings. Prospective exhorters were put on trial for a period before decisions to approve or reject were made based on reports from local superintendents and feedback from societies where they had been active. The reasons for refusal are not always categorically listed in the Association minutes. It is apparent that some were kept on trial or not allowed to proceed further because of doubts about their suitability of temperament or message, such as William Edward in Pembrokeshire, who seems to have been regarded as too much of a firebrand to be approved.[27]

Rescinding the permission granted to Elizabeth Thomas, if that is what happened, may not have been done simply because she was a woman, but possibly because of some of her opinions, which she expressed in very forthright terms in a letter to Harris in June 1742. This is a remarkable letter in many ways. As a native of south Cardiganshire in the mid-eighteenth century, her first language would almost certainly have been Welsh, but she wrote in articulate English. This was in keeping with the common practice amongst the more educated sections of Welsh society in the eighteenth century to correspond in English, so by

---

[26] CMA, Trevecka College/1 2945, p. 6, 3 February 1743; p. 109, 16 July 1744.

[27] CMA, Trevecka College/1 2945, p. 143, 22 January 1745; G. M. Roberts, 'Y Llafurwyr Cynnar' in G. M. Roberts (ed.), *Hanes Methodistiaeth Galfinaidd Cymru: Cyfrol I: Y Deffroad Mawr* (Caernarfon, 1973), pp. 264-5.

following this trend Elizabeth Thomas was giving an indication of her status. Cwmhowni, the farmhouse in which the Blaen-porth society met, was owned by Jenkin Lewis, who lived in Fareham in Hampshire but also owned property in London and Westminster. In his will, drawn up in 1741, he left his property in Blaen-porth to his niece, Elizabeth Thomas, daughter of Thomas Griffiths.[28] The fact that at least some members of her family seem to have held considerable property and had travelled beyond the confines of the immediate locality may help account for Elizabeth's level of education and self-confidence. However, Harris may have found aspects of her letter quite alarming, since she outlined her misgivings about some of the clergy:

> Any Body that has an Eye of faith may Easily perceive without any presumption that they was never called by Christ to preach the word, nor ministering the sacraments for they never knew any thing of the work of the spirit of God in their own hearts. They never was gifted, fitted nor own'd of God to convert any of their sins, neither did the Lord reveal them any of his hidden mysteries nor fitted them to go in and out before his people, neither had they any hand in this great work, and are these now fit to minister the sacraments to the children of God, or his own servants whome he has own'd to be his instruments to convert to build up his children in the faith?[29]

Elizabeth went on to say that she hoped to have the sacrament administered in their society, not by herself, but by one of the exhorters, insisting 'why should we not have the Liberty of

---

[28] NLW, SD/1770/220: Jenkin Lewis, Fareham, Hampshire (Blaen-porth), 1770. This is an example of the traditional Welsh practice of using the father's first name as the second name. Although several middle-ranking families were following the English trend and adopting fixed surnames instead at around this time, with a lot of sons of Johns and Williams becoming Joneses and Williamses, this family had yet to do so.

[29] CMA, Trevecka Ms 569, Elizabeth Thomas to Howel Harris, June 1742.

conscience seeing the government allows it'. This opinion suggests Dissenting sympathies and there is some indication that Elizabeth may have been a member with some local Dissenting cause. The superintendent for south Cardiganshire, William Richard, informed Howel Harris in September 1742 that 'Sister Betty Thomas' was threatened with excommunication by the Dissenters for receiving Methodists into her home.[30] William Richard was responsible for all of the societies from New Quay in south Cardiganshire to St Davids in Pembrokeshire, so there is no certainty that this was Elizabeth Thomas of Blaen-porth, but it does seem quite likely.

Although relations between Welsh Methodists and Dissenters became increasingly strained throughout the 1740s, during the early part of the decade several Dissenters were to be found amongst the society membership and Elizabeth may well have been one of them. However, it was not just Dissenters in the movement who argued along these lines, as several exhorters of the Anglican persuasion urged the Association to consider the benefits of being able to provide a full ministry to the societies. Such arguments for dissenting from the Church largely fell on stony ground in Association discussions and were consistently opposed by the eighteenth-century leaders. Harris himself remained steadfastly of the opinion that the Methodists should remain within the Church, unless forced to leave by the Church itself, so would be unlikely to welcome Elizabeth's comments regarding taking advantage of the protection granted by law to register as Dissenting meeting houses and administer the sacrament.[31]

Elizabeth then vanished from Methodist history to all intents and purposes, her pioneering role forgotten. The entry in Harris's diary which refers to her is not included in any of the

---

[30] CMA, Trevecka Ms 642, William Richard to Howel Harris, 12 September 1742.
[31] Tudur, *Howell Harris*, pp. 92-118.

published extracts of his diaries,[32] so this sole reference to the earliest Welsh woman Methodist preacher is buried in the manuscript version, the 284 volumes of which few venture to read.[33] She is not even named in most accounts of the early movement, but is described solely as the wife of Morgan Hughes, who was known to have married the heiress of Cwmhowni and to have settled there during the 1740s.[34] However, there is no doubt as to her identity, since, when Jenkin Lewis's will was proven in 1770, administration was granted to his niece and heiress, Elizabeth Thomas, wife of Morgan Hughes.[35]

Morgan Hughes had been a prominent figure in the Methodist movement and was the first superintendent appointed by the Association to oversee the societies in north Cardiganshire in 1743, having already established himself as a respected lay exhorter. He suffered a good deal of persecution for his Methodist activities, culminating in being arrested and put on trial in Cardigan in March 1743 for unlawful assembly. The case was thrown out when the prosecutor failed to appear on the day

---

[32] T. Beynon (ed.), *Howell Harris, Reformer and Soldier (1714–1773)* (Caernarfon, 1958); Beynon (ed.), *Howell Harris's Visits to London* (Aberystwyth, 1960); Beynon (ed.), *Howell Harris's Visits to Pembrokeshire* (Aberystwyth, 1966).

[33] G. Tudur, 'Papurau Howel Harris' in G. H. Jenkins (ed.), *Cof Cenedl XVI* (Llandysul, 2001), pp. 67-94.

[34] For instance, J. Evans, *Hanes Methodistiaeth rhan ddeheuol sir Aberteifi* (Dolgellau, 1904), p. 43; G. M. Roberts, 'Methodistiaeth Gynnar Gwaelod Sir Aberteifi', *Ceredigion*, vol 5, no 1, (1964), 8; G. M. Roberts, 'Y Llafurwyr Cynnar', p. 258.

[35] NLW, SD/1770/220: Jenkin Lewis, Fareham, Hampshire (Blaen-porth), 1770. Methodist historians often tended to concentrate on the extensive material within the Calvinistic Methodist Archive for their research and so did not consult the probate records which confirmed the name of Morgan Hughes's wife, also noted on the letter of administration granted after Hughes's death in 1792, NLW, SD/1792/9: Morgan Hughes, Blaen-porth, Cardigan, 1792.

and after a good deal of lobbying by the Methodists in support of Hughes, including through the influence of Marmaduke Gwynne of Garth, Breconshire, the future father-in-law of Charles Wesley.[36] Gwynne was on the list of JPs for Cardiganshire and had considerable influence which helped protect Methodists in the face of the law.

Despite this favourable outcome, Morgan Hughes ceased to be a Methodist exhorter the following year and his societies in north Cardiganshire fell under the care of William Williams of Pantycelyn.[37] It is not clear what lay behind this decision but, despite appeals from some of the society members who called for his reinstatement, the Association failed to agree in August 1744 on whether he should be permitted to continue to exhort and he seems to have withdrawn completely thereafter.[38] Harris's Assistant,[39] Thomas William, visited the Aberporth area in 1751, by which time Hughes was preaching in a small meeting house built at Cwmhowni for that purpose, but had declined an invitation to become pastor to a group of Congregationalists at nearby Troed-yr-aur.[40] Hughes had therefore certainly thrown in his lot with the local Dissenters after leaving the Methodist cause and it would be no great surprise if Elizabeth had followed suit, if she were not already a member. Yet Cwmhowni remained an important centre for local Methodists for years to come, suggesting that the couple

---

[36] CMA, Trevecka Ms 817, Howel Harris to Marmaduke Gwynne, 12 March 1743; Trevecka Ms 823, Marmaduke Gwynne to Howel Harris, 21 March 1743; CMA, Diaries of Howel Harris 98, 31 March 1743.

[37] CMA, Trevecka College/1 2945, p. 92, 27 June 1744.

[38] CMA, Trevecka Ms 1197, William Jones and eleven others to Howel Harris, 25 June 1744; Trevecca College/1 2945, p. 110, 12 August 1744.

[39] The Assistant was what was later called the superintendent minister.

[40] CMA, Trevecka Ms 2013, Thomas William to Howel Harris, 19 October 1751.

retained a close link to the revival.[41] Although Morgan continued to make use of the meeting house at Cwmhowni to preach, there is no mention of Elizabeth doing so. She was obviously gifted, literate and quite formidable, but even she was unable to continue to exhort in the movement once the rules of the Association were imposed. Membership with the Dissenters would have been unlikely to provide her with greater opportunities either, as there is no record of women being allowed to preach amongst them at this point. As has been noted many times, doors which opened for women could also close when a stricter form of organization was adopted.[42]

The only other known woman Methodist preacher in the eighteenth century was Jane Owens from Dolgellau in north Wales, although there may well have been others who simply do not appear in the documentary evidence. Jane Owens wrote to Howel Harris in 1770, seeking his advice and giving an account of herself as a schoolteacher and seamstress in the area who also spoke in the local societies.[43] Again, there was no suggestion of a more controversial public role and Jane seemed to be operating in an unofficial capacity at this point. Areas of north Wales had been slow to respond to attempts to import the Methodist message through missionaries from the South, so developing their own leaders and exhorters, like Jane Owens, was a vital element in establishing the movement in areas such as Dolgellau.

---

[41] John Thomas, a local Methodist and schoolteacher, notes in his diary hearing preachers, including William Richard and the Dissenter Benjamin Thomas, at 'Cwm' in Blaen-porth. NLW, Ms 20,516, 30 January 1757, 20 March 1757, 14 May 1757, 9 June 1757, 20 November 1757.

[42] *Lloyd*, p. 2.

[43] CMA, Trevecka Ms 2682, Jane Owens to Howel Harris 27 June 1770. The letter is transcribed in G. P. Owen (ed.), *Atgofion John Evans Y Bala: Y Diwygiad Methodistaidd ym Meirionydd a Môn* (Caernarfon, 1997), pp. 135-7.

In 1770, Methodism was still eyed with considerable suspicion in the north, where comparisons were made with the seventeenth-century Puritans who had turned the world upside down and executed a king who was descended from the Tudor family and thus of Welsh blood. North Walians referred to Methodists as Roundheads and Cariadogs, after Walter Cradock, the prominent Welsh Puritan, who had spent a year in the North, in Wrexham in the 1630s, and whose dangerous influence had obviously not been forgotten nor forgiven.[44] Jane Owens's letter testified to the continued opposition in the North: 'This is a terrible place against goodness', she announced. Society meetings would be drowned out by shouting from the outside and ferocious knocking on the door. Yet, Jane felt that she was being preserved by providence from the worst of the hostility since, although people threw stones and spat at her in the street as she went by, they invariably missed their target.[45]

Jane's words are translated here, because the letter was written in Welsh, suggesting that Jane was not of quite the same social status as Elizabeth Thomas. She may well have been one of the many women, men and children who were educated through the charity circulating schools set up by Griffith Jones from the 1730s to the 1770s, where the emphasis was on learning to read the bible in Welsh.[46] Certainly, several of the women who learnt

---

[44] For instance, in W. Roberts, *Ffrewyll y Methodistiaid, neu Butteinglwm Siencyn ac Ynfydog* (Shrewsbury, 1746), p. 29; J. Morgan-Guy, '"Tinkers and other vermin": Methodists and the established church in Wales 1730–1800' in D. W. Roberts (ed.), *Revival, Renewal and the Holy Spirit* (Milton Keynes, 2009), pp. 27-35.

[45] CMA, Trevecka Ms 2682, Jane Owens to Howel Harris 27 June 1770.

[46] For a history of the schools, see G. H. Jenkins, '"An Old and Much Honoured Soldier": Griffith Jones, Llanddowror', *Welsh History Review*, vol 11, no 4, (1983), 449–68; E. M. White, 'Popular Schooling and the Welsh Language 1650–1800' in G. H. Jenkins (ed.), *The Welsh Language before the Industrial Revolution* (Cardiff, 1997), pp. 324-37; W.

to read and write in those schools went on to teach in them. The religious motivation behind the charity schools proved beneficial to women since it ensured that it was considered just as important to save their souls and teach them to read. Education otherwise tended to favour boys who were regarded as having a more prominent role in society.[47]

Jane Owens wrote to Harris explaining her dilemma about how to proceed, being unable to afford to give up her livelihood as a teacher and thus not having the time to itinerate as a preacher in a way that she felt 'would be of benefit to them and me':

> And yet, I have no means nor anything to live on but that, and if I believed from the heart, I think that God would not allow me to be without anything that was necessary for my maintenance in this life. I believe that the Lord has some work from me to do, that I should not stop, and there is nothing established in my thoughts in this. I hope that you will consult God for him to lay me on the path most chosen by him. I am waiting on the voice of the Almighty to place me as would be most beneficial for him . . . I am trying to help some people as far as I can by the help of God, without which, I can do nothing.

One can hear echoes here of Elizabeth Thomas's scruples despite her preaching having great effect, probably because of the very fact that she was a woman. It is worth noting that Jane did not herself lay claim to the role of preacher, but instead stated that it was what others called her: 'There are many places around here where no exhorter is tolerated, and they accept advice better from a woman because she does not have that call

---

T. R. Pryce, 'The Diffusion of the "Welch" Circulating Schools in Eighteenth-century Wales', *Welsh History Review*, vol 25, (2011), 486-519.

[47] See E. M. White, 'Women, Religion and Education' in S. Clarke and M. Roberts (eds), *Women and Gender in Early Modern Wales* (Cardiff, 2000), pp. 210-33; and Linda Ryan's chapter (three) in this volume.

to exhort. And yet they say I am a preacher, but not everyone who is far away from me believes that.'[48]

She thus distanced herself from any direct claim to being a preacher, a term which it might have been rather too presumptuous for her to call herself. It is also interesting that the very idea of women exhorting was so inconceivable to some people that this in a way operated to her advantage and that she was tolerated in places where no male exhorter would be.

The first history of the Methodist movement in the Dolgellau area appeared in a series of articles between 1799 and 1813 in the journal *Trysorfa Ysprydol*, edited by Thomas Charles, recording the recollections of John Evans, born in 1723 and a longstanding member of the Bala Methodist society since the 1740s. In this account, the Methodist cause in Dolgellau owed much to a woman named Jane who had come to the area in 1766 to serve as a schoolteacher. All this accords with Jane Owens's letter of 1770, except that the name supplied by John Evans was Jane Griffith. Since he was used as a major source by nineteenth-century historians of the movement, it is this name which was repeated in some of the early published histories, including the three-volume account of the growth of Calvinistic Methodism in Wales by John Hughes.[49] Goronwy Prys Owen's suggestion that Jane Griffith and Jane Owens must be the same woman seems plausible, given the similarities and the unlikelihood of there being two female schoolteachers taking such a prominent role in the same small town at the same time.[50]

---

[48] In the original, Jane used the word '*pregethreg*', a colloquial form of '*pregethwraig*' which is the feminine form of the Welsh term for preacher: '*pregethwr*' or 'man who preaches'. There is no gender-neutral term for preacher in Welsh.

[49] J. Hughes, *Methodistiaeth Cymru, Cyfrol I* (Wrexham, 1851), pp. 505-6.

[50] It is also the case that Evans's memory was found in other instances to be not always completely accurate on all details. Owen (ed.), *Atgofion John Evans Y Bala*, pp. 31-2.

Elizabeth Thomas and Jane Owens are the only known examples of women preaching at any level in Wales during the early years of the evangelical revival. However, there were potentially other ways for women to show activism. They were of course expected to participate in the societies in the same way as men, which offered the opportunity to be heard in a semi-public setting. They are often mentioned as having provided hospitality for preachers and for those attending various meetings. There was a more informal, often domestic influence exercised by a number of Methodist women, especially perhaps those who belonged to fairly wealthy farming families who played host to societies and Association meetings. Catherine Pugh, for example, of Morfa Bach farmhouse outside Kidwelly, organized exhorters for the local society and provided food and accommodation for a flow of Methodist visitors attending meetings at the nearby chapel of ease, Capel Ifan, which was widely used by the Methodists.[51] She played an important role in making sure that local arrangements were in place, which was a significant element in the movement's progress.[52]

Mary Jones of Fonmon in Glamorgan seems to have performed a similar function for the supporters of Wesley, both before and after the death of her husband, Robert Jones, in 1742.[53] It is easy to overlook the level of organization that was needed to ensure

---

[51] T. Beynon, 'Morfa Bach, Cydweli', *Cylchgrawn Cymdeithas Hanes y Methodistiaid Calfinaidd/Journal of the Historical Society of the Presbyterian Church of Wales*, vol 16, (1931), 100-5.

[52] See, for instance, Obelkevich's comments on 'women's role' amongst the Primitive Methodists. J. Obelkevich, *Religion and Rural Society: South Lindsey, 1825–1875* (Oxford, 1976), pp. 243-4.

[53] CMA, Trevecka Ms 856, Howel Harris to John Lewis, 18 April 1743; 2685, Mary Jones to Howel Harris, 10 August 1770; 'Letters of the Revs. John and Charles Wesley and others, addressed to Mrs. Jones, of Fonmon Castle, 1745–1788', *WMM*, vol 21, (1875), 633-43; E. A. Morgan, 'The Wesleys and Fonmon Castle, Glamorgan' in *Bathafarn: the Journal of the Historical Society of the Methodist Church in Wales*, vol 9, (1954), 38-41.

that meetings went smoothly and that accommodation was provided for the visiting preachers. In the years before chapels were built, the movement relied heavily on the support of families of middling and lesser gentry rank who had sufficiently large farmhouses to offer as venues for meetings.

However, it is something of a stereotype to resort to the theme of women as the providers of hospitality and there were other more spiritual outlets for their energies and talents. One of them was hymn writing, which could be a means of conveying religious truths in a memorable fashion which, with repetition, might well have a longer-lasting effect than a single sermon. Specific hymns could also inspire in particular circumstances or might help express a particular sentiment, so they served an important function in the spiritual life of members. Most of the well-known Methodist hymn writers in the eighteenth century were male, with the notable exception of Ann Griffiths, from Dolanog in rural Montgomeryshire in mid Wales. She died at the age of twenty-nine, after giving birth to a daughter who also died. Although her early death meant that only some thirty verses of her work have survived, her hymns have been sung countless times and have had a substantial impact.[54]

Yet, in her own lifetime, they seem to have been transmitted only to a small group of fellow believers and were not recorded on paper. Famously, it was Ann's maid and confidante, Ruth, who recited the hymns from memory so that they could be preserved and published. Ann may well have been operating in the oral tradition which memorised popular songs and verses in the same fashion, but it may also show a certain reserve about seeking to broadcast her work further afield. Even when the hymns were first published, they appeared in a volume edited

---

[54] See S. Megan, *Gwaith Ann Griffiths* (Llandybie, 1982); A. M. Allchin, *The Furnace and the Fountain* (Cardiff, 1987); R. M. Jones, 'Ann Griffiths and the Norm', in B. Jarvis (ed.), *A Guide to Welsh Literature c.1700–1800* (Cardiff, 2000); Hodges, *Flame in the Mountains*.

by Thomas Charles, rather than under Ann's own name, and without her gender being disclosed.

It seems all too likely that there were other less heralded female hymn writers, inspired by the eighteenth-century revival, whose work has been lost without a trace. As with Ann Griffiths, a male mentor of some sort was often needed to ensure the verses were recorded and publicised further afield. One lucky survival is a hymn written by Dorothy Jones of Llanddarog in Carmarthenshire, which was preserved because the local exhorter, Richard Tibbott, committed it to memory and noted it down in his diary:

> *O disgwil ferch o disgwil di*
> *O disgwil fy Anwilid i*
> *Myfi a ddaw ith dynu mas*
> *O dan lywodreth pechod cas.*
>
> *Myfi yw y mab ath rhytha di*
> *O disgwil disgwil wrtho fi*
> *Mi ath gar di a chariad rhad*
> *Gwna it Angofio tu dy dad.*[55]

> Wait, girl, oh wait
> Wait my beloved
> I will come to pull you out
> From the rule of hateful sin.
>
> I am the son who frees you
> Oh wait, wait for me
> I will love you with free love
> To make you forget your father's house.

What is striking is that these verses are obviously written from a woman's perspective. Tibbott occasionally noted hearing Dorothy and the other girls in the society singing until the early hours of the morning and she may well have written verses

---

[55] NLW, Ms 18435B, p. 57.

which might be sung by the women of the society most especially.[56]

Letter writing could also be an active engagement with faith for Methodist women, with the eighteenth century proving to be a period of increased opportunities to acquire literacy for those below the level of the educated élite. The Methodist movement in addition provided them with a circle of contacts to whom to write, often for spiritual advice and to exchange pious sentiments. Many such surviving letters were written to Howel Harris by women who had met him during one of his preaching tours and were emboldened to contact him as a result. The correspondents often provided some sort of conversion narrative and an account of their spiritual experiences. Molly Williams, of Erwood in Breconshire, although she was the sister and sister-in-law of two Methodist exhorters, confessed that she was too shy to speak very much to Harris in person, but felt braver about putting her words down on paper in a letter.[57]

Others sent letters because they were located at a greater distance and could not communicate easily any other way. Mary Giles of Caerleon, near Newport in south Wales, wrote to Harris for the first time in 1740 to update him on her spiritual progress since their meeting in Caerleon, after which she said she came to feel:

> Like an owl in the desert till I became as an alien to my mothers children for when they seed me the one would sing and another would laugh but I could do nothing but cry woe is me for I ham undone for one time I would think that the earth was ready to swallow me up and another time I would think if I would cry to Death that I should never be pardoned.[58]

---

[56] NLW, Ms 18435B, p. 17, 19 August 1741.

[57] CMA, Trevecka Ms 940, Molly Williams to Howel Harris, 1 August 1743.

[58] CMA, Trevecka Ms 213, Mary Giles to Howel Harris, 2 February 1740.

There are obvious biblical influences here which reveal that women, like men, could relate their personal experiences to specific bible passages which seemed highly relevant to their condition at the time. One of the best examples of this is the surviving correspondence of Ann Griffiths, the hymn writer, who had an obvious depth of scriptural knowledge which she applied in her letters as well as her hymns, and, one suspects, in her daily conversation.[59]

Besides Ann Griffiths, one of the female letter writers who perhaps came closest to a sermon was Ann Harry, writing to John Belcher, the exhorter who had oversight of a group of societies in the South-east.[60] She wrote from the New Inn in Monmouthshire and seems to have been one of the Methodists under his care. Her address refers to a 'schoolhouse' suggesting that she may have been a teacher, which is not unlikely given the confidence in her writing. Letters from individual members usually found their way into the Trevecka collection because they were regarded as suitable for wider circulation, often because they gave what was considered to be a valuable account of spiritual experiences which might be a blessing to others.

It is easy to see why Ann Harry's letter might have been passed on for Harris, and possibly others, to read. There were two parts to the letter, but it is only in the second part that Ann came to the more practical everyday issues. The first section was full of Ann's hopes for the progress of the revival, expressed in lively language with colourful imagery. She wrote in very fluent, quite colloquial Welsh, very much influenced by the bible, which is tricky to translate in a way that completely conveys the original. She expressed a fervent hope that John Belcher would be 'like a spiritual fowler'[61] with one eye on the world and the other eye

---

[59] For English translations of her work, see Hodges, *Flame in the Mountains*.
[60] CMA, Trevecka Ms 1444, Ann Harry to John Belcher, 13 April 1746.
[61] A 'fowler' hunted wild birds. The suggestion here would seem to be that, like fowling, recruiting and watching over spiritual converts

'levelling along the middle of the Scriptural road through to the spiritual mark which is Christ'. She expected him to be 'in the middle of God's barn threshing his corn with the great flail in your hand striking out of the brains of the Hypocrites the knowledge which is in the head alone'. There were some quite conventional phrases about the fire of the gospel and the lamb of God, but what of the idea of throwing the water of God's grace to cool the pollution which boils in the cauldron of the hearts of sinners? What of 'hanging the Devil by his heels' with the young men gripping him by the waist and the grandfathers grasping his head and wringing his neck?[62]

At times Ann Harry took a familiar scriptural image and presented it with a slightly different twist, such as the idea of the old man being replaced by the new, which was extended by describing the old man physically ageing, 'his Tongue beginning to thicken and the New Man Speaking more and more clearly, and walking more and more agilely and the Old man with his arthritic hips losing his strength'. It paints a very vivid picture of the old man literally deteriorating, being superseded by the youthful, energetic, new man. There seems little doubt that this was a woman could have preached an engaging sermon! However, there is no evidence to suggest that she ever did so, but perhaps the society discussions and the opportunity to write letters like this may have provided her with an outlet to express her faith and communicate her thoughts.[63]

---

required a keen eye and careful approach. See M. Shrubb, *Feasting, Fowling and Feathers: a history of the exploitation of wild birds* (London, 2013).

[62] CMA, Trevecka Ms 1444, Ann Harry to John Belcher, 13 April 1746.

[63] For further discussion of these themes, see E. M. White, 'Women in the Early Methodist Societies in Wales', *Journal of Welsh Religious History*, 7 (1999), 95-108; White, *The Welsh Methodist Society*, pp. 207-16.

These examples show that there were at least some early Methodist women who were capable of analysing spiritual experiences and expressing themselves with reason and force. That was probably the case because of the greater possibilities to attain at least some measure of education during the eighteenth century. Women of this rank in society would have been highly unlikely to have had the capacity to write in this way prior to the advent of the charity schools. The circulating schools established by Griffith Jones between 1737 and his death in 1761 were continued by his co-worker and patron, Bridget Bevan, until her death in 1779. By the time Jane Owens was writing in 1770, they had already provided free instruction for a possible total of 250,000 pupils, at a time when the estimated population of Wales was around 490,000.[64] The schools helped create a generation of readers at exactly the time that the revival was seeking to make an impact and it is no wonder that Methodists were urged by their leaders to take advantage of the opportunity offered to learn to read.[65] In particular, the growth in literacy focused on greater knowledge of the bible, which helped lay the foundations for the preaching, hymn writing and letter writing which were so integral to the Methodist movement. The movement combined the importance of the written and spoken word, relying as it did so much on preaching and the recounting of spiritual experiences in the societies, but even that spoken word was very much dependent on familiarity with the written word of the bible.[66]

Elizabeth Thomas and Jane Owens operated within a small circle, so the effect of their preaching was inevitably limited. The society in the rural parish of Blaen-porth was unlikely to have had more than the twenty-five or so members which was

---

[64] G. H. Jenkins, *The Foundations of Modern Wales: Wales 1642-1780* (Cardiff, 1987), p. 377.
[65] For a discussion of similar themes in relation to English Wesleyan Methodism see *Ryan*.
[66] E. M. White, *The Welsh Bible* (Stroud, 2007), pp. 80-97.

average for the early societies in the South-west.[67] Dolgellau was a small market town in the thinly populated county of Merionethshire, so was also unlikely to attract large numbers to the society.[68] Although there was a gap of thirty years between their letters, both women were key figures in the formative period of the movement in their locality. This occurred later in north Wales than in the South, and it needed individuals like Jane Owens to emerge from within their own communities rather than to rely on missionaries from the South who were often regarded with greater suspicion.

In south Cardiganshire and in Merionethshire the language used by Methodist preachers would have been Welsh, since that was the only language of the bulk of the population. These western counties were amongst those where there was least knowledge of English. The best indication of this is the language adopted by the Established Church in these regions, since it had been obliged by law since the sixteenth century to provide public worship in Welsh where that was the language commonly spoken.[69] The vast majority of churches in Cardiganshire still used Welsh exclusively by the end of the eighteenth century, with only the parish churches in the towns of Aberystwyth and Cardigan operating bilingually.

The situation in Merionethshire was even more overwhelmingly monoglot, with only minor elements of English appearing in three churches in the county and then only when certain gentry families who favoured English, or visiting assize judges from England, were present.[70] Preaching in English would have been utterly pointless in these places. The use of Welsh by these early women preachers was therefore

---

[67] White, *The Welsh Methodist Society*, p. 143.

[68] Jenkins, *The Foundations of Modern Wales*, p. 289.

[69] I. Bowen (ed.), *The Statutes of Wales* (London, 1908), p. 150.

[70] E. M. White, 'The Established Church, Dissent and the Welsh Language' in Jenkins (ed.), *The Welsh Language before the Industrial Revolution*, pp. 252-3, 271, 276, 283, 285.

chiefly a matter of geography rather than gender. Had they been operating in a border county like Breconshire or Radnorshire, or in one of the long-established English-speaking enclaves of south Pembrokeshire, Gower or the Vale of Glamorgan, they would have been far more likely to use English.[71] However, the fact that their role was akin to that of private exhorters with a confined circuit of no more than two or three societies also played a part.

A prominent public exhorter like Howel Harris was called upon to visit a range of areas with different linguistic demands, so spoke in both languages depending on the location. He was based in Breconshire, where there was a greater tendency towards bilingualism. The key was the ability to communicate easily with the hearers, so the choice of language was pragmatic, which in most of Wales meant using Welsh alone. That ease of communication was part of the appeal of the Methodist movement and would also be true for Wesleyan Methodism as its influence grew in the nineteenth century. A greater measure of organization imposed by the central authority of the Association followed in the wake of the pioneering efforts of these women and, in both cases, their contribution came to an end, for reasons which are not wholly clear from the evidence. However, both evidently felt a strong sense of a call to serve God and their local community of believers. Elizabeth Thomas especially expressed a firm belief that some preachers were instruments called by God to do his work.[72] Although the groups they spoke to were small in number, there are suggestions that they had considerable effect on the hearers. Harris had learnt this for himself during his visit to Blaen-porth in the case of Elizabeth Thomas and Jane Owens believed that

---

[71] See the discussion of the Wesleyan Diana Thomas in Radnor and Aberystwyth, in chapter six.
[72] CMA, Trevecka Ms 569, Elizabeth Thomas to Howel Harris, June 1742.

for some people her words 'had been likely to work on them'.[73] The persistence of the cause in Dolgellau is an indication that foundations were laid by her efforts during this period.[74]

Although it has been suggested that women might preach with a distinctive female voice,[75] there is sadly insufficient evidence of the content of their preaching to be able to discern any signs of this with Elizabeth Thomas and Jane Owens. In each case, their voice survives only because it has been preserved by male colleagues and correspondents. Both showed a degree of reticence about their call to preach, at least in communication with Harris, but both also demonstrated considerable confidence in their commitment to their faith. Elizabeth Thomas's letter was opinionated and assertive, but on behalf of her society rather than herself. It has been suggested that women correspondents during the early modern period in general often apologised for their temerity in writing and also for bothering the recipient with the length and poor quality of their letters.[76]

Welsh Methodist correspondents showed similar traits and tended to sign themselves with phrases such as the 'your unworthy sister' used by both Elizabeth Thomas and Ann Harry, which was also frequently resorted to by Ann Griffiths

---

[73] CMA, Diaries of Howel Harris 72, 29 April 1741; CMA, Trevecka Ms 2682, Jane Owens to Howel Harris, 27 June 1770.

[74] Hughes, *Methodistiaeth Cymru, Cyfrol I* (Wrexham, 1851), pp. 505–6; G. M. Roberts, 'O Nerth i Nerth' in G. M. Roberts (ed.), *Hanes Methodistiaeth Galfinaidd Cymru, Cyfrol II: Cynnydd y Corff* (Caernarfon, 1978), pp. 126-7.

[75] See L. Shercliff, *Preaching Women: gender, power and the pulpit* (London, 2019).

[76] A. Laurence, *Women in England 1500-1760* (London, 1994), chapter eleven. See also J. Daybell and A. Gordon, *Women and Epistolary Agency in Early Modern Culture, 1450–1690* (London, 2016).

in her letters.[77] Jane Owens described herself as 'the weakest creature and the least of God's children' and signed as 'your unworthiest friend in the Lord'.[78] However, this was very much a Methodist convention, especially when writing to some of the movement's leaders, based on a self-conscious determination to avoid any hint of the spiritual pride which Methodists were often accused of indulging in by their enemies; it would not be out of keeping either for any committed Christian writer. It is not necessarily a peculiarly feminine characteristic, therefore, as the male correspondents followed a similar pattern of self-effacement: William Richard referred to himself as 'your weak unworthy and sinful brother', whilst Howel Davies, the Methodist leader in Pembrokeshire, signed off as 'your poor sinful, afflicted Brother in ye Great I am'.[79]

It is, therefore, perhaps in the work of female hymn writers of the period that a woman's voice is more easily detected.[80] In their case, there may have been a tendency to fashion verses to satisfy their own need for spiritual expression rather than to supply hymns which might be edifying for the Methodist societies as a whole, as male hymn writers like William Williams usually did.[81] They were always less likely to have their work publicised widely so were writing more for themselves and their immediate circle of friends. They may

---

[77] CMA, Trevecka Ms 569, Elizabeth Thomas to Howel Harris, June 1742; 1444, Ann Harry to John Belcher, 13 April 1746; Hodges, *Flame in the Mountains.*

[78] CMA, Trevecka Ms 2682, Jane Owens to Howel Harris, 27 June 1770.

[79] CMA, Trevecka Ms 1388, William Richard to Howel Harris, 2 January 1745; 1780, Howel Davies to Howel Harris, 30 January 1748.

[80] For a further discussion of this theme, see J. Aaron, *Nineteenth-century women's writing in Wales: nation, gender and identity* (Cardiff, second edition, 2010), pp. 13-22.

[81] E. Wyn James, 'The Evolution of the Welsh Hymn' in I. Rivers and D. L. Wykes (eds), *Dissenting Praise: religious dissent and the hymn in England and Wales* (Oxford, 2011), pp. 235-47.

have been inspired to help fulfil the needs of their women companions and thus devised verses to sing together to pass the time profitably as they walked to and from society and preaching meetings. Part of the appeal of the movement to women was the opportunity to extend their networks of friendship and singing together seems to have been a popular activity which helped strengthen the bonds of fellowship.[82]

Opportunities were therefore limited during the eighteenth century but the advent of the nineteenth century hardly threw open the doors for women preachers. Despite the founding of the Welsh Calvinistic Methodist Church in 1811, it was not until 1978 that the first woman, Pamela Turner, was ordained as a minister. However, some prominent women preachers did emerge during the nineteenth century, including the exceptional Sarah Jane Rees, known as Cranogwen after her birthplace in Llangrannog on the south Cardiganshire coast, which is around six miles away from Elizabeth Thomas's home in Blaen-porth. Cranogwen was a remarkably talented woman who proved to be a pioneer in many different fields.[83] The daughter of a sea captain from an area with a strong seafaring tradition, she rejected her parents' suggestion that she be apprenticed as a dressmaker and instead went to sea for two years, before gaining her master's certificate from a nautical school in London by the time she was twenty-one.

At the age of twenty-six, in 1865, competing against some of the most celebrated Welsh poets of the age, she became the first ever woman to be awarded the first prize for a poem in the National Eisteddfod. She also established considerable fame as a lecturer,

---

[82] White, *The Welsh Methodist Society*, pp. 209-10, 213-4.

[83] See G. Jones, *Cranogwen: Portread Newydd* (Llandysul, 1981); D. Beddoe, 'Rees, Sarah Jane [pseud. Cranogwen] (1839–1916), sailor, schoolmistress, and poet', *Oxford Dictionary of National Biography* (2007). https://www.oxforddnb.com/view/10.1093/ref:odnb/9780198614128.0 01.0001/odnb-9780198614128-e-48648 (accessed 5 August 2020).

including a tour of America. In 1878, she became the first female editor of a Welsh journal, *Y Frythones* (or 'The British Woman'), which was one of the first intended primarily for women.[84] An interest in temperance grew out of Cranogwen's commitment to her religious faith and she founded the South Wales Women's Temperance Union in 1901.[85] In addition to all these achievements, she emerged as one of the first well-established women preachers in Wales, despite continued misgivings about the idea of a woman preaching from a pulpit. Like her predecessors, Elizabeth Thomas and Jane Owens, Cranogwen had to demonstrate particular talents and an extraordinary call before being granted the opportunity to preach. Her notebooks give an indication of the content of her sermons and lectures, suggesting a structure and clarity, along with a vibrancy to what she was planning to say.[86] She was one of a select group of women who, by the late nineteenth century, were able to preach in public not just in private societies and the close circuits of their own movement or denomination. However, even at this stage, it seemed that few Welsh Methodist women could confidently call themselves preachers.

Conclusion

Early Methodism acknowledged the possibility that women could be 'stir'd up to speak', [87] although the first examples of woman preachers were largely overlooked when it came to writing Methodist history. The general expectation of lay participation in societies meant that women had further

---

[84] See S. R. Williams, 'The true "Cymraes": Images of women in women's nineteenth-century Welsh periodicals' in A. V. John (ed.), *Our Mother's Land: chapters in Welsh women's history, 1830–1939* (Cardiff, 1991), pp. 69-91.

[85] See Lloyd-Morgan, 'From temperance to suffrage?'.

[86] CMA, Personal papers of Sarah Jane Rees ('Cranogwen'); 14182, Sermon on the Book of Proverbs 29:1; 14183, notebook containing lectures; HZ4/65, A notebook containing notes on biblical characters.

[87] CMA, Diaries of Howel Harris 72, 29 April 1741.

opportunities to make an active contribution. The chance to acquire literacy through the eighteenth-century educational initiatives equipped them to analyse and express their spiritual condition with reference to the bible in particular. In some rare cases, they were able to share these insights with other members of the movement, both female and male, through hymns and exhorting. The process of accepting woman preachers was slow and halting, with some initial allowances seemingly withdrawn as the movement developed along more formal lines, a trend which might happen at different speeds as the Methodist cause, Calvinistic and Wesleyan, spread to different parts of the country.

6: 'Labouring for the Lord': What was the calling of the early Methodist women preachers 1760-1820?

John Lenton

The origin of this chapter goes back to my WHS lecture on John Wesley's original itinerant preachers delivered in Bradford in 2000.[1] At the end there was a question from Margaret Jones about women preachers. I did not really answer her enquiry, but undertook to look at the whole question later. This represents some kind of fulfilment of that promise. Acknowledgements are due to many friends who have assisted in different ways.

Definitions

'Calling' can be interpreted in two ways: the process by which women became preachers, their invitation from God to preach, and why they thought it came to them; and then what they actually did as preachers, the result of the original call. This will cover both, though spending more time on the second, the 'Labouring for the Lord'. This last was a phrase used by the women about what they did, especially in the journals and in their letters to each other.[2]

'Early' covers some of the first half of the nineteenth century as well as the eighteenth-century preachers. Looking back the two hundred years from the early twenty-first century the period up to 1820 is still 'early'. This chapter deals with Wesleyans, not Primitive Methodists or Bible Christians. 1760 was chosen

---

[1] J. Lenton, *'My Sons in the Gospel': an analysis of Wesley's itinerant preachers*, The WHS Lecture 2000 (Loughborough, 2000).

[2] For women in early Methodism see *Mack* and Burton, *Spiritual Literacy*.

because those English women who were Methodist leaders before 1760 such as Grace Murray or Sarah Perrin seem only to have exhorted rather than preached, in contrast to their later sisters.[3] It means there was a period of sixty years, half of which was in John Wesley's lifetime and half after his death. 1820 has been chosen as the end date because by 1820 both Primitive Methodists and Bible Christians were beginning to spread from their original heartlands, so that nationally women preachers could choose a different Methodist home.[4] For many women preachers we know little more than their name and where they lived. So the numbers mentioned here are much fewer than those who probably actually preached. For this research I developed a database of some sixty-seven women preachers of the period who were Wesleyans. They include thirty-five of those in Appendix A of Chilcote's 1991 book.[5]

Early Methodism has long been seen as a good example of Thirsk's law at work: 'In the breakup of old patterns and in the early stages of the forging of new ones, women were able to achieve a temporary position of influence in the early stages of the evangelical revival which was not sustained into the nineteenth century, when male ministers, trustees and administrators imposed a substantial measure of control'.[6] This chapter argues that the 'temporary' influence was still there in 1820 and later, at least in marginal areas, particularly rural societies where women were always important in Methodism.

---

[3] For Grace Murray see Best, *Tragedy of Errors*. For Sarah Perrin see Lloyd, 'Sarah Perrin', 79-88, and Lenton, 'Surviving Letters', 47-50. For the first woman Methodist preacher, and the different nuance of 'exhorting' in Wales, see pp. 57-61.

[4] For the Primitive Methodists see chapters seven and eight, and the Bible Christians chapter eight in this volume.

[5] *Chilcote 1991*. This book, with its appendices, set the standard for subsequent work by many others.

[6] D. Hempton, *The Religion of the People: Methodism and popular religion c.1750-1900* (London, 1996), p. 181 quoting Joan Thirsk in Ireland in 1993.

This argument about the permanence of the enlargement of the spheres of female influence can be found in many works. Hempton, Mack and Wilson all discuss this, in Wilson's case with particular regard to Mary Bosanquet Fletcher.[7] Mack suggested a concept of 'agency in which autonomy is less important than self- transcendence and in which the energy to act in the world is generated and sustained by a prior act of personal surrender'.[8] Which brings us to consider how the early women preachers were called.

Their call

This should be seen in two stages, first conversion, and second the 'call to preach'. As usual in general we know little, so have to reason from the few for whom we can find some evidence.[9] Of the sixty-seven women preachers only the conversions of twenty-eight and the calls of eighteen are known. Conversions are not always dated, and we do not always know whose preaching led to the conversion (four of the preachers here are unknown).[10] Twenty-one of the women preachers named the preacher by whom they were converted. Of these named preachers who were successful in gaining conversions, Mary Barritt appears four times, John Wesley and George Whitefield twice, but nobody else more than once. In the list are also preachers such as Thomas Maxfield, Joseph Benson, John Berridge, William Bramwell, and Samuel Bardsley. The dates of

---

[7] Ibid., p. 180; Wilson, 'Afterlife and Vocation'.

[8] Mack, 'Religion, Feminism and the Problem of Agency: reflections on eighteenth century Quakerism' in *Signs: Journal of Women in Culture and Society*, vol 29, no 1, (2003), 154.

[9] For the 802 male itinerants there were only 218 places of conversion: *JWP*, p. 51.

[10] For more discussion on the process of conversion see D. B. Hindmarsh, *The Evangelical Conversion Narrative* (Oxford, 2005).

the conversions range from the beginnings of Methodism in the early 1740s to as late as 1813.[11]

The call to preach is less well documented as with the male itinerant.[12] Of the eighteen of whom we know something, many were responding to the absence of a (male) preacher, not necessarily an itinerant.[13] Alice Cross, at her house at Booth Bank in north Cheshire, fixed the pulpit in their largest room. She was the leader of the society there. If the preacher failed to arrive, she occupied that pulpit in his place.[14] Similarly in Cornwall Ann Gilbert began preaching in 1771 when 'the preacher happened not to come'.[15] She went on to preach widely by general invitation, unlike Alice Cross who never preached outside Booth Bank.[16] Another in Cornwall who responded when no preacher came, and from that developed her call, was Mrs Elizabeth Collett at Gwinear. She was in Ann Gilbert's class, so had her as a role model. Then she moved to another village and persuaded her employer to have preaching in his house. One day the preacher did not come. The congregation 'having waited some considerable time, called to her to speak to them'. She gave out a hymn, and prayed, but they insisted she spoke. 'So she began speaking to them and the power of God came down among them'. They made her preach again and she was then invited to many other places.[17] Sarah Crosby at Derby in early 1761 found herself faced with a class which swelled in a week from twenty to two hundred. She preached to them and

---

[11] For the conversion of male itinerant preachers see *JWP*, pp. 25-6, 50-2. For biographies of some of these preachers see *DMBI*.

[12] *JWP*, chapter five.

[13] This was so with many male itinerants, see ibid., pp. 84-5.

[14] E. A. Rose, *Methodism in Cheshire to 1800* (Wilmslow, 1975), p. 33.

[15] Ann Gilbert's 'Narrative' in *AM*, vol 18, (1795), 44.

[16] Ibid., 42; Z. *Taft*, 1:49-51.

[17] Z. *Taft*, 2:120-4, quotations from pp. 121-2. It is interesting to find evidence about both the Cornish women Collett and Gilbert in William O'Bryan's writings: *Arminian (Bible Christian) Magazine*, vol 2, (1823), 113-14.

Wesley encouraged her, while trying to stretch his itinerants a little further in order to help her.[18]

Several were challenged by other preachers, both men and women. William Bramwell, the famous revivalist, was well known for his question: 'Why are there not more Women Preachers? Because they are not faithful to their call'.[19] It was that challenge which led to Elizabeth Tomlinson (later Evans), the original for Dinah Morris in George Eliot's *Adam Bede*, responding to the call to preach. Bramwell from 1793 encouraged Ann Cutler to come to his circuits to help him in revival. Some biblical texts struck home. Charlotte Berger was particularly affected by the text: 'The Spirit of the Lord is upon me, because he has anointed me to preach good tidings to the meek'.[20] Sarah Cox felt her mind continually applied by 'Cry aloud, spare not. Lift up thy voice like a trumpet'.[21]

Sometimes the call was from another woman preacher who asked them to travel with them. Mary Tooth and Sally Lawrence started by going with Mrs Fletcher. Mary Barritt had the younger Mary Tatham with her in the Nottingham circuit.[22] Charlotte Berger was called to assist the older Henrietta Webster.[23] Methodist women preachers were often determined to write about their experience in order to encourage others, though usually this became edited out by men who controlled

---

[18] For Sarah Crosby see *Z. Taft*, 2:23-115.

[19] Church, *More about the Early Methodist People*, p. 161 has the full account.

[20] J. Holland Brown, *Memoir of Miss Charlotte Sophia Steigen Berger of Saffron Walden* (London, 1879), p. 19. The quotation is from the KJV, Luke 4:13.

[21] *Z. Taft*, 1:72. Sarah Cox preached in Nottinghamshire and Leicestershire in the 1790s and early 1800s. The text is from the KJV, Isaiah 58:1.

[22] R. C. Swift, *Lively People: Methodism in Nottingham 1740-1979* (Nottingham, 1982), p. 46. For Mary Boardman and Catherine Smith see pp. 222-4 below.

[23] Brown, *Berger*, p. 21.

publishing.[24] At least two women went to Madeley to hear Mrs Fletcher and came away preachers. Mary Bosanquet Fletcher had encouraged them to speak in the tithe barn there, and having heard her call they took it to other places. This was how Diana Thomas of Kington,[25] and Susanna Knapp of Stourport, became preachers.[26] Mary Bosanquet Fletcher had already encouraged first Sally Lawrence and then Mary Tooth and turned each of them into preachers as they lived in her family.[27] Mary Barritt stayed with Mary Wiltshaw in 1799 and Mary Wiltshaw became a preacher as a result.[28]

Mary Barritt herself recounted her own call as linked to her conversion: 'I felt much concern for the happiness of my neighbours and took every opportunity of talking to and praying with and for them'. Later she found the challenge from Ann Cutler in 1792 reinforced that original call when Ann asked Mary in her own home 'if I thought I had any business at home'.[29] Charlotte Berger was challenged by the Anglican evangelical Thomas Scott in London in 1815.[30] Diana Thomas encouraged Mary Tooth to continue preaching after Mary Bosanquet Fletcher's death.[31]

---

[24] M. P. Jones, 'From "The State of my Soul" to "Exalted Piety": women's voices in the Arminian/Methodist Magazine 1778-1821' in R. N. Swanson (ed.), *Gender and Christian Religion* (Bury St Edmunds, 1998); Burton, *Spiritual Literacy*, pp. 171-5.

[25] *DMBI.*

[26] G. Hammond and P. Forsaith (eds), *Religion, Gender and Industry: exploring church and Methodism in a local setting* (Eugene, OR, 2011), p. 143.

[27] Ibid. chapter ten. See also Virgoe (ed.), *Angels and Impudent Women*, p. 118.

[28] Z. *Taft,* 2:184ff.

[29] *Taft Memoirs,* 1:26.

[30] Brown, *Berger,* p. 25.

[31] JRL, Fl/7/3/4 letter from Diana Thomas to Mary Tooth dated 12 February 1816.

Portrait of Mary Taft (née Barritt) praying in
Wesley Chapel in Whitby.[32]
The portrait in a typical pose is courtesy of the Oxford Centre for Methodism
and Church History, Oxford Brookes University.
It illustrates her ability to pray inquirers 'into the Kingdom'.

---

[32] The portrait is one of the few of early Methodist women preachers
to survive and deserves to be better known and more celebrated. The
Tafts were stationed at Whitby 1819-21. The portrait belonged to the
Methodist Clarkson family in Whitby for most of the nineteenth
century. They gave it to David Waller, a President who had
connections with the area, who gave it to the Bookroom, from where
it passed to the WHS. See *WMM*, vol 130, (1907), 538-9. Peter Forsaith
brought it to the notice of the author.

Sometimes the call came in ways which seem strange to modern preachers. Some women preachers were particularly affected by dreams. Charlotte Berger, at the time she was about to start preaching, had a dream:

> That there was a vast work appointed for her to do. It seemed that there was a vast iron machine, which I was required to lift up. Attempting to do this I found there were enemies opposing me, who had so altered the form of the machine as to cause me the greatest possible perplexity . . . Awaking and pondering over my dream the second verse of Isaiah 45 came to my mind 'I will go before thee and make the crooked places straight; I will break in pieces the gates of brass and cut asunder the bars of iron'.[33]

Mack has a whole chapter on 'the Methodist culture of dreaming'. Methodist women saw dreams such as this as justifying their continuing to preach despite opposition from within as well as outside their community.[34]

Two women, at least in their early days, suffered from fits, which were linked to preaching in that they were sometimes preaching while in a fit or trance. This was true of Elizabeth Dickinson of Staveley near Knaresborough who had visions where she was commanded to preach, and in preaching referred frequently to her visions.[35] More famously and with the clearest description of what happened was the much more long-lived preacher Sarah Mallet in Norfolk. Sarah, who always suffered from much physical illness, at the age of twenty-three began to have fits, during which she first told others to turn to God and soon began preaching from texts. For a month this continued to happen, with more and more coming to hear her. A few days after her final fit, her uncle asked her to preach in his chapel at Long Stratton. Soon she attracted Wesley's attention and

---

[33] Brown, *Berger*, pp. 22-3. The biblical text is drawn from the KJV.

[34] *Mack*, chapter six.

[35] Z. *Taft*, 1:181 onwards, especially pp. 184-6. She died at the age of twenty, having reportedly preached to thousands.

eventually received from him Conference's permission to preach.[36] It has been suggested that the seizures could be a form of epilepsy, but could also be a depressive illness, perhaps caused by an inadequate diet or even fasting.[37] Her modern biographer reports she continued to preach for another fifty-five years!

What was their calling? What did they do?

There were at least three main types of women preachers and preaching. The first category may be described as 'single place preachers'. Alice Cross is an example, but there were many others. Often, they were particularly in areas which had had no Methodist preaching previously. Women preachers settled in an area where Methodism might be not known or at least had little earlier success, began to preach in their own house and maintained a witness, often for a considerable time. Other examples included Elizabeth Baker (later Jordan) at Monmouth, Susanna Knapp in Stourport, Margaret Watson at Redcar, Sarah Lawrence at Coalport, Jeanne Bisson and Madame Perrott in Jersey, and Elizabeth Clarkson at Crakehall in the North Riding.[38]

Many other women preachers began in this way but proved so popular they went on to preach much more widely. Examples of this are Sarah Crosby at Derby in 1761, Mary Bosanquet originally only at Leyton and later at Cross Hall, Mrs Boyce and Mrs Grigson in Saham Toney in Norfolk, Mrs Webster and Miss

---

[36] East, *My Dear Sally*, pp. 20-5.

[37] Ibid. pp. 33-5. See also for similar American experiences A. Taves, *Fits, Trances and Visions: experiencing religion and explaining experience from Wesley to James* (Princeton, 1999). For fasting see *Ryan*, pp. 68-72.

[38] Z. *Taft*, 1:41-8 (Lawrence), 170-1 (Perrott), 2 178-180 (Watson), 180-3 (Clarkson); *WJW*, vol 24, p. 105 (Baker); *PWHS*, vol 28, (1951), 67ff; and *WMM*, vol 53, (1830), 861 (Bisson). For Knapp see E. Rowley, *Fruits of Righteousness in the Life of Susanna Knapp* (Worcester, 1866).

Berger in Saffron Walden in the nineteenth century.[39] Another example, but abroad, was Mrs Mary Gilbert in Antigua in 1781-6.[40] Mrs Collett twice moved to new parts of Cornwall. In each case she started a class, then invited the preachers to her house, made a room available for them and preached herself if for some reason no preacher turned up.[41] Sarah Perrin, preaching in Leominster while staying there in the 1740s, was possibly like this.[42] All these were very different from the male itinerant who was tied to a six week rotation around a circuit.

The second category were women preachers who were well known evangelists (to use a later term), who preached over wide areas, going from society to society like the men, but not necessarily or even usually following the circuit plan. They might well stay in one place for several weeks. Examples of this include Mary Bosanquet in the 1770s in Yorkshire, Elizabeth Hurrell, Sarah Crosby, Mary Barritt, Sarah Mallet, and Ann Cutler. Like the itinerants they stayed in Methodist houses and were fed by Methodists. Unlike them they had no Conference, though they might well, as Mary Barritt did, attend services and meetings associated with the (male) Conference each year.[43] They would stay longer in places which responded and might return again and again in future years. Sarah Crosby reported that in 1777 up until 4 December she had 'ridden 960 miles, kept 220 public meetings and around 600 private meetings'.[44] By

---

[39] For Mrs Boyce (née Sarah Mallet) and Mrs Grigson or Gregson see East, *My Dear Sally*. For Mrs Webster and Miss Berger see Brown, *Berger*.

[40] R. Glen, 'An early Methodist Revival in the West Indies' in *WMS*, vol 9, no 1 (2017), 36-56, at 52. Glen suggests Mary Gilbert may have preached with her husband in the 1770s as well.

[41] Z. *Taft*, 2:115ff.

[42] Lloyd, 'Sarah Perrin'.

[43] For Mary Barritt at Conference see *Taft Memoirs*, 1:95: 'My brother and I rode to Manchester Conference: we got in to hear Mr Pawson . . .' (July 1799).

[44] *Methodist Magazine*, vol 29, (1806), 567.

'public' meetings she meant services, as opposed to the 'private' meetings of Methodist classes and bands. By the 1790s we find in Barritt's correspondence that this kind of evangelism was being organized by some circuit superintendents, sometimes under pressure from lay leaders, but more usually because they had heard of the women's success. They would invite evangelists like Mary Barritt or Ann Cutler to come to their circuits.[45] As with male itinerants or Wesley himself there were certain households where they were always welcomed, such as Edward Wade's of Stourton Grange near Wetherby or the anonymous Quaker lady in Bainbridge in Wensleydale for Mary Barritt.[46]

These women were in their travels similar to the men, but they were not following the same regime of the circuit plan. They might stay in one place for a week and then proceed elsewhere, as opposed to the itinerant who typically never stayed in one place for two nights except at weekends in larger societies. Though there is no evidence in the form of letters that Elizabeth Hurrell and Sarah Crosby were similarly invited by Assistants, it seems likely that this is what had happened earlier with them. In the 1790s Mary Barritt's correspondence shows that after a while she was so sought after that she was able to choose, and to turn down or at least put off for a period many invitations.[47]

The third type were women who became local preachers rather than evangelists and went to their appointments on the plan (or their husband's appointments) rather than taking weekday or weeknight meetings. These preachers tend to be later, i.e. after 1785 or even after 1800, as Methodism settled down and most areas became covered by circuits.[48] There were more itinerants, the circuit plan became more fixed and controlling, and more local preachers were available generally, especially in urban

---

[45] *Taft Memoirs*, pp. 1:64-9; Z. *Taft*, 1:303-24.
[46] *Taft Memoirs*, 1:53-4, 65.
[47] See for examples the four different letters to her in ibid., 1:64-6.
[48] *JWP*, p. 139.

areas.[49] This meant it might well seem prudent for women preachers to marry itinerants or other local preachers and carry out a joint ministry.[50] These women often travelled with their husbands, helping them lead worship and using their protection. This was partly adapting to the circuit preaching plan as that became the norm for all Methodist services during the thirty years after Wesley's death. Circuits grew and covered more of the country but usually involved shorter distances.

Examples of this include Mary (Barritt) Taft, Mary (née Woodhouse) Holder, Jane Treffry, Sarah de Putron (formerly Eland), and Margaret Hainsworth (born Hargreaves).[51] All these five were wives of ministers, like Mary Bosanquet Fletcher before them. This group of ministerial wives might move every other year to a new circuit with the men they had married. Some such as Mary Taft preached in their own right as much or more than local preachers, possibly even as much as the average itinerant, though this seems in general unlikely. Others, like Mrs Sarah Stevens or Mrs Mary Wiltshaw, often supplied for their husbands when they were unwell.[52]

There were also some like Elizabeth Tomlinson or Sarah Mallet who became the wives of local preachers. Both Elizabeth Evans

---

[49] Local preachers and preaching plans have been insufficiently studied. See E. A. Rose, 'Local Preachers and the Preaching Plan' in G. Milburn and M. Batty (eds), *Workaday Preachers: the story of Methodist local preaching* (Peterborough, 1995), pp. 143-64.

[50] Marriage and change of name created difficulties for later historians. It was difficult in the twentieth century to make the link between Sarah Mallet (correspondent of Wesley) and Sarah Boyce (correspondent of Mary Tooth) until David East published his biography. There will be others who 'disappeared' waiting to be discovered.

[51] For these see Z. *Taft*, 1:100 (Holder), 2:194 (Eland), 2:222 (Hargreaves); R. Treffry jr, *Memoirs of Mrs Jane Treffry* (London, 1830); W. Jessop, *An Account of Methodism in Rossendale . . .* (Manchester, 1880), p. 293 (Hainsworth).

[52] Z. *Taft*, 1:159- 69 (Stevens), 2:184-93 (Wiltshaw).

(née Tomlinson) and her husband had their names on the Cromford preaching plan from 1819 to 1832. Their names were presumably on the Derby plan before 1819, since they had moved from Derby then.[53] In this period most local preachers were asked to preach every Sunday, often several times a Sunday.[54] Preaching wives could relieve the burden on their husbands considerably, whether ministerial or lay, and if the husband was unwell, supply for them. A slightly later example of a Wesleyan woman local preacher, who seems to have continued throughout the nineteenth century, is Mrs Fuller of the Swaffham circuit. She was a local preacher for almost sixty years and died in 1891.[55] The Swaffham circuit was one of those where Martha Gregson and Sarah Boyce were acting as local preachers in the 1820s and 30s, so it had women local preachers for most of the century. There were many of these local preachers who acted more widely as evangelists as well. Diana Thomas is a good example of this, a local preacher in the large Kington circuit on the Welsh borders,[56] but also preaching more widely, going for example to Aberystwyth, Machynlleth, Ledbury and Hereford, so could also be seen as a travelling evangelist. The survival of her (copied) diary for 1809 and 1810 shows that for those two years most Sundays she was preaching somewhere.[57] Sometimes she went with other preachers. If she was ill, they stood in for her. Yet in September 1809, she was in Neston in the Wirral, a long way from her area, and preaching in the week as well as on Sundays. On 29 January 1810 she

---

[53] *Methodist Recorder* (Winter 1896), 35-8.

[54] Rose, 'Local Preachers and the Preaching Plan' in Milburn and Batty (eds), *Workaday Preachers*, p. 156.

[55] There is a news cutting about her death inside the John Rylands Library copy of W. D. Lawson, *Wesleyan Local Preachers* (Newcastle-upon-Tyne, 1874).

[56] No circuit plan is known to survive, but her Journal shows this as she records that others went to fulfil her appointments if she was ill.

[57] Milburn and Batty (eds), *Workaday Preachers*, pp. 151-3.

preached three times in the day (and again on the Monday), four different sermons at two different places.[58]

How did early women preachers support themselves? In my research on early Methodist (male) preachers it soon became apparent that one of the tests for whether a man was an itinerant preacher or not was whether he was supported by the circuits. Frequently a name was added to the lists because in the surviving circuit stewards' accounts his name was to be found with a payment from circuit funds.[59] For women preachers this is not the case. No women were paid out of the Connexional or circuit accounts, or at least not for preaching.[60] Wives and daughters of male itinerants might receive payments from the Connexional Preachers' Fund.[61] Women preachers were not rewarded officially. So how did they survive?

Some women were wealthy in their own right. They owned property and had money. This was true of Mary Bosanquet Fletcher, Mary Tooth after Mary Bosanquet Fletcher had left most of her estate to her to maintain the cause in Madeley,[62] Charlotte Berger, Henrietta Webster,[63] Sarah Perrin,[64] and Martha Grigson.[65] All of them might well use some of that

---

[58] Hereford Archive and Records Centre, BH 28/1/7; this is William Parlby's exercise book, where he copies out sections of her journal.

[59] *JWP*, pp. 443-4, for example.

[60] It is possible some received expenses eg. for turnpike tolls. See M. Batty, 'The contribution of local preachers to the life of the Wesleyan Methodist Church until 1932, and to the Methodist Church after 1932, in England', University of Leeds PhD thesis, 1969, p. 28.

[61] *JWP*, pp. 109-10; C. Murray Norris, *The Financing of John Wesley's Methodism c.1740-1800* (Oxford, 2017), pp. 25-65.

[62] Drew University Library, Fletcher manuscripts 1306-5-3:05.

[63] Brown, *Berger*, p. 58 'persons of fortune'.

[64] Lloyd, 'Sarah Perrin'.

[65] Also Gregson, the daughter of one Anglican clergyman and the wife of another. Her husband was wealthy and after his death in 1829 she could still maintain a carriage. J. Lenton, 'East Anglian Women Wesleyan Methodist Preachers in Wesleyan Methodism to

money to support other women preachers as well as themselves, so Mary Bosanquet Fletcher at different times supported Sarah Ryan, Sarah Crosby, Anne Tripp,[66] Sally Lawrence and Mary Tooth, and Martha Grigson supported Sarah Boyce in her widowhood. Mary Woodhouse (later Holder), the daughter of a Whitby master mariner, was another who seems to have inherited money.[67] Eliza and Isabella Wilson were the sister and daughter respectively of Francis Wilson of Wharton Lodge near Wetherby. The Wilson family owned several farms near Wetherby.[68] Diana Thomas ran a successful milliner's business and combined her business journeys with preaching, rather as some male itinerants had earlier combined preaching with doctoring.[69] Mary Walsh married into money in the Gilbert family of Antigua.[70] Mary Parker in Norfolk was wealthy enough to build two chapels.[71]

On the other hand, Ann Cutler and Mary Barritt had no financial resources and were completely dependent on their hosts (Mary Barritt's brother John Barritt in the first instance for her). In a similar position were Ann Carr and Sarah Ryan; Sarah Lawrence was an orphan.[72] Mary Barritt might travel from one host to the next, and stay one night, five nights or several weeks.

1910' in *East Anglian WHS Bulletin*, (2008), 4-5; Hammond and Forsaith (eds), *Religion, Gender and Industry*, pp. 149-50.

[66] *DMBI.*

[67] *JWP.*

[68] I am indebted to my friend Shirley Martin who has researched this family extensively. See for example *WMM*, vol 31, (1808), pp. 373ff, vol 36, (1813), pp. 281-4; and vol 71, (1848), p. 936. The family is particularly confusing, because in the next generation there were two Rev. William Wilsons, one a son-in law and the other a son of Francis Wilson.

[69] *PWHS*, vol 14, (1924), 110-11.

[70] H. F. Gilbert, *Memoirs of the late Mrs Mary Gilbert . . .* (London, 1817).

[71] Lenton, 'East Anglian Women Wesleyan Methodist Preachers', 2.

[72] *DMBI.*

She and many other women preachers were dependent on who would provide them with food and shelter. Both Sarah Crosby[73] and Sarah Ryan seem to have been abandoned by their husbands. Admittedly the Tafts were better educated and had some money. Zechariah's brother was a doctor, so, after her marriage, Mary Taft had more resources.[74] One argument for marrying a husband was therefore financial support, as well as more access to the pulpit, especially if she married a husband who was a preacher and would therefore support her in both senses. Examples of this in this period include Sarah Mallet, Mary Barritt, and Sarah Perrin.[75]

Methodist women preachers in this period were typical of the class in which most Methodist leaders were found, small farmers, artisans, craftsmen, with some trades-people, such as Diana Thomas. A higher proportion seem to have had some money than among the male preachers, but a much smaller sample, so more difficult to be certain. Both men and women preachers tended to marry partners who were well-off, so the 'wealthy wives' tendency noticed for the male itinerants was matched by the wealthy husbands for the women.[76] In comparing these women preachers with the male itinerants we see another immediate difference. The Yarm circuit of 1768 showed a typical example of three male preachers travelling around a circuit of thirty-six societies calling at a different one every day and at the larger ones at the weekends. It was so regular that the preacher knew where he would be every day

---

[73] Ibid.

[74] E. Thompson, *'This Remarkable Family': a study of the Barritts of Foulridge 1750-1850* . . . (Barnoldswick, 1981), p. 10.

[75] Sarah Perrin married the important early preacher John Jones who became an Anglican clergyman. A. B. Sackett, *John Jones: first after the Wesleys*, WHS Publication no 7, (Broxton, 1972).

[76] *JWP*, pp. 46-9 for social class, pp. 101-6 for wealthy wives.

for the next six weeks at least.[77] Women preachers did not follow that system.

Most of these women preachers, that is forty-three out of the sixty-seven, are known to have been married. However, this does not necessarily relate to the period when they were preaching. Many spent a long period of widowhood (e.g. Mary Bosanquet Fletcher from 1785 to 1815) during which they continued to preach. If we analyse the forty-three we find that at least seventeen of these were preaching before they married. At least ten of them preached after their husbands died, or like Sarah Crosby they had been deserted by their husband.

Admittedly a few, like Fletcher, preached both as a single woman and as a widow (as well as throughout her marriage). So, though it might seem that most had a husband during their preaching careers, in fact most were usually not supported by a husband. Again, for several we do not know whether they were married, or, if they were, whether the husband was alive at the time the wife was preaching. Some, like Charlotte Berger or Mary Tooth, are known to have decided to be single and turned down a number of suitors.[78] Many Methodists, led by Wesley himself and supported by preachers such as Bramwell, argued that women preachers should not marry.[79] Of the forty-three who were married at least sixteen had children. This ranged from the 'numerous' family of Mrs Cock (Jane Bisson),[80] or the eleven children of Mrs Elizabeth Collett, down to Penelope Coussins' two children, one of whom died young.[81] Children

---

[77] Ibid., pp. 137-8.

[78] Brown, *Berger*, p. 23. For more on the proportions cf. E. Kent Brown, *Women of Mr Wesley's Methodism* (Metuchen, NJ, 1983), pp. 222-3.

[79] *Mack*, pp. 147-50. Wesley argued similarly against marriage for his male itinerants. But, having set the opposite example himself, they did not always listen to him and listened less as time went on: see *JWP*, pp. 92-3 and 107-8.

[80] Obituary in *WMM*, vol 62, (1830), 861.

[81] Z. *Taft*, 1:29ff, 2:115ff.

certainly made it more difficult for the women preachers to preach. It has been shown that in the years that Mary Taft gave birth she travelled to other circuits considerably less.[82] Some of those who married did not have children, usually because they were older, like Mary Bosanquet Fletcher.

Some of the preachers travelled little to preach, and often for the rest we do not know how they travelled. Many walked, just as the male local preachers usually did. Certainly Mary Barritt, in her early peregrinations, often walked as in her memorable journey to Hexham circuit and back in 1793-4:

> I pursued my journey over the mountains [from Middleham] to Reeth. As I travelled alone and on foot, I frequently kneeled down to supplicate the throne of mercy, for direction, comfort, and success and was much blest. This journey will never be obliterated from my mind, while reason and memory last.[83]

On the other hand, in 1794, in the Alnwick circuit she referred to 'her mare' on which she crossed a swollen river.[84] Riding a horse, as the male itinerants usually did, was therefore also an option.[85] Diana Thomas had a white pony which carried her to her appointments over the Welsh hills. Her riding whip was preserved into the twentieth century.[86] Mary Bosanquet Fletcher certainly rode on a number of occasions; Mary Barritt also, in her case usually on horses provided by friends. There were also those with money who might have some form of chaise, such as Mrs Gregson or Miss Berger.[87] Mary Barritt was sometimes transported in chaises or carriages belonging to her friends such as Edward Wade or Mr Jackson of Harewood.[88] She was also

---

[82] *PWHS*, vol 62, no 1, (2019), 32-3 table 4.
[83] *Taft Memoirs*, 1:28.
[84] Ibid., 1:36-7.
[85] For the male itinerants see *JWP*, pp. 127, 136-9, 142-4.
[86] W. Parlby, 'Diana Thomas of Kington, Lay Preacher in the Hereford Circuit 1759-1821', in *PWHS*, vol 14, no 5, (1924), 110-11.
[87] Brown, *Berger*, p. 47.
[88] *Taft Memoirs*, 1:65.

once transported in a farm cart which tipped her out![89] Travel could be a problem, for women as well as for male preachers.

Mack suggested that women were more eloquent about sanctification and the spiritual life than men: 'Methodists were in tune with women's interests in the deepest sense . . . because women had a profound affinity—whether cultural or inbred—with Methodist doctrines'.[90] Women have always formed a majority among Methodists. Sarah Crosby's letter book gives an interesting picture of how deep was the early Methodist woman preachers' spiritual life. This extract comes from a letter of 1765:

> My Soul shall live and die wrapt up in Him. I want to forget that I have a being and to know no existence but His . . . Lord correct me when I go astray! Unless my not speaking among the Brethren may be styled omissions forever. I have broke through that some time ago and are blest in speaking. I do not think it wrong for women to speak in public provided they speak by the Spirit of GOD. But at present I see myself just where I ought to be and just so employed. I think we want more abundant Life here. What a blessing it could be if the people in general were very simple & full of love.[91]

Most women preachers set themselves against any split or threatened division within Methodism. In the 1790s many Church Methodists, those who worshipped at the parish church and thought of themselves as at least as much Churchmen (or women) as Methodists, separated themselves from Methodism as it increasingly allowed the itinerants to administer

---

[89] 1811 in Lincolnshire: Library of Birmingham, Wolfson Centre for Archival Research, Mary Taft diary, p. 241.

[90] *Mack*, p. 133.

[91] Sarah Crosby's Ms Letter Book at Duke University, David M. Rubenstein Rare Book and Manuscript Library, Frank Baker Collection of Wesleyana and British Methodism, Bay 3356, Box 1, p. 38. Capitals as in original.

Communion and so was becoming more of a church.[92] Fletcher was in many ways a Church Methodist: the wife and then widow of a clergyman, who continued to reside in her late husband's vicarage for thirty years until 1815, she brought all her influence to bear on Methodists in Madeley so that most continued to worship every Sunday at St Michael's Madeley as she did, while still attending her own 'Methodist' services in the tithe barn beside her house.[93]

When in 1797 Alexander Kilham broke with Conference eventually to set up the Methodist New Connexion, Mary Barritt found the Leeds Conference 'a time of trial to my own mind as I was informed of many of my own spiritual children being on the eve of leaving the Methodist body and Joining Mr Kilham's party'. She did her utmost to dissuade them and indeed succeeded with the preacher Henry Taylor who would otherwise have joined Kilham.[94] Mary Barritt also had close contacts with the Revivalist Methodists. She stayed with the Broadhursts in Manchester. Her friend and mentor was William Bramwell, who invited her to all his circuits and put her portrait over his mantelpiece (probably not the one in the WHS collection at Oxford, shown earlier in this chapter). Bramwell had also intended to leave Methodism in 1803 together with Broadhurst and his Band Room Methodists and had actually resigned from the ministry. Again Mary was among those who influenced Bramwell to return. Conference received him back.[95]

---

[92] Lloyd, *Charles Wesley and the Struggle for Methodist Identity*, pp. 219-33. The Church said, correctly, that official Methodism was going away from them.

[93] D. R. Wilson, *Church and Chapel in Industrializing Society: Anglican ministry and Methodism in Shropshire 1760-1785* (New York, 2017).

[94] *Taft Memoirs*, 1:57-9.

[95] W. R. Ward, *Religion and Society in England 1790-1850* (London, 1972), p. 81. The Ms Conference Journal at JRL shows him leaving and returning at the same Conference, one of several examples of ministers over the years who technically resigned but never actually left.

In general women Methodist preachers stayed loyal in a time of division and disunion. In the early nineteenth century among both Primitive Methodists and Bible Christians, many of their women preachers had been brought up as Wesleyans. However, in most cases, it is difficult to prove that they had preached while they had been Wesleyans. Ann Carr, Martha Williams and Hannah Woolhouse seem to have been exceptions to this.[96]

During the life of John Wesley after 1761, and the thirty years after his death, there were at least ten and usually more women preachers actively preaching in the Connexion. Certainly, they tended to preach in private houses rather than chapels, and in small chapels rather than large ones at all periods. Not all preached in wide areas across the country. But, even after the Conference ban on women preaching to men in 1803, women such as Mary Bosanquet Fletcher, Mary Taft and many others continued to preach. It can also be shown that more women began to preach in every period, including after 1803. In the decade 1800-1809 there were at least nine women who seem to have begun preaching. Examples include Mary Tooth, Diana Thomas and Sarah Eland. In the next decade 1810 to 1819 another ten seem to have begun to preach including such as Charlotte Berger (who went on to the 1870s) and Mrs Henrietta Webster. The Conference prohibition on women preaching in 1803, except to other women,[97] does not seem to have altered what women preachers actually did. In 1820 at the end of this period being examined, there were at least twenty-two of these sixty-seven women preachers who were still preaching.

---

[96] D. C. Dews, 'Ann Carr (1783-1841) and the Female Revivalists of Leeds, a study in female preachers, secession and Primitive Methodism', in *From Mow Cop to Peake 1807-1932* (Leeds, 1982), pp. 19-27.

[97] *Minutes of the Methodist Conferences from the Beginning*, vol 2, (London, 1813), pp. 188-9.

Preaching

One of the acid tests of whether women were acting as preachers or not was whether they took texts. Exhorters famously did not.[98] For most women preachers we do not know enough to say whether they had texts, but we do know some of their texts. Paul Chilcote's Appendix H lists seventy-four known occasions when sermon texts of women preachers were recorded up to 1803.[99] These were from eight different preachers, and mostly those of Mary Taft and Mary Bosanquet Fletcher. I have added to this number, many being other texts used by Mary Taft.[100] I have found texts from five more preachers from the later period than Chilcote (who stopped in 1803), including a large number from Diana Thomas's Journal.[101] So thirteen of the sixty-seven preachers have known sermon texts. These now include such relatively unknown preachers as Rosamund Tooth, sister of the much better-known Mary Tooth, but also the well-known Elizabeth Evans, Jane Treffry, and Charlotte Berger, all of whom began preaching in the nineteenth century. If Rosamund Tooth took a text, then it seems likely that her better-known sister Mary, who modelled herself on her mentor and patron Fletcher, did also.[102] The same is true of most of the others in the sixty-seven. There is only one case, that of Ann Cutler, who we specifically know refused to take a text. However, her exhortations were so powerful, she was invited to so many places, and the letter in which Wesley

---

[98] Cf. the different usage of the term in Wales, explained in chapter five.

[99] *Chilcote, 1991*, pp. 317-20.

[100] Lenton, 'Mary Barritt Taft', 27-9, table 3.

[101] Hereford Archive and Records Centre, BH 28/1/7, William Parlby exercise book.

[102] Rosamund Tooth preached from 1 Peter 4:8 in 1828, during Mary Tooth's absence from Madeley. JRL, Letter from R. Tooth to M. Tooth, Fl/3/1/6, vol 3, Corr E-H.

himself had authorized her to preach has survived, that in her case there can be no doubt about her preaching.[103]

Whether women preached differently from men is not easy to ascertain.[104] Certainly they were diffident about their preaching and reluctant to do it in many situations, but so were many of the early male preachers.[105] Mack has an important chapter on 'men of feeling' and their self-portrait of the 'band of brothers'. She follows that with a section explaining how for some Methodist women, 'their religious activities were less oriented toward family life than towards the movement as a whole, including their relationship with other women'.[106] However, when we look at sermons like that of Elizabeth Evans (as Dinah Morris in *Adam Bede*) we can see that Evans was taking stories from her own life to make the impression she wanted, something all good preachers have always done, but because she was reimagining her time as a little girl this was different from the male preacher.[107]

As with the men, some, particularly those whom I described as evangelists, often preached outside, for example Mary Bosanquet in the quarry at Golcar near Huddersfield in September 1776.[108] Sarah Crosby preached to over five hundred people 'in a field, because no house could contain the people'.[109] Diana Thomas rather later preached in farm yards, market-

---

[103] Z. *Taft*, 1:301ff. Letter from Wesley to Ann Cutler, *JWL*, vol 8, p. 214 now in JRL.

[104] The suggestion of Liz Shercliff; see Shercliff, *Preaching Women*, especially chapter two.

[105] As Eryn White points out on p. 69.

[106] *Mack*, chapters three and four, quotation from p. 150. These women preachers such as Mary Bosanquet Fletcher and her friends thought nationally about the Connexion and Conference.

[107] P. W. Chilcote, *Her Own Story: autobiographical portraits of early Methodist women* (Nashville, 2001), pp. 177-81.

[108] Church, *More About the Early Methodist People*, pp. 142-3.

[109] *Chilcote, 1991*, p. 153.

places, village greens, fairs, crossroads and wayside corners.[110] Miss Berger and Mrs Webster once preached in a ship.[111]

Inside they often preached in ordinary houses, but it varied enormously. Staying in an inn in Harrogate in 1773 Mary Bosanquet found that the other residents insisted she speak to them in the ball-room! They were so affected they insisted she return the next Sunday, when a larger company assembled.[112] Inns were used quite often, as were barns and any other building where a meeting could be held. In 1797 Mary Barritt spoke to 'multitudes' in a dyehouse in Leeds during the Conference.[113] Charlotte Berger and Henrietta Webster opened what they called preaching rooms in Walthamstow and Holloway End in 1816 and promptly preached in them. But they also had meetings in their own house.[114]

Chapels, what Wesley called preaching-houses, were also frequently used. This was a period when chapels were being built, so the congregation who heard them in a house one year, might be in a chapel next year. These were mostly small ones in the country, but as larger ones were built, so women were asked to these as well. Ann Gilbert preached to 1,400 in the chapel at Redruth. Sarah Crosby in 1775 preached in the large chapels in Bradford and Halifax to thousands of hearers. Charlotte Berger and Henrietta Webster were invited to preach in the chapel at Poplar in 1819.[115]

Some preachers, as we have seen, stayed in one place, one area, or later one circuit. Others travelled widely. Take someone like Mary Bosanquet Fletcher. At first her preaching life seems relatively simple. She began at Leytonstone in the 1760s, moved to Yorkshire, where she certainly preached widely in the 1770s,

---

[110] Parlby, 'Diana Thomas of Kington', 111.
[111] May 1821; Brown, *Berger*, p. 49.
[112] *Chilcote, 1991*, p. 150.
[113] *Taft Memoirs*, 1:57.
[114] Brown, *Berger*.
[115] Ibid., p. 46.

moved to Madeley in 1781 and remained there until her death in 1815. And then we learn that she made an extensive tour of Bath, Bristol and Kingswood from December 1777 to April 1778. After her marriage, with her husband she went to Dublin for several months. In all these places she seems to have preached extensively. She returned to preach in Bristol in 1785.[116] If we had a complete roster of everywhere she preached it would be wider still. However, most women preachers tended to preach only in smaller areas; for example Mrs Elizabeth Clarkson is only known to have preached in Crakehall and the villages around it between Easingwold and Helmsley. There were sizeable areas which had no known women preaching. Scotland seems to have had only one known woman preacher, 'a female from the banks of the Spey' who conducted services at Elgin *c.*1817.[117] The South of England had a large gap with no women preachers from Cornwall to London.[118] Mrs Fletcher and others preached in the Bristol area. Penelope Newman in Cheltenham and the villages around, from where she is known to have come as far south as Stroud is one example, but otherwise the south Midlands had no known women preachers, apart from the minister's wife in Oxford, Mrs Sarah Stevens.[119] On the other hand, in the north Midlands and the North, especially Yorkshire, women preachers seemed to abound. At least twenty-three of the sixty-seven are known to have preached in Yorkshire. Norfolk was also a seedbed for women preaching. At

---

[116] There is no modern biography of Mary Bosanquet Fletcher. We are still largely dependent on H. Moore, *The Life of Mrs Mary Fletcher* (London, 1817).

[117] W. F. Swift, *The Romance of Banffshire Methodism* (Banff, 1927), p. 31.

[118] A Miss Morris of Eastbourne preached in that area between at least 1825 and 1841, and may have been preaching before 1820. C. C. Crisford, *A Golden Candlestick or Methodism in Eastbourne* (Eastbourne, 1913). I am grateful to Michael Hickman for this reference.

[119] Wife of William Stevens who was stationed in Oxford 1791-3. Methodism was relatively weak in both Scotland and the South of England outside Cornwall.

least seven are known to have preached in that county. We know all this largely because of Zechariah Taft's book *Holy Women*, published in Yorkshire in 1825.

Conclusion

Early Methodist women preachers were a significant group 1760-1820, even though it became more difficult for them to operate as they had previously after the Conference decision against them in 1803. In many rural areas in the North and elsewhere, women attracted crowds in the open air, maintained the witness in small cottage meetings, and were also able to fill large chapels. Though their existence was often written out by male editors, yet sufficient evidence of their presence across the country has remained. More (at present anonymous) women will be discovered by future research.

Today, the Methodist Church in Great Britain encourages men and women to become worship leaders, local preachers and ministers. The active presbyteral ministry is roughly half and half male and female. No figures are available for local preachers, but looking at circuit plans makes me think it is fairly equal. For worship leaders, again no figures are known to me, but circuit preaching plans seem to show more women than men as worship leaders. However, that equality is certainly not there for superintendents of circuits or Chairs of districts.[120] The Methodist Church still needs to be more inclusive and to encourage more diverse talents.

There are comparisons to be made with early Methodism, though obviously far fewer women than men preached. 'Exhorters', which is how most early women preachers began, have some similarities to modern worship leaders. Though in

---

[120] In 2018 out of thirty Chairs of district only seven were female. Of 395 superintendents 84 were women, both being less than a quarter of the total; *Minutes* (2018). See also chapter fifteen, and J. Lenton, '"The Cry of the Beloved": Methodist Women Ministers 1973-1996' in *The Shropshire Wesley Historical Society Bulletin*, vol 28, (2018).

Wesleyanism there were no women ministers, yet the leading women Methodist evangelists of the day such as Sarah Crosby, Mary Bosanquet Fletcher and Mary Barritt were clearly more effective than many of the male itinerants among their contemporaries, as can be seen by the crowds who came to hear them. We should celebrate more the women pioneers of Methodism's past, especially of this little understood and remembered period. Sarah Crosby, Mary Bosanquet Fletcher, Elizabeth Hurrell, Mary Barritt, Charlotte Berger and others are little known, but should be held up as examples of people who strove against the handicaps of their society to proclaim the message of Methodism to all. Inspired by the Arminian hymns of Charles Wesley and others, which they quoted frequently, they were certain that the call to preach was for them as well. They agonised over how they should 'labour publicly'. Fletcher stood for preaching on the pulpit steps rather than go the whole way in to the pulpit. When she wrote in 1803 to the Tafts she quoted this hymn by Isaac Watts:[121]

> O for that strong and lasting faith
> Which credits *all*, the Almighty saith:
> That claims the promise of the Son
> And feels the comforter its own.[122]

Mary Bosanquet Fletcher was claiming for Mary Taft and for herself, as representatives of all Christian women, the inspiration of the Holy Spirit, the Comforter, and the promises of Jesus.

---

[121] I am grateful to Martin Clarke for the reference, a 'methodised' variant of an Isaac Watts hymn; see https://hymnary.org/text/o for a strong a lasting faith (accessed 30 October 2019).
[122] Z. Taft, *Original Letters Never Before Published, on Doctrinal, Experimental and Practical Religion* (Whitby, 1821), letter 41, p. 85. Emphasis mine.

7: 'Labouring with Success': early Primitive Methodist women preachers[1]

Tim Macquiban

This chapter concentrates on an examination of the place and role of early women preachers, especially those who itinerated, i.e. were sent to circuits, in Primitive Methodism, one of the branches of Methodism in Britain which emerged from the revivals of the first decade of the nineteenth century.[2] Beginning in the camp meeting inspired by American evangelist Lorenzo Dow held at Mow Cop on the borders of Cheshire and Staffordshire in 1807, it emerged as a distinct movement with the work of Hugh Bourne and William Clowes coming together in 1811 and the formation of a separate circuit at Tunstall. From here preachers were sent out to the rest of the North of England, including Hull where the first Conference of the PM Connexion was held in 1820.[3]

Paul W. Chilcote, historian of Methodist spirituality, has, in considering the place of women in Methodist history, claimed that the 'memory of women has been lost . . . [they have] not been permitted a voice and therefore to shape our memory. This must be rectified for our Christian family ever to be truly healthy'.[4] Zechariah Taft, Wesleyan minister of the early nineteenth century, reflecting on the ministries of women in his time commented that 'many females, whose praise was in all

---

[1] An earlier version of this paper was published in the journal *The Ranters` Digest*, vol 20, (2019), 9-21.

[2] 'Early' means from the origins to the 1830s.

[3] *DMBI*, p. 281.

[4] P. W. Chilcote, *Early Methodist Spirituality: selected women's writings* (Nashville, 2001), p. 9.

the churches while they lived, have been suffered to drop into oblivion'.[5]

Amy Richardson (1872-1953) was a PM local preacher in Leeds whose name was not placed on the Leeds II circuit plan in 1896, even though authority was given to her to preach in 1896. This caused Colin Dews a hundred years later to suggest that 'the use and impact of female local preachers within Methodism . . . requires further research'.[6] That still remains the case, as is evidenced by the wealth of material, some new and hitherto unpublished, recently deposited in the Englesea Brook Museum of Primitive Methodism.[7] Dorothy Graham first introduced me to the importance of giving attention to the neglected and suppressed topic of women preachers in Methodism. She was a co-contributor of a chapter in the book *Workaday Preachers: the story of Methodist Local Preaching* published for the bicentenary year of 1996 (the first official Conference recognition of the office of local preacher).[8] One of our Englesea Brook volunteers and supporters, Margaret Gleave, has done valuable work on the significance of female preaching in the first fifty years of Primitive Methodism.[9] She points to the work of over two hundred women preachers among Primitive Methodists and Bible Christians as the two branches of Methodism who employed women preachers in the most sustained way.

This chapter will concentrate on some unpublished material in the 1828 collection of forms returned by preachers to Hugh and

---

[5] Ibid. p. 15 and *DMBI*, p. 21. Taft (1772-1848) was a great supporter of women preachers within the Wesleyan Connexion and wrote three pamphlets in their support.

[6] D. C. Dews, *Ranters, Revivalists, Radicals, Reformers and Revolutionaries: a celebration of Methodist local preaching in Yorkshire* (Leeds, 1996), p. 58.

[7] Englesea Brook Museum: Mss Reports of Itinerant Preachers 1828.

[8] E. D. Graham, 'Women Local Preachers' in Milburn and Batty (eds), *Workaday Preachers*.

[9] In an article entitled 'An Extraordinary Calling' in *The Ranters' Digest*, vol 15, (2017), 4-13.

James Bourne at Bemersley to highlight aspects of what such studies in the past decades have shown, namely the opposition to women preaching, the invisibility to its reality, and the deafening silence of the women themselves in the official records of the day. We will listen to the voices of three women in particular, Elizabeth Allen, Ruth Watkins and Mary Burks, whose testimonies and witness survive thanks to their doggedness in responding to the bureaucratic nature of early Primitive Methodism and its obsession with gathering data, a practice it shared with Wesleyans and later Methodists.

But first we need briefly to set the context for why within Primitive Methodism there was a place for women preachers in the earliest days of its development up to 1840 but why this too eventually proved as problematic as it did for the Wesleyans. Preaching plans, being the primary source of evidence for the appointments to which itinerant and local preachers were assigned in local circuits, have survived in only very limited numbers for the early period of Primitive Methodism. It is therefore difficult to give a reliable estimate of the full extent of female preaching, especially as their names were not always included even if they were used as preachers, evident from other records, such as the Minutes of Conference and the Connexional Magazines.[10] And yet, as Jennifer Lloyd has clearly demonstrated in her book on women preachers, they were present, challenging the patriarchal hierarchies with limited and diminishing success in the nineteenth century, 'never exercised in complete equality with their male colleagues.' As Elaine Kaye and others note, their contributions were valued but always limited by rules within the wider connexions which prevented them from exercising too much power.[11] David Hempton, however, claims that 'Methodism was comprehensively shaped by women in ways that we do not

---

[10] *Lloyd*, p. 2 and Graham, 'Women Local Preachers', p. 185.
[11] *Lloyd*, quoting p. 3 from E. Kaye, J. Lees, and K. Thorpe, *Daughters of Dissent* (London, 2004), p. 124.

fully understand', citing instances of their role as 'purveyors of hospitality, deaconesses, visitors, evangelists, prayers, exhorters, testifiers, class members and leaders and preachers who helped to define the character of the Methodist movement'.[12]

Anne Stott characterises the role of women in prophetic preaching as symptomatic of what Weber describes as indicative of the charismatic energy of a new religious movement in its earliest phase before it becomes bureaucratized. In the wake of industrialization and urbanization, such forms which thrived in a rural cottage environment gave way to a more domesticated role in which women were more confined to the home, the class and the classroom.[13] As they played a prominent and influential role shaping the early PM movement, it is essential to have more work undertaken on the role of female preachers and to unearth more evidence of its reality and significance. Lloyd`s thesis that female preachers were most useful in the conversionist period of the development of early Primitive Methodism does seem to fit the higher percentage of female itinerants before 1834 (as much as twenty percent) but more work needs to be done to critique the reasons behind this.[14] One key factor may be what Bourne observed when he met Elizabeth Evans,[15] whose preaching he admired, and who was the model for George Eliot`s Dinah Morris,[16] saying he believed that 'she had lost

---

[12] Hempton, *Methodism: empire of the Spirit*, pp. 138-39, 149-50.

[13] A. Stott, chapter six, 'Women and Religion', in H. Barker and E. Chalus (eds), *Women`s History: Britain 1700-1850: an introduction* (London, 2005), pp. 100ff quoting Weber`s *Sociology of Religion*, pp. 104-5.

[14] *Lloyd*, p. 4.

[15] *DMBI*, article on Elizabeth Ann Evans (1776-1848) preacher in the Midlands. The pulpit from which she preached at Wirksworth is exhibited in the Englesea Brook Museum.

[16] G. Eliot, *Adam Bede* (Edinburgh, 1890), vol 2, pp. 14-25.

some ground when entering the married state'.[17] Certainly, it caused some difficulties for the Wesleyans whom she left in the early 1830s (because of the stigma attached to women's ministry) to join the Arminian Methodists, though she subsequently returned to the fold.

Context

John Wesley's ambivalence towards women preachers is well recognized: he stated that 'we know not where it will end'. Yet he used Sarah Mallet among others and tolerated the initiatives of such as Mary Bosanquet in bearing fruit in the revival.[18] But the more exuberant revivals sparked by William Bramwell and others in Yorkshire and elsewhere in the 1790s were different, leading the Connexion after Wesley's death in 1791 to re-examine the role of women preachers. Such revivals were ably aided by women helpers. Of Mary Barritt, chief agent with Bramwell of the Nottingham revival of 1799-1800, it was said that 'It is at the peril of your soul that you meddle with [her]. God is with her—fruit is appearing wherever she goes'.[19] Phyllis Mack sees the 1790s onwards as a period of 'heightened gender consciousness in their campaign to publish women's life stories and spiritual writings.'[20]

When the first signs of opposition to women preachers arose in Wesleyanism, the women's cause found a champion in Zechariah Taft, whose *Thoughts on Female Preaching* nevertheless failed to sway the Wesleyan Conference of 1803 from severely

---

[17] Kendall, *Origin and History of the Primitive Methodist Church*, vol 1, pp. 142-4.

[18] *JWL*, vol 7, pp. 8-9. See also chapter six in this volume.

[19] Quoted in *Lloyd*, p. 47. For more information on the use of female preachers, of Ann Cutler and Mary Barritt, see J. Sigston's *A Memoir of the Life and Ministry of Mr. William Bramwell* (Leeds, 1820) written at the height of the PM acceptance of the ministry of women. Their example encouraged a new generation of those aspiring to be preachers.

[20] *Mack*, pp. 290-1.

restricting the use of women as preachers.[21] 'In general they ought not' was a judgement which became enshrined in Wesleyan practice for most of the rest of the century with some few but notable exceptions slipping under the connexional radar with local connivance for practical reasons.[22] Revivalist zeal gave way to a more cautious conservatism and the need to toe the establishment line in a revolutionary era.

But from the beginning, picking up many converts from Wesleyanism because it had set its face against revivalism and a more proper role for women, the PM Connexion, appealing to a poorer and more rural base, attracted a considerable number of women. Some of them were enlisted first as local preachers and then as itinerants in the first two decades from its emergence as the Camp Meeting Methodists in 1807 and the PM Connexion in 1811. Joseph Nightingale, erstwhile follower of Thomas Paine and ex Wesleyan, described the revivalists as 'simple, harmless, and well-meaning . . . but enthusiastical and ungovernable'. That is what the government feared.[23]

By 1818, twenty percent of all its preachers were women.[24] Hugh Bourne, the co-founder of Primitive Methodism with his experience of those female helpers in parallel movements such as Dorothy Ripley with Lorenzo Dow, saw the tremendous value of the contribution women could make in the rapid development of his movement.[25] Mary Dunnell, preacher for the

---

[21] Published Dover, 1803.

[22] See Graham, 'Women Local Preachers', p. 168 for full text of the 1803 Conference resolution.

[23] Quoted in J. S. Werner, *The Primitive Methodist Connexion: its background and early history* (Wisconsin, 1984), p. 27.

[24] Ibid., p. 142 drawing on W. F. Swift's article 'The Women Itinerant Preachers of Early Methodism' in *PWHS*, vol 29, (1953), 84.

[25] J. Walford, 'Remarks on the Ministry of Women' in W. Antliff (ed.), *Memoirs of the Life and Labours of the late Venerable Hugh Bourne* (London, 1855). Other parallel movements included the Magic Methodists with Nancy Foden and the Independent Methodists with Hannah Peacock.

Independents, was one of his earliest helpers. He praised her 'volubility of speech and flowery eloquence' when she spoke at the first August camp meetings held in the open air for evangelistic rallies to the hundreds gathered from all over the north Midlands and Cheshire.[26]

Such activity laid them open to the charge that they allowed the use of 'females to preach in promiscuous assemblies', in line with the assumptions of indecorous behaviour found in most of the anti-Methodist propaganda of the time.[27] Sarah Kirkland has the honour of being the first female preacher on a PM plan of 1814, aged only eighteen, and a 'travelling preacheress' two years later.[28] She attracted thousands to the camp meeting in Nottingham Forest, a feeding ground for the recruits gathered and harvested in the numerous preaching places being established in the very period Wesleyans were post-Peterloo closing ranks against such vulgar expressions of a religiosity which would not only bring notoriety but also risked losing credibility in an age of retrenchment. She was the only woman included in George Herod`s *Biographical Sketches* of ministers and preachers in 1855.[29]

The examples of some of those women as well as men who risked not only their reputations but also their security are amply evidenced in the *PMM* accounts of such women as Elizabeth Brownhill, Elizabeth Clifford, Mary Porteous and Elizabeth Smith.[30] There was a clear need to justify such activity as can be deduced from the article in the second *PMM* of 1821

---

[26] *Graham, 2010,* p. 67.

[27] Ibid., p. 74 and *Lloyd,* pp. 90-1.

[28] *DMBI* (accessed 10 August 2020).

[29] G. Herod, *Biographical Sketches of Some of those Preachers whose Labours Contributed to the Origination and Early Extension of the PM Connexion* (originally published London, 1855, reprinted Stoke-on-Trent, 2002). Nottingham Forest was a large open area north of the city centre, half way to Basford.

[30] *Graham, 2010,* pp. 22, 41, 46.

when a piece appeared entitled 'The Female Preachers' Plea'. Already many viewed such preaching as dangerous and divisive, a view highlighted by the departure of Ann Carr who split off in 1822 founding the Female Revivalist Society with its own chapel in Leeds, nicknamed the 'Jumping Ranters'.[31]

Some new evidence

We now hear three voices which come from the obsessive collection of data and publications which from early days marked out the PM Connexion in its projection of a self-identity as a growing movement keen to bureaucratize the charisma of the founding fathers in ways which prevented its demise. They come from a collection of 186 returns following on from a minute of the 1827 Conference relating to preachers, [32] requiring all preachers to make a return, with their dates and places of birth and conversion, as well as dates and places of service as both local and travelling preachers, with forms sent out from the Book Room at Bemersley.[33]

While they are mostly the completed forms, there is supplementary material given by some who had not received the forms or chose to add to the account. As yet, they have not been fully analysed and cross-checked against other listings. I have extracted the only three identifiable returns out of 186 from women preachers (despite their numbers being around twenty percent of the total). The male language of the minute clearly implied that they were not expected to make the returns even though the minute said it would only take them thirty minutes to complete!

---

[31] Ibid., p. 64.

[32] *PM Minutes,* (Bemersley, 1827).

[33] James Bourne, brother of Hugh, was responsible for the production of all forms and printed material in the 1820s, printed on the press at Bemersley, Staffs. He was book steward for the PM Connexion from 1824.

Elizabeth Allen (1803-1850)[34]

Her form stated:[35] writing to

Mr James Bourne, Book Steward, Bemersley near Tunstall, Staffordshire

Grimsby Circuit 2 April 1828

Dear Brother and Farther [sic] in Christ,

Grace and peace be multiplied upon you from God the Farther and from our Lord Jesus Christ. My design in writing in this manner is. In looking at the Minutes of the last Conference held at Manchester, I find that each preacher is requested to give an account where he has travelled. But as the females Preachers are not mentioned in this minute, I did not know whether it was my duty to write or not. But I have been told that two printed forms has come into the Circuit to be filled up with the above mentioned and Bro [Robert] Atkinson says he lost one on account of which he advises me to write a few lines by way of letter. [36] Here they are at your service, and do with them as you think proper after so many reasonings about the matter whether to do it or whether I should not. I hope you will excuse it coming so late. I remain your unworthy sister in the kingdom and partner of our Lord Jesus, Eliz. Allen.

I Elizabeth Allen was converted at or near Coathillin the parish of Lazonby and County of Cumberland in the year 1820 and as a local preacher my name never appeared upon the plan till that same quarter that I was taken out to travel which was by the Hull Circuit at the Sept. 1824 Q[uarte]r Day. But I did not enter upon my labour till the last of Octbr. Or the first of Novbr. 1824 being then 22 years of age. I travelled in that Circuit till the 25 December in all 2 years and 3 months. Then was removed to Louth in Lincolnshire and travelled there till Christmas with the exception of a few days being ill. When

---

[34] *Graham, 2010,* pp. 6-7. She was on the stations from 1825 until 1834.

[35] Englesea Brook Museum, Mss Reports of Itinerant Preachers 1828 135.

[36] Robert Atkinson e.m. 1821, in Grimsby circuit 1827-29, died 1858.

leaving Louth I came to Grimsby where I am at present and am labouring with success. May the Lord grant we may have an abundant harvest of preccious souls gathered to the standard of the cross which may be the crown of our rejoicing in the day of the Lord, the grace of the Lord Jesus Christ be with you. E. Allen

NB When I am removed from this Circuit which I expect will be before winter is over if you could get me into some easy circuit I would be much obliged to you as I have been ill and am weak at present.

Subsequently, she itinerated till 1835, including missions to Scotland and Ireland. She was assigned to circuits in Hull (six months) and Pocklington (six months) in 1829, Preston Brook for the two following years, then Tunstall for two years, followed by her last station at Macclesfield. It was there that she married John Vernon and ceased to itinerate. She continued however to preach on the circuit plan until her death in 1850, aged forty-seven, leaving her husband and two children. It is recorded that she often preached in the open air due to the large crowds attracted by her preaching because of its novelty value.[37]

Ruth Watkins (1803- ?)

Her form stated:[38]

Pursuant to the order of the Annual Meeting or Conference of 1827, I transmit the following account of myself:

I Ruth Watkins was born at Earlswood in the county of Monmouth and was brought up to the occupation of Dress Makeing. At the age of twenty-one I was converted to the Lord. My conversion took place at Earlswood in or about the month of February 1824. Began to labour as a local preacher November 1824 and did continue till March 1825 which was about five months. On the 24 March I was taken out to labour as a travelling preacher in the Primitive Methodist Connexion

---

[37] *Graham, 2010*, pp. 53-4, *DMBI.*
[38] Englesea Brook Museum, Mss Reports 153.

by the Tunstall Circuit; and an account of my itinerant labours is contained in the following table:

24 March 1825, Tunstall Remaining three years one week.

Soon after, in 1829, she sailed as a missionary to America, accompanying William Summersides, his wife and two children, William Knowles and Thomas Morris, arriving in New York in July of that year. Regular reports were sent back and printed in the *PMM* of her and their experiences. Her brother Nathaniel also travelled west and settled in Canada as a preacher where she was also based from 1831 in New Albany in Nova Scotia.[39] She suffered ill health and became disillusioned because of the lack of support from the PM society at home.

Mary Burks (1796-1837)[40]

Her form stated:[41]

Primitive Methodist Connexion 18[28 crossed out]31

An account of the itinerant and other labours of me Mary Burks.

I Mary Burks was born at Gringley in the county of Nottingham and was brought up to the occupation or employment of a House Keeper. At the age of twenty-three, I was converted to the Lord. My conversion took place at Stockwith in Lincolnshire in or about the month of April 1819. I began to labour as a local preacher in June 1820 and continued till March 1822 which was about one year and nine months. On the seventh of March I was taken out to labour as travelling or itinerant preacher in the Primitive Methodist Connexion by the Scotter circuit, and an account of my itinerant labours is contained in the following table:

---

[39] Nathaniel Watkins e.m. 1829, 1831 in Canada, disappears. W. Leary, *Some Lincolnshire Methodists* (Loughborough, 1998).
[40] *Graham, 2010,* pp. 20-1. Also spelt Birks; e.m. in 1822 and last stationed in 1834.
[41] Englesea Brook Museum, Mss Reports 193.

18 March 1822	Scotter circuit	17 December 1822	nine months
26 December 1822	Louth circuit	26 June 1823	six months
6 July 1823	Scotter circuit	23 June 1824	one year
6 July 1824	Lincoln circuit	26 June 1826	two years
6 July 1826	Grimsby circuit	24 December 1826	six months
1 January 1827	Hull circuit	26 June 1829	two years six months
1 January 1830	Grimsby circuit	26 June 1830	six months
6 July 1830	Louth where I am now		

I have sent two years subscription money of my entrance

Primitive Methodist Connexion Louth Circuit 1831

To the Preachers and members of the Fund called the Primitive Methodist Preachers Fund assembled at the District Meeting at Grimsby and at the Conference in Leicester.

Dear Fathers and Brethren, Grace and Peace be with you, Amen.

I Mary Burks, desirous of becoming a member of your Fund being myself considered eligible first as to age being thirty-five years, of good health and a sound constitution. I now offer myself as a candidate for the said fund. I was informed that a minute was passed last conference giving me the privilege of entering the said fund as from last Conference (if these my present documents should by you be received) by sending my entrance and this year's subscription money. An Account of my birth, conversion, commencement of my ministerial labours, and the circuits in which I have laboured, you will find annexed with this document. I remain your sister in the Gospel of the Redeemer, Mary Burks. Louth 9 February 1831

Approved by the Quarter Board at Louth 4 April 1831

William Byrom, President

William Ball, Secretary

Fortunately, a plan survives for the Scotter circuit in the Circuit Plan Scrapbook at Englesea Brook for the quarter November 1821 to January 1822. On this, 'M. Burks' is listed as preacher number fourteen. She was planned for nine appointments in five places (including Epworth) over seven Sundays. Like most plans of the 1820s, there was a reminder printed at the bottom of the plan that 'N.B. Every preacher is reminded affectionately requested strictly to attend his [sic] Appointments, or provide a proper substitute'.[42]

It was said that because of her tall stature (over six feet?) her powerful voice and forceful personality, she was a very impressive figure who attracted large crowds. When in the Hull circuit she was reported to have asked the Hull quarterly meeting to buy her an ass for her appointments. Whether this was caused by the rigours of travelling already taking their toll upon her, by 1834 she was far from well. After Hull she served in Lincoln for six months, then another six months in Hull, a year and a quarter in Louth, then a year and three quarters in Malton, a year in York, and two years again in Hull, a total of ten appointments in fourteen years! She then retired to East Stockwith in the Scotter circuit where she resided with her father. She remained a class leader and local preacher till her death in January 1837, aged forty-one. It would be interesting to find out whether she was able to acquire any of the benefits of her subscription to the Preachers' Fund (assuming that she was accepted).[43]

William Suddard(s)[44]

Sometimes the voices of women preachers are filtered through their husbands or colleagues to ensure that their presence and contribution is not overlooked. This was the case with William

---

[42] Englesea Brook Museum, Circuit Plans Scrapbook no 36, November 1821 to January 1822.

[43] *Graham, 2010,* pp. 20-1 and *PMM,* vol 18, (1837) pp. 451ff.

[44] W. Leary, *Ministers and Circuits in the PM Church: a directory* (Loughborough, 1990), p. 204. He entered the PM ministry in 1823 the same time as his wife Jane. They were married in Newcastle in August 1823. He is recorded as having left for New York, presumably with his wife.

Suddard(s), born in Bradford in 1804, a PM itinerant in the Hull circuit by 1824 who had been a local preacher with the Wesleyans from 1820. In 1827 he accompanied William Clowes to a missionary meeting in Scotter. Soon after he was able to become the missionary he hoped to be. He wrote this in his return to the Connexion, where his form stated:[45]

> At which time [1824] I peaceably withdrew feeling an impression upon my mind of it being my duty to go abroad as a missionary; at the instigation of some of the Wesleyan Preachers, I offered myself for foreign labours in their Body. My wife being in the habit of Preaching—the Conference, nor yet the Missionary Committee could sanction my going out unless she would cease from acting in that public way—Mr Zechariah Taft informed the Conference 'She would preach and go where she would'—upon which it did not appear practicable for me to go.

And so he had jumped ship and re-joined the PM Connexion in the Hull circuit. But there is no record of whether his wife continued to preach or to support him beyond 1824; informally, though, she is given as being on the stations in the Hull circuit in 1823. She then would only have been permitted to preach in the same circuit and not to itinerate at all. He is listed in the *Minutes of Conference* as itinerant in the Hull circuit in 1825 and 1826 and may have withdrawn from the stations before emigrating with his wife Jane (see below) to the States, drawn there by Rev. George Cookson, a native of Hull. He served in New York and Philadelphia, this time as part of the Methodist and then Protestant Episcopal Church, latterly as rector of Grace Church, Philadelphia, where he served for over forty years.[46]

Jane Ansdell (1801-1892) had played a vital role in the introduction of Primitive Methodism to Hexhamshire and

---

[45] Englesea Brook Museum, Mss Reports 80.
[46] See entry for Suddards in Leary, *Ministers and Circuits*, p. 204. Additional information supplied by Shirley Martin. Suddards died in 1883.

Weardale in the 1820s, and was one of the preachers from Shotley Bridge who went at the invitation of John Gibson to Hexham to preach in October 1822. She was there accompanied by another travelling preacher, William Suddards, sent from Stockton to Hexham, whom she married in 1823. They had two children born in 1825 and 1827. I can find no evidence that she continued to preach after her marriage in Britain but she was a preacher in America and Canada.[47]

Other women preachers

But what of those missing from the records? I cite but a few to instance the way in which the record is sadly incomplete, two for whom much is known and one for whom little.

Another female preacher known in the North East was Mary Porteous (1783-1861), born in Newcastle, wife of a seaman whom she married in 1807, and becoming a class leader and Sunday School teacher with the Wesleyans. She joined the Primitive Methodists and resisted the call to preach for some years but eventually at the age of forty-one became a local preacher. She was called to be a travelling preacher in 1825 but delayed her start for a year because of family commitments when she went to Whitby. Even though the Conference resolution of 1827 laid down that 'no married female shall be allowed to labour as a travelling preacher in any circuit except that in which her husband resides', she was allowed to travel, to circuits in Ripon (two years), Carlisle (three years), Hexham (two years), then a gap of a year and working in North Shields, Sunderland and Durham until in 1840 she ceased to itinerate because of ill health.[48] Her work was earlier interrupted by injury sustained in her travels. She wrote in a letter: 'We have

---

[47] *Graham, 2010*, pp. 8-9. Ansdell is also spelt Ansdale.
[48] Ibid., pp. 41-2.

some five jumpers in the shire. I feel delighted in being among them but have not yet learned to jump with them'.[49]

Mary Peat is listed in a plan of the Welton circuit in north Lincolnshire for October 1824 to January 1825. She is listed separately after the Preachers' Names and those of Exhorters under the heading Women. She is the only one so listed. She is not included in the listings made by Graham in her *Chosen by God* nor in Leary`s *Some Lincolnshire Methodists*.[50] Her inclusion here shows how incomplete the records are. As yet no further information has been found for her. She may have married and moved elsewhere.[51]

Elizabeth Russell (née Smith, 1805-36) was born in Ludlow, and brought up by her grandmother after she was orphaned. Apprenticed as a dressmaker she went to London and worked for an actress. Then later she moved to Water Stratford in Buckinghamshire where she worked for a local vicar. In a troubled spiritual state, she returned home to Ludlow in 1824 where she had a conversion experience under PM preaching, even though the local 'cause was low`. Encouraged to pray, she did so, causing 'a stout man to fall as one shot in battle'. This was taken as evidence of the power of her calling, encouraged by Sarah Evans,[52] confirmed by the quarterly meeting which sent her as a local preacher to a new mission in Presteigne, Radnorshire, possibly with the status of a hired local preacher. She walked the thirty miles from Ludlow, unafraid of what she had to do in order to maintain herself. Giving up her dressmaking earnings, she was given an allowance of two

---

[49] G. Milburn, 'The Ranters in Hexhamshire' in *Hexham Historian*, vol 2, (1992), p. 30.

[50] *Graham, 2010*; Leary, *Some Lincolnshire Methodists*.

[51] Circuit Plans Scrapbook no 42, October 1824 to January 1825 at Englesea Brook.

[52] Leary, *Ministers and Circuits*, p. 68. S. Evans is recorded as entering the ministry in 1826 at Hopton Bank, and Prees Green in 1826-7 but she disappears after 1828.

guineas a quarter (half of what her male colleagues could have expected).

She was subsequently stationed in the Brinkworth circuit for four years (serving there with dedication during the cholera outbreak of 1832) and then to Darlaston where she married fellow preacher, Thomas Russell. Sadly, when a daughter Julia was born she died at sixteen months old, closely followed by Elizabeth's own death after a short illness and return to her native Ludlow, where she died early in 1836. Her husband Thomas stationed in the South was not present for the funeral. As her obituary later recorded, 'though but a weakly woman, she overcame opposition with her plain firm method', such as the opposition of clergymen, rowdy youths and noisy musicians, especially while in the Brinkworth district of Wiltshire where a female preacher was quite a novelty. She was particularly skilled in opening up new places which led to chapels being built.[53]

Three things stand out from the accounts of her work as characteristic of the contribution she and other women preachers made in these early days:

- *Her diligence and frugality*—perhaps this is shorthand for not costing the local cause as much as others with family ties and responsibilities;
- *Her consent to open mission*—breaking new ground through this extraordinary call with a sense of novelty and fresh enthusiasm;
- *Her enduring trouble and affliction in a thinly inhabited country*—again possibly shorthand for being prepared to go where others hesitated because of family ties.

The series of letters written by Elizabeth to her colleague and mentor Sarah Evans in the period 1826 to 1828 are indicative of the reality that she too was 'labouring with success', as she recalls in February 1828: that 'In the branch we are doing well. I

---

[53] *Graham, 2010*, pp. 46-7; *DMBI*.

have lately joined a good number of members;[54] and we are building a new chapel. Our societies are growing in grace. We long for greater work. The congregations daily increase'. The year before she had reported on the arrival of Sister Welch[55] in Ludlow on her way to Hopton Bank. 'I am thankful that I am able to take up my appointment again'. She had been in Hopton Bank for six months, then sent to Prees for six months and back to Hopton Bank for another year before a year in Presteigne. Next she reverted to local preacher status.[56] But where was her record in the 1828 return of itinerant preachers? Lost on the road from Radnorshire to Ludlow and on to Bemersley? Or never delivered to that branch of a sparsely populated county? Or simply disregarded because she was a hired local preacher rather than fully on the stations? Fortunately we have extracts from her letters in the *PMM* to tell of the reality of her perseverance in the face of great difficulties in a key area of mission.

In 1828, after her grandmother's death, she was transferred from her work in the Ludlow and Presteigne branches to Brinkworth in Wiltshire with five male colleagues. Here too she had a 'zeal for missionary labours'. In 1829, she moved to Wootton Basset in Berkshire where it 'was recorded that her preaching talents as a female are more than ordinary; her way is perfectly open, and she has been very useful'. A classic assessment and understatement by a male colleague! She is reported as giving a speech at a missionary meeting at Broadtown in the Brinkworth circuit in December 1829.[57] In the 1830 Conference report re-stationing her for an unprecedented third year in the Brinkworth circuit, this assessment was given: 'Elizabeth Smith is attentive to discipline; a general family visitor, very peaceable; her preaching generally acceptable; not

---

[54] 'Joined' means that she had admitted them to the society.
[55] *Graham, 2010*, pp. 54-5, spelt also Welsh; e.m. at Hopton Bank and Prees in 1826-7 and was transferred to Presteigne in 1828.
[56] *PMM*, vol 18, (1837), 139-41.
[57] *PMM*, vol 11, (1830), 278-80.

addicted to long preaching; preaches a full, free and present salvation; is successful in the conversion of sinners; her general conduct good; and she has been useful here.'[58]

One wonders whether such understated praise given for outstanding work is a recognition of the threat that her 'labouring with success' posed to her male colleagues. Her subsequent marriage to Thomas Russell, an itinerant preacher imprisoned for his beliefs, and work together in Hampshire, Berkshire and then Staffordshire are equally remarkable in the rapid growth of the causes in these parts. She survived scarlet fever in 1833 only to have her daughter Julia succumb to smallpox in 1835. She herself died the following year. Over one thousand people attended her funeral in the new chapel in Ludlow.[59]

Conclusion

We can from the evidence presented begin to see that a pattern has emerged which, in the main, fits with the conclusions drawn by Graham, Lloyd and Stott of the contribution made by women preachers among the early Primitive Methodists. More than the male counterparts, female preachers were likely to be young, less than twenty years old, and overwhelmingly at the time of stationing single. Maybe some were wanting to move in defiance of parents or to make a break from family ties? Most came from poor backgrounds in agricultural settings or cottage industries. Their length of tenure on those stations was as short, and sometimes shorter (a quarter or two in some instances), as their male colleagues'. Sometimes these were cut short for reasons mainly of illness or for marriage. Their lives were counter cultural in orientation, suited to a predominantly cottage religion centred on labouring households. Compassion

---

[58] *PMM*, vol 18, (1837), 179 in 'Memoir of Elizabeth Russell'.

[59] There is a memorial at Englesea Brook Chapel graveyard to Thomas Russell, her husband, (1815-1907) who entered the ministry in 1829 in the Brinkworth circuit. See Leary, *Ministers and Circuits*, p. 182.

through family visiting and hospitality through shared meals were key concepts, cutting across the usual social norms and boundaries. Their role was predominantly evangelistic and revivalist. They were engaged in conversations concerning the state of the soul, especially at times of illness or approaching death, talking of their own feelings and telling of their conversions. They were usually moved on once a society had been formed. The novelty value of their presence offered much in the attraction of converts and recruits to the movement. Though we have little direct evidence, by inference we can confirm Obelkevich's lists of characteristics of early Primitive Methodism in Lincolnshire; its preachers preached the 'three Rs', that is, ruin, repentance, and redemption; and their preaching was 'plain, pithy, pointed and practical'.[60]

Once ceasing to itinerate, they were sometimes continued as hired local preachers to assist in circuit missions and special services. That was the situation for Ann Brownsword, daughter of a farmer and innkeeper at Englesea Brook, sister of Thomas the boy preacher, who itinerated until she married Charles Abraham, a druggist, in Burslem where she settled and continued as a local preacher. She had been the cause of the conversion of many rough Bolton factory workers prior to her stationing in the Tunstall circuit in 1821 and was highly commended for her work by Hugh Bourne.[61] For many, as Mack concludes, 'the missionary project became a family project' as women retreated into dictated domesticity.[62] More work still needs to be done in testing the Stott hypothesis that public preaching was abandoned for the domestic world as plebeian village evangelists became respectable middle-class philanthropists. While this may fit neatly with the experience of Wesleyanism, I would want to query whether it sits well with the continuing egalitarian nature of Primitive Methodism.

---

[60] Obelkevich, *Religion and Rural Society*, pp. 223-4.
[61] *Graham, 2010*, pp. 15-16.
[62] *Mack*, p. 298.

Stott`s conclusion that 'a cottage religion centred on the labouring household' allowed more scope for female agency fits well with the situation of Primitive Methodists in the earlier part of the nineteenth century.[63]

Other contributions especially chapter eleven of this volume will set out when the rot set in and male ascendancy prevailed against such earlier aspirations and experiences. Perhaps how women were allowed (by men) to read their bibles may determine whether such reading empowered and liberated them or rather constrained and suppressed their God-given gifts as male readings predominated from the pulpit. If only we had the authentic voices of women preachers in printed sermons from the early nineteenth century to demonstrate whether they did, as was experienced later, speak from a position of a less powerful group with stories and narratives of changed lives in the language of their hearers. Carlyle wrote that: 'The history of the world is but the biography of great men.'[64] The historiography of Primitive Methodism needs to be revised to include the stories of such women as we have described, hewn from the materials amassed by men and retold. Only then can we honour their contribution to the extraordinary growth of this movement in its first twenty years, thanks to the evangelistic efforts of those who 'laboured with success' in their realization of the extraordinary call they had heard, but who were not able to stay the course in the changing circumstances of a Connexion whose charisms were blunted by the onset of denominational rectitude and respectability.

---

[63] See Stott, 'Women and Religion' in Barker and Chalus (eds), *Women's History*.
[64] Shercliff, *Preaching Women*, p. 42.

8: The Women Itinerant Preachers of the Bible Christian itinerancy, 1815-1907: their status and their work

Colin C. Short

> Ye Heralds of truth, Sent forth by the Lord,
> Both antient and youth, Who publish His word;
> Ye Sons and ye Daughters, Selected by grace,
> Be strong and courageous, And each fill his place.[1]

The Bible Christian (BC) branch of Methodism was the child of William O'Bryan, a Wesleyan local preacher who broke away from the Wesleyan Methodists in the Stratton Mission in north Cornwall and north-west Devon in 1815.[2] The movement spread through Cornwall and the South West, with presences elsewhere, including London,[3] and merged with the Methodist New Connexion and the United Methodist Free Churches in 1907. Catherine O'Bryan, who had been preaching along with her husband in his freelance missionary work since 1812, was the first woman preacher 'in connexion with William O'Bryan'.[4] Their daughter Mary became one of the early woman ministers with the Bible Christians. Her gravestone records her as sixty

---

[1] Catherine O'Bryan, wife of William O'Bryan, founder of the Bible Christians. First verse of a poem appended to *BCMin* (1820), p. 18 as one of two poems entitled 'Address to the Preachers'. It later appeared as hymn nineteen in the 1824 BC Hymn Book and so survived in the Connexion until 1888. C. C. Short, *O'Bryan's Hymns* (Oxford, 2006).

[2] *Shaw and Short*. Prior to June 1818 O'Bryan was called Bryant.

[3] T. Shaw, *The Bible Christians 1815-1907* (London, 1965).

[4] *Shaw and Short*, p. 88. The 'in Connexion with' phrasing is from the title page of the annual *BC Mins* (1819–27) issued after a Conference equivalent to an Annual General Meeting.

years a minister.[5] The Bible Christians and another early nineteenth-century Methodist branch, the Primitive Methodists, employed women ministers.[6]

This chapter explores the story of the BC women ministers, using official documents, including the *Ms Journal*,[7] and other sources to examine their status and work, and how that changed. The situation of the final cohort of four women ministers that emerged in the late nineteenth century is scrutinised. In exploring the ministry of these women, I follow historians such as Jennifer Lloyd[8] and David Shorney,[9] though sometimes reaching different conclusions.[10] This chapter offers a similar picture to the description of the early PM women itinerants in the last chapter. It also portrays the declining trend of female preaching amongst the Bible Christians, as we will also see with Primitive Methodists in chapter eleven, except for a final late cohort of BC women itinerants, as described below.

Their status

The BC Connexion deployed both women and men as ministers; indeed, if we include supernumeraries,[11] they were never without a woman minister. The Connexion's *Digest of the Rules, Regulations and Usages* referred only to 'itinerant preachers', regardless of gender, as did the *Minutes of Conference* and the

---

[5] In the Shebbear Methodist Church burial ground, north Devon, adjacent to the outside wall of the vestry. Her name as a minister first appeared in the *BCMin* (1823); she died in 1883.

[6] Official usage was 'itinerant preacher', but 'travelling preacher' was commonly used.

[7] JRL, 'Bible Christian Manuscript Journal 1824-52', Previous index reference MAW Ms 817; Calkin Reference GB 146. It is cited as '*Ms Journal*' by year (the later pencil pagination is unreliable).

[8] J. M. Lloyd, 'Women Preachers in the Bible Christian Connexion,' *Albion*, vol 36, no 3, (2004), 451-81; and *Lloyd*.

[9] *Shorney*.

[10] See also D. M. Valenze, *Prophetic Sons and Daughters* (Princeton, 1985), and *Field-Bibb*.

[11] A retired minister no longer sent to work in a circuit.

statistical tables; thus, in 1853 the two itinerant preachers stationed at Luxillian[12] were George Batt and . . . Mary Ann Taylor.[13] In popular usage, both men and women itinerant preachers were known as 'ministers'.[14] The core doctrinal statement read: 'We believe that God calls women as well as men to publish salvation to their fellow creatures.'[15]

A central question is: what was the process for appointing a BC itinerant preacher, and how were women treated? There were four factors:

- they were perceived as called by God and tested by the BC Connexion;
- they were recognized at an Annual Conference, listed annually in the *Minutes of Conference* and in due course 'received into full connexion';
- they were stationed;
- they were paid.[16]

These factors applied to the women itinerants as well as to men, though with variations as we will see.

On their calling, Christian believers will have no problem with the sense of a calling from God; others may describe this as an inner compulsion arising from within a religious community; either way, such personal conviction had to be given

---

[12] The nineteenth-century spelling of Luxulyan, a parish north east of St Austell in Cornwall, and William O'Bryan's home parish. Used always in this spelling by the Bible Christians.

[13] *BCMin* (1853), pp. 6, 8. There were twelve chapels and thirty-nine local preachers.

[14] By 1900 'itinerant' was dropped from the *Minutes* but not from the *Digest* 1892 or 1902.

[15] *Digest*, §44 p. 49f. I quote from the *Digest* (1902), here identical to the first, 1838, edition. The wording covered the work of local preachers as well as of itinerants.

[16] This factor gainsays Lloyd's statement, 'by 1910 no woman had achieved permanent entry into the professional ministry of any formal denomination.' *Lloyd*, p. 270.

opportunity in that community's processes. Unfortunately, few biographies or obituaries of the women ministers exist. For inner compulsion we might, however, quote Ann Mason, who, after speaking informally in small meetings, recalled that: 'I thought it cannot be that I am called upon to preach, but . . . I yielded to obey, and He assured me it was His will; and I felt it was "wo [sic] unto me" if I preach not the Gospel.'[17]

Betsy Nicholls 'gave herself to the work' (of ministry) out of conviction that it was her way forward.[18] Ann (sometimes Annie) Guard Carkeek:

> Felt a call to higher service when still young but there seemed to be no opening in the Wesleyan Church for women in the ministry at that time. She offered herself to the Bible Christians for missionary work abroad in 1893 . . . Suddenly she was offered work in the Blaenavon Circuit . . .[19]

This was in 1892, to work as a hired local preacher (they were usually unpaid).[20] These accounts are not untypical of what might be called, Christian 'call to service' narratives, and like many of them, throw little light on the processes by which that call was then fulfilled.

It has been generally assumed that in the William O'Bryan era, until his separation from the movement in 1829, he was the leader who called men and women into itinerant ministry and thus gave them recognition. This was certainly true in the case of James Thorne, the movement's second minister;[21] but it is difficult to find clear evidence on women ministers. Several had a spiritual relationship with the O'Bryan family that could call

---

[17] A. and H. Freeman, *A Memoir of the Life and Ministry of Ann Freeman* (Exeter, NH, 1831), p. 20. The biblical reference is to 1 Corinthians 9:16 (KJV).

[18] *BCMag* (1862), 138.

[19] C. J. Appleby, 'Ann Guard Carkeek' in *Journal of the Cornish Methodist Historical Association*, vol 9, no 3, (1999), 106-10.

[20] Her further story is considered below, pp. 115-17.

[21] *Shaw and Short*, p. 83.

William and Catherine 'father' and 'mother'; in the sense no doubt as 'father, mother in God'.[22] This is at best circumstantial evidence, but there was one case where William O'Bryan's role in the calling was explicitly identified. Elizabeth Gay appears on the list of appointments in the first BC *Minutes of Conference* in 1819 as stationed at Dock (Devonport), but has 'desisted' in 1820.[23] In 1828 she brought a charge against William O'Bryan, declaring she had been injured by him, 'in having been taken out to travel from her situation'.[24]

In 1827, as William O'Bryan's rule of the Connexion was waning, a more formal process for calling itinerant preachers was agreed.[25] The question was posed, 'As it has been feared that some have been sent out too soon to travel, what can be done to prevent it in future?'[26] The answers included:

1. Let all candidates make known their intentions to the Leaders' meeting,[27] [or] the Society in which they meet: and let them make known their intentions to one quarterly meeting at least,[28] previous to that at which they undergo their examination,[29] in order that there may be a fair opportunity for all to express their minds on the matter.

---

[22] See for instance Margaret Adams' letters to Catherine in *BCMag* (1825), 70, 357. At this time the *BCMag* was called the *Arminian Magazine*.

[23] *BCMin* (1819), p. 7, (1829), p. 3.

[24] *Ms Journal* (1828).

[25] *BCMin* (1827), p. 11f.

[26] A veiled criticism of O'Bryan, or the preachers wresting a little more control from him.

[27] The meeting of the itinerant preachers with the local church leaders and local preachers.

[28] The quarterly meeting was the circuit administrative meeting comprising all the preachers and representatives of the local Societies.

[29] The implication is that this was an oral examination.

This represents a major new initiative in controlling the sincerity and preparedness of all ministerial candidates. The second answer was specific to women:

> 2. In case of taking out females, let the Assistant preacher converse with them closely on the nature and importance of the work, and let them also be proposed at a quarterly meeting and let none be sent out without the sanction of the Quarterly meeting.[30]

There was no explicit reference to an examination, unless it be understood within 'the sanction'. But again, the power to regulate the ministry was being reverted to the people and the itinerant preachers in the woman candidate's home circuit. It was a major step forward.

Margaret Pinwill[31] who went to her first circuit in 1836,[32] serves to illustrate both the process at work, and its flexibility. While her father was living on Guernsey she took the few opportunities to preach that came to her as a lay person without knowledge of the Guernsey Norman-French patois. This led to a minister there inviting her to consider the ministry:

> It was as though the message came, if not in so many words, yet in effect, 'The Master is come and calleth for Thee'.[33] In almost total ignorance of what was before her, she . . . gave herself to the work to which others thought she ought to be devoted . . .[34]

The process established then took over. She sailed for Plymouth in March 1836, presumably with a letter of introduction from her pastor, and was quickly sent to the Isle of Wight. At the

---

[30] *BCMin* (1827), p. 11f.
[31] *Ms Journal* entries for 1836 and *BCMin* 1836; her obituary spelt her 'Pinwell'.
[32] *Mills*, p. 46.
[33] John 11:28 (KJV).
[34] *BCMag* (1876), 195, her obituary written by her husband. 'Almost total ignorance' may imply the inadequacy of the preacher's conversation!

Conference later that year, being recommended by her pastor, she was confirmed as 'on trial', and continued on the Isle of Wight.[35]

While this sort of process appears to be the norm, other 'flexibilities' emerge, which the *Ms Journal* reveals. The year before Margaret Pinwill, Elizabeth Samseders's name appears. The decision recorded is that 'she receive an appointment if needed but her name not to appear on the Minutes as she has not been duly recommended'.[36] This is the only time her name is recorded and she never appeared in the printed *Minutes of Conference*. The same year as Margaret Pinwill appears (1836) Eliza Wheeler is 'to have an appointment but her name not appear on the Minutes';[37] she does, however, appear from 1837.[38] At the end of the nineteenth century, at a time when no women had offered for ministry for many years, Eliza Giles came forward. Her offer proceeded according to the 1827 Rules, but after such a long time the Conference was minded to review their processes. In 1894 new Regulations were approved, and three further women were admitted 'on trial'.

Itinerant preachers were tested, both by the challenges of the work, and by report of the lay officials of the circuit in which they were serving. From the start of the Connexion the male itinerant preachers were subject to annual approval. They were under the discipline of Conference and had to provide annual certificates from their circuit stewards as to their calling and their response; any shortcomings were examined. Such details appear not in the printed *Minutes* but in the *Conference Ms Journal*.[39] Women were not exempt from this. The *Ms Journal*

---

[35] This is inferred from the *Ms Journal* entries; she was received on trial in 1836.

[36] *Ms Journal* (1835) entries.

[37] Ibid., (1836) entries.

[38] For a similar process with a man see *BCMin* (1825), p. 4.

[39] Certificates were examined annually at Conference all through this period with the exception of two years before William O'Bryan's

reveals their certificates too had to be produced. Thus in 1833 the women itinerant preachers listed were:

Elizabeth Dart
Ann Arthur Guest
Ann Brown
Elizabeth Carne
Catherine Harris
Jane Bray
Ann Potter
Fanny Tremain
Mary Husband

After each name there appears . . . 'Certificate produced and approved'. For at least all the period covered by the *Ms Journal* (1824-52) they were being treated exactly the same as the male itinerant preachers.

Although a hierarchy is applied to the male itinerant preachers 'on trial' from the first *Minutes* (and probably earlier), determined by years-of-travel in the ministry, at first the women were simply listed. Then in 1828 the question was posed, 'How long shall our Females travel On Trial?' The answer decided was three years, and three new names are listed as 'Females . . . on Trial'.[40]

Oft-quoted with respect to the BC women itinerant preachers is question four of the first (1819) BC *Minutes of Conference*: 'What are our thoughts on female preaching?'[41] Three further questions follow, 'But do not many object to female preaching ?' 'What is the chief objection to Women's preaching?' and 'But does the above Scripture (1 Cor. 14:34, 35.) prohibit Women, from giving pious public instruction?' As with the Connexion's doctrinal statement, these provisions concern women *preaching*

---

separation from the Connexion in 1829, when they were examined in the districts (groupings of circuits). See the *Ms Journal*. Regrettably none survive, for either men or women.
[40] *BCMin* (1828), p. 6.
[41] *BCMin* (1819), p. 4.

rather than itinerant ministry specifically.[42] As Chilcote has shown,[43] women's *preaching* was recognized by John Wesley, albeit as something done in extraordinary circumstances, and yet done often enough to be widely known in the eighteenth century.[44]

In 1827 'W. L. B.' (possibly itinerant William Bailey) published in the (BC) *Arminian Magazine* 'Some questions on the subject of women preaching',[45] but still without addressing the issue of women's ministry. In fact, the Bible Christians never provided an *apologia* for women's ministry. Most women preachers were local preachers, who were neither noted by Conference nor listed in the *Minutes*; they were not sent (other than within their own circuit); and they were normally unpaid.[46] This distinction has sometimes been overlooked. Field-Bibb declares the 1819 argument refers to 'female ministry', a clear misunderstanding. Lloyd shows no awareness that the 1819 discussion does not justify women's ministry.[47]

---

[42] The longer discussion by O'Bryan in the 1823 (BC) *Arminian Magazine* still does not explicitly justify women *ministers*.
[43] *Chilcote, 1991*, cf chapter four in this volume.
[44] *Chilcote, 1991*, p. 182: 'From Cornwall to the North Yorkshire Moors, and in Ireland as well, women's voices were raised in proclamation of the Gospel they felt called to preach.'
[45] *BCMag* (1827), 134-40.
[46] We know little of BC women local preachers. BC preaching plans are quite rare, and women are often disguised by the use of initials. Joanna Brooks was a significant early local preacher in north Cornwall (see Shaw, *Bible Christians*, p. 20f). Later in the century, Lois Thorne on her final return from the China mission in 1901 effectively became a travelling local preacher-advocate for that mission. *Mills*, pp. 56ff.
[47] *Field-Bibb,* p. 16; Lloyd does not discuss the 1819 debate in detail; Valenze does not draw extensively on BC literature. Chilcote's *Methodist Defense* prints BC documents but does not consider this question.

Most probably the real reasons for the BC employment of women itinerant preachers were as pragmatic as John Wesley's acceptance of women preaching. I would identify them as:

- they were perceived to be called by God;
- they proved to have an effective ministry;
- there was a shortage of men;
- they demanded attention — in the sense that they drew a crowd.

Notably, the concept of an 'extraordinary call' is absent from the 1819 justification. We see this in the final sentence of the answer to question four in the 1819 *Minutes*:

> We believe, we ought to praise God, that the kingdom of darkness is shaken, and the kingdom of the Redeemer is enlarged, *whoever* be the instrument God is pleased to use; and that we dare not be so insolent, as to dictate to HIM, who HE shall employ, to accomplish HIS gracious purposes.[48]

No hint there of anything exceptional about women preaching![49]

BC ministers were not ordained in an ecclesial act which involved a necessary laying-on of hands. Among Methodists, only the Wesleyans and the New Connexion practised laying-on of hands.[50] However, all the BC male ministers were recognized in a formal order of service, called their 'reception into full connexion'. Nevertheless, in time, the word 'ordained' entered their vocabulary.[51] This was a public service; one report

---

[48] *BCMin* (1819), p. 4f. Emphasis in the original,

[49] 'Unlike John Wesley and Zechariah Taft, the 1819 BC Conference did not consider that there was anything *extraordinary* in God's call to women to preach.' *Shorney*, p. 317.

[50] A. R. George, 'Ordination' in *DMBI*, p. 260.

[51] The earliest reference found is in the report of the reception service at the 1854 Conference *BCMag* (1854), 357: 'It struck us that the formal laying on of hands was all that was wanting to make this a thoroughly scriptural ordination'; 'scriptural' refers to 2 Timothy 1:6.

notes that 'The President gave a charge to the Brethren before a large congregation on the evening of Tuesday 29 July 1828'.[52] Developing forms can be traced in the reports of the service in the *BC Magazine*.[53] Regular features include the ministers' testimonies, and the invitation to the congregation to affirm the reception: in the earlier services to . . . 'signify your approval of what we have already done'.[54] The implication is that Conference received into full connexion but the people confirmed that. From the beginning and through the middle of the century the word 'ordination' is not used. Not even a handshake is mentioned.

At the end of the nineteenth century the Bible Christians issued a *Book of Services*,[55] which included a *Service for the Public Reception of Ministers into Full Connexion*. In this service the congregation is being asked 'to ratify the decision of the Conference.' The congregation approves 'by a show of hands' and a bible and the hymn book are presented. The order occupies four pages. Its title page carries no heading, the open-together second and third pages are headed . . . RECEPTION OF MINISTERS // INTO FULL CONNEXION while the final page is headed . . . ORDINATION SERVICE. A new term has been introduced. By the 1902 *Digest* each candidate who has completed their period 'on trial' is examined in a Conference

---

[52] *Ms Journal* (1828).

[53] The service was not always reported.

[54] This form of words comes from the *Ms Journal*. It was varied in the service, but always had the same intent. Thus in 1868, 'They have been brought before the Examining Committee . . . and heartedly received by the Conference. And now they are brought here to be received by this large congregation . . .' *BCMag* (1868), 410. This was at Ebenezer Chapel, Shebbear, the service was on Friday 31 July.

[55] The small number surviving of this very rare book seem to exhibit minor differences, perhaps indicating several editions. The version quoted was used from October 1897 at High Street Chapel, Penzance, and is in the Penzance deposit in the Cornwall County Record Office, MR/PZ/125.

committee. If then an itinerant preacher is approved, . . . 'he [sic] is received into full connexion, first in Conference, and then in the public congregation.' The *Digest* supplies an outline order of service, headed thus:

ORDINATION SERVICE

The following is the order of the Ordination Service: [56]

With this explicit heading, the perception of what is being done in the service has changed. The order which follows is the same as the 1897 order. Although by around 1900 the Bible Christians considered their male ministers to be ordained, no Anglican, probably no Wesleyan, would call the service 'ordination'. No mention is ever made of hands being laid,[57] no handshake even seems to be required. The usage reflects an imprecise, ambiguous even, BC usage, and a very low theology. But were women involved in such services? Specifically, were the final cohort of women itinerant preachers considered to be ordained?

At the 1828 reception service,[58] it was 'the Brethren' who were to be addressed; but there are no recorded occasions when such wording was used when women came into full connexion. In all the *Digest* references to the service, the pronoun-references to the participants in the service are always male. After the introduction of the 'on trial' period for women itinerant preachers, there was the paper transaction in the *Minutes of Conference*, but there is no BC record of a woman involved in the service. Where a local newspaper existed and reported the BC Conference (the two conditions were not always met, such was the 'small-place' nature of the Connexion), and a woman or women might have been involved in the service, there is no independent reference to women being involved.

---

[56] *Digest* (1902), p. 44.
[57] Any idea of an Apostolic Succession—the notion that the laying-on of hands provides a spiritual succession that goes back to the Apostles—would have been alien to the Bible Christians.
[58] The first time the service merited a reference in the *Ms Journal*.

But what about the final cohort of women at the end of the nineteenth century? Sadly, the same result emerges. Eliza Giles for instance was received into full connexion in 1894 at Bristol. The *Magazine* does not mention her as present at the 'ordination service'. Like all the other women itinerants there is no independent evidence to identify her as present; this is also the case for Lillie Edwards, the only one of the three other late nineteenth-century women who was received. In late nineteenth-century BC usage, they were not 'ordained'.

BC itinerant preachers, men and women, were paid by the circuit in which they were stationed.[59] Most local preachers were unpaid, though hired local preachers did exist, and towards the end of the Connexion Lillie Edwards began her ministry in this way.[60] The women's pay, though, was a pittance, and half their male colleagues. In 1820 male itinerant preachers were paid three pounds a quarter, women, one pound ten shillings (£1.50), but both were required to pay one pound per annum into the Preachers' Fund.[61] Other additions applied to the men, and other deductions appeared from time to time. By 1902, the male itinerant preachers were on an advancing scale, beginning as a probationer at twenty-five pounds per annum, rising to one hundred per annum for 'the

---

[59] This contradicts Lloyd, 'Women Preachers in the Bible Christian Connexion', p. 467. Evidence for circuit payment of ministers is found in Mary Thorne's letter to Ebenezer Thorne 17 January 1865 (*Shaw and Short*, p. 225), William O'Bryan's annoyance at a circuit paying a minister he had dismissed in 1824, and the duties of a circuit steward, 'paying quarterly the salaries and allowances of the Preachers' in *Digest*, (1902), p. 32.

[60] C. P. Burnham and C. C. Short, 'Lillie Edwards (1863-1937): A female Methodist Superintendent minister' in *PWHS*, vol 60, part 2, (2015), 65.

[61] *BCMin* (1820), pp. 6, 16. In 1825 the women ministers were only required to pay ten shillings (£0.50) to the Preachers' Fund *BCMin* (1825), p. 8.

superintendency of a circuit'.[62] Again various additions might apply. Probationer women received eighteen pounds per annum, rising to twenty-four pounds on reception into full connexion.[63] There is inequality here typical of the era, and, in perception at least, a lesser status. Several of the final cohort seem to have left the itinerant ministry for the better paid role of evangelist.[64]

At the second Conference in 1820 when the question of 'travelling preachers marrying' was raised, the answer contained the following words:

> We recommend to our itinerant brethren, who intend to marry, to choose their partners from among our sisters, who have dedicated themselves to the service of God, by coming forward as travelling preachers: and we do agree that those preachers who so marry, shall be entitled to the first support from the connexion.[65]

As worded the advice was directed to men, although it was also giving permission to women ministers within the discipline of Conference. What should happen to the women with respect to

---

[62] The BC usage of 'pastor' was beginning to wane in favour of the more common Methodist term 'superintendent'. The 1902 Rules still used pastor in most places.

[63] *Digest* (1902), p. 144. There is always difficulty in comparing Methodist ministerial remuneration with others as the value of provided-accommodation is hard to assess. However, 'Working-class incomes in 1900 seldom exceeded one hundred pounds per annum and most were considerably less.' J. F. C. Harrison, *Late Victorian Britain 1875-1901* (London, 1990), p. 68, which might suggest that BC ministers at the top of the range were not too badly paid, although by 1900 they were hardly working-class. Yet the women's income was very low, illustrating what Harrison says, 'Women's inferior status in the world of work was emphasized by inequality of remuneration' p. 164.

[64] Lloyd, 'Women Preachers in the Bible Christian Connexion', p. 479 with reference to Lily Oram.

[65] *BCMin* (1820), p. 7.

their ministry remained undefined, nor was there ever any advice to a woman itinerant preacher who might wish to marry outside the ministry. Many men followed the 1820 advice. Not all the women itinerant preachers' marriages were to male itinerant preachers.[66] It may be that some early disappearances of women itinerant preachers might be ascribed to love.

The 1820 resolution implies support for married ministers, though unspecified. Soon a question arose as to its meaning, in the case of James and Catherine Thorne. James was the second BC minister in seniority. After he married itinerant preacher Catherine Reed in 1823,[67] Catherine continued to be stationed as Catherine Thorne in 1824 and 1825, alongside her husband.[68] But Mary Thorne's 1865 letter to her son Ebenezer reveals a darker side to the treatment of a woman minister when she married:

> He (James Thorne) had full consent of the Conference, was appointed to London where your Aunt was a travelling preacher. The Circuit stewards received orders [from William O'Bryan, that is] not to provide any house, furniture or lodgings for them, or to allow him a wife's salary; so your Aunt continued to work on in her plan, and thus had her salary as a single woman till near her confinement and then the stewards were imperatively forbidden to allow them anything . . . Mr. Reed sent his daughter £5 as a present and thus helped them through.[69]

This is William O'Bryan's daughter writing about her father's treatment of her brother-in-law, for she was married to Samuel

---

[66] Examples, with page references in *Mills*, include Mary Elson (p. 23f), Eliza Jew (p. 35f), Mary Lyle (p. 38), Betsy Reed (p. 48f) and Martha Hutchings (as Hatchings p. 33f), who married the lighthouse keeper on St Agnes, Scilly, and was the ancestor who prompted Mills's compilation of the women ministers.

[67] *Mills*, p. 51.

[68] *BCMin* (1824), p. 7, (1825), p. 7.

[69] Mary Thorne to Ebenezer Thorne 17 January 1865, *Shaw and Short*, pp. 223-7, at 226.

Thorne. Such treatment reveals that in spite of the 1820 resolution, in the early days women ministers who married could not expect to be treated well.[70]

Once that bad example become known, it would seem likely that it would be accepted that no women itinerant preacher should continue in ministry after Conference had given her permission to marry. It seems to have become an unwritten rule, as I can find no formal statement of it.[71] In every other case that I can identify the former women itinerant preacher ceased to be stationed or paid, albeit many still exercising an effective ministry as local preachers alongside their husbands.[72] Such inequality was, of course, of its time.[73]

2. The work of the Bible Christian women itinerant preachers

'Being sent' lies at the heart of the work of a Methodist itinerant preacher. Chilcote has shown that many eighteenth-century women preachers travelled and preached extensively, but usually of their own volition, often by invitation.[74] In contrast, the women BC ministers were stationed in circuits by the annual Conference.

---

[70] The Thornes's situation might be viewed as an early part of James Thorne's growing dispute with William O'Bryan in the late 1820s, culminating in O'Bryan's departure from the Connexion in 1829: see *Shaw and Short*.

[71] It is not explicit in the *Digest* (1902), except that rules dating from 1894 provided that a women itinerant preacher who retires due to illness shall only receive an annuity if she be unmarried — which is far from being the same thing.

[72] For example, Ann Arthur Guest (a minister 1820-41), who married the minister James Brooks in 1841; Ann continued as a local preacher 'as long as her health would allow'. *Mills*, p. 26f.

[73] Harrison, *Late Victorian Britain* chapter eight, 'The Woman Question', pp. 157–83 outlines the diminution of the employment status of women that had been happening through the century, albeit not a uniform picture, p. 165.

[74] E.g. Lenton, 'Mary Barritt Taft', 17–23.

Thus, when the BC work began in St Austell in July 1818, Ann and Sarah Cory were sent to preach in the open air in a field above the town. The crowd-pulling effects of women's preaching recalls what Christians might see as the work of the Holy Spirit at Pentecost.[75] When the first *BC Minutes of Conference* appeared in 1819, Sarah was still appointed to the circuit, but Ann had already moved on. With the 1819 *Minutes* and through to 1823 a note follows the stations: 'Our Sisters to change under the direction of the General Superintendent' (O'Bryan).[76] He sent the women itinerants to be pioneer evangelists where he perceived the needs of the gospel; thus the appointments printed in the *Minutes* to the end of the O'Bryan era in 1829 do not indicate that the women stayed there all year. This evangelistic itinerancy was an important element in the work of the early women ministers.

The moves of Ann Mason (later Freeman), from north Devon, in her first sixteen months of ministry can be found in her Journal.[77] She had begun to preach in February 1817, as a local preacher, at a time when there was just one BC circuit. In September that year it was divided into three, with another formed from the 'Boylite' work in west Cornwall, absorbed that year.[78] So she was sent to begin her ministry at Probus, east of Truro, in March 1818, moved to Yealmpton in the South Hams, and then worked around St Austell, all in different circuits. By the first Conference in 1819, already worn out by her efforts she was stationed as a supernumerary at Shebbear. In 1821 she was appointed to Dock (Devonport), but never went. Nevertheless, in 1822 she returned to the work in the St Austell area. After a year she was sent to London, where her colleagues were Henry Freeman, William Strongman and Catherine Reed.[79] Her journal

---

[75] Acts 2:1-14.

[76] E.g. *BCMin* (1819), p. 7, (1820), p. 6, etc.

[77] Freeman, *Memoir of Ann Freeman*, which includes excerpts from her journal.

[78] See *Shaw and Short*, phase 7, pp. 90-4.

[79] *BCMin* (1823), p. 7.

shows that she was primarily an evangelist.[80] She married Freeman and in August 1824, they left the Bible Christians for the Quakers.

Mary Ann Werrey was sent from 1820 to at least five appointments in five years.[81] We know no details of her first two stations, St Keverne (1820) and Truro (1821).[82] Whether she reached Truro may be doubted, for at her own request, she was sent to Scilly in 1821.[83] There her work as an evangelist was so effective that senior minister William Mason was sent to help her.[84] Two men were then appointed in 1822.[85] She was moved to Guernsey in March 1823,[86] and worked so effectively as an evangelist that the minister Samuel Smale was sent out in May to help.[87] He and Mary O'Bryan were appointed by Conference later that year and Mary Ann was moved on to Jersey.[88] 'Many were converted' on Guernsey and she preached to large

---

[80] See for instance 5 May 1822, 'With my sling and stone I am resolved to go forward, knowing it is wo [sic] unto me if I preach not the gospel': the biblical reference is to 1 Corinthians 9:16 (KJV); and cf. p. 100, n. 17 above. See also 3 May 1824, 'I spoke to the people in the street again, and was graciously assisted in proclaiming the liberty of the gospel'. Freeman, *Memoir of Ann Freeman*, pp. 41, 68.

[81] *Mills*, pp. 66–8.

[82] *BCMin* (1820), p. 5 and (1821), p. 5.

[83] *Mills*, p. 70 says that she went to Scilly in 1822, with the agreement of Conference. Although her name is in the list of women ministers that year she does not appears on the list of appointments. D. P. Easton, *A History of the Nonconformist Churches on the Isles of Scilly* (Isles of Scilly, 2009), p. 55 quotes the 1909 *United Methodist Magazine* to the effect that she was stationed at Truro in order to be free to go to Scilly. Whatever happened, it is possible that it was an appointment made by William O'Bryan himself.

[84] F. W. Bourne, *The Bible Christians: their origin and history 1815–1907* (London, 1905), p. 104.

[85] *BCMin* (1822), p. 6.

[86] Bourne, *Bible Christians*, pp. 119ff.

[87] Ibid. p. 122.

[88] *BCMin* (1823), p. 7.

numbers in the open air on Jersey.[89] She disappeared from Jersey, but reappeared in Northumberland. She moved north to Edinburgh, albeit no longer a BC woman itinerant preacher, but still an evangelist.[90] Recently James Bowen has completed her story. He has shown her continued life to be varied, but still to include work as a freelance evangelist.[91]

The BC Connexion sent its women ministers in the early days as pioneer evangelists, conscious of their novel appeal. There is evidence, notably with the examples of Ann Mason and Mary Ann Werrey above, that some of these women were conscious of a calling to be evangelists, for they continued that work after leaving the Bible Christians. Yet the initial pioneer evangelistic role of the women seems to have waned. The long-standing women itinerant preachers became more circuit ministers than evangelists. The three women listed in 1850 exemplify this in different ways.

Catherine Harris became a women itinerant preacher in 1825 and served in twenty-five appointments, some as a supernumerary, but only on three occasions for more than two years, before retiring in 1853.[92] She began in the era of women itinerant preachers serving when the BC movement was a charismatic community and retired in what had become an institutional church.[93] She died in 1896, aged 89.[94] In 1835 she was specifically appointed to Devonport with a male pastor, to

---

[89] *Mills*, p. 66.

[90] C. C. Short, *Durham Colliers and West Country Methodists* (Kidderminster, 1995), pp. 11–13.

[91] J. M. Bowen, 'A Dream Fulfilled: The Life of Mary Ann Werrey . . .' in *PWHS*, vol 61, no 6, (2018), 274-9.

[92] *Mills*, p. 27f. It should be noted that in the early days the male itinerants also were often moved after only a year.

[93] For this change, and in particular O'Bryan's inability to cope with it, see *Shaw and Short*.

[94] Her longevity, albeit long supernumerary, means that the Connexion was never without a women minister.

revive a failing circuit.[95] After one year she was moved on; the work done. Yet nothing I can discover of her later ministry seems to have had an evangelistic priority.

Mary Ann Taylor was active 1832-53, when she became BC minister Paul Robins's second wife, and returned with him to his work in Canada.[96] She had been sent to twelve circuits in twenty-two years, staying two years in six of them and three years in two. These longer stays suggest a circuit ministry rather than a pioneer evangelistic one, and no revival is reported in these circuits.[97] Certainly in Canada she did not exhibit the evangelistic effectiveness that Robins's first wife, the former itinerant preacher Ann Vickery (1820-30), achieved.[98]

The third women itinerant preacher in 1850 was Ann White (1834-50). She was sent to ten circuits, but twice does not appear on the stations. Her ministry in two extended appointments (with a colleague) reflects the evangelistic focus of the early women itinerant preachers. At Week St Mary (1837–9) membership numbers rose,[99] new chapels were opened,[100] and Ann was left so tired that her third year there was as a supernumerary. Tenterden (1844–7) too saw evangelistic success; indeed at Woodchurch F. W. Bourne, the third 'leader'

---

[95] Bourne, *Bible Christians*, p. 269.

[96] *Mills*, p. 55.

[97] Bourne has no references to revivals at the relevant times in her circuits, and I would not be prepared to describe such membership increases as occurred as signs of evangelistic revival. *Mills*, p. 55 notes her unusual extended stays, but records no report of evangelistic activity.

[98] Mary Ann does not appear in S. B. Leetooze, *The Damascus Road: short biographies of the preachers who served the Canadian Conference of the Bible Christians 1832-1884* (Bowmanville, ON, 2005), pp. 213ff.

[99] *BCMin* (1836–9).

[100] Rehoboth (1837), Bethel (1838), W. Cocks 'Week St Mary Circuit Celebrates 150 Years' in *Old Cornwall*, vol 9, no 8, (1983), 377–90, and Week St Mary (local tradition).

of the Connexion, was converted.[101] Later in 1850 she married Rev. James Roberts,[102] and therefore left the itinerant ministry.[103] In 1854 the couple transferred to the South Australian BC Church.[104] There Ann continued to preach, often attracting larger crowds because of her gender.[105] In 1867/8 she was listed as a circuit minister; this may not have been the only occasion.[106] The South Australian BC historian regards her as a significant woman who made a major contribution to South Australian society.[107]

One further aspect needs to be noted: initially the women were sent without training.[108] The Bible Christians never had a ministerial training institution.[109] Some background as a local

---

[101] M. B. and C. P. Burnham, 'The Making of an Evangelical Minister: The Early Years of Frederick William Bourne (1830–1905)', in *PWHS*, vol 60, no 5, (2016), 199-213.

[102] Roberts had become a minister in 1832 of the break-away Arminian Bible Christians of 1829, and was one of those accepted back in 1835. See *Shaw and Short*, step 2, pp. 140–4.

[103] *Mills*, p. 65f.

[104] O. A. Beckerlegge, *United Methodist Ministers and their Circuits* (London, 1968), p. 198.

[105] E. Curnow, *BC Methodists in South Australia 1850–1900* (South Australia, 2015), pp. 122, 236.

[106] Ibid., p. 293.

[107] Ibid., p. 58.

[108] Men's training, a course of study while on trial, existed by the late 1840s: Obituary of John Mackrell, *BCMin* (1850) p. 5f.

[109] References to formal ministerial training at Shebbear School are misunderstandings. Potential male ministerial candidates were frequently sent there to improve their education, studying generally under the headmaster and theologically under the governor (Shaw, *Bible Christians*, p. 69), but not yet on trial as ministers. Witness Richard Trembath, who came to Shebbear in those circumstances but died there, (G. P. Dymond, *Thomas Ruddle of Shebbear* (London, nd), p. 53) and never appeared in *BCMin*; and Francis Clapp, who stayed three years at Shebbear, but whose reception into full connexion was four years after he began circuit work (Beckerlegge, *United Methodist*

preacher was generally the case,[110] but whereas the men were required to study while on trial, the course of study was published annually in the *Minutes,* the women were not included in that course until the emergence of the final cohort in the 1890s.

The first edition of *A Digest of the Rules, Regulations and Usages of the . . . Bible Christians* in 1838 referred to the women itinerant preachers with the words, 'They do not, however, take part among us in church government; they are entitled to attend meetings for business, but not to vote.' Exactly the same wording persisted through to the 1902 *Digest*.[111] In David Shorney's words . . . though women might preach, men would always govern.[112]

However, prior to the 1831 Deed that established the form of the Connexion, women itinerant preachers attended district meetings and Conference. There is only a little evidence of them speaking. In 1828 Ann Cory and William O'Bryan 'consulted together' over a matter of contention,[113] and at the same Conference the *Ms Journal* explicitly records Elizabeth Gay saying the single word, 'Yes'![114] James Thorne records a London

---

Ministers and their Circuits, p. 47). In 1897 the Connexion began discussions with the University College of South Wales and Monmouthshire, Cardiff, to send students there, *BCMin* (1897), p. 47f. John H. Squire, a Cardiff native, went after two years at Shebbear in 1898, achieving two degrees, Beckerlegge, *United Methodist Ministers and their Circuits,* p. 222. As union with the MNC and the United Methodist Free Churches approached (1907) some candidates went to the former United Methodist Free Church Victoria Park College in Manchester (e.g. William Chivers in 1904; Beckerlegge, *United Methodist Ministers and their Circuits* p. 46. No women were ever given further education.

[110] E.g. *Digest 36.1,* (1902), p. 37.

[111] From which the words are quoted: *Digest* (1902), p. 49.

[112] *Shorney,* p. 310.

[113] *Ms Journal* (1828).

[114] On this point I disagree with *Shorney,* p. 320.

district meeting from 5-8 July 1825 with eleven ministers present, four of them women itinerant preachers.[115] However, from 1831 to 1896 the women were excluded.[116] In 1896 a rule was added to the 1894 regulations governing women ministers, 'Female Preachers are expected to attend the District Meetings, and take part in the business, without the power of voting'.[117]

The situation with respect to the sacraments is not entirely clear. Did BC theology explicitly associate 'ordained' with an exclusive male right to administer the sacraments? The 1838 *Digest*[118] sits on the fence: BC itinerants in full connexion were 'wholly devoted to the work of ministry, preaching and administering the sacraments'.[119] No distinction was made between men and women. In January 1824 Mary O'Bryan wrote from Jersey to her father William about Communion. In his response he seems to have encouraged her to administer it:

> Exclude every scruple of [*a word is missing from her transcript*] on man's account — women have souls as well as men. As often as you can make it convenient and the people do, without hesitation. I doubt not Jesus will be there, and that will be better than all the Bishops in England. Yea, He hath promised to be where two or three are met in His name. Therefore if you at that time meet in His name, you may be sure to be right, and cannot be wrong.[120]

Yet until the end of the century, it seems few women itinerant preachers did. We lack enough preaching plans or biographies

---

[115] J. Thorne, *A Memoir of James Thorne* (London, 1873), p. 203, quoting James Thorne's *Journal*.

[116] *Shorney*, p. 320.

[117] *Digest* (1902), p. 51.

[118] Published Shebbear (1838); the *Digest* (1902) differs only in punctuation.

[119] *Digest* (1902), p. 45.

[120] Cornwall County Record Office, Mary O'Bryan Thorne Ms Journal, X241/8. Not everyone interprets this as explicit approval to celebrate, nor evidence that she ever did. The biblical reference is to Matthew 18:20.

of the women ministers to be clear about Holy Communion. Not all plans even indicate when the men were celebrating Communion. Similarly, the early women ministers do not seem to have baptized. Shorney refers to the total absence of any entry by a woman itinerant preacher in the twenty-seven BC baptism registers from before 1837 at the Public Record Office;[121] and there is no case of women itinerant preachers baptizing among the Cornish circuits for which I have baptismal records. What we are seeing is the women ministers' work being limited by more than just rules about governance. Perceptions about the 'right' work for men and women ministers might have been influenced by presumptions about the 'priestly' roles in ministry in celebrating the sacraments.

The women ministers were subject to many pressures, both emotional and physical. Most of these women were young. They were called to the work of ministry because of their deep and enthusiastic experience of Christian salvation. Theirs was, nonetheless, hard, potentially dangerous work, and subject to much ridicule. Examples of the physical pressures and dangers might be found in several of their stories. Mary Toms was sent to the Isle of Wight by deck passage, that is, without any effective shelter from the sea, and arrived in Cowes wet and dishevelled, but could find no accommodation.[122] Later on the same island Mary O'Bryan, 'was besmeared with rotten eggs'.[123] Mary Ann Werrey, on her arrival in Northumberland found 'nothing but abuse' and took care then to identify herself with the authorities for some protection.[124] Fifteen of the women itinerant preachers had breaks in their service, sometimes more than once, before returning to the work. Ann Mason explicitly identified her break as due to exhaustion. We can only surmise that that was the case with all fifteen; such a number is high, in

---

[121] *Shorney*, p. 320.

[122] Bourne, *Bible Christians*, p. 133f.

[123] Ibid., p. 257.

[124] Short, *Durham Colliers and West Country Methodists*, p. 11, no 7, p. 18 and a further private conversation with the late Geoff Milburn.

a total of about seventy-eight (nineteen percent),[125] and does not include those who stood down and then did not return to the work.

The appointments of Elizabeth Dart, the first woman BC minister,[126] were (# highlights periods not stationed):

1817	St Ervan		2 years
1819	Kilkhampton		1
1820	Kilkhampton	Supernumerary	1#
1821	Buckfastleigh	Supernumerary	1#
1822	{not known}		1#
1823	Bristol		1
1824	Monmouth Mission		1
1825	Kilkhampton	Supernumerary	2#
1827	St Ervan		1
1828	Jersey		1
1829	London		1
1830	Devonport		1
1831	Mevagissey		1
1832	Mevagissey	Supernumerary	1#

On 22 March 1833 she married Rev. John Hicks Eynon, who had been converted by her preaching; he died on 22 March 1888. Her inactive times reveal that for six of her fifteen years (forty percent) she was not serving fully. There is little evidence why,

---

[125] The number is open to question; for example, the *Ms Journal* reveals occasions when a name is brought forward for admittance on trial, but not as per rules. Often then the woman is stationed, but not listed in the printed *Minutes*.

[126] *Mills*, p. 19f.

but one guesses that she found the pressures of the work great.[127]

Often in early O'Bryan days the woman itinerant preacher was the only minister working in a circuit. Lloyd cites one such appointment (Elizabeth Gay, at Dock in 1819), but there were others. [128] The annual nature of the *Minutes* conceals some. But Mary Ann Werrey was sent to the Scilly and Jersey stations on her own, and set out alone for Edinburgh, arriving first in Northumberland.[129] Mary Toms was sent to the Isle of Wight, to be followed by Catherine O'Bryan and Eliza Jew,[130] all before any man appeared there—but he was soon supplied. Thus, William Mason was sent to Scilly and Northumberland, and Samuel Smale to Guernsey to follow the pioneer evangelism of Mary Ann Werrey.[131]

In his history of the Bible Christians F. W. Bourne gives the impression that a male minister was necessary to establish a local BC church.[132] Though no rules or regulations required it, a man would invariably be sent to consolidate the pioneer work of a woman.[133] Perhaps the perception was that women should

---

[127] Male itinerants also suffered pressures. Losses of both women and men were high, particularly in the early days. A random perusal of Beckerlegge, *United Methodist Ministers and their Circuits*, will reveal the reality.

[128] Lloyd, 'Women Preachers in the Bible Christian Connexion', p. 462.

[129] Short, *Durham Colliers and West Country Methodists*, p. 11f. Northumberland became for a while a BC circuit. Mary Ann established a meeting at Belford, and four others in the area soon followed. Short, *Durham Colliers and West Country Methodists*, p. 14.

[130] Lloyd, 'Women Preachers in the Bible Christian Connexion', p. 462, in spite of her assertion about Elizabeth Gay, quotes the query emanating from the Isle of Wight asking whether all Bible Christians are women; p. 458, quoting (BC) *AM* (1823).

[131] Bourne, *Bible Christians*, pp. 104, 122.

[132] Ibid., p. 137: James Thorne on the Isle of Wight.

[133] Or women, in the case of the Isle of Wight.

not govern groups that included men (even though men were allowed to govern groups that included women). One of the reasons William O'Bryan had been expelled from the Wesleyans for the first time was that he had trespassed on the prerogative of the superintendent to establish local churches.[134] The unwritten practice of the Bible Christians was echoing the Wesleyans, although these had no women ministers. However, some BC women did establish local churches.[135]

Whatever the cause, there were seeds of discontent here. Mary Ann Werrey had arrived in northern Northumberland in 1823. In 1824 William Mason, the Connexion's third minister, arrived to be her pastor. In language echoing William O'Bryan's own story, the *Ms Conference Journal* reveals the tension arising between Mary Ann Werrey and William Mason, 'she refused to take a plan or in any way to be directed by him, even only once a week'.[136] No wonder; Mason had taken over 'her' mission. Bowen has shown that in her later work outside the BC Connexion there is independence of spirit. [137]

Elizabeth Gay was stationed at Dock (Devonport) on her own in 1819, and although baptisms took place during that time she did not register any of them, and may not have baptized.[138] All were registered by either William Mason, stationed in St Neot, some twenty miles away, or William Lyle, who had lately come in from the 'Boylite' work.[139] Possibly Lyle at least was 'imported' to register, or even do, the baptisms, which seems demeaning. By Conference in 1820 she had 'desisted'.[140] Six years later the itinerant preacher William Metherell was given

---

[134] *Shaw and Short*, pp. 47–50.
[135] For examples of women establishing local BC churches, see *Mills*, pp. 11, 19, 20, 52, 62, 67.
[136] *Ms Journal* (1825) entries.
[137] Bowen, 'A Dream Fulfilled'.
[138] *Shorney*, p. 315. See also the discussion on baptisms on p. 111.
[139] *Shaw and Short*, pp. 90-4. Lyle is not in the 1819 *BCMin*.
[140] *BCMin* (1820), p. 3.

permission to marry her, and two years later (1828) they brought a charge to Conference against William O'Bryan.[141] The matter is reported thus in the *Ms Journal* . . .

> Q4: Do we consider that Elizabeth Metherall [sic] has been injured?
>
> A: Yes.
>
> Q5: Does she wish to have the matter explained who has injured her?
>
> A: (She answered) Yes.
>
> Q6: How has she been injured?
>
> A1: In having been taken out to travel from her situation, which induced her to give up her school and sell her goods and in the end obliged to return to her own resources.

From answer A1, it seems that Gay was called into the ministry by William O'Bryan and then sent to run the Dock Mission. She was obliged to leave her school (she must have been a teacher) and 'sell her goods and in the end obliged to return to her own resources'; probably discontinued without compensation. When this charge was brought, in 1828, the rift between the Conference and O'Bryan was rapidly deepening.[142] Conference ruled for Elizabeth,[143] but William's name does not re-appear from 1828. Whether compensation came is not known.[144]

Lloyd called Gay's appointment 'exceptional',[145] and 1819 was still early in the BC Connexion's life. So perhaps Dock in 1819

---

[141] *Ms Journal* (1828) records the case.

[142] See *Shaw and Short,* a major theme of the study.

[143] *Ms Journal* (1828) entries.

[144] Their baby son was baptized at Breage BC chapel in June 1829. Transcript in the hands of the author. Breage was soon to become a centre of the 1829 Arminian Bible Christian schism. See *Shaw and Short.*

[145] Lloyd, 'Women Preachers in the Bible Christian Connexion', p. 462.

was 'experimental', albeit a failure from Gay's point of view. It was an experiment which was repeated, with mixed success. It thus becomes another insight into the way that William O'Bryan seems to have been unable to cope with the progress of the Bible Christians from charismatic community into institutional church.[146]

After a long time with no women candidates (or at least none accepted),[147] four women offered successfully as itinerant preachers in the 1890s. Their basic details are:

Name	Entered ministry	Full connexion?	Last appointment	Destiny
Eliza Giles	1890	1894	Dalwood 1897	by 1898 resigned
Lily Oram	1894	Not received	London Jubilee	by 1895 resigned
Ann G. Carkeek	1894	Not received	Blaenavon	1895 evangelist
Lillie Edwards	1894	1897	Hastings 1903	set aside in 1908

Only Lillie Edwards persisted in the ministry, until finding that there was no place for women's itinerant ministry in the new United Methodist Church, created in 1907.[148]

We know little about Eliza Giles, the first to emerge. Her name simply appears in the 1890 Conference minutes as stationed on the Isles of Scilly. She was received into full connexion in 1894.[149]

---

[146] *Shaw and Short*, a recurrent theme.

[147] As far as the printed *Minutes* reveal. The loss of the *Ms Conference Journal* for the period leaves us unsure whether any women came forward but were declined.

[148] *Lloyd*, p. 267.

[149] There is confusion about her status including her date of reception e.g. *Lloyd*, pp. 264-5. Lloyd and Field-Bibb recorded 1893, at St Austell, but it was 1894, at Bristol. *Mills*, p. 25.

By 1897 she was in her fourth appointment at Dalwood in east Devon. It was a single minister station, albeit 'under the general oversight of Br. Daniel', thirteen miles away at Crewkerne.[150] But she resigned before a year's experience of that arrangement was over.[151] Perhaps she found the arrangement, or Brother Daniel, intolerable. There was no official obituary as she resigned. Joan Mills simply lists her stations.[152] However, she had an important influence on the training of the members of this final cohort. In 1893 the *President's Circular* noted 'That the Connexional Committee consider during the year the subject of the employment of female preachers, in order that the position of Miss Giles may be determined at the next Conference'.[153] As a consequence, in 1894 a new body of 'regulations with regard to the admission and employment of female preachers' was established.[154]

They covered the application process, the creation of a reading and study course, and the absence of circuit and district examinations. The regulations further define probation at four years, salary and preachers' Annuitant Society Regulations. There are no regulations about marriage, unless it be assumed that the rules were the same as applied to men—the need to make application to Conference.[155] As far as we know, none of the final cohort sought to get married, although it might be a reason why Eliza Giles resigned. Any payment from the preachers' Annuitant Society would cease on marriage.[156] Two important requirements were that:

---

[150] *BCMin* (1897), p. 16.

[151] *BCMin* (1898), *President's Circular*, p. 5.

[152] *Mills*, p. 25.

[153] *President's Circular* (1893), p. 8.

[154] *Digest* (1902), p. 50.

[155] Although those regulations are written with the male pronoun.

[156] *Digest* (1902), p. 51. The effect of this was that any payment being made from the fund after the woman had ceased her active ministry would end if she married.

All candidates are expected to pursue during their probation the course of reading and study laid down by the Examining Committee ... [and] ... before any probationer can be received into full connexion she must have had a certificate from the Quarterly Meeting of each Station on which she has laboured during her probation, as to her Christian character, acceptability as a speaker, and general fitness for the work, and produce a medical certificate as to health.[157]

The examining committee interpreted the reading and study to be the same as the men; thus in 1895 results appertaining to 'two young women' were reported, probably Eliza Giles and Lillie Edwards. Both 'fell below the minimum'.[158]

These regulations provide a much more formal pattern of candidature and employment than was ever previously the case, and they are by and large, stricter than those for men, for example with respect to health.[159] And, although the salary of a woman was less than a man, the woman itinerant's circuit was expected to pay two pounds five shillings (£2.25) per quarter into a fund administered by the Preachers' Annuitant Society, as a consequence of not having to pay any 'Children's Salary'.[160]

The same year as these regulations were adopted the other three women of the final cohort were accepted. The existence of these new regulations cannot have encouraged these applications as they happened at the same Conference. However, possibly the knowledge (through the BC grapevine) of their imminent adoption encouraged three women already in the service of the Connexion—as all three were—to offer as candidates for the

---

[157] Ibid., p. 50.

[158] *President's Circular* (1895), p. 5.

[159] *Digest* (1902), p. 50f, section 44: parts three (the need for a medical certificate as to health) and nine (failure of health and access to the Preachers' Annuitant Society) have no real parallel for men 'on trial'.

[160] Ibid., no 6. The children's salary was an extra payment made to married men with children for children's expenses, including education.

women's itineracy. No other women candidates came forward after 1894.

The *BC Magazine* for 1893 first reveals Miss Oram working as an evangelist in south Wales.[161] On acceptance for the ministry she was sent on trial to London (Jubilee) circuit, a single-chapel circuit with normally only one itinerant preacher,[162] a strange and difficult situation to which to send an evangelist from south Wales. She resigned during the year without any reference in the *President's Circular*.

Ann Guard Carkeek came from west Cornwall, was converted within the Wesleyans and seems to have become a Bible Christian to fulfil a call to full-time ministry.[163] She was working as a hired local preacher in Blaenavon in south Wales from 1892. When she offered for the ministry in 1894 she continued to serve in the same circuit,[164] but as an itinerant preacher on trial. However, the Conference Committee were unable to find her a station in 1895, and she became a Connexional evangelist.[165]

Before entering the ministry Lillie Edwards served as a hired local preacher in Ashford and Tenterden (1890–2), and an evangelist during each of the following years at Kilkhampton and London (Waterloo Road).[166] On acceptance for the ministry she was sent initially to Sevenoaks, on her own. Again on her own she served in the two small St Mawes and Hastings circuits as sole itinerant preacher (1898-1903 and 1903-1908).[167] Her work in each was as an ordinary circuit minister: she 'governed' both circuits, baptizing and celebrating Communion. As the compiler of the circuit preaching plan, she directed men, albeit

---

[161] *BCMag* (1893), 238.
[162] *Mills*, p. 44.
[163] Appleby, 'Ann Guard Carkeek'. See also *Who's Who in Methodism* (London, 1933) p. 285, for Annie Carkeek's later history.
[164] *Mills*, p. 44.
[165] *President's Circular* (1895), p. 11.
[166] Burnham and Short, 'Lillie Edwards', 64-73.
[167] *Mills*, p. 23.

local not itinerant preachers. Though the polity of the United Methodist Church after 1907 did not recognize her, she seems to have carried on doing the work until she herself decided to retire![168]

Evidently the BC Conference found it difficult to station these women. Lillie Edwards's circuits were all small. Although a woman's salary was less than a man's, perhaps the quarterly levy the circuits had to pay to the Children's Salary fund was a disincentive. Maybe the difficulty reflected Victorian prejudice against women at work. Or perhaps even the BC people had been persuaded (by the Oxford Movement or developments in their sister Methodist branches) that ministers were necessarily men?[169] Women's ministry was to be exercised in other ways, such as the deaconesses who were emerging elsewhere within Methodism. Or perhaps circuits perceived women ministers as evangelists, and felt they did not need an evangelist in that role.[170]

Conclusion

This study has examined the status and the work of the BC women itinerant preachers. This cannot be read as one of progress towards a sacramental priesthood, other than as a false

---

[168] Burnham and Short, 'Lillie Edwards'. Until 1911 the official United Methodist Church record showed 'Supply' at Hastings e.g. *UM Church Minutes of Conference* 1908, p. 62. When she retired in 1911 a man was appointed; ibid., (1911). This qualifies Lloyd's remarks, *Lloyd*, p. 268.

[169] In the late twentieth century one chapel in west Cornwall identifying itself as 'Bible Christian' declined to allow women preachers and required segregation of the genders in the congregation. It was unique, but perhaps indicative of how attitudes had changed.

[170] Male ministerial prejudice should be added if Jennifer Lloyd's story (Lloyd, 'Women Preachers in the Bible Christian Connexion', p. 473) about cheering at the 1869 Conference when Elizabeth Dymond's retirement was announced were true. It seems improbable and is based on hearsay.

start on that pilgrimage. There remains some doubt as to whether the early women BC ministers did celebrate the sacraments of baptism and Holy Communion. Among the final cohort Lillie Edwards did, but one example does not make a principle. What is the case though is that the BC women ministers do not have a positive place on the trajectory that Field-Bibb seeks to trace towards women's priesthood. Indeed it might be argued that using a Connexion committed to a 'priesthood of all believers' theology does not seem to serve her purposes well.[171]

Although BC women ministers were equal in many respects to the men, the explicit exceptions being in governance and pay levels, their status in practice reflected the inequalities of the era. The phrase 'of the era' may well represent one significant way of telling the story of the women ministers in the BC Connexion. While not denying that women's ministry was a radical intrusion into the accepted norms of the era, it is only with some imagination that the story can read as one of women's assertion of their rightful place. Governance issues probably led to one bad missional practice in the earlier period. This is the way that women sent as pioneer evangelists had their role supplanted by a man sent to take over the work. It was demeaning, and caused tensions. We cannot be sure how many of the women ministers who had very short ministries found the reality difficult. Yet it was again a story of its era: the practice loosely parallels the way in which, at the time, a woman's property became her husband's on marriage [172]

---

[171] The doctrine declares that all believers share equally in the grace of God; all may minister equally the things of God. It is one of the foundational doctrines of Methodism. One consequence is that the sacraments are not the exclusive ministry of a priestly class, although church order and discipline may make it appear so.

[172] This inequality was not addressed until Acts in 1870, 1882 and 1893. C. P. Hill, *British Economic and Social History 1700-1975* (London, 1977), p. 234. That practices once seen as acceptable become

It would be a mistake to tell either the marriage story or the women ministers' stories without an understanding of the era. Since there was a long period in which the Bible Christians had no active woman minister, there was no place for a BC woman minister in the story of the movements for women's electoral reform and family reform. There is no evidence for engagement with these movements by the final cohort either. Women's itinerant ministry can also be seen as a pragmatic response to circumstances. With the early Bible Christians 'the call of God' as perceived by the women coincided with the vision of William O'Bryan to use his wife Catherine as a preacher. Yet women's preaching is part of the Church's story from very early days, as has been male leadership, and under that leadership women's preaching has been from time to time tolerated.[173] I have deliberately referred here to preaching. Women's ministry is different again, and the Bible Christians took on board that difference without too much hesitation and followed the path into women's ministry, for pragmatic reasons.

It can also be read as part of the evolution of the BC movement from charismatic community into institutional church. In the early, charismatic, days of the BC movement the work of the women ministers was to be pioneer evangelists, a work which coincided with the developmental needs of the new movement. The major challenge for an evangelist is to how generate an audience, and the women did this very readily.[174] Women's open-air preaching by Bible Christians (and Primitive Methodists) drew the crowds. With the passing of time, and as the more settled circuits and meeting places and times of an

---

unacceptable with the passage of time is a measure of social evolution.

[173] By John Wesley for instance, see chapter four in this volume.

[174] We might conclude exactly this in the work of the PM women ministers. E. D. Graham, 'Chosen by God: the female travelling preachers of early Primitive Methodism', The WHS Lecture 1993, in *PWHS*, vol 49, (1993), 77-95.

institutional church developed, women ministers entered circuit ministry, and their number declined.

The story of the women BC ministers is also one of discontinuity. In terms of active ministry there was a long gap between the retirement of Elizabeth Dymond in 1869,[175] and the arrival of Eliza Giles in 1890; only the supernumerary (i.e. not active) Catherine Harris filled the gap. The BC Conference saw fit to revise its regulations before Giles was received into full connexion. And when the United Methodist Church was formed in 1907, the new Church had no women ministers.[176] Such discontinuities add strength to the view that the Bible Christians were of their era.

For the final cohort, we need to take seriously their personal stories. Eliza Giles is the most important as the first woman to offer for the BC ministry for many years. Unfortunately we know nothing about her life other than the bare outline of her ministry. In particular, we have no knowledge why she resigned after eight years' service.[177] The other three women share two features in common. They all came forward in the same year, perhaps prompted by the new rules being introduced that year. This may have been facilitated by the second fact that they were all already working for the Connexion. Yet only one of them, Lillie Edwards, persisted in the itinerant ministry. In this period the Wesleyans, the United

---

[175] *Mills*, p. 22.

[176] Perhaps Lillie Edwards remains the only BC woman minister to fulfil Wesley's extraordinary circumstance criterion.

[177] Two speculations have been made above: the breakdown of a ministry relationship, or marriage. In the absence of any other data either speculation is possible.

Methodist Free Churches and the Primitive Methodists had all started their Deaconess Movement.[178]

It might be possible that half this final cohort either mistook their calling or perhaps, the BC system allowed them, or even pushed them, to move into the wrong calling. In their case, the move into itinerant ministry was a false move and their true ministry was only achieved by trial and error. There might be other ways to read the story of the final cohort. Certainly, there were pay issues: why should someone earn more as an evangelist than a minister?[179] Yet the ordinary members of the Connexion were, seemingly, not over-enthusiastic either. The new experience of a Methodist Church of several branches coming slowly but inexorably into one, and the pressure-never-acknowledged-but-there, that the right way to do things was that of the larger Methodist churches, may have pushed women ministers out of the vision.[180]

Perhaps the final judgement on the final cohort must be that it was a relative failure. Lillie Edwards certainly made a considerable mark on the small circuits in which she served. But the Methodism of the era was against her. Perceptions of ministry were changing, the desire for Methodist union was dominant, and the pressure to conform to the 'old Connexion' and their ways must have been strong. What had begun as pragmatic and suffered the discrimination of its era probably succumbed to the different pressures of a different era.

---

[178] The Methodist Church, The history of the Methodist Diaconal Order, Wesleyan Deaconesses. https://www.methodist.org.uk/about-us/the-methodist-church/the-diaconal-order/the-history of-the-methodist-diaconal-order/ (accessed 25 April 2020).
[179] Lloyd's point about pay, *Lloyd*, p. 266, with respect to Lily Oram cannot be gainsaid.
[180] See R. Currie, *Methodism Divided: a study in the sociology of ecumenicalism* (London, 1968), p. 232.

9: Catherine Stephens Smith (1813-84): from Wesleyan Methodist minister's wife to radical holiness preacher

David Bundy

Little is known of the early life of Catherine Stephens Smith. Her husband Thornley Smith (1813-91) mentioned in his published memoir of her that she was born in Ryde, Isle of Wight, came from a 'once very respectable family', was orphaned young and raised by older brothers; was Anglican but experienced Methodist conversion in 1832. Thornley had originally hoped to marry her, but since she was considered too weak for missionary service, he married Elizabeth Cowper who died returning from the mission field.[1] When she married this WM minister and returned missionary on 4 April 1848, Catherine inherited three surviving children from his first marriage.[2] Catherine and Thornley had at least five children, the last birth being in 1861.[3] She remained a modest Methodist minister's wife until 1861 and her encounter with the wife of an American evangelist, Elizabeth Finney,[4] English reformer Josephine

---

[1] *Smith*, pp. 2-4, 16-17.

[2] George, Marianne, and Thornley. George became a Congregational minister, Marianne married a Wesleyan missionary in Ceylon/Sri Lanka, Edmund Rigg, and Thornley became a farmer in the Transvaal.

[3] Westmore, Catherine Hannah (both of whom are mentioned later), Ann b. 1852, Sophia b. 1853, and James b. 1861. There may have been other pregnancies, but these are not mentioned in the *Memoir*. Catherine Smith therefore had a sizeable family to care for.

[4] Elizabeth Ford Atkinson Finney was the second wife of Charles Grandison Finney. She was a widow, principal of the Atkinson Female Seminary, Rochester, New York (1841-8). They were married by Asa Mahan, the first President of Oberlin College. *Lloyd*, pp. 177-8. On Finney see W. Kostlevy, 'Finney, Charles Grandison' in Kostlevy

Butler,[5] and an American evangelist of the radical holiness movement, Mary Morse Boardman.[6] Under their tutelage and following their examples, she became a preacher herself, with her husband's support. This is her story.

Women preachers in the second half of the nineteenth century faced many difficulties. Heeney observed: 'Women's sphere in the late Victorian Church was decidedly subordinate, limited and controlled everywhere by the authority of men.' Lillian Lewis Shiman made it more explicit: 'Well-bred ladies did not put themselves forward nor did they take any active role in public affairs . . . Most men wanted a pliable, docile wife who would not jeopardise her husband's position through unorthodox behaviour'.[7]

A volume of essays on women's roles in society, edited by Josephine Butler, friend of Catherine and Thornley Smith,

---

(ed.), *The A to Z of the Holiness Movement* (Lanham, MD, 2020), pp. 113-14.

[5] Josephine Butler was a campaigner for women's rights, vigorous proponent of the Salvation Army, and friend of the Boardmans (note 6). H. Mathers, 'The Evangelical Spirituality of a Victorian Feminist: Josephine Butler, 1828-1906' in *Journal of Ecclesiastical History*, vol 52, no 2, (2001), 282-312.

[6] Wife of William Edwin Boardman, an accomplished theologian, prolific writer, preacher and organizer; see Mrs Boardman, *Life and Labours of the Rev. W. E. Boardman*, preface by the Rev. Mark Guy Pearse (New York, 1887). For more on the holiness movement see chapter ten.

[7] B. Heeney, 'The Beginnings of Church Feminism: women and the Councils of the Church of England, 1897-1919' in Malmgreen (ed.), *Religion in the Lives of English Women*, p. 260; L. Lewis Shiman, '"Changes are dangerous": women and temperance in Victorian England' in Malmgreen (ed.), *Religion in the Lives of English Women*, p. 193.

included discussions of medicine, education, and science, but did not dare address church limits on women.[8]

The situation within Methodism was more complicated as has been demonstrated by John Lenton, Jennifer Lloyd, and Dorothy Graham; and within Nonconformity generally as has been discussed by Deborah Valenze and Linda Wilson.[9] The 1803 *Minutes of Conference* made the perspective of that assembly clear: 'Shall Women be permitted to preach among us? A[nswer]: We are of the opinion that, in general, they ought not'. There was a loophole in the legislation:

> But if any woman among us thinks she has an extraordinary call from God to speak in public, (and we are sure it must be an *extraordinary call* that can authorize it,) we are of the opinion she should, in general, address her *own sex*, and *those only*. And upon this condition alone, should any woman be permitted to preach in any part of our Connexion.[10]

Two levels of permission were required. The first was approval of the superintendent and quarterly meeting for preaching in the circuit where they lived. To preach in another circuit, 'they shall have a *written* invitation' both from the 'Superintendent of such Circuit' and a note from the 'Superintendent of their own Circuit'.[11] No evidence has been found that Catherine Smith ever sought permission. In actuality, during her most active years, 1873-8, she would have had to do nothing more than ask

---

[8] J. E. Butler (ed.), *Woman's Work and Woman's Culture: a series of essays* (London, 1869).

[9] J. Lenton, 'Labouring for the Lord: women preachers in Wesleyan Methodism 1802-1932 — a revisionist view' in R. Sykes (ed.), *Beyond the Boundaries: preaching in the Wesleyan tradition* (Oxford, 1998), pp. 58–86; Graham, *Saved to Serve*; Lloyd; Valenze, *Prophetic Sons and Daughters*; L. Wilson, *Constrained by Zeal: female spirituality amongst nonconformists, 1825–1875*, Studies in Evangelical History and Thought (Milton Keynes, 2000).

[10] *Minutes of Conference*, vol 2, (London, 1863), p. 187 [emphasis in original].

[11] Ibid., p. 187 [emphasis in original].

her husband who was superintendent of the circuits to which he was stationed.[12] Following the models of Catherine Booth[13] and Hannah Whitall Smith[14] (both of whom she knew), and her friends Elizabeth Finney (wife of Charles Grandison Finney) and Mary Morse Boardman, she began to speak, testify, and preach. Like Elizabeth Finney, and unlike the other women, she spoke mostly to women.

One of the categories of preaching exercised by women has not received much attention. That is, Methodist women preaching only to women. Of the scholars mentioned above, only Lloyd mentions the phenomenon, and that only briefly.[15] Catherine Smith is a case study of the processes required for a woman and her husband, Thornley Smith, a WM minister, to arrive at the practice of her becoming a preacher in the radical holiness movement, speaking almost exclusively to women. An important issue: what is to be considered preaching? In this chapter, speaking, testifying, and biblical/doctrinal exposition as part of an established public programme is considered 'preaching.' It was not limited to a discourse given in a chapel or church. There is no information regarding the use or non-use of manuscripts during the preaching. This chapter argues that

---

[12] Thornley Smith was superintendent, 1873-5, of the London Bethnal Green circuit, *Minutes of Conference* (1873), p. 52; 1875-6, Colchester circuit church in the same First London district, *Minutes of Conference* (1875), p. 40; 1876-9, Uxbridge and Rickmansworth still in the First London district, *Minutes of Conference* (1876), p. 43. In the *Memoir*, there is no mention of superintendent status or of the matter of asking permissions in her own or other circuits. Thanks to John Lenton for this information.

[13] Co-founder of the Salvation Army. G. A. Patzwald, 'Booth, Catherine Mumford' in Kostlevy (ed.), *A to Z of the Holiness Movement*, pp. 22-3.

[14] Quaker radical holiness co-revivalist with her husband Robert Pearsall Smith. M. E. Dieter, 'Smith, Hannah Whitall' in Kostlevy (ed.), *A to Z of the Holiness Movement*, pp. 274-6.

[15] *Lloyd*, pp. 177-8. The central case was Elizabeth Finney.

it was within the burgeoning radical holiness movements, after 1870, that Catherine Smith found her voice, and that the networks were important for supporting her transition from minister's wife into various forms of public ministry, including preaching. These networks provided many women with opportunities for developing a public voice.[16] Catherine's case provides an example of a person moving from more 'separate spheres' to less 'separate spheres', transitioning to more complicated spheres, both confirming major tenets of the 'two spheres' thesis and requiring nuancing of that theory.[17] In the *Memoir* penned by her husband, it appears that this transition was stressful for them both.

Sources for Catherine Stephens Smith

Primary sources for the life and work of Catherine Smith are this *Memoir*, secular newspapers and radical holiness movement periodicals, data in Methodist sources related to the career of her husband, and census records for 1851-81. No publications by her have been identified. Remarkably, there are few

---

[16] See the studies of D. Bundy, 'Radical Holiness Becomes a World Christian Movement: The Influence of Isabella Sarah Leonard in Great Britain, Australia and Singapore, 1881-1892' in W. Kostlevy and W. Thornton jr (eds), *The Radical Holiness Movement in the Christian Tradition: a festschrift for Larry D. Smith*, Studies in the History of World Christianities, vol 1, (Lexington, 2016), pp. 53-67; P. Pope-Levison, 'Pentecost in the Churches: Women in the Pentecostal League of Prayer' in *WMS*, vol 10, no 1, (2018), 46-65; and D. Bundy, 'Sophia Chambers, Founder of the Holiness Church: A Case Study of Victorian Entrepreneurial Religious Leadership' in *WMS*, vol 11, no 1, (2019), 24-9.

[17] L. Davidoff and C. Hall, *Family Fortunes: men and women of the English middle class, 1780–1950* (London, 1987). The ambiguities of this framework have been recognized by the authors and numerous studies have chipped away at its viability, but the concept remains a foil for much work in women's studies. See Vickery, 'Golden Age to Separate Spheres?', and E. Gordon and G. Nair, *Public Lives: women, family and society in Victorian Britain* (New Haven, 2003).

references in Methodist historiography to the career of Thornley Smith,[18] despite his significant publishing record.[19] Mentions of Catherine Smith in newspapers and religious periodicals are few.

The account of the life of Catherine Smith was not the first memoir written by Thornley Smith, a prolific writer of such. Numerous missionaries,[20] and Methodist women,[21] as well as Syriac scholar and WM minister, John Wesley Etheridge,[22] received his attention. So did his parents, Hannah and Captain George Smith.[23] As well, he published a small book about his first wife, Elizabeth Cowper Smith (1811-47), who accompanied him to South Africa as a WM missionary wife; she became ill there and died on board ship returning to the UK.[24] As with his earlier efforts, the *Memoir* about Catherine Smith was a blending

---

[18] I. E. Page, 'The Late Rev. Thornley Smith' in *The King's Highway: a journal of scriptural holiness*, vol 20, (1891), 357-8; and obituary: '(1) Thornley Smith,' in *Minutes* (1892), pp. 13-14. Neither provides much data. Extremely useful for determining ministry locations is: W. Hill, *Hill's Arrangement of Ministers and Probationers with Circuits* (London, 1887).

[19] For example, he is not in *DMBI* (accessed 25 June 2019).

[20] T. Smith, *Memoir of the Rev. Thomas Laidman Hodgson, Wesleyan missionary* . . . (London, 1854); Smith, *The Earnest Missionary: a memoir of the Rev. Horatio Pearse, late General Superintendent of the Wesleyan missions* (London, 1864); Smith, *Memoir of the Rev. John Whittle Appleyard, Wesleyan missionary in South Africa* . . . (London, 1881).

[21] Smith with J. H. Lord, *Memorials of* . . . *Emma Loutit, wife of* . . . *J[ames] Loutit* . . . (London, 1867); Smith, *Walking in the Light: a memoir of Mrs Hannah Bairstow* (London, 1868).

[22] Smith, *Memoirs of Rev. John Wesley Etheridge: including extracts from his writings, correspondence and poetry* (London, 1871).

[23] Smith, *Won at Last: or, memoirs of Captain George and Mrs Hannah Smith* (London, 1870).

[24] Smith, *Memorials of Mrs Elizabeth Smith, wife of the Rev. Thornley Smith, including brief notices of the Wesleyan missions in South Africa and some occurrences connected with the recent war in that country* (London, 1848).

of spirituality and data, designed to contribute to the reputation of the person as an ideal Christian, a model to be imitated, and a person to be remembered by those who knew her.[25] The data were taken from letters, written by Catherine or by acquaintances about her, WM records and Thornley's memories. The use of the letters gives her a voice in the narrative. The work generally fits well into the profile of the Victorian 'domestic biography' described by Tolley, as well as the 'quiet and uneventful' biographies of women discussed by Atkinson.[26]

The *Memoir* is less than straightforward. Catherine is presented in two ways. On the one hand, she is presented as quite complex and learned. She read widely in scholarly as well as popular religious and reformist literature, eschewed fiction, led class meetings, ministered to ordinary and 'fallen women,' advised him in his writing, edited his texts, preached, developed friendships with famous Methodists, participated in the radical holiness movement networks, and experimented with new theological ideas. On the other hand, this interpretation was set in the narrative of a woman who was timid, quietly submissive to her husband and the church, always had faith and did not think too deeply, did not influence his writing and thinking, daily promoted the welfare of her family and children, prayed continuously and effectively, gave spiritual blessing to all who she encountered, struggled with life and duties cheerfully, suffered without complaint, comforted her husband in his illnesses, attended more than the usual number of prayer and evangelistic meetings, and encouraged women through letter-writing and in private meetings in homes; during church services she was always there prayerfully supporting her

---

[25] *Smith,* pp. v-ix, presents his rationale for writing the volume.
[26] C. Tolley, *Domestic Biography: the legacy of evangelicalism in four nineteenth-century families* (Oxford, 1997), pp. 117-61; J. Atkinson, *Victorian Biography Reconsidered: a study of nineteenth-century 'hidden' lives* (Oxford, 2010).

husband, and sent their children to the mission fields as offerings to God.

The text thus presented contrasting visions of Catherine Smith. The narrative of the ideal Victorian minister's wife seems oddly out of sync with the other track of the account. Two items were appended to the account of her life to reinforce the narrative of the ideal Victorian minister's wife. The first was the text of 'The Wise Woman', a sermon by John Kilner, former missionary and the Missionary Secretary of the WM Missionary Society, delivered at her funeral. The 'Wise Woman' takes care of 'her house', the scene of 'the silent outflow of her influence.' Supportive church work is fine if it remembers the headship of the man; evangelism and mission undertakings by women are to be done in the home.[27] Kilner earlier made much the same argument regarding missionary wives. He insisted they were to be missionaries themselves in the private sphere, providing an example to the 'heathen; they were to work only with women'.[28] Also appended to the volume was a sermon by Thornley Smith, 'The Redeemed in Heaven', insisting on the heavenly destiny of a life lived as the ideal 'Christian mother.'[29] Both appendices presented Catherine in the same way. In the eyes of Kilner and probably others of his colleagues, this is what gave her (and him) power and worth; it was the identity they desired for her.

---

[27] J. Kilner, 'The Wise Woman: A discourse delivered at Holly Park Church . . . on the occasion of the decease of Mrs. Thornley Smith', in *Smith*, pp. 235-58.

[28] J. Kilner, *Remarks on Christian Women's Work in Heathendom* (London, 1874). See *Lloyd*, pp. 211, 237, and C. C. Bennett, 'Women's Work: The Role of Women in WM Overseas Mission in the Nineteenth Century' in *Methodist History*, vol 32, no 44, (1994), 234. John Kilner, e.m 1847, Wesleyan Methodist Missionary Secretary 1877-88, was an interesting choice by Smith for his non-missionary wife.

[29] T. Smith, 'The Redeemed in Heaven,' in *Smith*, pp. 259-73.

UK radical holiness movement networks 1860-73

In 1860, a process of religious and cultural realignment began for Catherine and Thornley Smith. Their theology, the networks in which they participated, and religious activities began to change. The radical holiness movement networks in which they came to participate promoted:

1. A relativization of denominational identity;

2. Involvement in radical holiness movement networks;

3. Using the term 'Baptism with the Spirit' in place of sanctification, entire sanctification, or Christian perfection;

4. Ministry to, and or, with the poor (ethical and social commitment);

5. Belief in faith healing (healing was included in the atonement);

6. The acceptance of women preaching, not only as 'an extraordinary call';

7. Self-supporting 'Faith Mission' (to nominal Christians and non-Christians everywhere);[30]

8. Philo-Semitic;[31]

9. Pre-millennial eschatology.

This cluster of ideas was not always proclaimed with the same enthusiasm within the diverse sectors of the networks. There was no magisterium or committee of ministers to determine or

---

[30] The radical holiness movement networks merged the 'self-support' concepts of William Taylor (Methodist Episcopal Church dissident) with the 'faith' mission tradition of Europe best known through the work of Georg Müller of Bristol (Brethren). See D. Bundy, 'Pauline Missions: The Wesleyan Holiness Vision' in C. Yrigoyen jr (ed.), *The Global Impact of the Wesleyan Traditions and Their Related Movements*, Pietist and Wesleyan Studies, vol 14, (Lanham, 2002), pp. 13-26.

[31] The Missions to the Jews were European-wide (primarily) mission networks which worked to convert Jews to Christianity. These reacted against oppression of the Jews and sought their conversion as part of their Christian millennial expectations. T. Smith, *Memoirs of Rev. John Wesley Etheridge*, pp. 145-55, 161-75, 212-27.

enforce orthodoxy. These adaptations or changes did not occur all at once in most participants in the radical holiness movement networks. The developments in Catherine's and Thornley's perspectives took place over a number of years; developments will be mentioned as they occur in the narrative of Catherine's shift from Methodist minister's wife to radical holiness preacher.

In 1859, Thornley Smith was appointed to Bolton, where he was under the guidance of the Rev. John Hannah (1792-1867), tutor at Didsbury College, who served as Chairman of the Manchester and Bolton district and who became a lifelong friend. Thornley soon became a leader in multi-denominational prayer meetings to foster community and renewal of the churches.[32] This prepared the way for the invitation by the ministers to Charles and Elizabeth Finney who arrived in 1861, probably with the approval of Hannah. Catherine Smith served as a class leader.[33] Finney's meetings in Bolton were the only successful evangelistic/holiness campaign of his second foray into the UK.[34] Thornley Smith was chair of the first meeting.[35] He was not immediately impressed with Finney or his preaching. Despite having anticipated that Finney's 'ministry would be accompanied with power from on high . . .' at first his manner seemed somewhat stern and his style of preaching by no means attractive. However, 'In a few days . . . the Spirit swept away all prejudice' and the crowds required a larger meeting place. He reported: 'Both Mr. and Mrs. Finney spoke often on the subject of Christian holiness, or entire sanctification, and Mrs. Smith saw that there was a blessing for her which she had not yet realized.'

---

[32] 'Union Prayer Meetings' in *Patriot* (17 November 1859), 741.
[33] *Smith*, p. 57.
[34] K. J. Hardman, *Charles Grandison Finney: revivalist and reformer* (Durham, 1987), pp. 437-9.
[35] 'The Revival Services' in *Bolton Chronicle* (14 January 1860), 5.

Catherine Smith experienced 'entire sanctification'; Thornley was clear that it was not 'absolute perfection' but 'Christian perfection'. He noted that the women's meetings transcended class lines and that 'my wife joined her [Elizabeth Finney], and they became as sisters'.[36] The *Memoir* changed tone. Thornley devoted sixty pages to the first forty-eight years of her life; he devoted 173 pages to her last twenty-three years. The turning point was the Finney encounter and the beginning of a more public role.

Elizabeth Finney preached only to women.[37] Thornley Smith was not allowed to attend; the fact that he asked permission to attend (and was refused) suggests he was not offended at the idea of being preached to by Elizabeth Finney, or maybe he was just curious. He implied that because Catherine had 'read many of the standard works on the subject', she also was speaking to the women,[38] but no definitive evidence has been found. In the newspapers the women, except for Elizabeth Finney, were unnamed. At the end of the three-month Finney visit, the women decided to give Elizabeth Finney a monetary gift and flowers. The *Bolton Chronicle* described the scene of the women's meeting in the Temperance Hall; the narrative focused on the role of Catherine Smith: 'every nook and corner being filled . . . There must have been 1000 of the fair sex present, including every age, grade, sect, and relationship . . . The tea was well managed . . .' At the end of the tea, 'Mrs. Finney, accompanied by some of the more active workers in connection with her, took

---

[36] *Smith*, pp. 61-3.

[37] For a complimentary description of the women's meetings, see 'The Revival' in *Bolton Chronicle* (25 February 1860), 8; reprinted as: 'The Revival Movement in Bolton' in *The Constitution* (1 March 1860), 4. Only Elizabeth Finney was named.

[38] *Smith*, pp. 62-4.

their places on the platform, when Mrs. Thornley Smith was called to preside.'³⁹

A letter of appreciation was read by a fellow leader Elizabeth Best. Then she deferred to Catherine:

We now ask you to accept . . . a small tribute of love from all classes who have attended your meetings . . . Mrs. Smith then gave the signal for a general rise, and then from a bouquet which stood on the table drew forth a glittering purse . . . containing 50 guineas, which she presented to Mrs. Finney on behalf of the Bolton ladies, as a small thank-offering and acknowledgement of her valuable services in conveying instruction to many who have attended her meetings.⁴⁰

After the Finney meetings, Thornley points out Catherine's resuming domestic responsibilities, but noting she gave the pre-baptismal instruction to eighteen candidates, 'from her lips', hosting teaching sessions in her home.⁴¹ Smith never commented on his own feelings or spiritual developments during this period. But there is an important hint. He was part of the Evangelical Alliance British delegation to the 1862 Geneva meeting, where he met 'rationalists' and Protestant 'Puseyites', learning of Lutheran State Church persecution of German Methodists. He then wrote to Catherine that a 'new reformation' is needed, 'a baptism of the Holy Ghost'.⁴²

During the next few years in Lincoln and Huddersfield the Smiths slowly entered the British radical holiness movement networks. They renewed their friendship with William Arthur.⁴³ Smith preached (1864) alongside Thomas

---

³⁹ 'Farewell Meeting to Mrs. Finney' in *Bolton Chronicle* (31 March 1860), 5.
⁴⁰ Ibid., 5.
⁴¹ *Smith*, p. 67.
⁴² Ibid., pp. 68-71.
⁴³ Ibid., pp. 23, 80. Arthur (1819-1901, e.m. 1838), a former Missionary Secretary, was author of the Wesleyan classic adopted also by the radical holiness movement networks and Pentecostals: *Tongue of Fire;*

Champness,[44] and hosted John Hannah and John Kilner.[45] Money was received from Cuthbert Bainbridge (1840-72), part of the Newcastle mercantile family, wealthy landowner and champion of holiness causes, for the new chapel.[46] Finney and the experience of Bolton were on his mind.[47] The next appointment was at Maidstone, where Catherine again became a class leader.[48] There she also became lifelong friends with Josephine Butler, who was already well integrated into radical holiness movement networks.[49] Influenced by Butler, Catherine became engaged in the battle against the Contagious Diseases Act, 'and from that day made it her own.'[50] What precisely that meant for her was not explained, but normally it involved

---

or, the true power of Christianity (London, 1856). *DMBI* and T. Bergman, 'Arthur, William' in Kostlevy (ed.), *A to Z of the Holiness Movement*, pp. 6-7.

[44] On Champness, see *DMBI* and W. Parkes, 'Champness, Thomas' in Kostlevy (ed.), *A to Z of the Holiness Movement*, p. 50.

[45] *Smith*, pp. 80-3.

[46] Ibid., p. 85. Bainbridge was closely connected to William Pennefather, an Anglican with strong Brethren and radical holiness movement sympathies who founded the Mildmay Conference Centre, hospital, and Deaconess order. He with Bainbridge provided support for the Boardmans, Mahan and Robert Pearsall and Hannah Whitall Smith to move to the UK. D. Bundy, 'Keswick and the Experience of Evangelical Piety' in E. L. W. Blumhofer and R. H. Balmer (eds), *Modern Christian Revivals* (Urbana, IL, 1993), pp. 118-44. T. B. Stephenson, WM minister and orphanage founder, was a mutual friend of Thornley Smith, Bainbridge and William Pennefather. T. Smith, *Memorials of Mrs. Elizabeth Smith*, pp. 66-8; *Smith*, pp. 137-8, 142.

[47] Ibid., p. 96.

[48] Ibid., p. 102; other places where she served as class leader included: 90 (Huddersfield), 131 (Swansea), 170 (Rickmansworth, Uxbridge).

[49] An essay is in process regarding the radical holiness movement networks of Josephine Butler. On the Maidstone meeting and Catherine Smith, see 'Contagious Diseases Act Meeting of Women at the Corn Exchange' in *Maidstone Telegraph* (16 April 1870), 5.

[50] *Smith*, pp. 116, 129, 130, 179, 180, 191.

writing and speaking publicly against the Act. No written or published texts have been identified. This was not unusual; most women active in struggles for the rights of women remained anonymous.

This activism, both as class leader and as an anti-Contagious Diseases Act campaigner, continued during their ministry in Swansea.[51] She encouraged revivalist efforts (October 1870) in the local Anglican church led by Robert Aitken, whose son William H. M. H. Aitken would soon be a colleague of the Smiths in radical holiness movement revivalism.[52] In response to Aitken's campaign, as in Bolton, they were ready to relativize denominational priorities to 'unite with Christians of other denominations' for 'extending the kingdom of the Lord.'[53]

London: radical holiness movement neighbours

The move to Bethnal Green, east London, in 1873, placed them in the midst of the developing radical holiness movement networks of London. The Smiths met the Boardmans and Asa Mahan, first President of Oberlin College, USA, at a Woodford (near London) garden party in the early spring of 1873.[54] 'From that day [they] became our much-loved friends.'[55] It was on the basis of discussions with William Boardman that Thornley Smith, on 23 December 1873, recounted 'I made a full surrender of myself to Christ, and realized a power which no words can possibly describe. It was the rest of faith . . .' He reflected that

---

[51] Ibid., pp. 129-31.

[52] On the Aitkens, see *DMBI* which unfortunately does not mention their radical holiness movement participation.

[53] Ibid., pp. 121-2.

[54] Mahan, a prolific radical holiness movement author, joined Boardman in England in 1872, editing, writing and speaking at holiness conventions until his death in 1889.

[55] Ibid., pp. 138-9. The Boardmans were well known because of his book, *The Higher Christian Life* (London, 1859, second edition 1871). They moved definitively to London in 1873. William died in London, 1886; Mary, in 1904. Both were prolific authors.

'As a minister I have known the theory of Christian holiness . . . but I never experienced it before.'[56] Thornley and Catherine Smith now publicly shared the radical holiness movement understanding of 'baptism with the Holy Spirit.' Mary Boardman would have been the ideal person to mentor Catherine as a preacher. Her struggle with preaching to mixed gender audiences is recounted in the biography of her husband.[57] Following a traumatic experience in Cincinnati, she wrote on women preaching, analysing the biblical passages about women and making most of the exegetical moves that later radical holiness movement and feminist scholars would make.[58]

Holiness conventions (1874-8)

The Boardmans were engaged, for several years (1869-1870, 1873-1886), in holding holiness conventions throughout the UK. The Thornley Smiths became allies in the project, although the details of that process of involvement remains unclear. Thornley Smith gave no hint of his religious evolution in the presentation of Wesley's theology,[59] but his religious experience of 1873 guided by the Boardmans led to their increased identification with and broad participation in the radical holiness movements after 1873, all the while working within the Wesleyan Church even after his official retirement in 1879.[60]

---

[56] *Account of the Union Meeting for the Promotion of Scriptural Holiness held at Oxford, August 29th to September 7th, 1874* (London, 1874), p. 365.

[57] Mrs Boardman, *Life and Labours of the Rev. W. E. Boardman* (1887), pp. 146-8.

[58] Mrs Boardman, *Who shall publish the glad tidings?* (Boston, 1873).

[59] T. Smith, *Christian Theology; a selection of the most important passages in the writings of the Rev. John Wesley, A.M. arranged so as to form a complete body of divinity with a biographical sketch* (London, 1871).

[60] *Smith*, pp. 183-7. Smith was asked by two different publishers to update Adam Clarke's *Commentary* (p. 102); Catherine assisted with the research and edited his texts. They maintained good relationships with prominent Wesleyans including William Arthur (pp. 23, 80,

Being friends with the Boardmans put them at the centre of the British radical holiness movement networks.

Smith did not speak at the Union Meeting for the Promotion of Scriptural Holiness at Oxford (1874).[61] However, he was part of the inner circle of the radical holiness movement networks. His fellow Methodist, Isaac E. Page, published an obituary of Smith in the WM Southport convention periodical *The King's Highway*.[62] He reported Smith 'was present, with other Wesleyan ministers, at the great Oxford conference for the promotion of holiness.' Both Page and Smith were part of a morning bible study and prayer meeting focused on 'the baptism of the Holy Ghost' that included key leaders of the holiness networks: Dr Asa Mahan, George Pearse,[63] and Lord Radstock.[64] 'When the meeting closed Thornley Smith took the writer's arm, and said with feeling, 'O my brother, if I could but begin my ministry afresh under a power like this!' God gave

---

140), John Kilner (pp. 83, 132, 164, 186), and T. B. Smithies, (p. 211), as well as Methodist publishers. On Smithies, see *DMBI*.

[61] *Account of the Union Meeting*.

[62] W. Parkes, 'Page, Isaac E.' in Kostlevy (ed.), *A to Z of the Holiness Movement*, p. 225.

[63] George Pearse, Brethren holiness, was a founder of the China Inland Mission and long-time administrator. He became a missionary in France and was crucial in the development of the radical holiness movements there. He later became a missionary in Algeria: G. Pearse and J. B. Pearse, *The Bible Women in France* (London, 1874); J. K. Cooley, *Baal, Christ and Mohammed: religion and revolution in North Africa* (London, 1963), pp. 251-9. Pearse was a frequent writer in radical holiness movement periodicals, for example, G. Pearse, 'The Gift of the Holy Spirit' in *The King's Highway*, vol 5, (1876), 349-50, as well as a radical holiness movement biblical commentary: G. Pearse, *Étude sur l'épître de saint Paul aux Romains* (Paris, 1875).

[64] On Lord Radstock, see H. H. Rowden, 'Waldegrave, Granville Augustus William, third Baron Radstock (1813-1913)' in *Oxford Dictionary of National Biography* (Oxford, 2004), vol 56, pp. 767-8.

him years of work after that . . .'[65] Thornley Smith testified: 'I returned home consecrated for service, and in the full rest of faith.'[66] The Oxford 'Ladies' Meetings' included many testimonies of unnamed women. These were led by Hannah Whitall Smith and Mary Boardman; it is probable that as a close friend of Mary and an experienced speaker, Catherine would have been among the testifiers.[67]

At the Brighton 'Convention for the Promotion of Scriptural Holiness' (1875), Thornley Smith was the only Methodist prominently on the programme; he, Asa Mahan (Congregationalist) and C. B. Sawday (Baptist minister) led a 'Conversational Enquiry Meeting.'[68] Smith did not cover his own involvement in *A Christian Mother*, but he did mention that Catherine took members of the church to Brighton, that she agreed 'with the teaching of Pasteur Monod'[69] and Dr Asa Mahan, 'and when opportunity was given, she was not backward in bearing her testimony . . .'[70] She would have spoken at the sessions organized for women under the leadership of Hannah Whitall Smith at the convention, meetings which attracted as many as two thousand women, and which men were allowed to attend, but which were on the programme

---

[65] I. E. Page, 'The Late Rev. Thornley Smith' in *The King's Highway*, vol 20, (1891), 357-8. Smith died on 2 August 1891.

[66] *Account of the Union Meeting*, p. 365.

[67] Ibid., pp. 289-325. Only the two leaders were mentioned by name.

[68] *Record of the Convention for the Promotion of Scriptural Holiness held at Brighton, May 29th to June 7th, 1875* (Brighton, 1875), pp. 254-5.

[69] Pasteur Théodore Monod (1836-1922) participated in the Broadlands, Oxford, and Brighton holiness conventions of 1874-5. He was a popular speaker in holiness conventions throughout Europe, and edited a French radical holiness periodical, *Libérateur*. See Anon., 'Monod, Théodore' in S. Macauley Jackson (ed.), *The New Schaff-Herzog Encyclopedia of Religious Knowledge* (London, 1910), vol 7, pp. 473-4; Anon., 'Monod (Théodore)' in F. Lichtenberger (réd.), *Encyclopédie des sciences religieuses* (Paris, 1882), vol 13, pp. 140-1.

[70] *Smith*, pp. 145-6.

as 'Meetings for Ladies, exclusively.'[71] None of the names of speakers at these sessions, besides Hannah, were mentioned in the *Record*. Later Thornley Smith served as a chair of the London Moody-Sankey Crusade in August 1875.[72]

Radical holiness life in the orbit of Bethshan

The Smiths became Philo-Semitic and premillennialist largely through their friendship with John Wilkinson: 'Formerly I could not accept his views, but for the last ten years or more, I have seen cause to entertain the blessed hope of Christ's coming, as did Mrs. Smith also, who read much on the subject.'[73]

The first published widely circulated expression of commitments to the theological perspectives of the radical holiness movement cause were in the Commentary on 1 Peter which was praised by radical holiness movement reviewers for its premillennial and holiness perspectives.[74] The Smiths became engaged with radical holiness ministries to the poor, and to exploited women. They supported temperance ministries, and also through financial contributions and active participation existing ministries, including the Salvation Army, Dr Thomas John Barnardo, founder of Barnardo's Homes for Children, T. B. Stephenson, Miss Annie MacPherson, founder and director of an Industrial Training School for poor children

---

[71] *Record of the Convention for the Promotion of Scriptural Holiness . . . Brighton*, pp. 120, 254-5.

[72] Among the newspaper notices, for example: 'The Expected Visit of Messrs Moody and Sankey to the East of London' in *East London Observer* (30 January 1875), 5; 'Moody and Sankey at the East End' in *East London Observer* (17 April 1875), 7; 'Messrs Moody and Sankey in Bow End Hall' in *East London Observer* (24 April 1875), 5.

[73] *Smith*, pp. 172-9. [John Wilkinson, 1824-1907] *God Answers Prayer: some experiences in the life and labours of John Wilkinson* (London, 1902) and S. H. Wilkinson, *The Life of John Wilkinson, the Jewish Missionary* (London, 1908).

[74] T. Smith, *Expository Lectures on the First Epistle of St Peter* (London, 1878). See for example the anonymous review in *Penuel*, vol 3, (1878), 124.

in London, and Miss Coles, founder of the 'Orphan House'; and Catherine continued her activism against the Contagious Diseases Act with Josephine Butler.[75] The Smith family also continued to financially support Methodist projects.[76] After the Smiths retired in 1879, they chose to live in the London Finsbury Park circuit which allowed them to live near the Boardmans, their radical holiness movement colleagues and ministries, and John Kilner. The Smiths, despite their prominence in radical holiness movement networks, were neither speakers at the Southport (WM) holiness convention nor in the meetings leading up to the opening of the convention in WM chapels. This, and the fact that Thornley Smith's contributions to their periodical, *The King's Highway*, were infrequent and toward the end of his life, is evidence of a fissure in the overlapping British radical holiness movement networks.

The Smiths became involved in the healing ministry at Bethshan (Healing Home, London, formally established 1882) with the Boardmans and Elizabeth Baxter. Thornley Smith reported regarding Catherine: 'She had read of faith-healing, had been to Bethshan, and knew several cases in which prayer had been answered in a very remarkable way.' After injuring her shoulder blade in a fall in 1883 she first went to a doctor. Then she went to Bethshan again:

> I there prayed audibly and asked God that my shoulder might be healed, and that I might have the use of my arm again. I just trusted in the Lord that He was both able and willing to answer my prayer, and, returning home, I told them that my arm was cured. But no one had faith to remove the bandages and on the following Sunday morning I felt that I could not go to the chapel, as they caused intolerable pain. I asked

---

[75] *Smith*, pp. 34, 158 (temperance ministries); p. 192 (Salvation Army); p. 193 (Barnardo, Stephenson, Miss Annie MacPherson, Miss Coles); p. 130 (Contagious Diseases Act).
[76] *Report of the Wesleyan Methodist Thanksgiving Fund, 1878-1883* (London, 1883), p. 23 (while superintendent of Uxbridge and Rickmansworth circuit). Thanks to John Lenton for this reference.

Catherine [Hannah Smith] to take them off; she did so, and I cannot forget the relief I felt in having my arm set at liberty . . . I have had no bandage since, and I can use my arm just as I did before.[77]

'Jehovah Rophi—the Lord thy healer' became 'one of my wife's mottos.'[78] She was a proponent of faith-healing but she 'did not exclude the use of means or think that medical skill was to no avail'.[79] Smith reported that American Baptist minister A. J. Gordon's book on healing, 'which we read with interest, contains much that is valuable on the subject of faith-healing.'[80] In the *Memoir*, there are numerous other accounts of her healing after being ministered to and prayed for by the Boardmans.[81] Catherine's daughter Catherine Hannah Smith continued the relationship with Bethshan after Catherine's death.[82]

Catherine Smith's extensive reading became focused on literature of the radical holiness movements. She served as class leader in various societies to which Thornley was assigned, and in diverse situations. Sometimes the classes were quite large. From his brief comments it seems that her efforts were uniformly well received.[83] Catherine led confirmation classes for significant numbers, and the descriptions of this are of

---

[77] *Smith*, p. 201. Catherine Hannah Smith b. 1851 King's Lynn, living with her parents aged thirty and a teacher in the 1881 census, was the oldest daughter of Catherine Stephens Smith and the other 'Catherine' who removes the bandage in the quotation.

[78] Ibid., p. 203. See also W. E. Boardman's earlier publication, *'The Lord that Healeth Thee': (Jehovah-Rophi)* (London, 1881). The biblical reference is to Exodus 15:26.

[79] *Smith*, pp. 201, 205-7.

[80] Ibid., p. 206. A. J. Gordon, *The Ministry of Healing; or, miracles of cure in all ages* (London, 1882).

[81] *Smith*, pp. 188, 201-207, 219.

[82] Miss T. Smith [Catherine Hannah Smith] 'Keeping God Waiting' in *Thy Healer and Faith Witness*, vol 6, (1889), 139.

[83] *Smith*, p. 38 (Plymouth, c.1853-6); p. 57 (Bolton); p. 90 (Huddersfield); pp. 101-2 (Maidstone); p. 131 (Swansea).

preaching.[84] After 1873, the Boardmans and the Smiths collaborated in holiness conventions throughout England. Catherine and Mary spoke at the women's meetings, although Catherine is not often named in the newspaper accounts. The pattern was that Mary Boardman would give a short homily and Catherine (and other women) would speak. For example, there were 'bible readings' and 'preaching' by the women at Cambridge 3-8 July 1876. Thornley Smith observed:

> One of the afternoon services was intended particularly, though not exclusively, for females, . . . my wife spoke, as if inspired on the blessedness to families of full consecration on the part of the mothers. It was her own experience, and she knew nothing that could influence the minds of children for good so much as parental consistency in all walks of life.[85]

During 1875-6, Thornley was sent to Colchester. The Smiths invited William and Mary Boardman for a holiness convention, 22-3 April, which was 'attended by the power of the Spirit in a remarkable manner.'[86] Their son was commissioned as a missionary and Thornley noted that 'Westmore spoke in a spirit worthy of his mother'.[87] The months that Thornley Smith reported Catherine to be ill were months when the Boardmans did not travel far from London, and no records of women's meetings led by Mary Boardman have been identified during those periods.[88] The Boardmans were solicitous during

---

[84] For example, p. 191.

[85] Ibid., p. 168.

[86] 'Colchester' in *Banner of Holiness*, vol 1, no 33, (1876), 522.

[87] *Smith*, p. 164. Westmore S. Smith (1849-1925) b. Dartford, educated at Woodhouse Grove and Kingswood, e.m. 1875, went as a missionary to the West Indies, returning 1902.

[88] Ibid. The schedule of William Boardman has been pieced together from secular newspaper records and reports of meetings in radical holiness movement periodicals and those of sympathizers.

Catherine Smith's final decline and were present at the funeral; William Boardman participated.[89]

Conclusion

While much of Catherine's involvement in speaking to groups could have been incorporated into the WM regulation of an 'extraordinary call,' that term does not appear in the *Memoir*. Her speaking in Wesleyan contexts was only in defined roles of class leader or confirmation teacher in her husband's 'parish'. Outside of Wesleyan circles, her involvement included work against the Contagious Diseases Act and preaching primarily, but not always, in women's only meetings, under the leadership of Mary Boardman and Hannah Whitall Smith.

Catherine Smith (along with her husband) was prominently part of the network of radical holiness persons after 1873. There were close friendships with William Arthur, William and Mary Boardman, Elizabeth Finney, T. B. Stephenson, Cuthbert Bainbridge, T. B. Smithies, and Josephine Butler. The biography mentions relationships with Charles Finney, Thomas Champness, W. H. Aitken, William Gluyas Pascoe,[90] Asa Mahan, Hannah Whitall Smith and Robert Pearsall Smith, John Rattenbury,[91] Catherine Booth, Miss Annie MacPherson, and John Wilkinson, as well as D. L. Moody and I. Sankey, among others.[92] The intensity of these relationships is often impossible to define from the references in the *Memoir* and confirmatory sources have not often been found. The Smiths were well known in the larger holiness circles, not only because of their participation in holiness conventions and but also because of Thornley's reputation as a Methodist scholar, as well as his radical holiness books and publications on radical holiness

---

[89] Ibid., pp. 219-24.

[90] Pascoe (b. 1838, e.m. 1860-95) was a Welsh-born WM minister, active in the Southport convention; Hill, *Hill's Arrangement of Ministers and Probationers with Circuits* (London, 1963), p. 409.

[91] *DMBI.*

[92] *Smith.*

spirituality in prominent holiness periodicals.[93] At the same time close relationships were maintained with prominent Wesleyan Methodists.

Thornley Smith did not discuss explicitly or offer an *apologia* for her or his involvement in the radical holiness movements. In the *Memoir* of Catherine, it is 'hidden' in plain sight, as might be expected from studies of 'Victorian biographies of hidden lives.'[94] Perhaps he wished to avoid corporate shame or have Catherine's reputation as a minister's wife diminished by WM readers. He was influenced by the 'two spheres' theory, as much or more so than Catherine. Catherine courageously transcended the strictures placed on ministers' wives, with the cooperation and help of her husband. Thornley was supportive of her efforts to cross the boundaries; but as clearly felt constrained by them. Her experience is confirmatory of the power of the 'two spheres' theory.[95] The roles of men in support of wives transcending these social boundaries also deserves attention.

Not only did the gender and ecclesial boundaries shift. Catherine (and Thornley) Smith's theology became identical with that of radical holiness movement networks:

1. Conversionist;
2. Baptism with the Holy Spirit;
3. Relativizing denominational identity;
4. The acceptance of women preaching, not only as 'an extraordinary call';
5. Faith healing;
6. Faith mission support;

---

[93] These included: *The Christian's Pathway to Power, Penuel, Banner of Holiness, Divine Life,* and *The King's Highway.* Articles and accounts of his work also appeared in the radical holiness movement-promoting *Christian Herald* and until the healing controversies (1885) in *The Christian.*

[94] Atkinson, *Victorian Biography Reconsidered,* p. 3.

[95] Vickery, 'Golden Age to Separate Spheres?'.

7. Ministry to and or with the poor as a core ethical and social commitment;
8. Philo-Semitic;
9. Pre-millennial eschatology.

Thus, they moved from being simply WM to being promotors of the theology, religious experiences and networks of the radical holiness movements, while continuing to function as Wesleyans.[96] In their story, one finds an older couple who had worked hard to be seen as proper Wesleyans but who evolved in their commitments as their experiences and understandings of religion and society changed. The structure of the *Memoir* suggests they struggled with the new acceptance and opportunity within the radical holiness movement networks. They both became involved in the networks' efforts at religious and social renewal, but the biggest challenge was breaking the perceived taboo by accepting a public role for women; that included preaching/speaking to women. But it can be said that when her husband heard her preach, he was proud.

---

[96] Catherine Smith presents a different paradigm than the women studied by Lenton in 'Labouring for the Lord', and in *Lloyd*. Her approach was also different from the later deaconesses examined in Graham, *Saved to Serve*. These women ministered within Methodism, sometimes stretching the boundaries of Methodism to create space for their ministries, but not developing new theological categories to sustain their work.

10: 'Promised Ground': Phoebe Palmer's British Visit 1859-1863

Tim Woolley

A minister once said to us 'Mrs. Palmer, how do you get people to believe so easily?' Our reply was 'Because we never attempt to persuade anyone to appropriate a promise, until we have reason to know they are on *promised ground.*' The promise 'I will receive you' is only applicable to those who, through the enabling grace of God, separate themselves from the spirit of the world.[1]

Phoebe Palmer, offering an explanation of her preaching of entire sanctification at Newcastle-upon-Tyne on 12 October 1859.[2] The comparatively select group of writers on the life and ministry of Phoebe have often approached her through particular interpretive lenses. For Timothy L. Smith, credited for 'rediscovering' Phoebe after years of neglect, it was as a socially engaged revivalist that her 'crowning achievement' can be found.[3] Elaine Heath encourages us to consider her as a mystic who could 'become the patron saint for contemporary Methodists who are drawn to the new monasticism'.[4] Most recently Justin A. Davis contends that as a key figure in the development of Protestant theology Phoebe takes both a share of the credit for Pentecostalism and of the blame for

---

[1] P. Palmer and T. C. Oden (ed.), *Phoebe Palmer: selected writings* (New York, 1988), p. 263.
[2] Explained in more detail in this chapter as a process by which consecration, faith and testimony brought about a 'second blessing' through baptism of the Holy Spirit.
[3] T. L. Smith, *Revivalism and Social Reform: American Protestantism on the eve of the Civil War* (Nashville, 1957), pp. 169-71.
[4] E. Heath, *Naked Faith: the mystical theology of Phoebe Palmer* (Eugene, OR, 2009), p. 2.

fundamentalism.[5] This study focuses on Phoebe as a preacher of entire sanctification, a mass communicator of theological ideas in Britain, visiting from America with an equally distinctive message and method and assesses her legacy with particular focus upon the praxis of her presentation of those ideas.

Phoebe Worrall was born into a Methodist family in 1807 in New York City. Her father Henry was English and had been converted in Bradford in 1785 at the age of thirteen by the preaching of John Wesley who later gave him his first membership ticket.[6] In 1826, aged nineteen, Phoebe married a doctor, Walter Palmer, and in 1831 the couple went to live with her older sister Sarah Lankford and her family. Sarah introduced Phoebe to entire sanctification: growing up in a Methodist household, Phoebe must have been familiar with the doctrine if not the experience.[7] Phoebe began to yearn for this experience. After ten years of marriage and the death in infancy of two of their first three children, Palmer's yearning was intensified when on 29 July 1836 she and Walter endured a shattering experience. Phoebe rocked her fourth child, eleven-month-old Eliza, to sleep and placed her in her crib before retiring to her own room. Soon after, she heard screaming from the nursery and came running. A careless maid had tried to refill an oil lamp without putting it out. When the flames shot up, she had thrown the lamp away from her. It had landed in the crib, splashing burning oil all over the child. Phoebe cradled the infant in her arms but within minutes, Eliza was dead.[8]

---

[5] J. A. Davis, *Schleiermacher and Palmer: the father and mother of the modern Protestant mindset* (Eugene, OR, 2019).

[6] C. White, *The Beauty of Holiness: Phoebe Palmer as theologian, revivalist, feminist, and humanitarian* (Grand Rapids, 1986), p. 1.

[7] Sarah Lankford (1806-1896) was herself a significant figure in the holiness movement who after Phoebe's death married Walter Palmer. See J. A. Roche, *The Life of Mrs Sarah A. Lankford Palmer: who for sixty years was the able teacher of entire holiness* (New York, 1898).

[8] R. Wheatley, *The Life and Letters of Mrs. Phoebe Palmer* (New York, 1884), pp. 30-2.

Portrait of Phoebe Palmer (née Worrall).
Accessed via digital collections on-line.[9]

Almost exactly a year later on 26 July 1837, on what she ever after referred to as her 'Day of Days', Phoebe testified to the experience of entire sanctification. She determined from that day forward to devote herself entirely to God. To many modern minds her thought process at this point is an uncomfortable one since she began to believe that Eliza's tragic death, along with the death of her first two children,[10] was a sign of divine judgement that she had been too dedicated to them:

> My precious little ones, whom God had taken to himself, were then brought to my recollection, as if to admonish me relative

---

[9] Image available via digital collections
https://digitalcollections.nypl.org/items/79c1ff9c-c2a5-9f57-e040-e00a18061f18 (accessed 20 July 2020).
[10] Alexander (b. 1829) died after eleven months, whilst Samuel (b. 1830) lived just seven weeks. The Palmers' other children were Sarah (1833-1918), Phoebe (1839-1908) and Walter (1842-1885).

to making the sacrifice. I thought how fondly I had idolized them. He who had said, 'I the Lord your God am a jealous God', saw the idolatry of my heart, and took them to himself.[11]

From this Phoebe took that with regards to husband Walter, 'neither should this, the yet dearer object, be withheld',[12] and that he was to be an adjunct, but not a barrier, to her serving God first and foremost. Thus began a period of thirty-seven years when Phoebe Palmer, a woman with no formal training, exercised the ministry of a theologian, hymnodist, preacher and writer with the full support of Walter. Her public ministry began with leading of the Tuesday meetings for the promotion of holiness which had been begun by her sister, Sarah and which were instrumental in a revival in interest in the doctrine which spread beyond the bounds of Methodism and saw the beginning of the holiness movement. The meeting had been composed of women from two New York Methodist churches since 1835 but Phoebe joined it and became leader by 1840. It was effectively a Methodist class meeting with emphasis on entire sanctification at a time when there was a concern amongst some that the doctrine was being lost as a Methodist distinctive. At first only women attended these meetings, but eventually Methodist bishops and hundreds of clergy and laymen from other traditions began to attend as well.[13] In the same year as she began to lead the Tuesday Meetings Phoebe began to accept invitations to preach which soon were forthcoming from across the United States and Canada.

Phoebe was already widely known amongst British evangelicals before she and her husband Walter set sail aboard the steamship City of Baltimore on 4 June 1859, bound for

---

[11] P. Palmer, *Faith and its Effects: or, fragments from my portfolio* (London, 1856), p. 54. The biblical quotation is from Exodus 20:5 (KJV).
[12] Ibid.
[13] White, *Beauty of Holiness*, pp. 161-5.

Liverpool.[14] The Palmers had intended to visit England before. As early as 1845 they had planned a trip with American Methodist bishop Leonidas Hamline and his wife which never occurred;[15] this visit before her name was well known here was most likely planned more as a pilgrimage than a preaching tour. In 1856 at the invitation of some sympathetic ministers and laypeople a visit was once again mooted but it would be another three years before the Palmers crossed the Atlantic. Prominent amongst those encouraging their visit was Rev. Robert Young, that year serving as President of the Wesleyan Conference.[16] As will be seen, Young was to be one of the Palmers' most vocal advocates during their 1859-63 visit.

By the time of her visit, American editions of Phoebe's many books had been in circulation in Britain for a number of years and some of her major works had been reprinted in the UK. Phoebe's most popular and thorough exposition of her theology, *The Way of Holiness,* had appeared in a British imprint in 1845 just a couple of years after its first American edition,[17] and was republished in 1852. In 1857 the intended publication of a six volume British edition of Phoebe's works was

---

[14] Palmer and Oden (ed.), *Phoebe Palmer,* p. 259.

[15] H. Raser, *Phoebe Palmer, Her Life and Thought* (New York, 1987), p. 128. The passion for evangelism of Robert Young (1796-1865; e.m. 1820) which led him to support Phoebe's visit was described thus: 'The salvation of souls was regarded by him as absolutely necessary, and was expected with a steadfast faith. His thoughts, plans, consultations, and public labours were incessantly directed to this end.' Anon., *Wesley and His Successors: a centenary memorial of the death of John Wesley* (London, 1891), p. 184. Sadly, Young had to become a supernumerary at the Conference of 1860 due to paralysis.

[16] Palmer, *Four Years,* p. 694.

[17] P. Palmer, *The Way of Holiness: with notes by the way: being a narrative of religious experience resulting from a determination to be a Bible Christian* (London, 1845).

announced.[18] This included *The Way of Holiness,*[19] . . . and *Faith and its Effects,*[20] . . . both with laudatory prefaces by Wesleyan minister Thomas Collins (1810-1864, e.m. 1832). Subsequent years also saw the appearance of *Entire Devotion to God,*[21] and *Incidental Illustrations of The Economy of Salvation, Its Doctrines and Duties,*[22] which is described by Charles Edward White as a 'nearly four-hundred-page grab bag of letters, anecdotes, exhortations and reflections in between.'[23]

A key work of Phoebe's is *Promise of the Father,* which I have not yet found in a British imprint, but which is apposite to an examination of her as a public speaker and was published on the eve of her UK visit in 1859.[24] Raser has argued that Phoebe wrote this book as a justification of her own ministry after a period of its growing and expanding during the 1850s.[25] In it, Phoebe deftly defined preaching using an Old Testament text: 'Thus, (Nehemiah vi. 7) it is said, "Thou hast appointed prophets to preach." Hence prophets were preachers, and to prophesy is to preach.'[26] In identified preaching with prophesying, Phoebe was free to claim this as a faithful course

---

[18] Wheatley, *Life and Letters,* p. 498.

[19] P. Palmer, *The Way of Holiness: with notes by the way: being a narrative of religious experience . . . First English edition, reprinted from the thirty-fourth American edition. With preface by the Rev. T. Collins* (London, 1856). Alexander Heylin, publishers of the 1856 edition, in claiming it to be the 'first English edition' were overlooking the edition published by S. W. Partridge in 1845. See n. 16 above.

[20] Palmer, *Faith and Its Effects.*

[21] P. Palmer, *Entire Devotion to God: a present to a Christian friend* (London, 1857).

[22] P. Palmer, *Incidental Illustrations of the Economy of Salvation: its doctrine and duties* (London, 1858).

[23] White, *Beauty of Holiness,* p. 31.

[24] P. Palmer, *Promise of the Father: or, a neglected specialty of the last days. Addressed to the clergy and laity of all Christian communities* (New York, 1859).

[25] Raser, *Phoebe Palmer,* p. 200.

[26] Palmer, *Promise of the Father,* p. 42.

of action for women, setting it apart from the formal activity understood as the male domain of preaching, and leaving the reader in little doubt as to which she understands to have fidelity to the intentions of Christ:

> But, in fact, the word *preach*, taken in connection with its attendant paraphernalia, oratorical display, onerous titles, and pulpits of pedestal eminence, means so much more than we infer was signified by the word *preach*, when used in connection with the ministrations of Christ and his apostles, that we were disposed to withhold our unreserved assent to women's preaching in the technical sense. But . . . we wish to state unequivocally, that in a scriptural sense we believe all Christ's disciples, whether male or female, should covet to be endued with the gift of prophecy; then will they proclaim, or, in other words, *preach* Christ crucified, as far as in them lies, under all possible circumstances; and it is thus only that the command of the Head of the church can be obeyed — 'Preach the gospel to every creature.'[27]

Phoebe's defence of female preaching in *Promise of the Father* relied substantially on John Fletcher's doctrine of dispensations and in particular on his understanding of the meaning of the day of Pentecost,[28] yet whilst that debt goes entirely unacknowledged, Mary Bosanquet Fletcher is held up at length as a prime example of how women are empowered by God in public speaking: 'may not every pious Churchman and Methodist say, "Would to God all the Lord's people were such prophets and prophetesses'?"'[29] Phoebe also gave a lengthy description of the ministry of Mary Taft, reflecting on the level of recognition afforded her partnership with husband

---

[27] Ibid., p. 86. The biblical quotation is from Mark 16:15 (KJV).

[28] See L. W. Wood, *The Meaning of Pentecost in Early Methodism: rediscovering John Fletcher as John Wesley's vindicator and designated successor* (Lanham, MD, 2002), pp. 113-44.

[29] Palmer, *Promise of the Father*, p. 106. The quotation is based on Numbers 11:29, though there is no reference to 'prophetesses' in the KJV.

Zechariah: 'And it is only thus that it may be apologized for, that the devoted Mrs. T. was not on one occasion recognized as a fellow-helper with her husband, the Rev. Dr. Taft.'[30]

The case Phoebe made in the book was a focussed one, relating not so much to the right, as the *responsibility*, of women to teach and preach in church. It did not touch on questions of ordination or the wider role of women in the public or domestic sphere. As will be seen both by her own definition and by any reasonable understanding of a ministry of proclamation, Phoebe's activities in Great Britain and elsewhere came within the remit of preaching.

Upon landing in Liverpool, the Palmers were met by William Thorneloe, Wesleyan minister in Prescot who had read of their impending arrival in the *Guide to Holiness* magazine, which Phoebe was to take over publishing and editing on her return to America.[31] The sense of a long-awaited pilgrimage was inescapable in the early weeks of the Palmers' British visit, with trips to Wesley's Chapel and grave as well as the Surrey Music Hall to hear Charles Haddon Spurgeon preach. On their way to London Phoebe was moved to journey through Birmingham, final home of Hester Ann Rogers who she described as a 'burning and shining light' to her ever since childhood.[32] Phoebe was clearly steeped in early Methodist history and folklore and this comes across in her accounts of the British tour in a number of places, as will be seen below.

---

[30] Ibid., p. 89. The doctorate was a confusion with Zechariah's brother Henry who was both a doctor and a Methodist itinerant preacher.
[31] Begun in 1839 by New England Methodist Timothy Merritt with the encouragement of the Palmer sisters, *The Guide to Holiness* remained in print until 1901 and was edited by Walter and Sarah Palmer after Phoebe's death. In 1862-3 it carried regular reports of the Palmers' British tour. White, *Beauty of Holiness*, pp. 92-4. Thorneloe e.m. 1834 and died 1862.
[32] Palmer, *Four Years*, p. 28.

After nearly a month of tourism, formal services began at Bowden and Altrincham in Cheshire with moderate success. But it was a letter from long term correspondent of the Palmers', Robert Young, now Chairman of the Newcastle-upon-Tyne district, which began their work in Britain in earnest. Responding to his invitation to preach, the couple journeyed to the North East in September and stayed for thirty-five days in Newcastle where crowds of up to two thousand were drawn to Brunswick Chapel. In the Palmers' own account of their tour *Four Years in the Old World* (1866) the numbers of respondents in each place are recorded.[33] A figure of thirteen hundred 'justified' is recorded for the Palmers' time in Newcastle, after which they moved on to Sunderland, where another thirty-five days drew even bigger crowds and produced a harvest of 'seekers' justified and two hundred sanctified. The Palmers then moved on to North Shields where a total of 4,345 names were reported 'given in'. By July 1860 1,593 new members were reported in Wesleyan circuits across the district, with another 1,851 on trial.[34] It was at these meetings in the North East of England that the Palmers made the most impact both in terms of numbers of respondents and, as will be seen, in terms of influence.

Between the end of their North East campaign and October 1863 when they returned home Phoebe and Walter Palmer visited fifty-one towns and cities of varying sizes in England, Scotland, Ireland, Wales and the Isle of Man, drawing large crowds and recording significant responses in most places they visited. As Oden has noted, throughout their travelling, Phoebe 'tirelessly tracked down the Wesleyan connections, reminiscences and historical sites.'[35] She wrote to the Hamlines in December 1859 of her excitement at being in Wesley's study, moved from the Orphan House in Newcastle to the North Shields estate of local

---

[33] *Scotland*, p. 137.
[34] Ibid., p. 126.
[35] Palmer and Oden (ed.), *Phoebe Palmer*, p. 264.

dignitary Solomon Mease.[36] The account of the Palmers' visit to Epworth in May 1861 in *Four Years* is replete with extracts from Wesley's Journal and descriptions of Wesley sites in the area far outweigh reports of the meetings held daily during a week-long campaign.[37]

When the Palmers visited Madeley in January 1862 it was purely intended to be a pilgrimage to see the sites associated with the life of John Fletcher. Thanks to a number of local admirers, most notably the then vicar of Madeley, George Edward Yate (1825–1908), who had read a number of Phoebe's books, the Palmers were persuaded to stay in the area for three weeks. They conducted meetings in the barn in the vicarage grounds and across the Wesleyan circuit, resulting in the addition of nine hundred members to the Madeley circuit and four hundred to the adjacent Wellington circuit, in what was the second most successful time of her four years in Britain.[38] That Phoebe gives a lovingly detailed account of all she saw in Madeley in *Four Years* once again underlines both the sense of pilgrimage for her in the trip and the importance to her of the Fletchers as a model of partnership in ministry; she refers to the work of 'Mr and Mrs Fletcher' frequently in the narrative and emphasizes both Mary Bosanquet Fletcher's ministry during her widowhood and her lasting reputation in the locality.[39]

What was it then that the Palmers were presenting? Key to Phoebe Palmer's theology is a modification of entire sanctification, introducing the concept of what became known as 'The Shorter Way'. This was a process with three distinct steps. For Phoebe the first step to entire sanctification was *entire*

---

[36] Ibid., pp. 264-5.

[37] Palmer, *Four Years*, pp. 455-63.

[38] H. Raser, '"Holding Tightly to the Promise of the Father": Phoebe Palmer and the legacy of the Fletchers in mid-nineteenth-century Methodism' in Hammond and Forsaith (eds), *Religion, Gender and Industry*, pp. 173-88.

[39] Palmer, *Four Years*, pp. 516-34.

consecration, 'a perfect and entire yielding up of all to Christ, an entire trust in Christ, and a continuous reliance on Christ, for all needed grace under every diversity of circumstance or experience.'[40] It is a once-and-for-all surrender of 'body, soul, and spirit; time, talents, and influence; and also, of the dearest ties of nature',[41] which must be reaffirmed daily. Such self-sacrifice underpinned a determination that 'we give ourselves at once wholly and for ever away to [God's] service, in order that we may be unto him a peculiar people, zealous of good works, not living to ourselves.'[42]

The second step to entire sanctification was to *exercise faith.* According to Phoebe, in 2 Corinthians 6:16-7:1 God promised to receive the offering of those who separate themselves from all evil through entire consecration. If believers entirely consecrated themselves to the Lord, they could trust that God had sanctified them. Whether or not one felt any different after devoting every area of one's life to the Lord was for Phoebe of no importance since it would be wrong to question whether God had sanctified the heart: such a doubt would be a lack of trust in the written word of God.[43] Here Phoebe arguably adopted a biblicism beyond Wesley's own high view of scripture and the concept of 'orthopathy' or personal renewal, important both in the 'warmed heart' experience of Aldersgate Street and in the theology of Pentecostalism to which the holiness movement subsequently gave birth, was largely absent from her thought.

The third step in the sanctification process was *testimony.* The work had already occurred, but it must be ratified as believers

---

[40] Palmer, *Incidental Illustrations,* p. 131.
[41] P. Palmer, *The Way of Holiness* (New York, 1843), p. 135. There is an echo here of Phoebe's interpretation of her experience as a bereaved mother.
[42] Palmer, *Faith and its Effects,* p. 15.
[43] Palmer, *The Way of Holiness,* pp. 85-6; Palmer, *Incidental Illustrations,* p. 151.

publicly bear witness to what, on the basis of scripture, they know God has done in the heart. While John Wesley had *suggested* that those who received the blessing should tell other believers, Phoebe *asserted* the 'binding nature of the obligation to profess the blessing'.[44] She taught that Romans 10:9-10 ('if thou shalt confess with thy mouth the Lord Jesus, and shalt believe in thine heart that God hath raised him from the dead, thou shalt be saved' [KJV]) required public profession as well as the faith of the heart for God's work to be effective. Not to tell others was to withhold the honour due to Christ; thankfulness for God's mercy required outward acknowledgment of inward grace.[45]

As a Methodist Phoebe recognized the importance of singing theology and the immediacy of the Shorter Way is captured well in her hymn 'The Cleansing Wave',[46] which first appeared in the *Guide to Holiness* magazine in 1871:

Oh, now I see the crimson wave!
The fountain deep and wide;
Jesus, my Lord, mighty to save,
Points to His wounded side.

Refrain:
The cleansing stream I see, I see!
I plunge, and, oh, it cleanseth me!
Oh, praise the Lord, it cleanseth me!
It cleanseth me, yes, cleanseth me.

---

[44] Palmer, *Incidental Illustrations*, pp. 148-50.

[45] Ibid., p. 114.

[46] Phoebe wrote a number of hymns, of which this was by far the most popular, appearing in 246 hymnals, including as recently as 1985 in the *Seventh-Day Adventist Hymnal*. Her hymns do not appear in any hymn books authorized by any of the branches of British Methodism, although her hymn 'O! when shall I sweep through the gates' was included in I. D. Sankey's widely used *Sacred Songs and Solos* (London, 1878); J. Julian, *A Dictionary of Hymnology*, vol 2, (New York, 1907), p. 1585.

I see the new creation rise,
I hear the speaking blood;
It speaks, polluted nature dies,
Sinks 'neath the cleansing flood.

I rise to walk in Heav'n's own light,
Above the world and sin,
With heart made pure and garments white,
And Christ enthroned within.

Amazing grace! 'tis Heav'n below
To feel the blood applied,
And Jesus, only Jesus know,
My Jesus crucified.

Here there was found no sense of waiting or struggle. Despite her own travails following Eliza's death, for Phoebe it would seem that the priority of what she discerned from scripture took precedence over her own experience. The tune, incidentally, was written by Phoebe's daughter Phoebe Knapp.[47]

In the United States and Canada in the 1840s and 1850s Phoebe had preached alone and the British tour seems to have been the first occasion when she and Walter publicly operated a team ministry. It is unclear why this is, but it seems to have been a successful pattern they continued on their return to America. An article published in a Cincinnati Methodist women's magazine *The Ladies Repository* in 1866,[48] along with accounts in *Four Years in the Old World,* give an idea of how this new way of working reflected her theology of sanctification through the conduct of services. Evening meetings commenced with a hymn, often a Charles Wesley composition: the opening service at Brunswick began with 'Come Holy Spirit, Raise Our Songs',[49]

---

[47] See n. 6 above.

[48] J. A. Roche, 'Mrs. Phoebe Palmer' in *The Ladies' Repository; a monthly periodical, devoted to literature, art and religion* (Cincinnati, 1866), 66-7.

[49] Palmer, *Four Years,* p. 95; *John Wesley, A Collection of Hymns, for the use of the people called Methodists* (London, 1850), p. 596.

whilst on Good Friday 6 April 1860 at Penrith the service commenced with 'And Can it Be.'[50] Sometimes other composers' work was used, albeit still from John Wesley's hymnal, such as Anne Steele's 'Almighty Maker of my frame' (Stroud, 7 October 1860).[51] Prayers were then offered, often by a local minister. Walter then read a passage of scripture; Acts 2 was often chosen but at Penrith Romans 12 was read, and Walter made some comments, usually merely 'a few easy and pertinent remarks' according to *The Ladies' Repository*. Then in the words of Phoebe 'we urged the imperative claim, by virtue of God's infinite mercy in giving his son for a lost world, as a reason why there should be an unreserved, immediate and unconditional surrender of the whole being to God on the part of all present.'[52] Phoebe made an appeal for entire consecration on the basis of faith in the sacrifice of Christ as outlined in the scriptures — highlighted for example in Romans 12:1 (KJV): 'I beseech you therefore, brethren, by the mercies of God, that ye present your bodies a living sacrifice, holy, acceptable unto God, which is your reasonable service.'

The Ladies' Repository recorded that Phoebe 'may occupy twenty minutes or even an hour' and it would be easy to imagine that this was a high-pressure, hard sell approach to revivalism, but the description of her preaching in the magazine cautions against that:

> She is calm and free from vociferation and is rarely vehement . . . in her communications there is more of logic than rhetoric. She does not . . . attempt any severe or protracted reasoning but reaches her conclusions in a way that is simple, direct and vigorous . . . her discourses are replete with Scriptural illustration and her design is transparent . . . Circumstances influence the matter and length of her discourse.

---

[50] Palmer, *Four Years* p. 299.
[51] Ibid., p. 342; Wesley, *Collection of Hymns*, p. 651.
[52] Roche, 'Mrs. Phoebe Palmer', 67.

A contemporary account of her preaching in Carlisle in 1860 from the Wesleyan newspaper *The Watchman* described Phoebe's preaching as 'addressed more to the understanding than to the feeling of her audiences.'[53] Harold Raser opines that 'Palmer was simply a gifted and by 1866 well-polished public speaker who offered a clear and simple message in the common vernacular of "respectable revivalism"'.[54]

Having implored her hearers to the *entire consecration* of their lives by *faith* in God's Word, Phoebe then invited their immediate response through coming forward to receive prayer and then immediately giving their *testimony* of their salvation or sanctification. An example of this is found in the Palmers' account of their stay in Newcastle:

> A local preacher was the first to hasten to the communion-rail and was the first to receive 'the tongue of fire.' Would that you could have heard his clear, unequivocal testimony, as with a holy boldness, which perhaps scarcely was more than equalled on the day when the holy flame first descended on the Pentecostal morn, he spake as the Spirit gave utterance . . . surely now, as in the early days of the Spirit's dispensation, Pentecostal blessings bring Pentecostal power.[55]

The language used in this description is probably not a reference to glossolalia but rather reflects Phoebe's frequent exhortation to her hearers to be baptized 'with an inward baptism of fire' which stemmed from her modification of Wesley's pneumatology. Phoebe identified the experience of entire sanctification with being baptized in the Holy Spirit. In this, once more without ever acknowledging so, she followed John Fletcher who described:

> The still more abundant life, the life of the adult or perfect Christian, imparted to him when the love of God, or power from on high, is plentifully shed abroad in his believing soul,

---

[53] Palmer, *Four Years*, p. 216

[54] Raser, *Phoebe Palmer*, p. 119.

[55] Palmer, *Four Years*, pp. 96-7.

the day that Christ baptizes him with the Holy Ghost and with fire, to sanctify him wholly, and seal him unto the day of redemption.[56]

At the conclusion of the testimonies, which were often repeated by Walter so that the whole congregation could hear them, the respondents were further invited to confirm their experience by singing an appropriate hymn: at Manchester in April 1863 the choice was Charles Wesley's 'Come O My God the Promise Seal',[57] with its final verse beginning:

> Tis done! Thou dost this moment save,
> With full salvation bless;
> Redemption through thy blood I have,
> And spotless love and peace.

The official response of Wesleyan Methodism to the Palmers' visit was varied. In August 1860 the *WMM* reported approvingly of almost fourteen hundred names taken down at the Newcastle meetings, almost all of whom had been visited in their homes.[58] At the Wesleyan Conference that year, however, in a sermon preached by the President Samuel Waddy, concern was expressed at 'the damage which may be done to the position and usefulness of . . . ministers in having recourse to revival schemes.'[59] Such fears of undermining the pastoral office

---

[56] J. Fletcher, *A Third Check to Antinomianism: in a letter to the author of Pietas Oxoniensis* (Bristol, 1772), p. 45.

[57] Palmer, *Four Years*, p. 673; Wesley, *Collection of Hymns*, p. 396.

[58] *Scotland*, p. 125.

[59] S. D. Waddy, *Ministerial Support. London Conference, 1860. The substance of the official sermon and ordination charge [on Heb. 13 v17] of S.D.W.* (London, 1860), p. 7. Waddy (1804-1876; e.m. 1825) was not opposed to *revival* in and of itself. His presidential address concluded with the hope that 'the blessing of God will come down upon us, and this will be the year of the "Great Revival."' His opposition to revival 'schemes' likely reflected his adherence to Bunting's concept of the pastoral office, forged at Waddy's first attendance at Conference in

were seemingly not shared by the significant number of Wesleyan ministers who invited the Palmers to minister in their circuits and hosted them during their stay, and Phoebe and Walter were always scrupulous in ensuring that they never ministered anywhere without a formal invitation.

In 1862 the Wesleyan Conference issued a decree banning superintendents from allowing pulpit access to persons 'not amenable to our regular discipline.'[60] Whilst the inappropriateness of the preaching of women was not mentioned as such in the resolution, and the Palmers were not cited in the debate,[61] a familiar and thus-far fairly ineffective response from the Wesleyan authorities to revivalist visiting preachers was being offered. In reaction to the visit of Lorenzo Dow the famous question twenty at the Wesleyan Conference in Liverpool in 1807 was asked and in no uncertain terms answered:

> Q: Have our people been sufficiently cautious respecting the permission of strangers to preach to our congregations? A: We fear not: and we, therefore again direct, that no stranger, from America or elsewhere, be suffered to preach in any of our places, unless he come fully accredited; if an Itinerant Preacher, by having his name entered on the Minutes of the Conference of which he is a member; and if a Local Preacher, by a recommendatory note from his Superintendent.[62]

This minute had to be invoked again in 1847 regarding another American visiting preacher, James Caughey, but it did not prevent his frequent visits. Indeed, he was present in the UK a number of times during the Palmers' stay and Phoebe recorded the Palmers dining with him in Sheffield in September 1863 just

---

1829, at the height of the Leeds organ case. A. Waddy, *The Life of the Rev. Samuel D. Waddy* (London, 1878), pp. 82, 268.

[60] *Minutes* (1862), pp. 326-7.

[61] R. Carwardine, *Trans-Atlantic Revivalism: popular evangelicalism in Britain and America, 1790-1865* (Westport, CT, 1978), pp. 184-5.

[62] *Minutes*, vol 2, (1813), p. 403.

before their return to America, being fulsome in her praise: 'He is an apostle to many in this country. Hundreds, I am sure, claim him as their spiritual father.'[63] That the 1807 decision had to be restated once more in the 1862 prohibition, and plenty of Wesleyan pulpits remained opened to the Palmers until their departure in the autumn of 1863, implies that the view expressed by a correspondent to the *Revival* magazine that such a Conference decision could only be the act of 'a few mistaken persons' and 'not the voice of the body'[64] was a stubbornly held one by those Wesleyans open to the possibilities of revivalism.

Now equally as committed to connexional propriety as the Wesleyans and with their own revivalist origins in the visit of Lorenzo Dow seemingly a fading memory, [65] the 1862 PM Conference also directed 'station authorities to avoid the employment of revivalists, so called.'[66] Elsewhere it was a different story. The Methodist New Connexion had responded quickly to the arrival of Dow when at their Conference at Hanley in 1806 a resolution was passed stating 'that no person except the Circuit and planned Local Preachers, shall be allowed to preach in any of our societies, without first obtaining permission from the Circuit Preachers.'[67] However, the New Connexion's prohibition was rescinded at their Leeds Conference of 1807. For some the need to obtain permission from the circuit preachers had perhaps smacked too much of the Wesleyanism that they had left, and so less draconian guidance replaced it with the advice that: 'As it was designed solely to prevent improper and designing men from introducing themselves upon our Societies in consequence of the abolition of the law it is earnestly recommended to all our people to

---

[63] Palmer, *Four Years*, p. 693.
[64] Carwardine, *Trans-Atlantic Revivalism*, p. 185.
[65] Werner, *Primitive Methodist Connexion*, pp. 45-50.
[66] *PM Minutes* (London, 1862), p. 28.
[67] *MNC Minutes* (Hanley, 1806), p. 6.

consult with the preachers and leaders in any case which may appear doubtful.'[68]

This thus left it to local circuits to make their own mind up about revivalism, which ironically for a church with no culture of female preaching now gave Phoebe opportunities in New Connexion circuits which were, officially at least, closed to her in the parent body. There were also plenty of invitations forthcoming from the branches of the newly emerged Reform movement in the North and Midlands in the last fifteen months of the Palmers' stay in Britain. The Wesleyan Reform Union magazine reported that in Walsall 'Revival services were held in our new chapel, conducted by Dr. and Mrs. Palmer of America, which were attended with glorious success.'[69]

For Phoebe the delight of her visit to the town in February 1863 had been two-fold: tales of Wesley's treatment at the hands of the mob in 1743 had made it a place 'noted in my mind since childhood'.[70] She was also gratified that in the twenty-six days she spent at the Reformers' Whitmore Street chapel, opened the previous year with a visit from Caughey, 'all labouring as one in bringing the unsaved to Jesus, Wesleyan, New-Connection, Primitive and Free-Church Methodists, have mid-day and evening assembled.'[71] Occasionally on their tour of Britain Phoebe had recorded the support of other free churches in the work alongside Methodists, but the result of their final meetings held in Nottingham in June and July of 1863 yielded the widest harvest of all: 'a total of upwards of six hundred persons who have recorded their names, amongst whom are Wesleyans,

---

[68] *MNC Minutes* (Nottingham, 1807), p. 15.
[69] *The Wesleyan Reform Union Magazine*, vol 3, (London, 1863), 24.
[70] Palmer, *Four Years*, p. 630.
[71] Ibid., p. 632. Whilst at Ventnor on the Isle of Wight in the summer of 1860 Phoebe recorded being aware of a place of worship belonging to 'Bible Christians' but I have found no evidence she ever preached in any of their chapels whilst in Britain. Ibid., p. 298.

Nonconformists, Primitives, Independents, Baptists, Episcopalians, and even Roman Catholics.'[72]

When Phoebe died in 1874 aged sixty-six, she was probably the most famous Methodist woman of the nineteenth century. Yet she was soon all but forgotten, and her memory widely recovered only when Timothy L. Smith published his seminal book *Revivalism and Reform* in 1957.[73] Since then Phoebe's adaptations to the theology of entire sanctification have continued to be controversial and their dismissal by some Wesleyan theologians has contributed to her neglect,[74] along of course with her inconveniently being merely an untutored woman. However, the importance of her theology as the foundation for later developments are increasingly being recognized. Thomas Oden, for one, describes her as the 'missing link' between Methodist and Pentecostal theology and believes that she was one of the most important women theologians of all time.[75]

In the context of the focus of this volume, what is the legacy of Phoebe Palmer as a Methodist woman preacher in Britain? It would be hard to argue that her theological significance in her lifetime in the UK matched that of her influence in her native America, where amongst a growing interest in entire sanctification in the latter half of the nineteenth century 'Hers was likely the loudest voice, contributing most to the holiness movement and its future growth.'[76] In Britain as Bebbington has observed, there was 'a tendency in the later nineteenth century

---

[72] Palmer, *Four Years*, p. 684.

[73] Smith, *Revivalism and Social Reform*, p. 82.

[74] William J. Abraham, for example, admits to dismissing Phoebe as 'a minor, derivative nineteenth century theologian who at best had offered a crude oversimplification of the theology of John Wesley and early Methodism' until he encountered Elaine Heath's work — Heath, *Naked Faith*, ix.

[75] Palmer and Oden (ed.), *Phoebe Palmer*, p. 14.

[76] Davis, *Schleiermacher and Palmer*, p. 148.

to lose sight of the distinctive Methodist teaching of holiness altogether' illustrated by the fact that just three years after the Palmers' departure an article on holiness in *The MNC Magazine* showed no trace of the Wesleyan theological tradition whatsoever.[77]

This is not of course to say that Phoebe's ministry had no impact in the UK. Not to be dismissed is the experience of those who heard her and responded in her meetings. Using the figures quoted in *Four Years in the Old World,* Nigel Scotland has calculated that a total of 18,556 people were justified and 590 sanctified.[78] It has to be noted at this point that there were occasions when contemporary reports of Phoebe's impact were queried and not only by those opposed to revivalism: after their visit to Stroud in Gloucestershire in 1860 a correspondent to the *Revival* magazine claimed that the Palmers had exaggerated their success, a view which was endorsed by the editor who claimed that it was 'very possible that their perception of events may be highly tinged by their earnest desires, and that transient impressions may be taken for prominent results.'[79] For herself in *Four Years In The Old World* Phoebe was to claim 250 who received 'pardon or purity' at Stroud and with the benefit of hindsight she did not hesitate to include in the book alongside her successes more modest figures, such as the early meeting at Bowden where a response of only thirteen was disappointing. Nevertheless, in many places her ministry resulted in transformed lives and the addition of many new members to Methodist churches.

The most significant impact of Phoebe's British visit, though, had to do arguably with what we might now call 'the optics' of a husband and wife team ministering together. This can be highlighted by contrasting the Palmers' visit with another

---

[77] D. Bebbington, *Holiness in Nineteenth-Century England* (Carlisle, 2000), p. 67.

[78] *Scotland,* pp. 137-8.

[79] *Lloyd,* p. 179.

American female Methodist evangelist to have exercised an itinerant ministry in the UK in the 1840s, African American preacher and abolitionist Zilpha Elaw. Beginning in Ramsgate and Canterbury, in late 1840 Zilpha moved north to Pontefract in Yorkshire at the invitation of the Primitive Methodists. In February 1841 she was in Leeds, then Bradford and Hull, moving in August 1841 to Liverpool. She also preached in Manchester, Glossop and Stockport, Huddersfield and Newcastle where, although she remained in the area for over a year, she had a very different experience than that of the Palmers, described it as 'very barren and rocky soil to work upon; for the wickedness of the people is great.'[80]

There are many similarities between the two women. Like the Palmers, Zilpha ministered in Wesleyan, Primitive, New Connexion and Free Methodist chapels; like Phoebe she also faced opposition because of her sex,[81] being told by Liverpool North circuit superintendent minister John Davis that not only did the Wesleyans not allow women to preach but that 'there is nothing in the Scriptures that will allow for it.'[82] In a similar although in a less developed way to Phoebe, Zilpha's defence of female preaching draws on prophetic biblical imagery, notably the fulfilment in the book of Acts of Joel's prophecy (2.28-29) meaning that 'the Christian dispensation has for its main features the inspirations of the holy prophetic Spirit, descending on the handmaidens as well as on the servants of God.'[83]

---

[80] Z. Elaw, *Memoirs of the Life, . . . of Mrs. Zilpha Elaw* (London, 1846), p. 156.

[81] If, as seems probable, she experienced racism whilst in the UK, Zilpha chose not to emphasize it in her memoirs, instead claiming that her account was a spiritual one, focusing not on the 'features of my outward person' but on the 'lineaments of my inward man, as inscribed by the Holy Ghost' — ibid., p. 51.

[82] Ibid., p. 147. Davis e.m. 1802 and died 1852.

[83] Ibid., p. 124; the reference is to Acts 2:18 (KJV).

Unlike for Phoebe though, for Zilpha marriage meant not partnership but willing subjection; Zilpha had been widowed in 1823; her unbelieving husband Joseph had opposed her ministry and it is unlikely that she would have been able to follow her call to visit England had he lived. She wrote in her memoirs:

> The boastful speeches too often vented by young females against either the paternal yoke or the government of a husband, is both indecent and impious—conveying a wanton disrespect to the regulations of Scripture . . . That woman is dependent on and subject to man is the dictate of nature; that the man is not created for the woman, but the woman for the man, is that of Scripture. [84]

It is perhaps significant that after her second marriage to Ralph Shum in London in 1850 Zilpha's public ministry appears to have ceased.[85] In contrast, the Palmers' meetings modelled a very visible dynamic in which Walter played an important but clearly secondary role. Here a woman was in primary focus, even as a man, her husband, was also alongside her on the platform. Such an idea was hard for some to credit even on her rediscovery in the twentieth century—Smith underplayed Phoebe's role by reference to her 'testimony and prayer meetings . . . held in connection with her husband's campaigns.'[86] More recently, Lloyd has claimed that 'the form of their interdenominational meetings was designed to undercut any suggestion that Phoebe was taking the lead and doing anything more than exhorting.'[87] From both her writings and contemporary reports of her ministry though, it seems clear

---

[84] Ibid., p. 61.

[85] By the time of the Palmers' visit Zilpha had been widowed again and was living in Mile End, London where she was 'a class leader and most consistent member of the Wesleyan Society in the St George's circuit.' *Methodist Recorder* (12 September 1873); *Scotland*, p. 65.

[86] Smith, *Revivalism and Social Reform*, p. 82.

[87] *Lloyd*, p. 178. On 'exhorting' see also pp. 98-110, 118 in this volume.

that for Phoebe the public proclamation of the gospel was not 'an extraordinary call' upon her as a woman, or in Zilpha Elaw's phrase 'the extraordinary direction of the Holy Ghost, in reference to female evangelists',[88] but rather an expression of her argument in *Promise of the Father* that she had not only a *right* but a *responsibility* equally as Spirit-led and as irresistible as Walter's to publicly proclaim Jesus Christ. In *Promise of the Father* this is underlined by her admiration for the ministry of Mary Taft as 'fellow-helper' to Zechariah and her willingness to credit the influence of Mary Bosanquet Fletcher's praxis as a preacher over John Fletcher's inspiration as a theologian.

Phoebe's greatest legacy from her British tour is that a combination of the inspirational nature of the Palmers' partnership in ministry and opposition to her pre-eminent role led directly to a significant holiness movement beyond Methodism led by a wife and husband. The Rev. A. A. Rees, minister of the independent Bethesda Free Church in Sunderland, responded to the Palmers' visit to the North East by publishing a pamphlet *Reasons for Not Co-operating in the Alleged 'Sunderland Revivals'.*[89] Since Rees was to later play host to D. L. Moody, his objection was clearly not with revivals *per se*, but quoting Shakespeare and Milton,[90] as well as the apostle Paul, Rees argued that the idea that both Walter *and* Phoebe could have a public ministry in this revival was an anathema. Phoebe could not speak publicly, he contended, because for women 'their station in life demands modesty and humility, and they should be free of the ostentation of appearing so much in public as to take part in the public services of teaching and praying.'[91] Rees's pamphlet reached the manse of a New

---

[88] Elaw, *Memoirs*, p. 147.
[89] A. A. Rees, *Reasons for Not Co-operating in the Alleged 'Sunderland Revivals': in an address to his congregation* (Sunderland, 1859).
[90] Ibid., p. 5.
[91] Ibid., p. 9.

Connexion minister in nearby Gateshead, and his wife read it with fury.

Having long been a devotee of Phoebe's books the enraged ministerial spouse, Mrs Catherine Booth, wrote a rejoinder, *Female Teaching*. It was first published in December 1859.[92] She attended one of Palmers' meetings in the town in June 1860,[93] and in that year she began to speak publicly in her husband's church—initially as Phoebe did with Walter alongside her and then in his stead when he was unable to fulfil his appointments. Catherine Booth's defence of Phoebe's argument was rooted in Methodist theology—she quoted Adam Clarke directly in three places, including in a defence of female ministry that had the same moorings as the one offered by Zilpha Elaw, that 'according to the prediction of Joel, the Spirit of God was to be poured out on the women as well as the men, that they might prophesy, that is teach.'[94]

In 1861 Catherine sent a copy of her pamphlet on request to the editor of the *Wesleyan Times*, Dr James Stacey (1818-1891, e.m. 1839) who was also the Methodist New Connexion's President of Conference. Stacey's negative reply, which included his disparagement of her use of Clarke as an authority ('his reputation does not and cannot stand high'),[95] added to Catherine's already growing disillusionment with the New Connexion. Her disenchantment was shared by her husband William when his written request to Stacey for permission to become an itinerant evangelist for the New Connexion was denied at their 1861 Conference in Liverpool, leading to his

---

[92] C. M. Booth, *Female Teaching: or, the Rev. A. A. Rees versus Mrs Palmer, being a reply to a pamphlet by the above gentleman on the Sunderland revival* (London, 1861). The second edition is the earliest imprint known to have survived.
[93] *Scotland*, p. 133.
[94] Booth, *Female Teaching*, p. 10. This is a reference to Joel 2:28-9.
[95] F. St. G. de L. Booth-Tucker, *The Life of Catherine Booth* 2 vols (London, 1892), vol 1, p. 353.

resignation from its ministry. Catherine and William then began to exercise a similar ministry to the Palmers in Cornwall, invited by a New Connexion colleague and also preaching in Wesleyan chapels. It was at St Ives in late 1861 that Catherine received a letter from Phoebe. Replying with approval to the news that the Booths had left the New Connexion for an itinerant evangelistic ministry, Phoebe's letter reads in places like a Pauline epistle: 'We rejoice in what the Lord is doing by you. Glory be the Triune Deity! My faith grasps great blessings for you. I do not doubt but the Captains of the Armies of Israel will go out before you and permit you to see multitudes saved.'[96]

At this point the Palmers were in Liverpool and facing a large number of preaching commitments with Walter ill, Phoebe sought Catherine's help:

> My object in writing to you now is to ask whether your devoted husband and yourself will be able to come and take our place. I have sometimes thought that we might in some way be permitted to work into each other's hands and thus increase the revenue of praise to our Lord and make our union in heaven the sweeter.

As the Booths' ministry was beginning to grow in St Ives they were unable to join the Palmers in the North West, but the letter was a mark of the high regard the two women held each other in, and an example of Phoebe encouraging Catherine as a woman preacher and affirming the Palmers' own model of ministry that the Booths had begun to emulate. Whilst Phoebe may have been quickly forgotten in British Methodism, her memory lingered on for the Booths and their followers. In 1870 Catherine's pamphlet, still in print in revised form, became the theological foundation to sanction full authority in leadership to women in the Salvation Army, the movement that Catherine and William founded in 1865. As late as 1900 Phoebe's book

---

[96] Ibid., pp. 453-5; includes both quotations.

Entire Devotion to God was still being published in London by Salvationist Publishing and Supplies.[97]

Phoebe Palmer's preaching during her visit to Britain brought many onto what she described as 'the promised ground' of acceptance of God's pledge of full salvation. Although the influence of her reinterpretation of Wesleyan holiness theology may not have been lasting within British Methodism, that of her theory and praxis of female preaching upon Catherine Booth certainly was. Phoebe wrote to Catherine at St Ives in 1861: 'Doubtless the time hasteneth when truth, in relation to the gift of prophecy as entrusted to the daughters of the Lord Almighty, must triumph. Then, perhaps those who have endured the crucifying process as pioneers in this work will not be forgotten.'[98]

The continued role of women officers working alongside their male counterparts in 131 countries throughout the world in propagating the still-held doctrine of the Salvation Army that it is the privilege of all believers to be wholly sanctified, is, one suspects, a legacy with which Phoebe Palmer would be content.

---

[97] Palmer, *Entire Devotion to God* (London, 1990).
[98] Booth-Tucker, *Life of Catherine Booth*, vol 1, p. 454.

11: 'Survival of the Fittest': what led to the decline or 'extinction' of Primitive Methodist female preachers, 1807-1907?

Jill Barber

> In the early days of our denomination there were female itinerant preachers. They have become extinct as a class, through the operation of the law of the survival of the fittest.[1]

The fate of female preachers in the PM Connexion is a terrible warning that freedoms can be lost as well as won. At the start of the movement, not only were female preachers actively encouraged, but over one hundred women were appointed as itinerant preachers between 1813 and 1844.[2] Yet by the end of the century there was not one. Given that female preaching was such a distinctive feature of early Primitive Methodism, how did such a promising beginning go so badly wrong? Were women preachers, as William Bowe claims, intrinsically inferior to men, or is it, as Jennifer Lloyd perhaps provocatively suggests, that 'this is not a history of progress, but, like much of

---

[1] W. Bowe, 'The Position of Woman in the Church', fourth paper, in *PM Quarterly Review*, vol 7, (1885), 440.

[2] The origins of Primitive Methodism can be said to date from 1807, when the first camp meeting was organized at Mow Cop by Hugh Bourne. This grassroots movement spread rapidly from north Staffordshire across Britain. (The first missionaries, including the female preacher Ruth Watkins, arrived in America in 1829, but the Primitive Methodists struggled to survive, and separated from the British Conference in 1840). Excluded by the Wesleyans, the name 'Primitive Methodists' was first used in 1812, reflecting a choice to follow the earlier, purer form of Methodism started by John Wesley in 1739. In 1932, the Primitive Methodists united with the Wesleyans and United Methodists to become The Methodist Church in Britain.

women's history, of doors opening and closing according to men's needs and concerns'.[3]

While 'survival of the fittest' was used above to refer to itinerant preachers, this was part of a wider debate at the time (1885) about the role of women in the church, specifically with regard to the 'propriety' of women preaching. In the official record, the 'extinction' of female itinerant preachers can be dated to 1862, when Elizabeth Bultitude retired after thirty years in ministry, but this needs to be considered alongside the decline in women exercising their call to preach in other ways, such as local preachers. In 1907, when a question was asked about the current situation, the answer was, 'We have a few women's names still on the plans, but they are mostly "mothers in Israel" who have long ceased to preach. It is rarely indeed that we have put a young sister on the plan.'[4] Female preaching will be considered here in its widest sense, as Primitive Methodism was a largely working-class movement led by lay people and, as we shall see, the distinction between itinerant and local preachers was very fluid, for both men and women.[5]

The aim of this chapter is to look at the reasons for the decline, if not 'extinction', of PM female preachers by 1907, and the barriers they faced. Key factors will be examined, which have been identified as helping to create or develop a 'hostile environment' for women preachers. These cover the impact of internal changes, such as the movement from open air worship

---

[3] *Lloyd*, p. 2.

[4] H. B. Jeffs, 'Our Women and the Centenary', in *Primitive Methodist Leader* (28 February 1907), 1.

[5] 'In view of the missionary nature of Primitive Methodism it is interesting to note that anyone possessing any speaking ability was soon pressed into service first as a local preacher and then as an itinerant. The call to preach sometimes came from an overwhelming conviction of the young woman herself, sometimes because of a need for someone to minister in the local situation and sometimes because the church authorities simply 'put her on the plan'.' See Graham, 'Chosen by God' (1993), 82.

to chapel building, increasing governance, and the desire for upward social mobility and respectability. Then we will look at cultural factors which affected women, such as the pressures of marriage and motherhood, expectations of a woman's place, and Victorian values and attitudes towards the 'weaker sex' which led to a reduction in self-confidence.

Finally we will see how these were compounded by the church through its use of scripture, a perceived conflict between religion and politics, and the way it engaged with social justice and women's rights. Against this backdrop, the extent to which women, including female itinerant preachers, were able to overcome these barriers, or 'go under the radar', will be assessed. To set this in context, there will be an overview of what happened after 1907. In conclusion, we will review causes for the decline of female preaching and ask what lessons can be learnt from the past.

The decline in female preaching: from mission to maintenance

Firstly, the decline of female preaching in Primitive Methodism shows a strong correlation with the move from mission to maintenance, from evangelism to chapel building, which took place from the 1850s, after the deaths of the founders.[6] As missionaries, speaking in cottages or the open air, women proved hugely successful. They had a curiosity value, drawing large crowds who flocked to see this unique spectacle, especially as the preachers were mostly young women.[7] For example, George Herod recalled going to hear Sarah Kirkland at East Bridgford, near Nottingham, in 1817:

> We remember a young woman's invitation to go and hear a
> little woman called a Ranter preach . . . Curiosity led us to the

---

[6] William Clowes died in 1851, and Hugh Bourne died in 1852.

[7] E. D. Graham, 'Female itinerants of early Primitive Methodism, with special reference to those stationed in missionary situations' (2005). http://www.methodistheritage.org.uk/missionary-history-graham-female-itinerants-2005.pdf (accessed 10 June 2020).

place. Her chapel was a barn, and she had an old gig for a pulpit. When we reached the place it was crowded with people, but with much ado we got within the walls; however, it was impossible to get a sight of the preacheress; but at last we observed two poles reared against the principal beam; we immediately climbed them, and took our seat on the beam, where we had a full view of all that was passing.[8]

As preaching moved from the open air into chapels, the focus was on ministering to the converted rather than making new converts, and female evangelists became increasingly seen as surplus to requirements.[9] Building projects were male preserves, and then there was the question of manses. Once chapels were built, the next step was housing for the ministers. While it was acceptable for a female itinerant preacher to lodge with a local family, it was quite a different matter for her to become a householder, especially if she was young and single.

Along with the chapel building, Methodism began to change from a movement to an institution, with a greater emphasis on rules and regulations.[10] Emma Quarton, a lace maker from Nottingham, was twenty-one when she became a PM travelling preacher in 1841, but it was to be a short-lived appointment. It appears that Emma soon fell foul of the circuit authorities, and the following year she 'disappears' from the stations. So what went wrong? The minutes of the circuit meeting in Preston Brook, Cheshire, record the following:

> In our judgement Sister [Quarton] does not conform to rule in plainness of dress, with regard to her cap, watch guard[11] and bag, and we request her to conform in future.

---

[8] Herod, *Biographical Sketches*, p. 320. The Primitive Methodists were also known as 'Ranters' because of their enthusiastic style.

[9] Valenze, *Prophetic Sons and Daughters*, pp. 11, 274-8. The greatest period of chapel building was 1850-79.

[10] This change was codified in 1903, when the PM Connexion changed its name to the PM Church.

[11] This was a ribbon used to attach a watch to a dress.

Resolved that T. King speak to E. Quarton respecting her superfluous dress, and the necessity of keeping her promises and that if she do not improve she go home.

It seems that Emma did not conform, so she went home. We do not know what it was about Emma's 'superfluous' dress the circuit leaders took such exception to, but perhaps there was too much lace.[12]

By 1885, in an increasing desire for acceptance by more established churches, the Primitive Methodists were looking to the Wesleyans for their rules: 'Our Wesleyan friends adopt the best course. They neither forbid nor encourage female preaching, but make the conditions for admissions into their pulpits so stringent that only women of unquestionable piety and talent can expect to occupy that position.'[13]

Significantly, while women were allowed to preach, they were not given any place in church governance, so the rules were universally decided by men. It was not until 1899 that the formidable Mary Bulmer became the first woman delegate to the PM Conference.[14] The extent to which men developed a stranglehold on leadership and decision making, which effectively silenced women, is highlighted in some fascinating correspondence around the PM centenary in 1907. The connexional planning committee consisted of one hundred

---

[12] E. D. Graham, *Chosen by God: a list of the female travelling preachers of early Primitive Methodism* (Broxton, 1989), p. 19. J. Barber, 'More Hidden Voices: Ann Hirst and Emma Quarton' in *The Ranters' Digest*, vol 19, (2019), 20-4. Emma Quarton was stationed by the PM Conference who met in June 1841 to go to Prees Green, but it is unclear if she actually went, and she then 'disappears' from the stations. She returned to her home town, where she worked as a lace mender in Broad Marsh, one of the poorest areas of Nottingham.

[13] T. Parsons, 'The Position of Woman in the Church', fifth paper, in *PM Quarterly Review*, vol 7, (1885), 682.

[14] E. D. Graham, 'Two Primitive Women Preachers' in *PWHS*, vol 56, (2007), 54.

members, all men. The list of preachers invited to participate in the celebratory camp meeting, included not a single woman, despite the fact that female preachers played such a significant role in the genesis of the movement.[15]

Class and respectability

Another factor which served to silence women was the growing 'respectability' of the Primitive Methodists, as they moved away from their roots and became effectively middle class. The exclusion of women was justified on the grounds that the question of women in relation to public preaching 'is not one of inferiority, but of propriety'.[16] In the wonderful set of magic lantern slides taken at the Centenary Camp Meeting in 1907 it is astonishing to see the PM preachers wearing top hats.[17]

In their desire for respectability, the Primitive Methodists were only following the path already travelled by the Wesleyans. In the 1820s, the Wesleyans were naming their new chapels Brunswick and Hanover after the royal family, keen to dispel fears that Methodists were republicans. At a time when Methodists increasingly wanted to show their loyalty to the government, female preaching could be disruptive.[18] A letter to the *Bath Chronicle* in 1828 voiced outrage about a woman preacher at a camp meeting on Combe Down, calling her words 'perverted' and 'debased', and her practice of holding up her hands 'degrading, common place' and 'vulgar'.[19]

---

[15] H. B. Jeffs, 'Our Women and the Centenary' in *PM Leader* (28 February 1907), 1; letters re 'Our Women and the Centenary' in *PM Leader* (7 March 1907), 147.

[16] J. Macpherson, 'The Position of Woman in the Church', first paper, in *PM Quarterly Review*, vol 7, (1885), 239.

[17] A set of these slides is in the collection at Englesea Brook Museum of Primitive Methodism.

[18] *Lloyd*, p. 6.

[19] *Bath Chronicle* (5 June 1828). Camp meetings which gathered large crowds were seen as a threat to law and order. Women preachers

Women's passion for preaching the gospel was no longer seen as an asset, but was turned against them. One PM minister claimed in 1885, 'No doubt the crass ignorance, the vulgar zeal, the unseeming boldness exhibited by some women preachers of late have pained many pious souls, and have led them to denounce the whole thing.'[20] Part of the problem was education, or a lack of it.[21] As Primitive Methodism became more conformist and respectable the status of the travelling preacher was raised. In the early years evangelism and saving souls were considered more important than a formal education. For example, when ministerial training was first proposed there was opposition from the Cambridge circuit, on the grounds that 'what they would gain in Light they would lose in Heat.'[22] However, as demand for more educated ministers increased, in 1865 the first training scheme for ministers was set up at Elmfield College in York. It was only for men.

Marriage and children

In the early days of the movement, female preachers were young and predominantly single.[23] Marriage became another

---

were particularly subversive because they were not 'respectable' and threatened the status quo.

[20] Parsons, 'Position of Woman', 682.

[21] According to her son, Rebecca Brining (1803-66) could not write. As Rebecca Tims she was a female itinerant preacher, reverting to local preacher status after her marriage. *PMM*, vol 47, (1866), 427.

[22] R. Dolman, 'Rough Informal Energy: The story of Primitive Methodism', a talk given at Castle Street Methodist Church, Cambridge (31 May 2007). https://www.castlestreet.org.uk/rough-informal-energy-the-story-of-primitive-methodism/ (accessed 20 June 2020).

[23] Obituaries in the *PMM* show that some girls started preaching as young as thirteen or fourteen. Elizabeth Elliot of Oswestry was only fifteen when she drowned on her way to take a preaching appointment. https://www.myprimitivemethodists.org.uk/content/people-2/lay-

barrier to female preaching, particularly after 1827 when the PM Conference passed a resolution that married women should not preach in circuits other than where their husband resided. Mary Porteous was a notable exception, gaining a special exemption as her husband was a seaman.[24] It is no coincidence that the peak in numbers of itinerant female preachers was in the year before this resolution was passed. This meant that women were forced to retire when they got married, and no longer able to travel as itinerant preachers. By the end of the nineteenth century, attitudes had hardened against married women having any preaching role at all, even as local preachers. Robert Bryant, a PM minister, made a distinction between unmarried and married women claiming that, it is *wives* rather than *women* who are told by Paul to be silent in church.[25]

Children were another barrier to female preaching. It has been estimated that in 1818, one in five PM preachers was a woman.[26] They were mostly single, with an average age of about twenty. Once women were married, they could find themselves either pregnant or giving birth for the next twenty years, so how did they manage to preach at all? Hannah Scofield of Chesterfield (1806-1837) was converted at the age of fourteen and soon put on the plan. As well as being a local preacher, she was a class leader, led prayer meetings, visited the sick and gave hospitality to visiting preachers, as well as being an exemplary wife and mother. What makes Hannah's story incredible is that she did

---

people/surnames-beginning-with-e/elizabeth_elliot_1810-25_of_oswestry (accessed 11 June 2020).

[24] J. Lightfoot, *The Power of Faith and Prayer exemplified in the Life and Labours of Mary Porteus* (London, 1862).
https://www.myprimitivemethodists.org.uk/content/people-2/primitive_methodist_ministers/p/mary_porteous_nee_thompson (accessed 20 June 2020).

[25] R. Bryant, 'The Position of Woman in the Church', third paper, in *PM Quarterly Review*, vol 7, (1885), 431.

[26] Werner, *Primitive Methodist Connexion*, p. 142.

all this with four young children, and when she died, the day after giving birth to her fifth child, she was still only thirty-one.[27]

The story of Mary Lee, in the 1840s, illustrates the pressures that women faced, and their male counterparts did not. Mary was called to preach, but her husband was also a preacher. With a large family, on a Sunday Mary would take the three youngest children with her, often walking eight or nine miles to her appointment. During the hymn before the sermon, Mary would sit in the pulpit and breastfeed the baby, so that it would sleep through the sermon. The congregation found the sight of Mary cradling her baby in her arms 'as she prayed that the Everlasting Arms might enfold the babes in Christ', a wonderful illustration of God's love for them.[28] As the century advanced, and perhaps Victorian sensibilities became more important than hearing the gospel, babies in the pulpit became unacceptable, effectively barring many younger women from preaching.

'Angel in the house'

As the PM church became more conscious of how it was seen by the outside world, and more anxious to conform, its male leaders became heavily influenced by changing cultural attitudes to women in contemporary society. The term 'Angel in the house' was first coined in a poem by Coventry Patmore, published in 1854, and became a well-known description for the expected role of a woman in the late Victorian period. It defined the ideal of womanhood, the perfect wife and mother. The poem contained the lines, 'Man must be pleased; but him to please is woman's pleasure.'[29] Two years later, in a lecture on 'Woman, Her Position and Mission', William Antliff used words that are uncannily similar. 'Man loves woman for his own sake rather

---

[27] Obituary, *PMM*, New Series, vol 8, (1838), 253-7.

[28] W. M. Patterson, *Behind the Stars* (Queensland, 1974); first published in *PM Leader* (1911).

[29]

https://en.wikipedia.org/wiki/The_Angel_in_the_House#The_poem (accessed 11 June 2020).

than hers; she loves him more for his sake than her own.'[30] As PM editor, President of Conference, and Principal of the Sunderland Institute, William Antliff was hugely influential in the church. He emphasized that women's education should be, 'for the sphere they will have to fill'. Woman's role was that of 'helpmeet' and should be one of self-sacrifice.[31]

Articles in the connexional magazines focused on a woman's place, upholding the principle that God had ordained women and men to occupy 'separate spheres'. Just as a woman's province was the home, in the outside world her sphere was also confined to the domestic, presiding at bazaars and tea meetings. The highest accolade for Hannah Bowe, a lifelong Methodist, was that 'her knitting needles were truly consecrated'![32]

In 1885, the Primitive Methodists held a symposium on 'The Position of Woman in the Church'. All six papers were written by men, and they were all ministers. In answer to the question, 'What then becomes of the abnormal unity claimed in relation to female preaching?' James Macpherson declared that apostle, prophet and teacher are masculine nouns in the Greek, while helper is a feminine noun, hence woman's role.[33] Another contributor, Thomas Greenfield, allowed that while a woman's role should be restricted to teaching women and children, 'they may also convey valuable lessons to men in covert style by oblique and unobtrusive hints'![34]

---

[30] W. Antliff, *Woman: her position and mission* (London, 1856).

[31] https://www.myprimitivemethodists.org.uk/content/people 2/primitive_methodist_ministers/a-2/william_antliff_dd (accessed 13 June 2020).

[32] Obituary of William Bowe in *PM Minutes* (1913), p. 16.

[33] Macpherson, 'The Position of Woman in the Church', 234. For Macpherson see *DMBI*.

[34] T. Greenfield, 'The Position of Woman in the Church', second paper, in *PM Quarterly Review*, vol 7, (1885), 244.

Survival of the fittest

Charles Darwin, who published his *Origin of Species* in 1859, can also be seen as a contributor to the decline of female preaching, as his theory of evolution was used to justify the exclusion of women on the grounds that they were constitutionally weaker, and unsuited to the rigours of preaching. It is true that the health of many of the early women itinerant preachers broke down under the strain, but this was also true of men. The fact that the itinerancy of many female preachers was short-lived was used against them, but an analysis of the early preachers identified by Dorothy Graham points to marriage rather than illness as the more likely reason for their 'disappearance' from the stations.[35]

Elizabeth Bultitude used her own example to stress that women could withstand the rigours of itinerancy. 'In all the thirty years I only missed two appointments, one when there was a flooding rain and the other, a heavy thunderstorm; and being planned out of doors, I did not think it wise to go. I have walked thousands upon thousands of miles during the thirty years. I have visited from ten to forty families in a day and prayed with them. I have preached five and six times in the week and three and sometimes five times on the Sabbath.'[36]

Viewing women as the 'weaker sex' was nothing new. In his 'Vindication of Female Preaching' (1823), the BC William O'Bryan said this in their defence:

> Some have said women have not so strong intellectual powers as men have. Perhaps, in general they have not. But some women have minds as well informed as the generality of men,

---

[35] Figures show that slightly more women than men retired from the ministry on the grounds of ill health, but it seems that the Connexion also used this as an excuse to phase out female itinerant preachers in the move towards respectability. E. D. Graham, 'Chosen by God: the female itinerants of early Primitive Methodism', University of Birmingham PhD thesis, 1986, p. 175.

[36] *PMM*, vol 72, (1891), 564-5.

witness queen Elizabeth . . . Has every man who is called to preach, natural abilities sufficient to govern a kingdom?[37]

To survive, female preachers had to prove, not just that they were as good as men, but that they were better. Hannah Maria Knowles was described as having 'a mind of unusual strength'. In 1832, on a mission in Ohio, she travelled two hundred miles in a wagon with a sick baby. Her preaching caused such a sensation that 'the word ran like fire among dry stubble'. A local newspaper said that comparing Hannah's preaching to that of the most brilliant male preachers (such as Lorenzo Dow) must stop the mouths of those who try to use scripture to say that women should not preach the gospel.[38]

Use of scripture

Scripture has been used throughout history to justify personal and cultural prejudice, and it was a key weapon in the arsenal of those who fought to extinguish female preaching. As H. B. Kendall, the PM historian, memorably said in 1907, 'With an eye on woman preaching, the texts were beaten and pounded incessantly, like the tins and kettles which were clashed to drown the preacher's voice at a camp meeting.'[39]

For Hugh Bourne, and John Wesley, scripture had to be balanced with experience. If the converting work of the Spirit was in evidence, then the preaching was of God, whether the preacher was male or female.[40] Hugh Bourne was once asked in Glasgow, 'You allow women to preach in your churches! How

---

[37] *Lloyd*, p. 76.

[38] J. Barber, 'Hidden Voices: Hannah Maria Knowles, "A Mind of Unusual Strength"' in *The Ranters' Digest*, vol 18, (2018), 16-23. She had been an itinerant preacher from 1825 as Hannah Maria Shatford before she married William Knowles. The couple went as PM missionaries to America in 1829.

[39] H. B. Kendall, 'The Old Wells and the New' in *PM Leader* (24 January 1907), 1.

[40] Graham, 'Chosen by God' (1993), 78.

do you reconcile this with St Paul's statement on the question?' To this came the prompt reply:

> The men have monopolised the preaching for upwards of eighteen centuries, and you must admit that on the whole they have made very badly out; and suppose now you permit the women to try and see if they cannot do better than the men have done. At any rate, God owns them in the converting work, so we had better not interfere with them.[41]

In 1802, when the Irish Conference passed a resolution banning women from preaching, it was on the grounds that 'it is contrary both to Scripture and prudence that women should preach'. The Wesleyan, Zechariah Taft, wrote his defence of female preaching in the same year. He began by citing 1 Corinthians 1:27 (in the KJV): 'But God hath chosen the foolish things of the world to confound the wise, and God hath chosen the weak things of the world to confound the things which are mighty.'[42] Unwise, perhaps, as it fed into the argument that women were weak and foolish. It was a text that both Hugh Bourne and William O'Bryan avoided, choosing instead to focus on Acts 2:17, 'Your sons and your daughters shall prophesy' (KJV). However, as the century progressed, it was Paul's words that were used to beat women into submission: 'Let your women keep silence in the churches: for it is not permitted unto them to speak' (1 Corinthians 14:34, KJV).

Lack of self confidence

In the early years of Methodism, women had the courage to defy convention and rebel against the rules. Women like Ann Carr, who left the Primitive Methodists to form her own Women's Church in Leeds when male leaders tried to control what she was doing, and Elizabeth Evans who left the

---

[41] Kendall, 'The Old Wells and the New', 1. John Lenton (p. 92) and Eryn White (p. 99) also discuss the compatibility of women preaching with St Paul's recorded views.
[42] *Lloyd*, pp. 48-50.

Wesleyans in 1832 to join the Arminian Methodists in Derbyshire, when her name on the preaching plan was replaced with an asterisk.[43] However, as the nineteenth century progressed, the constant message that female preachers were unfit, unscriptural and brought the church into disrepute, took its toll. Lack of self-confidence led many women to accept that their role was not in the pulpit but pouring tea.[44]

Female preachers had always been subject to self-doubt. Hugh Bourne had even used women's reluctance as a sign of their call to preach. Mary Porteous was so conscious of her 'weak abilities', that when she took her first service she had a panic attack in the pulpit and thought she would fall over the edge. She thought she could not go on and preach, but she announced a hymn and prayed hard, and went on to become a preacher who, according to Kendall, when compared with her male colleagues in the Ripon circuit in 1828-30, 'did not come behind any of them in piety and zeal, and she excelled most of them in preaching power'.[45]

Lack of self-confidence was seen as a virtue in women, as it kept them humble, and they were much less likely to challenge the male leadership. Rebecca Brining was praised because, 'in church affairs she knew her place and kept it. She sowed no seeds of discord'.[46] It was said approvingly of Hannah Scofield that when asked to preach 'she felt reluctance', and 'in the pulpit she always appeared with great timidity.'[47] Women preachers were also subject to far more scrutiny than men. Accounts of female preaching usually concentrated on how they looked and spoke, not what they said. It was said of Elizabeth Swinton that

---

[43] Milburn and Batty (eds), *Workaday Preachers*, p. 170; *Lloyd*, p. 102.
[44] 'Mother in Israel' was a term of approval used for PM women, usually indicating their role in providing hospitality for visiting preachers, or running bazaars.
[45] Lightfoot, *Power of Faith and Prayer*.
[46] Obituary of Mrs Brining in *PMM*, vol 47, (1866), 427.
[47] Obituary of Hannah Scofield, *PMM*, vol 19, (1838), 253-7.

many were induced 'to come and hear her, or rather see her, wherever she preached', because of 'the singularity of her dress and appearance'.[48]

A letter from Wilfrid Callin, a PM chaplain in World War One, to his sister Eva in Douglas, in the Isle of Man, shows how little confidence women had in taking on leadership positions when the absence of men forced churches to turn to women to fill the gaps. Callin writes encouragingly from the trenches, 'With regard to the Primary Superintendency, I am in favour of you taking it on . . . and I know you can do it as well as, or better than, anybody else there'. However, he cannot resist a reminder that she belongs to the weaker sex, 'so long as you are well'.[49]

Women's lack of self-confidence also stemmed from the fact that as time went on, the stories of the early female preachers were not just forgotten, but deliberately erased from connexional histories, robbing them of role models. In his *History of the Primitive Methodists* (1823), Hugh Bourne gives an account of an incident in Huddersfield in 1820, when Susannah Perry and William Taylor were arrested and thrown into prison for preaching in the market place. When John Petty rewrote the PM connexional history in 1860, he removed Susannah's name from the account, replacing it with William Taylor and 'another'. In his account of their trial he describes them as William Taylor and 'a fellow colleague', implying that both preachers were male.[50]

Social justice

The final factor which I believe contributed to the decline of female preaching relates to the increasing failure of the church to engage in politics and social justice, particularly with

---

[48] Obituary, *PMM*, vol 34, (1853), 444-6.

[49] Englesea Brook Museum, Callin Papers, letter from R. W. Callin to E. Callin, 7 May 1918.

[50] J. Petty, *The History of the Primitive Methodist Connexion* (London, 1860).

women's rights. In her study, Valenze highlighted the impact that the move from cottage preaching to chapels had on women's issues, meaning that 'the grievances of women and their families no longer reached the pulpit'.[51] Hugh Bourne, who famously ejected a member from the PM Conference in 1821 for being 'a speeching radical', saw politics as a distraction from the work of saving souls.[52]

This was a separation of religion and politics, which began in the opening years of the century, with the Wesleyan obsession to be seen as loyal citizens, who posed no threat to the establishment or the status quo. Dorothy Ripley (1767-1831) was born in Whitby, where her father was a local preacher, and she met both John Wesley and Sarah Crosby who stayed in her home.[53] When she was a girl, she encountered a woman being abused by a group of sailors, which gave Dorothy a lifelong passion to help the oppressed, particularly women. But by the time she felt God was calling her to preach, Wesleyan attitudes to female preachers were hardening. When Dorothy told the church that God was calling her to go to America to preach freedom from slavery, she was met with blank refusal.[54]

Without the support of the church, Dorothy became an independent evangelist. Not only did she get to America, but she became the first woman to preach to Congress in the newly

---

[51] Valenze, *Prophetic Sons and Daughters*, p. 11.

[52] J. M. Turner, 'Methodism in England 1900-1932' in Davies, George and Rupp (eds), *History of Methodism in Great Britain*, vol 3 (1983), p. 330. Turner notes that although many individual Primitive Methodists were active in politics, the official pronouncements of the Church tended to the pietistic.

[53] Sarah Crosby visited Whitby in 1774 and 1775. *Chilcote, 1991*, pp. 153-4.

[54] D. Ripley, *The Extraordinary Conversion and Religious Experience of Dorothy Ripley* (New York, 1810); Ripley, *The Bank of Faith and Works United* (New York, 1819); 'Dorothy Ripley (1767-1832) Believe it or Not', https://personalpedia.wordpress.com/2008/06/10/dorothy-ripley-1767-1832-believe-it-or-not/ (accessed 10 June 2020).

built Hall of Representatives. Seeing herself first as an evangelist, she took the gospel into the strongholds of slavery, and published the terrible conditions she witnessed, including the story of Rosa an enslaved girl she befriended. She even took up the cause of the native Americans, living alongside them, and preaching wherever she could.[55] In 1818, when the American evangelist Lorenzo Dow arrived in Liverpool to take part in a PM mission, Hugh Bourne was most unhappy to find that Dorothy had come with him, but she went on to preach at the opening of the first Primitive Methodist chapel in Nottinghamshire, at Bingham, to huge crowds.[56] But despite, or perhaps because of, speaking out against injustice wherever she found it, this remarkable woman was never recognized as a preacher by the church into which she was born.[57]

Methodism in the eighteenth century was at the forefront of a new movement for social justice. John Wesley set up the first free medical dispensary in London in 1746, and published one of the earliest anti-slavery tracts in 1774. In the first half of the nineteenth century PM local preachers became the first trade union leaders, campaigning for better wages and working conditions for miners and farm labourers. They led the Chartist movement, fighting for suffrage for all (men). However, by the end of the nineteenth century, Primitive Methodism was

---

[55] E. A. Everson, '"A Little Labour of Love": The Extraordinary Career of Dorothy Ripley, Female Evangelist in Early America', Georgia State University PhD dissertation, 2007; L. C. Warner, *Saving Women: retrieving evangelistic theory and practice* (Waco, TX, 2007).
[56] J. Walford, *Memoirs of the Life and Labours of Hugh Bourne* (London, 1856; reprinted Stoke-on-Trent, 2002) vol 2, pp. 44, 48. Walford thought Bourne was 'dissatisfied' with Lorenzo Dow for allowing Dorothy Ripley to travel alone with him, as it might cause scandal for the Primitive Methodists. Women preachers were not allowed to travel with male preachers to appointments to avoid accusations of impropriety, but this put women at increased risk.
[57] Herod, *Biographical Sketches*, p. 188; W. Clowes, *The Journals of William Clowes* (London, 1844), p. 191.

lagging behind social change rather than leading it, particularly in the area of women's rights.[58] As an article in the *PM Leader* stated, 'We may be Radical in our politics, although even there we look askance at the suffragette, but the last thing we have any intention of doing is to confer the denominational franchise on our women.'[59]

Another PM minister wrote, 'The tendency of the age is unquestionably in the *direction* of equality'. But it seems the church could only go so far, as woman was still tainted with the sin of Eve. 'The elevation of woman . . . means the lifting her from the servile, secluded, abject position to which sin and slavery had sunk her, into a position that approaches *more nearly* to an equality with man.'[60] 'Frances', writing in the *Primitive Methodist Leader*, complained that young PM women were leaving the Connexion for other organizations, such as the Salvation Army, because they were afforded a wider role there—not relegated to arranging weekly teas and bazaars.[61]

This was a huge missed opportunity. Women, denied the opportunity to have their voice heard in the Church, voted with

---

[58] Primitive Methodism was obsessed with pietistic morality e.g. temperance and Sabbath observance, rather than human rights. M. Johnson, 'The National Politics and Politicians of Primitive Methodism: 1886-1922', University of Hull PhD thesis, 2016, pp. 33-34, 148. Connexional publications remained silent regarding women's suffrage. None of the PM MPs openly opposed women's suffrage. But support was really for full adult suffrage. Although extending the vote to women householders was sometimes promoted as an initial concession, it was preferred that women received the vote within the context of universal adult suffrage. The militant suffragettes' tactics were condemned by most because of their use of violence. https://hydra.hull.ac.uk/assets/hull:15456a/content (accessed 11 June 2020).

[59] Jeffs, 'Our Women and the Centenary', 1.

[60] Bryant, 'The Position of Woman in the Church', 425.

[61] *PM Leader* (14 February 1907), 98.

their feet. Ethel Annakin (1881-1951) was born into a leading PM family in Harrogate. After leaving home to train as a teacher, she joined the emerging Labour Church in Liverpool, finding an inclusive church with a heart for the poor, committed to equality and social justice. She became increasingly active in supporting women's suffrage, and was in great demand as a speaker. In 1905, she lectured in south Wales on socialism and women's suffrage, and the following year became one of the national speakers for the National Union of Women's Suffrage Societies, speaking at as many as two hundred public meetings a year. She later organized the Women's Peace Crusade, speaking to half a million people in the last year of the war.[62] Although Ethel did address the PM Conference in 1927, the Church failed to appreciate, or make use of her outstanding gifts as a speaker, and her passion for campaigning. William Younger, a future President of the PM Conference, acknowledged this loss, saying in 1913:

> Mrs Philip Snowden, is one of the most remarkable women of this generation. She is now in great demand at all meetings of national significance, and has become famous in the United States. It is amazing that Primitive Methodists all over the country do not see the value of her services, and secure her for great gatherings, where she could represent the church of her girlhood with distinction.[63]

Decline or extinction?

We began with the contention that female preachers became extinct during the nineteenth century, but was it true? Although the PM Conference never made an active decision to stop employing women as ministers, no women were accepted after

---

[62] https://www.myprimitivemethodists.org.uk/content/people-2/lay-people/surnames-beginning-with-s/snowden-ethel-nee-annakin-1881-1951 (accessed 12 June 2020).

[63] W. Younger, *Christian Messenger* (1913), 53. Ethel Annakin married Philip Snowden in 1905. He became Chancellor of the Exchequer in 1924.

1844, and the last woman in active ministry, Elizabeth Bultitude, retired in 1862 after thirty years in ministry. However, many women who felt a call to ministry found ways to go under the radar, and continue to exercise their gifts as preachers, especially in the first half of the nineteenth century.

Sarah Kirkland, the first PM female travelling preacher, no longer appears on the stations after her marriage to fellow preacher John Harrison, in 1818. However, in practice they continued to exercise a joint ministry in Hull, as John records in his Journal, 'We separated, that we might be more useful, and by so doing we succeeded in opening two places each night.'[64] As young people thrown together in testing circumstances, it is not surprising that many female itinerant preachers married their male colleagues. In fact, Bible Christians were actively encouraged to do so, recognizing that this was a way for the church to benefit from the gifts of the women preachers without having to pay for them. This enabled many of the early female itinerant preachers to continue their ministry after marriage, although not only was their contribution unacknowledged, but it was exercised entirely in their husband's name.

For example, William Knowles and Ruth Watkins were the first PM missionaries who went to America in 1829. With them, but unnamed, was William's wife Hannah. As a married woman Hannah was invisible, but as a single woman she had been an itinerant preacher and met William when they were both stationed in the Isle of Man.[65] Hannah disappears from the record, but to William's credit, in his Journal he makes it clear that she was by far the more successful preacher. When Hannah preached at Eaton, Ohio, 'while she was speaking, the power of God came down in such a manner, that every man, woman and

---

[64] *PMM*, vol 62, (1881), 292. See also pp. 105-6 for a similar system amongst the Bible Christians.

[65] In Leary's *Ministers and Circuits*, she appears as 'H. Shatford', assumed to be male, and in 1827 (the year she married) is marked 'disappears'.

child, sprang at one moment from their seats.' Whereas when William preached he 'did not see anything uncommon among the people'.[66]

Ministers' wives were often expected to be unpaid curates, and this could involve unauthorized preaching. Ann Howson (1809-92) was locked in her room by her Quaker family to prevent her marriage to an impoverished PM minister, John Hirst. After a dramatic escape and flight to Leeds, they were married by special licence in 1831. During their first winter, John was caught in a snowstorm and could not get home. Rather than abandon the service, Ann decided to read a sermon, and then began to speak herself. Her words were so inspiring that there were immediately demands for her to be put on the plan as a preacher, a calling she fulfilled for over sixty years. When John was appointed to the Belper circuit in 1852, members complained to their representative on the stationing committee, 'You have accepted a travelling preacher with nine children'! 'Yes', was the reply, 'but I have got you two travelling preachers'.[67]

Another outlet for women was to become hired local preachers, who in practice were no different from travelling preachers, but were employed by a circuit or district rather than Conference and so had less security. Ann Tinsley was a PM travelling preacher who moved in and out of ministry depending on her marital status. In 1828 at the age of nineteen, she was stationed as an itinerant preacher in a lead mining area. Here she met John Longmire, but on marrying him she had to retire. By 1837, Ann found herself a widow with a young child, and was employed by the Scotter circuit as a hired local preacher, with a salary plus an allowance for her child. When she married again (twice) her

---

[66] 'American Mission, 1831: Journal of W. Knowles, 1831' in *PMM*, vol 13, (1832), 91-6, 135-8.

[67] Barber, 'More Hidden Voices'.

husbands were both itinerant preachers, which enabled her to pursue a joint ministry, albeit in their name not her own.[68]

Other women, while 'extinct' in the official record, made a career for themselves as special preachers. Emma Quarton, summarily dismissed as an itinerant for her 'superfluous dress', went back to Nottingham where she worked as a lace mender, but through the *PMM* we can see she was in great demand in the 1850s as a special preacher at anniversaries and chapel openings.[69] Women preachers might not have their names on the plan, but their preaching could always be relied on to bring in the money.[70] In Leeds, when funds were short, 'Sister' Scupham was the chosen preacher: 'it being the time appointed for the Quarterly Collection, and our Circuit Funds being low, we wish to enlist your services as we know you can command a good congregation and collection.'[71] Similarly, when Ann Hirst preached at Boston in 1841 it was noted that the collection was thirty pounds, compared with five pounds the previous year.[72]

While women were denied official recognition, and excluded from the itinerant ministry, it was always open in the PM Church for women to become local preachers, and when female itinerants retired, they did not stop preaching, but reverted to local preacher status. However, despite evidence that female preaching was increasing in the Wesleyan Connexion in the last two decades of the nineteenth century, in the PM Connexion, which had been the first to fully embrace women as preachers

---

[68] Graham, 'Two Primitive Women Preachers', 46-50.

[69] For example, Cromford in 1854.

[70] PM preaching plans show that women's names were often excluded, indicated by initials only; Kendall, *Origin and History of the Primitive Methodist Church*, vol 1, p. 208.

[71] Letter dated 28 February 1855, quoted by E. D. Graham, 'Women Local Preachers' in Milburn and Batty (eds), *Workaday Preachers*, p. 177.

[72] *Lloyd*, p. 158.

and evangelists, numbers declined.[73] Far from being encouraged to preach, women were now actively discouraged. Instead their role was seen to be as Sunday School teachers and fund raisers. By the 1880s even the demand for women as 'special' preachers had waned, as women were expected to run bazaars and tea meetings. It seems shocking that in 1907 a local preacher could declare, 'Many churches that will allow a coloured man or a converted clown to occupy the pulpit without a question, shut the door against a woman.'[74]

An example of the hostile environment that had developed in regard to women preachers is revealed in a PM publication in 1902, in which even God's approval is seen to be partial:

> It is a far cry from present-day conditions to the time when females were included among the travelling preachers of our Church . . . Altered circumstances have seemed to forbid a reestablishment of the custom, but in the early years of our history the conditions were, no doubt, favourable to its adoption, and in instances not a few it was signally owned of God.[75]

Against a picture of official 'extinction' and inexorable decline, there is one woman who emerges like a light from the tunnel. Mary Bulmer was accredited as a local preacher in 1891. Highly regarded, she at times acted as a hired local preacher and even a travelling preacher in all but name. In 1899 she was called to step into the breach in the Stanley circuit on the death of both its ministers, acting to all intents and purposes as its superintendent minister. Mary continued to work in the Stanley circuit for two years as a travelling preacher, even if not recognized and stationed as such by the Connexion.[76] Women like Mary ensured that, against all the odds, while PM female preaching certainly declined, it never became 'extinct'.

---

[73] Lenton, 'Labouring for the Lord', pp. 74-7.
[74] *PM Leader* (7 March 1907), 147.
[75] *Christian Messenger* (1902), 183.
[76] Graham, 'Two Primitive Women Preachers', 51.

Postscript: continuity and change after 1907

Reflection around the Centenary in 1907 appears to have been a watershed moment for women in the PM Church, even if change was to be painfully slow. At the Centenary Camp Meeting in 1910, one woman was invited to preach, the redoubtable Mary Bulmer. In 1917, the new President, Rev. Tolefree Parr, insisted that:

> More and more should we enlist the splendid genius and intuitive wisdom of women, no longer should she stand in the outer courts or be confined to menial tasks. Leadership as well as service was her right. Let the Church not lag behind the State in her welcome of woman.[77]

Women's role in the Church improved although it continued to be secondary to that of men.[78] An order of deaconesses called 'Sisters of the People' was established in 1914, which after the first World War began training women for foreign missions and encouraged a greater use of female local preachers.[79] In 1921, although Rev. George Armstrong confirmed that there was nothing in the Church's constitution to bar women from the ministry (in response to a question from a woman delegate), no action followed. It was not until the Conference of 1930, following a passionate speech by one of its ministers' wives, that Primitive Methodism approved an 'investigation' into how it could 'satisfy the needs of women in its Church' and redress their 'feeling of inferiority'.[80] In 1924, the first woman was nominated, though unsuccessfully, for the post of Vice

---

[77] *Christian Messenger* (1917), 787.

[78] Johnson, 'National Politics and Politicians', p. 198. (See also pp. 85-7, 148-52, 198-201).

https://hydra.hull.ac.uk/assets/hull:15456a/content (accessed 11 June 2020).

[79] *PM Leader* (28 May 1914), 366; (3 February 1921), 69.

[80] *Lancashire Evening Post* (23 June 1930), 3; Johnson, 'National Politics and Politicians', p. 199.

President of Conference.[81] In 1931, the PM Conference unanimously approved the ordination of women ministers.[82] Methodist Union the following year put a stop to further progress as the idea of women ministers was unacceptable to the Wesleyans, who had no history of female itinerant preachers. It was to be a long wait until the Methodist Church that emerged from Union ordained its first woman ministers in 1974.[83]

Conclusion

While the early female preachers of Primitive Methodism are celebrated today as a pioneering example of inclusion, it is clear that from the very start women were never accorded equal status with men. Female itinerant preachers were expected to do the same work as men, and no differentiation was made in their ability to preach the gospel and open missions, but they were always paid less than the men. When men received four pounds four shillings a quarter, women received just half that at two pounds two shillings.[84] Only men were appointed superintendent ministers, by a Conference made up entirely of men.[85] As time went on, women were excluded from preaching and leadership, which were seen as higher status roles.

It is clear also that the exclusion of women's voices in the governance of the church, which became an exclusively male preserve, has to bear a large share of the responsibility for the decline of female preaching. In seeking to learn lessons from the past, we need to make sure that the leadership of the church is

---

[81] Johnson, 'National Politics and Politicians', p. 148.

[82] *Portsmouth Evening News* (24 June 1931), 16.

[83] https://www.methodist.org.uk/about-us/news/latest-news/all-news/methodist-church-celebrates-40-years-of-women-s-ordination/ (accessed 11 June 2020); *Field-Bibb,* pp. 25-38, explains the convoluted debates among Wesleyans from 1922 to 1932 on the issue of women in the ministry.

[84] Graham, 'Female itinerants' (2005), 6.

[85] Until Mary Bulmer was admitted to Conference in 1899.

representative of its members. As we have seen, a lack of diversity can lead to fossilised ideas, attitudes and prejudices. The lack of education and training also played a large part in marginalising female preaching, as women, many of whom were servants and dressmakers in the early years of the movement, became less equipped to preach to increasingly middle-class congregations. Opportunities for access for all to learning and development continue to be as important today.

Were women preachers inferior to men? Evidence to the contrary can be seen in the example of Hannah Knowles, and countless others whose obituaries in the *PMM* reveal the impact of their preaching on people's lives. It could be said that women preachers had to be better than men, and were certainly subject to more scrutiny. The achievement of many women who juggled preaching and other church work with looking after husbands and children is astonishing and truly inspirational. Yet it could be true to claim it was the 'survival of the fittest'. Annie Swales (1815-95), a PM local preacher in Pickering, Yorkshire, for sixty years, is a good example. In 1864 she said this about her experience of continuing to preach against the odds:

> I have felt the pulpit has been my right place for twenty nine years, and sometimes I have had to contend with people that have tried to assail me saying it is not right for a woman to preach and so on, but God Himself has interposed and they have been convinced.[86]

Women had to be strong to face and overcome opposition, but more insidious was the way that cultural changes about 'a woman's place' led to attitudes which were embraced by the

---

[86] *Lloyd*, p. 147. In the 1861 census returns, Annie gives her occupation as 'Primitive Methodist local preacher'. Her son John became a PM minister.
https://www.myprimitivemethodists.org.uk/content/people-2/primitive_methodist_ministers/s-2/john-swales (accessed 12 June 2020).

Church, and undermined women's self-confidence. The rewriting of connexional histories, and the fact that women's voices were excluded from the connexional journals (which show a lack of any writing by women until the 1890s), played a key part in this.[87] Indeed, one of the most important reasons why the 1907 Centenary can be seen as such pivotal point in halting the decline of female preaching, was the publication of a new connexional history, in two volumes, by H. B. Kendall, *The Origin and History of the Primitive Methodist Church*, written specially for the Centenary. Looking back to tell the story of the Church in its first hundred years, Kendall resurrected the hidden and disregarded stories of the early female preachers, highlighting their contribution to the origins and mission of the movement. Magic lantern slides were even produced of women like Sarah Kirkland, Mary Porteous and Elizabeth Bultitude. Suddenly, Primitive Methodists discovered a new pride in this forgotten part of their history, and young women, for the first time in decades had role models, which could now inspire them to become preachers themselves.

Sadly, the failure to listen to women's concerns and hear women's voices had by 1907 already led many young women, like Ethel Snowden, to seek opportunities outside the Church for speaking out for social justice and women's rights. As we have seen, some joined the Salvation Army, others the Independent Labour Party. Although the Church gave lip service to social and political justice, including women's suffrage, words did not lead to action. When individual women spoke out they often found little support from the Church. The PM MP, Jim Simmons, considered that he 'could be a more effective evangelist from the Socialist platform' and 'could preach the "Politics of Christ" more effectively from the political soapbox than from the pulpit.'[88] This was an issue which affected men as well as women, but PM men had opportunities

---

[87] Johnson, 'National Politics and Politicians', pp. 85-6.
[88] J. Simmons, *Soapbox Evangelist* (Chichester, 1972), pp. 58, 172.

to learn their public speaking within the Church as local preachers. Not only were women deterred from preaching but, arguably as a result, there was not one PM woman MP within the life of the Church.[89]

There is some truth in the claim that the story of female preaching is about 'doors opening and closing according to men's needs and concerns'.[90] By 1907, the male leadership of the Church was waking up to the fact that a declining membership meant it needed to look at new ways of being, which meant revisiting its history. But it was left to a minister's wife to say, 'I am convinced that our church has lost immeasurably in practically silencing women so far as preaching goes, and will never recover its lost glory until it is realised that in Christ there is neither male nor female.'[91]

If we are to learn from the past, perhaps we need to go further and ask whose call is not being recognized, whose voice is not being heard today? For in Christ there is neither male nor female, black nor white, old nor young, gay nor straight, and the Spirit of Jesus, and perhaps John Wesley and Hugh Bourne, continues to call us to break down barriers by speaking truth to power.[92]

---

[89] In 1931, Dorothy Woodman (1902-70) became the first, and only, PM woman to stand for Parliament, although unelected. She was a member of the Labour Party. Johnson, 'National Politics and Politicians', p. 202.

[90] *Lloyd*, p. 2.

[91] E. Pearce, Letter re 'Our Women and the Centenary' in *PM Leader* (7 March 1907), 147. Both this quotation and the final paragraph of this chapter allude to Galatians 3:28: 'There is neither Jew nor Greek, . . . neither male nor female . . .' (KJV).

[92] The 'perennial task of the church is to maintain a dynamic balance between the spirit and structures'. P. W. Chilcote, *She Offered them Christ: the legacy of women preachers in early Methodism* (Eugene, OR, 1993), p. 123.

12: What's extraordinary about my call? A reflection on the preaching ministry of ordained women from the 1970s to the present

Christina Le Moignan

As has been said, the year 2019 marked the 350th anniversary of the birth of Susanna Wesley, often referred to as 'the mother of Methodism'. We celebrated it by having the conference entitled 'An Extraordinary Call' about women preachers in Methodism and pondering the part these women played in Methodist history. This reflection seeks to bring the story up to date by way of an assessment of my own place in that history.

Susanna's second son, John Wesley, has always seemed to me a curious mixture. On the one hand he was the born organizer, with everything cut and dried, and pretty clear boundaries. On the other, there was the gospel imperative and if that meant ignoring boundaries, then so be it; the gospel took precedence. If people would not come to hear the gospel in church, then Wesley himself must take to preaching outside. Thus, on 2 April 1739, he famously 'submitted to be more vile, and proclaimed in the highways the glad tidings of salvation'.[1] As far as others were concerned, if people Wesley had never dreamed of were being used and blessed by God in roles hitherto reserved for the clergy, including women, then he must accept such people.[2] The God Wesley served was a limitless God, whose love is of unfathomable depth, and of unlimited extent. Such a God is in human terms extraordinary; so he may well call extraordinary people to do extraordinary things.

---

[1] *WJW*, vol 19, p. 46.

[2] See chapter four in this volume.

Personal history

Perhaps at this point some personal background would help.[3] Like all Methodist ministers, I began my preaching ministry as a local preacher. I was accredited as such in 1971, and, when the ordained ministry became open to women in the British Methodist Church, I offered as a candidate in 1972. After training at Wesley House in Cambridge, I was ordained in 1976. I was a circuit minister in three circuits,[4] and in 1989 was asked to join the staff at Queen's, Birmingham, an ecumenical theological training college for Anglican, Methodist and United Reformed Church ministers.[5] After seven years at Queen's, I became Chair of the Birmingham district, from which I retired after eight years in 2004. During that time, I was President of the Conference for the year 2001-2. Both as a Chair of district and as President, I was the second woman to fill these roles, the first, in each case, having been Kathleen Richardson.[6]

Positive discrimination

I think that being a woman was certainly one reason for my appointment to Queen's; the number of women students was rising quite rapidly, and there was a fairly limited pool of

---

[3] Christina Le Moignan was born at Harrogate in 1942. She was educated at the Methodist Edgehill School in north Devon and Somerville College, Oxford, where she read Classics. She went to Nigeria, to Ibadan University, where she taught and also gained a PhD in Political Science. She was accepted for the ministry in 1973. She is the author of *Following the Lamb: a reading of Revelation for the new millennium* (Peterborough, 2000) [Editors' note].

[4] Hunts Mission, Southampton and Gosport,

[5] See A. Chandler, *Anglicanism, Methodism and Ecumenism: a history of the Queen's and Handsworth Colleges* (London, 2018).

[6] Kathleen Richardson (née Fountain), entered the Wesley Deaconess Order in 1961 and e.m in 1976. She became the first woman Chairman of a district in 1987 and the first female President in 1992; see *DMBI*.

potential women tutors to choose from.[7] I also guess that members of the Conference were on the lookout for women as potential Presidents. I was one of the first women to be accepted for the ministry in 1973 and I think that there has certainly been an element of positive discrimination in the course of my ministry.[8] Methodists are a generous and inclusive people, and, I believe, regularly thought 'we must have a woman' (on such and such a committee).[9] This was much more than mere tokenism. I honoured it and was genuinely grateful for it; and I do also think that positive discrimination as a practice is justified as a way of building up expertise in under-represented groups.

Nevertheless, I found it personally uncomfortable: it had the feeling of being promoted beyond one's pay grade; and that was worse if the committees were ecumenical, with most members representing churches without women priests. On the other hand, there were definite perks to positive discrimination, the most signal example being invited in 1980 to be part of the group representing the British Conference at the General Conference of the United Methodist Church in the United States.[10] More fundamentally, I have learned an enormous

---

[7] In 1989 there were thirty-two women among the ninety-six candidates for the ministry accepted that year; see *Minutes* (1989). Up to 1987 only an average of sixteen female candidates were accepted each year.

[8] Thirty women were accepted as candidates in 1973. Fifteen of those were Deaconesses who were sent straight into circuit ministry.

[9] In 1980, for example, I was appointed to the Doctrinal Committee; see *Minutes* (1980), p. 11. It consisted mostly of College tutors (it was nine years before I became a tutor). I was the only woman on a committee of thirteen and the most junior in terms of ministry. It may have been partly because of my doctorate (only two of the men had one), though as this was in Political Science it was hardly relevant.

[10] The General Conference of the United Methodist Church, which has representatives from all over the world as well as all the

amount from the opportunities that have been put in my way, which I think I should never have had had I been a male minister.

Preaching in theological training

Certainly, preaching was an important element in my theological training. I think no-one who trained at Wesley House in my time will forget sermon class, in which a student preached to the whole college in the chapel. The sermon was commented on in strict order by a 'manner' critic, a 'matter' critic;[11] then by any other student who wished to contribute, and the staff in a set order, beginning with the most junior and ending with the Principal, who then pronounced the benediction, after which we all dispersed.[12] The preacher was not invited, or expected, to speak at any point in the process. I am not sure how effective this was as a teaching method, but it undoubtedly left us in no doubt of the importance of preaching. As to women students' experience of this, I do have one cherished memory of our student organist choosing to play, as his pre-service voluntary for the first woman doing her sermon, 'Thank heaven for little girls'.[13] I rather think the staff decided that this fell into the category of things they 'had not really heard'!

By my third year at Wesley House preaching training was less formal, and certainly by the time I was teaching at Queen's it was entirely done on the basis of a sermon preached in a local

---

Conferences in the US, meets every four years. In 1980 it was held in Indianapolis.

[11] The manner critic concentrated on how the student preached e.g. volume, speed of delivery, gestures if any, etc. The matter critic concentrated on what was said (and unsaid) and its organization.

[12] The Principal of Wesley House in 1973 was Gordon Rupp who retired in 1974 and was succeeded by Michael Skinner who introduced less formality; K. B. Garlick, *Garlick's Methodist Registry* (London, 1983).

[13] A 1957 song associated with Maurice Chevalier.

church, and listened to by one or two students plus a tutor, with a de-brief afterwards.

Preaching in circuit

As a circuit minister, I have to confess that it was not easy to give preaching its proper preparation time, given the multiple demands of ministry. They do not spend much time in college telling you about ministry as dealing with a country chapel which has no damp-proof course, or how best to handle administration. I had to keep reminding myself how significant preaching was in terms of ministerial service offered: an hour spent in pastoral visiting would be one or two person-hours of ministry; an hour spent in leading worship might be sixty hours.

Preaching to a congregation that you get to know also has its pastoral element. It is obviously an abuse of the pulpit to say anything that has an identifiable application to individuals, but nevertheless, one's preaching is informed by an awareness of what is on people's minds and hearts. All this, of course, is by no means applicable only to the ordained; local preachers also have many other things to do, and if they spend a long time in a circuit may get to know local congregations very well indeed. But, to stress my primary point, being entrusted with proclaiming the Word of God is an amazing honour, and it needs all the preparation we can give it.

An extraordinary call?

Rather belatedly, we come to the subject of 'call'. What was extraordinary about the call in my case? If I talk (now) mostly about ordained ministry, that is because, when I began at least, women ministers were a good deal rarer than women local preachers. I was conscious that my call was extraordinary both in other people's eyes and in my own—but not for the same reasons. For me being a woman was nothing amazing, I shared that characteristic with half the human race. What was extraordinary was the call to be a minister.

293

By contrast, most other people saw nothing very extraordinary about ministers; but the idea of a woman being a minister was unfamiliar to say the least. I always wore a dog-collar when I was working, because I think that visual signals about who one is are useful; and when I was walking round the community I used to have the slightly unnerving experience of being looked at just beneath the chin—'is that really a dog-collar I'm seeing?' Children were more straightforward, and said 'coo, are you a vicar?'—to which my usual response was 'more or less'.

While for most non-church-goers a woman in a dog-collar was of only mild interest, for one's own people, and for ecumenical colleagues, it was of course a different matter. The unfamiliar on the whole is treated with reserve. Against that, Methodists, I think, are in general a kind and accepting people, and my experience was that people often went out of their way to make women ministers feel included. Yet, however kind people are, being in a small minority is not restful; you are different, and therefore obvious. At the inspired suggestion of Brian Beck,[14] who was a tutor at Wesley House while the first women were training there, we went on a periodic retreat with the Roman Catholic Sisters of the Assumption.[15] Suddenly one was in a place where it was normal to be female, and it was bliss.

Resistance to ministry?

More important than the mild discomforts of being in a minority was the question of whether people were prepared to accept the ministry of ordained women, because you cannot minister to people who do not want to be ministered to. I remember my pleasure, mixed with relief, when someone said after one of my first funerals, 'you can see me out any time'; and the even greater reassurance of one of my stewards saying, a few months into my first appointment, 'we wondered what

---

[14] Brian Beck, e.m. 1957, was Tutor at Wesley House 1968-80 and then became Principal. He was later Secretary of Conference (*DMBI*).
[15] At Hengrave Hall, near Bury St Edmunds.

having a woman minister would be like, but it's just the same really'.

Of course, probably one never really knows who is staying away, but I was not conscious of a significant problem, certainly within the Methodist Church, of being unacceptable simply because I was a woman. I am aware that by no means all of my women colleagues would be able to say the same. Even for myself, I think it would be fair to say that some of my ministerial colleagues were not wholly at ease with me at the beginning. Some ministers' wives viewed me with a degree of suspicion, but on the whole, I was not conscious of that reaction lasting long.

Some ecumenical colleagues I think had more deep-seated issues with women ministers, though as some of them would never have accepted Methodist ministerial orders as adequate anyway, that probably made little practical difference. In any case, significantly more of my ecumenical colleagues were genuinely supportive. Only very rarely did I feel hurtfully discriminated against, and that may well have been a useful experience in making me a bit more sensitive to people who suffer far greater discrimination than I ever did for what they are, whether in gender, race or sexual orientation. You find yourself saying, 'but it's not my fault that I'm a woman', (or 'black', or whatever it is), and then saying, 'but what am I doing sounding apologetic about who I am?' That is not a good place to be.

Different or the same?

But let me go back to my steward's conclusion that it is 'just the same really' having a woman 'minister'. Is it really just the same, and if it is, should it be? I think in the 1970s and 1980s, when ordained women were quite unusual, we did tend to downplay differences, and go for the 'just the same really' option. When one of the tutors at Wesley House said, 'we are going to treat you just like the men', and took it for granted he was paying us a compliment, we thought, 'well, let them get used to us first, and if we want to complain about being treated as something we are not, we can do it a bit later'. All this was in the days before political correctness; nor had feminist theology become at all mainstream. But being an honorary male was not what we were, or felt.[16] I still clearly remember putting on the first clerical shirt that did up what, for me, was the right way, and that was not until the ordination of women in the Church of England made it worthwhile for such shirts to be produced.[17] 'Gosh, I feel human', I said (I think out loud), a human being recognized for the gender that she was.

Because, of course, gender is important. I do think, for a number of reasons, that the ordained ministry is more complete if it includes women presbyters than if it does not. There is a theological importance about this; having women ministers allows the whole human race, and not just half of it, to be represented in a significant part of the ministry of the whole church. It avoids a dissonance between the church's membership as a whole, which is considerably more female than male, and an entirely male ordained leadership. Symbolically it seems to me quite important that the up-front person should sometimes be a woman.

Pastorally men may be quite as gifted as women. They are probably more chary, and wisely so, of physical contact with women; whereas if I was visiting a bereaved man, for example, I would generally feel no unease about sitting by him and putting a hand on his arm. In the leadership of churches, too, I think there tends to be some difference in style between men and women. More men than women, I guess, are most at ease with a 'lead from the front' style, though we can probably all

---

[16] For the lack of difference between male and female ministers' views see J. M. Haley and L. J. Francis, *British Methodism: what circuit ministers really think* (Peterborough, 2006), p. 130.

[17] Anglican women were first ordained in March 1994.

quote women ministers for whom this is certainly the preferred option.

Might it be that women's accumulated experience of 'keeping the family happy' is reflected in meetings in a greater desire to let everyone have their say than to get home quickly? In this example, and in other ministerial matters, of course, gender is only one factor among many; one ministers with the person one is, and personality is a highly complex matter.

Conclusion

The Methodist Church, both in its membership and in its congregations as a whole has always been more female than male, and it is right that its ordained ministry should represent that preponderance. But perhaps my primary concern that the ministry should be open to women, as well as men, lies in my conviction that everyone who has something to offer to ordained ministry should be able to make that offer. The church needs that, and I truly believe God wants it.

13: A Call in Context: the Extraordinary becomes Ordinary

Judith Maizel-Long

This chapter offers an account of the call to the ministry of Word and Sacrament of this writer as one of the earlier of the women presbyters in British Methodism. In it I consider my own experience of the call, complicated by wishing to be a follower of Jesus though brought up as a liberal Jew. More general factors in the resistance to the ministry of myself and other women in the Methodist Church are discussed, as well as the encouragement received, sometimes from unexpected sources, male and female.

In my experience, women strengthened and supported one another's ministries though belonging to diverse denominations, and in all places I observed through my lifetime how candidates for women's ministry rejected by one denomination moved to another where their gifts could be acknowledged and used. A succession of women has been called to preach and advocate for themselves and other women the joint ministries of preacher and minister of Word and Sacrament in continuity between the ministry of Susanna Wesley and ordained ministry of women in Methodism and other churches, in a progression to the present day.

When does an 'extraordinary' call become an 'ordinary' one? John Wesley described the ministry of lay men and women as an 'Extraordinary Call', as detailed in earlier contributions to this book. In contrast, my call to ministry happened as the Extraordinary was becoming ordinary in the late twentieth century and the early years of the new millennium.

The experience of a call

In 1971, on a summer Sunday evening in the small historic city of Durham, soon after term had ended, in Elvet Methodist Church, being the larger of two Methodist churches in the city, Stuart Rhodes, Methodist chaplain to the University of Durham,[1] preached to a mixed Methodist congregation of townspeople and university students, both postgraduates and a few undergraduates who were hanging around after term had ended. I was one of those undergraduates. The context of that service was that Methodist Conference in 1971 had just resolved, after passionate discussions taking place for twenty-five years, to open the presbyteral ministry to female candidates on the same basis as their male counterparts. The 1971 Conference passed the brief preparatory legislation for the selection of female candidates for ministerial training. That was the Methodist way of creating an equal ministry.[2] More recently it has been the anniversary of the first ordinations of female presbyters in 1974 which has been celebrated.

Stuart Rhodes preached that summer evening of 1971 on discipleship, saying notably that any Christian who takes their faith seriously should ask himself, and equally now herself, whether God wants her or him in the full-time ministry of the church. The invitation to women as equals to men was conscious and deliberate in Stuart's sermon. Aged nineteen and a history undergraduate, I was thrilled and confused at the same time. It was the beginning of my call to serve God in ordained ministry, but there were some major issues for me yet to resolve.

---

[1] J. Stuart Rhodes served subsequently as minister of Wesley Memorial Church, Oxford, 1975-80, and then Chair of the Stoke-on-Trent district.

[2] *Field-Bibb*, pp. 63-6; J. M. Turner (ed.), *Methodism and Ministry: the ministry of women and men, unity and the future of Methodism. Articles by Rupert E. Davies* (Peterborough, 1993), pp. 23-4.

The rock from which I was hewn

Looking solely at my maternal family, I was, so I gather, absolutely typical of Methodist student ministers in the 1970s. I was a first generation university graduate, who had grown up in a strong Methodist area, a Midlands mining village. There was a Methodist influence in preceding generations, a PM great-grandfather, and grandmother, and a grandfather who had considered offering for the ministry after Methodist Union in 1932.

The Jewish side of the family was my father's. His mother, daughter of a Lithuanian rabbi, graduated in dentistry in Paris before the First World War. She married a Riga timber merchant with international contacts, specialising in sourcing Baltic timber to export to London. It was grandfather's far-sightedness and prudence that ensured the Maizel family's safe migration from Latvia to England by 1938. My father, Dr George Maizel, had a medical vocation and pursued his studies in Edinburgh where there was a greater internationalism than in London medical schools, and acquired a slight Scots accent. My father's secondary education was delivered in Hebrew, so understanding the Hebrew bible, he opted to become a liberal Jew and a socialist.

With the establishment of the National Health Service in 1948, he chose to become a general medical practitioner in an area of shortage. My mother shared his idealism in politics, and had qualified as a state registered nurse because her family did not have the means to send her to study medicine. Her deep satisfaction was being a writer and public speaker, and a teacher of nursing, from whom I inherited or caught a way with words. Both parents had a love of books and theatre which balanced their vocation in medical and nursing care. In the mining community where I grew up, both parents were highly regarded because of their compassionate and knowledgeable ways, and for encouraging young people to fulfil their ambitions.

I have also discussed with my sister how our parents' generation, young adults during the Second World War, were deeply traumatised but brushed that under the carpet. My mother was first married aged twenty-three, her husband, an RAF officer, went missing in action a few months later. Within months, she learned that she was widowed, and my older sister was born. My father's trauma was the loss of friends and family members apart from his parents in the Holocaust, where eighty percent of Latvian Jews 'perished', in the euphemism of the time. My mother lost her faith though my father did not. My older sister was on a different journey, and the eight-year gap was more significant then than now.

My parents did not object to me going on occasional exploratory visits to the parish church and the Methodist church with school friends. The worship in the historic parish church followed the Prayer Book of the Church of England, and was relatively formal and remote. I was more comfortable in the Methodist church with warm and friendly people and (for my younger self) more comprehensible and participatory worship.

Religious experience

In my mid-teens I flirted with atheism which was a regular topic in my school debating society. In one such debate I was arguing for atheism, but found that the argument that I was making did not convince me. It seemed to me that I suddenly felt a presence, that of the loving mind behind the universe. It was not a choice that I made, it was simply the most comprehensive explanation of 'life, the universe, and everything'.[3] It was my own experience of the 'warmed heart'. Theologically, I would say that at the age of fourteen, this was the point at which I came to belief in God. As we have reflected, even as a teenager I had to find my own arguments for the existence of God and for Christian belief.

---

[3] The title of a novel in the series by Douglas Adams, *The Hitchhiker's Guide to the Galaxy* (London, 1980).

My mother, Clarice Maizel, who knew that I was drawn to Christianity, was a lapsed Anglican for many years. Many of her generation had been persuaded, by popular writers like George Bernard Shaw and H. G. Wells, that belief in God was untenable in the light of scientific knowledge. My mother had not converted to Judaism, yet was very anxious that I should not disown or deny Judaism, so that if I were asked 'are you Jewish?' I should always say 'yes'. As she told me, the real tragedy of the German Jews was that many went to the gas chambers not knowing anything about Judaism. If asked, I always say that I am Jewish, a follower of Jesus the Jew.

I never broke that promise, and I will continue to keep it for the rest of my life. I also promised that I should visit Israel and spend some months there before making a formal decision to be baptized, which I do not regard as a repudiation of Judaism.

Following Jesus — the influence of teachers

Jesus had become real to me through a kind and loving primary school teacher, Mrs Attwood, who read to us the stories of and about Jesus, drawing our thoughts particularly to how Jesus spoke with individuals in the Gospels, kindly to those who were distressed, and sternly to those who needed to change their attitudes. I remember, when to our class of nine-year-olds, she shared dramatically the story of Jesus's conversation with the woman at the well (John 4), in a simplified form.[4] And I thought, 'who could not love this Jesus who knows all about us and still loves us?'

Later, it was our secondary school Head of Religious Education, Ann Wood, who inspired me to see a bigger view of what Christianity was about. A Congregationalist lay preacher in Sheffield, Miss Wood took seriously the challenges of the modern world and taught our group of fourteen-year-olds in 1965-6 about Dr Martin Luther King and Dietrich Bonhoeffer before they were widely known in churches in Britain. Aged

---

[4] John 4:5-42.

about fifteen, in the school library I came across a copy of Leslie Weatherhead's controversial book *The Christian Agnostic* which argued a case for liberal Christianity.[5] Now I would argue with Leslie Weatherhead on his uncritical modernism, though then I was excited by the progressive version of Christianity before I went to university. Miss Wood influenced me to look for the Student Christian Movement (SCM) and its publications when I arrived in Durham. I had joined the SCM and Methsoc, the student Methodist society, in the first week of term. In due course both the SCM and the Methodist Church were to employ me.

I went up to Durham University to read history. I spent most of my time reading Christian theology and spirituality, and being involved with two groups, the flourishing MethSoc, and also a small SCM group. My mentors there included Ruth Etchells, later to be the first woman principal of the Anglican theological college, St John's College, Durham. Ruth lent me a copy of the newly published *Jesus the Jew* by the Jewish scholar Geza Vermes.[6] I chose the religious options in my degree, which was broad enough to include courses on Christendom and Islam, Reformation and Counter-Reformation. I was really rather lucky to be awarded an upper second-class degree in history.

The power of my call

Why was the call to the ministry of Word and Sacrament so strong for me? It made more sense of who I felt myself to be, with my interests and gifts, than any other plan for my life. It is only in retrospect that I see how well my parental influences prepared me for ministry, though the diversity induced in me a long identity crisis—was I Jewish or Christian, even agnostic or atheist? I had a motivation to tell people about the Jesus that I

---

[5] L. D. Weatherhead, *The Christian Agnostic* (London, 1965). Leslie Weatherhead was President of the Methodist Conference in 1955.
[6] G. Vermes, *Jesus the Jew: a historian's reading of the Gospels* (Minneapolis, 1973).

had come to know, seeing him in those many and varied people who love him, the one who reveals the loving character of God.

When I first received the call, mediated by Stuart Rhodes, it was as if a new door had opened in my life that had not existed before. I was blessed in the early autumn of 1971 when a young Methodist ministerial couple, Michael and Maureen Bowman, came to the Worksop circuit with modern ways, and became my support and interlocutors in issues of faith and theology.[7]

Iona

The months after I heard the call from Stuart Rhodes, in the autumn of 1971, began a period of crisis for me. I developed an unidentifiable condition, in retrospect probably Myalgic Encephalomyelitis (ME), not then medically identified, which left me physically exhausted, and the university agreed for me to have a year off. Thankfully after about six months I began to recover, but then my father, afflicted by a sudden depressive episode, took a fatal overdose. That was the major event of my early adulthood. The university took me back with wonderful pastoral care, and in Lent 1973 I went as a member of a chaplaincy group to a residential week at Iona Abbey, home of the Iona Community. In that week, two notable things happened. First, I received physical healing, not suddenly, but rather it was more like the turning of a corner following on from receiving the laying on of hands in a service of prayer for healing. The second event was that in the service of commitment when the resident Church of Scotland minister, John Harvey, gave me a sentence of scripture, which was a calling to ministry.

I went home to stay with my mother and told her about the Iona experience. She told me that when she visited my grandfather in London, he confided that he had never believed in God. I asked that, as she had asked me not to be baptized until after

---

[7] Michael Bowman e.m. 1968 Worksop circuit 1971, a supernumerary minister in the Chesterfield circuit in 2020.

my grandparents were dead, would she free me from that promise? She did so. I called to see Michael Bowman the next day, and three days later I was baptized in the Methodist Church at the age of twenty-one. Over the next years, through the influence of Michael Bowman and Ruth Etchells, and reading theology books that I took home, my mother revisited the Christian faith of her youth, and became a member of the Methodist Church.

Working out my vocation

Though now a baptized Christian, I still had unfinished business in my Jewish heritage. After graduating from Durham University, I went to Israel to spend the summer working in a kibbutz in northern Galilee. I spent four weeks in a small factory at Kibbutz Dafna close to the Syrian border, and then travelled around, visiting my father's surviving schoolfriends, and also staying in hostels and visiting the Christian and Jewish sites accompanied only by the bible, a guidebook and some temporary companions. There was one proposal of marriage (declined). I found in Israel that I was both a Jew and a Christian. If these things contradict, I concluded, it is in the minds of other people not mine. Some Israelis said, 'yes, you are Jewish', others said, 'no, you are not'.

In the following few years I tried alternatives to offering for church ministry: secondary history teaching; a secular job selling women's sportswear in a big London store; historical research; and organizing a large conference in Coventry Cathedral for the SCM. None of these things were quite right. So I went to my minister at Hinde Street Methodist Church in the West End of London, and started the ball rolling to become a local preacher, and to candidate for the Methodist ministry.

'What's a nice Jewish girl like me doing in a place like this?'[8] this quotation is how I began my testimony to Synod in 1978 in

---

[8] 'What's a nice kid like you doing in a place like this?' is sung by Sammy Davis jr as the Cheshire Cat in the Hanna-Barbera cartoon

my candidating year. As intended, it raised a laugh and caught the attention of the Synod. I was accepted at the age of twenty-six, and sent to study at Queen's College, Birmingham.

Was feminism part of the call to ministry?

Some opponents of equal ministry of women in the church have blamed the feminist movement for changing the doctrine and practice of the churches. Those of us in the post-war generation grasped that our mothers had had a tougher time than we did in the 1960s and 1970s. I learned that my very clever mother, brought up in a working-class family, was not able to stay at school after the age of sixteen because a university education was beyond her parents' means. Such mothers wanted better prospects for their daughters.

Was feminism a factor in my call to ministry? Not directly at all in my first twenty years. My parents encouraged my sister and me to have a career, as my mother had in nursing and in writing. My paternal grandmother may have been one of Europe's first women dentists, but her husband refused to let her convert her French qualifications to a British one, because he believed that it would reflect unfavourably upon him. (My father was on his mother's side, and tried to help her obtain Scottish qualifications). The one feminist book that I read as a teenager was my older sister's copy of Simone de Beauvoir's *The Second Sex*.[9] At the age of thirteen I was too young truly to understand it, but it strengthened in a general way my conviction that women are equal to men, but widely treated unjustly.

The experience of our mothers

There was no explicit interaction of feminism with my religious thinking, but I did think in terms of finding a career as vocation,

---

adaptation of *Alice in Wonderland* of 1966. That is the tune which has stuck in my mind since childhood.

[9] S. de Beauvoir, *The Second Sex*, trans. and ed. H. M. Parshley (London, 1953).

following the pattern of my parents, who held what was probably still a minority view for daughters in 1970.

In the circles of educated, thinking people who read serious newspapers and were sympathetic to progressive and liberal causes in the 1960s, supporters of the Labour and Liberal parties (and progressive Conservatives), sympathy to the equality of men and women was widespread. It was generally accepted that girls had as much right to be educated to the level of their ability as boys. Women had proved their calibre in the two world wars. After the Second World War, feminism was not a popular cause anywhere, and militancy was thought to be an unattractive quality in women.

Generally, progressive people believed in progress because of the ways in which they had seen the effects of growing economic prosperity and increasing levels of education as Britain after 1944 opened free and compulsory secondary education to all. Religious faith was beginning to falter, but belief in progress seemed to be unassailable. What appeared to be bastions of female oppression seemed to be retreating everywhere. My mother was approached by fellow members of the Labour Party to stand as member of Parliament for the Bolsover constituency in 1965 because the other candidate, Dennis Skinner, was thought to be too left-wing.[10] She decided against a political career.

Discovering and owning feminism

I discovered feminism as a postgraduate student in London when I came across the book *Man Made Language* by Dale Spender,[11] an Australian linguist who analysed the masculine

---

[10] Dennis Skinner, MP for the Bolsover constituency 1970-2019.
[11] D. Spender, *Man Made Language* (London, 1980). This classic book on the relationships between language and power convinced me that to change the power balance between men and women, it is necessary also to change the language. Reading it was an intellectual conversion to feminism.

bias of the English language as its rules were devised to begin from the normative 'Man'. I was also persuaded by hearing Pauline Webb speak to an SCM conference,[12] and in consequence I became convinced that feminism, which I understand to be the movement for the equality of women and men, is entirely compatible with Christian faith.

In my twenties in London I became known as a Christian Feminist, and my sister recalled something that I had forgotten—in church when everybody said 'amen' at the end of some prayers, little Judith aged seven said loudly 'and our women!' It appears that I became aware that there was an issue about the status of women at a young age. Evidently I was first exposed to ideas of the equality of women through my mother, sister, teachers, and observation of the lives lived by women and men close to me. I was fortunate to have felt encouragement by my father, and my mother who had been exposed to convictions of female equality by her teachers at a girls' grammar school in the 1930s. These teachers would have been suffragists as younger women, twenty or thirty years beforehand.

The experience of women in the churches ran parallel with these stories of opportunity and frustration. One consequence for me was my involvement with groups of Christian feminists, mainly of women who argued for inclusive language in church. Notably our members included Mrs Margaret Davies (prominent in Women's Work of the Methodist Church), and Janet Morley, poet and liturgist. The group wrote to the editorial committee for *Hymns and Psalms*. Influence of the group showed in small ways in the preface to *Hymns and Psalms* (1983), the Methodist Faith and Order Report on Inclusive Language and Imagery of God (1992), and in the *Methodist Worship Book* (1999).

---

[12] P. Webb, *World-Wide Webb: journeys in faith and hope* (Norwich, 2006), p. 90. At that time, Pauline Webb was one of the few visible Christian feminists. She was Vice President of the Methodist Conference 1965; Vice Chair World Council of Churches.

I hope to write an article on the subject of this 'inclusive language' pressure group at a later date.

Affirmation and resistance to women in the ordained ministry[13]

During my theological studies at Queen's College I found our tutors unanimously supportive of women's ministry. However, other attitudes existed in the church, even among fellow students. There was one Sunday in my second year when, as I occasionally did, I drove a fellow ministerial student to a preaching appointment in my little Hillman Imp. I was disheartened when he used a story about how dreadful women drivers are as a sermon illustration. It was also bad manners as he would not have been able to take the appointment if I had not driven him! I was not in a mood to challenge him directly, as I expected to be mocked for taking a joke too seriously.

Then the same evening I attended an evening service conducted by a superintendent minister, who told a joke about the pettiness of women. At the end of the service I was furious and emotional, but because of the intensity of my annoyance, compounded by the morning's experience, I didn't trust myself to challenge the superintendent face to face at the end of the service. Instead, the next day I wrote a letter to him, but stupidly did not keep a copy. I wrote politely to him, about the uses of humour, and that perhaps certain types of joke which are based on caricatures of people are put-downs and not appropriate in the pulpit. The following morning my tutor challenged me, saying that a superintendent minister had a complaint about me, saying that I was not suitable for ordination. This was deeply wounding, but as the superintendent minister would not produce the letter that I had written to him, nothing came of it. I had not shared this story for many years, and surprised myself recently by the intensity of feeling it still provoked. This indicates that questioning my call or ministry can be a tactic

---

[13] See also Lenton, '"The Cry of the Beloved"'.

used to maintain social control by members of a dominant group.

The only other uncomfortable experience at college was when we were given details in our penultimate term of our first appointments. The Principal told me that there had been an ideal appointment for me, a university chaplaincy, but it was decided to send me elsewhere because the superintendent in that circuit disagreed with the ordination of women. Instead, I was sent to Leeds, with a wonderfully affirming superintendent, but a difficult appointment (the kind that any experienced minister might have declined). Leeds was a bracing appointment in an inner city and housing estate area. One family resigned from membership over the appointment of a female minister.

And a little later, I was challenged when attending the induction of a new Anglican colleague as I entered the vestry to put on my cassock. 'Who are you and what are you doing here?' one of the priests asked in an aggressive manner. I made the obvious reply about being the local Methodist minister. The challenger withdrew but did not apologise, muttering something about American feminists. By this point, I found his rudeness amusing (though contrary to the gospel). Compensations for this were the warm welcome and affirmations I received from Methodists, Anglicans, Baptists and Catholics. I was always welcome to pop into the Catholic Social Club in an evening where there was competition to buy me a lemonade, and I was given the same respect given to Catholic religious sisters. They said of me, 'Reverend Judith is like Sister Joseph' (headteacher of the Catholic primary school), 'but less fierce'.

When my five-year appointment was drawing to an end, I was hoping for one less stressful. In that year, 1988, ministers were not permitted to contact circuits with vacancies. I must have had a fierce reputation as a feminist, as there was no telephone call for the first fortnight. I was very grateful to the Barnsley circuit when they telephoned me, and I had a happy time there. By this point, ordained women were less of an oddity, as there were female deacons in the Church of England, and during my time in Barnsley, the Church of England 'priested' women and the Vicar of Dibley appeared on television.

In 1995 I accepted a superintendency and moved south. I will not name the circuit; I was the first female minister they had had and the first superintendent. With most of my churches I got on swimmingly, and with most of the leadership. But there was a minority group who took against me and organized some dubiously legal procedures not to agree to my re-invitation. The Chair of district was retiring and did not want to take the matter up. A former President looked into the matter but it was decided not to pursue it, as after some anxiety (as a move could have forced my husband to become unemployed) I was employed by the South East Institute for Theological Education as Director of Mission and Pastoral Studies.[14]

Training ordinands and student ministers for the United Reformed Church, the Methodist Church, and the Church of England was a happy time in my life and ministry. I have been delighted with the progress of all SEITE students, and have no small satisfaction to see that they are offering notable leadership in their churches. I confess not a little pride to see some exercising senior leadership roles in these churches, twenty years on.

I would say that, by 1999, the period of strangeness of women's ministry was coming to an end, or it may be that I was getting the seniority and respect that meant that I was no longer vulnerable. There is one cameo from 2002. The Institute at the beginning of the academic year had a weekend school in Butlins Hotel, Margate for our Anglican, Methodist, and URC ministerial students. We worshipped together in a nearby Catholic church. At the weekend's Sunday morning Eucharist, I was the presiding minister. There was just one ordinand who

---

[14] Based in Chatham, Kent.

would not come up to receive from me, a first-year female Anglican. There was a stir in the congregation at this snub. I did not take it personally. It was part of the theology of her home parish that Free Church ministers are not 'properly' ordained. My ministry was being rejected as a Methodist, not as a woman! Very quickly, the Catholic priest who was our host came up and kneeled before me for a blessing which I gladly gave.

Is the struggle over for women's ministry?

I would that it were so, but a meeting with a black female Methodist presbyter recently persuaded me that wherever there is an 'out' group with less power or status, they are vulnerable to unjust treatment by those who retain power, probably unseen by the majority who may be complacent. Unlike sixty years ago, we generally do not believe in the inevitability of progress. Like Martin Luther, we must recognize that because of fallen human nature, there will always be sin in the church. The church inhabited by sinners will always be in need of repentance and reform. Luther wrote in Latin *'Ecclesia semper reformanda'*.[15] Our task in our time, I suggest, is firstly to recognize and support those women and men who are called to preach God's liberating Word; and secondly to challenge the structures of injustice (in the church and in the world) which try to prevent their holy calling. That calling unites us through the centuries with all the women honoured in this book.

---

[15] Meaning 'The church always needs to be reformed'.

14: Called to Lead

Michaela Youngson

I chose the title for this reflection 'called to lead' some weeks ago, and as often is the case when you send your sermon title ahead, you get to the week before and the Holy Spirit has other ideas! So were I to begin again I would call this talk 'When the laughter changed sides'. I will come to why shortly, but the subtitle of both these names is 'reflections on women's leadership in the church today'.

'Today' is a very dangerous word with a readership of historians. What does today mean? I could talk about the leadership of Queen Hatshepsut who was Pharaoh in ancient Egypt, and in order to assert her power wore the false beard of the Pharaoh. But you might say, that is a little bit previous to today, but what is today? Is it since Methodism ordained women?[1] Is it modernism, post-modernism, wherever we are now? As I am not sure what 'today' is, this reflection is going to be somewhat kaleidoscopic rather than linear.

The laughter changed sides

In June 2014 I was privileged to organize the celebration in Wesley's Chapel of forty years of women's ordained presbyteral ministry within the life of the Methodist Church. We had ordained into the diaconal ministry for much longer and we must never forget that.[2] I am sure deacons get as grumpy when

---

[1] Sunday 30 June 1974.

[2] The separate Methodist churches before 1932 used different terms for receiving deaconesses into their order, though the (British) United Methodists used the term 'ordination' from 1917. The Methodist Church after union 'ordained' its deaconesses from 1936. See Graham, *Saved to Serve*, pp. 347, 402-3.

313

we forget that, as I do when Anglicans state that we have had women priests for only twenty-five years!

At the celebration service the redoubtable Dr Pauline Webb (since gone to glory) spoke about the debates in the Methodist Conference leading up to that momentous decision in 1971,[3] when women's vocations were no longer sacrificed on the altar of ecumenical unity.[4] Conference decided that women can be ordained as presbyters within the life of the Church. As Pauline talked about the debates she said, 'I knew we were winning when the laughter changed sides.'

There is a moment in progressive change, when it is the status quo that becomes recognized as ridiculous rather than the new idea. Finally, those who had for years stood up in the Conference and offered reasons why it would be ridiculous for women to be ministers were the ones being laughed at. When their statements became the statements to be mocked, the laughter changed sides.[5] That is a powerful statement about change in society, in the Church. It is when the status quo becomes ridiculous and the laughter changes sides that justice rolls down like a river.

The power of the role model

In Mary Beard's book *Women and Power*, she invites the reader to exercise their imagination; she invites them to close their eyes and think of a doctor, a priest, a prime minister, a president, lots of roles of leadership.[6] And she asks 'who is it that comes to mind?' It is an exercise in examining our unconscious bias. Use your imagination; who is it that comes to mind when you hear those words? Time and time again, whether we like it or not, it will be a male image that we have in our head when we think

---

[3] *Minutes* (1971), pp. 11-12; *Field-Bibb*, pp. 63-6.
[4] Webb, *World-Wide Webb*, p. 79.
[5] For a description of the process over the years see Turner (ed.), *Methodism and Ministry*.
[6] M. Beard, *Women and Power: a manifesto* (London, 2017), pp. 53-9.

of that. So even though the barriers of academia or the barriers of the church have been broken down, somehow it is the lack of role models that keeps things the same, that stops the culture changing, even when the law has changed.

A lot has happened in the Methodist Church since women were ordained. There have now been six women Presidents. I was at the Conference in 1992 when Kathleen Richardson became the first, and that was the year I had been accepted to go to college to train, and so almost twenty years after the decision to ordain women we had our first woman President.[7] And in the twenty-five years since, we have had five more. That might be argued to be rather slow. There has been a good deal of commentary on having three women in a row, Loraine,[8] myself and then Barbara Glasson.[9] I long for the day when nobody needs to comment any more, when this is not a story, when it is just normal, as opposed to 'when are we getting back to normal and having a bloke?'[10]

One of the important things about cultural change that enables women to feel that they can be part of the leadership of any organization or any society, let alone the Church, is the availability and visibility of role models. I am going to share some of my role models with you before I mention some of what I am seeing in the church today in terms of women's leadership.

Whilst it would be tempting to consider Hatshepsut as a role model, I will resist the temptation! I am writing a novel about her at the moment. I have been writing it for about five years, so do not worry, it is not going to be in the shops in time for

---

[7] Kathleen Richardson, e.m. 1976, President 1992.

[8] Loraine Mellor, e.m. 1995, President 2017-18.

[9] Barbara Glasson, e.m 1994, President 2019-20.

[10] The Methodist Conference elected Richard Teal to be the President of the Conference for 2020-1 and has now designated Sonia Hicks to succeed him in 2021. This is worthy of comment as she is the first black woman presbyter to be elected to that office in the British Methodist Church.

Christmas. The story is about her and Miriam, and asks the question 'what if?'[11] What if the Pharaoh at the time of the people of Israel had been a woman? What would have driven her to make the decisions that put the people of Israel in that position?

I am not sure I have ever thought of Susanna Wesley as a personal role model, though I can see why she was for so many women across generations. Her domestic circumstances make me shudder and I have every sympathy for someone whose only way to get some peace is to throw their apron over their head as a signal to the family to leave her alone. Susanna's determination to educate her children, girls and boys, whilst enduring poverty and the absences of her husband, is admirable and I am grateful I do not face the limited choices that were open to a woman of her time. Susanna does inspire me in her approach to prayer. She was not casual about prayer and as a liturgist, this matters to me. She did not adopt a 'God as my best mate' attitude when praying but acknowledge God as the 'Sovereign Ruler of the Universe'.[12] In this, she models something that I aspire to.

You may have heard of Dame Ellen Wilkinson. She is one of those stories that we have stopped telling about Methodist women. She was the daughter of a local preacher in Manchester, and her church helped raise the money to send her to university. Ellen became the first Labour woman Member of Parliament to take a seat. Another had been elected, but she was Fenian and would not take the vow, and so Ellen became the first female

---

[11] Exodus 2:4-10.
[12] 'Enable me, O God, to collect and compose my thoughts before an immediate approach to Thee in prayer. May I be careful to have my mind in order when I take upon myself the honour to speak to the sovereign Lord of the universe.' Susanna Wesley, many internet sources, including: http://www.cometothefire.org/alethasjournal/2019/7/30/the-fruit-of-one-mothers-prayers (accessed 10 July 2020).

Labour MP. She became the MP for Jarrow, and led the Jarrow March. She was there at the front, Red Ellen: very short red hair, and it was not only her hair that was red! She went on in the post-Second World War government to be the Minister for Education, and it is said that she worked herself to death for the cause of universal education. She passed the law which provided school milk to primary school children.[13] I will not mention the other woman with Methodist roots who got rid of school milk!

Even as a card-carrying Marxist, Ellen said, 'Methodism never leaves you, it is a fire that runs through your veins'. For me she is an extraordinary role model who represents what is in my Methodist DNA, the passion for social justice, and the value of every single human being. She recognized the value before God of every person; and the willingness to go beyond your own comfort to work for a better world. You will not be surprised to know that she was a suffragette and embodied the willingness to put yourself on the line, to speak out against the status quo, to point out that the status quo is ridiculous, and to wait for the laughter to change sides. So Ellen Wilkinson is one of my role models.

Another of my role models is Christina Le Moignan, who was my tutor when I was at Queen's College.[14] Christina was one of the women to be ordained in the first years following the Conference decision. She went on to be President of the Conference, as well as being Principal of the West Midlands Ministerial Training Course and Chair of the Birmingham district. Like Kathleen Richardson, and Alison Tomlin, she showed those of us following behind that there are no structural limits to the roles that women can undertake in the life of the church. Each brought her own style and particular way of doing things and helped me to see beyond the ranks of male leaders,

---

[13] L. Beers, *Red Ellen: the life of Ellen Wilkinson, socialist, feminist, internationalist* (London, 2016).

[14] See chapter twelve in this volume.

that would sit on the Conference platform year in and year out, to a vision of a church in which all can offer their gifts and have that offer enthusiastically taken up by a church willing to change.

Lastly, I want to mention the Reverend Nicola Jones.[15] At the age of sixteen I went to the London weekend with the Methodist Association of Youth Clubs. Onto the platform of the Royal Albert Hall Nicola entered, wearing a clerical collar and preached; and she was extraordinary. But it was not really the quality of the preaching, or even her presence or stature that stood out to me, it was that collar. I had never seen a woman wearing a clerical collar before. No-one in my home church had ever said 'women cannot preach'; it was not something we talked about. I never asked the question. I had seen lots of women lay preachers in the pulpit in my home church in east Yorkshire, but I had never seen a woman dressed as a minister. The minute that Nicola walked onto the stage I thought, 'Oh, that is what I am going to do', and God's call on my life was clear and direct. I needed the leap of imagination, I needed to go beyond what I knew and what I had already seen, I needed the role model and that moment.

I went 'on note' as a local preacher at sixteen.[16] I mean God help those poor congregations . . . because at that age I knew everything! I know a lot less now. It took me seven years to become fully accredited as a lay preacher because I moved house five times and job four times, and got married. That is how it is for young people. But along the way people were very encouraging. The kind of everyday sexism you get in the church was definitely there, but no-one at any point said 'you should not be doing this', or questioned God's foolishness in putting me into that kind of role. What made the difference for me was seeing with my own eyes someone who looked a bit like me,

---

[15] E.m. 1980.
[16] The first stage of local preacher training, being given a note to preach by the circuit superintendent to accompany another preacher.

who shared my gender, that allowed me to think 'Oh, that is what I am going to do'. Culture change takes longer than changing the rules. Culture change comes through seeing role models, through encouragement, through active investment in people who may be not the norm, to become a new norm.

You can rely on HIM to hit the nail on the head

Mary Beard's book, *Women and Power*, includes the cartoon of Miss Triggs. She is there in a boardroom and the quote underneath reads: 'That's an excellent suggestion, Miss Triggs. Perhaps one of the men would like to make it.'[17]

It is an experience many women share. It is not usually said quite so starkly but you know, a minute after you have spoken, a man says the same thing and everyone says, 'Well, that is a really good idea', and you think you are invisible. In my book, *The Weaver, The Word and Wisdom*,[18] I offer reflection based on that experience, inspired by the story of Miriam's death in Numbers 20 and the reactions to it of the people of Israel.

At the very beginning of Numbers 20 it reads that the people of Israel were in the wilderness of Zin, in the place called Kadesh and Miriam died. It helps to know that chapter 19 is all about water; water for cleansing, water for the animals, water for the people. Chapter 20 states that Miriam died, and the next sentence states that, 'There was no water'.[19] There is a tradition that Miriam was the water diviner for the wandering tribes, and in their grief no one else could find the water. This is 'diviner's intervention'.

> I am the water diviner.
> I am the founder of the solution.
> I am the word in season,
> the wisdom not of Solomon,

---

[17] Beard, *Women and Power*, p. 7.
[18] M. Youngson, *The Weaver, the Word and Wisdom: worshipping the triune God* (Werrington, 2007).
[19] Numbers 20:1, 2 (KJV).

but of Bathsheba, of Miriam,
of Mary Magdalene.
Written out of history,
written out of the canon,
written out of minutes and reports.
Unheard, unrecognized,
unseen yet somehow
undaunted.
Go and find your own water.
Go and find your own solution.
Go and find your own word of wisdom.
I am woman, and I will write my own history.
I will write my own canon.
I will write my own account of the things that
Matter.
Ignore me at your own risk.

The culture in the Methodist Church has not yet changed enough, not to fully embrace the role of women, lay and ordained, in leadership. In all areas of equality, diversity and inclusion there is still work to do. My perception is that we took our foot off the gas in 1972. After a long campaign, the advocates of women's ministry achieved their goal. Women were going to be ordained, job done.

A group of women ministers began meeting at an annual gathering, and after a while formed two camps. One was of women who had fought the fight, had got women's ordination sorted out, and were in campaigning mode still, the fruit of which was the report to the Conference *The Cry of the Beloved* which called for the Church to work more proactively for the full inclusion of women at all levels of the Churches' life and for a change to the predominantly exclusive language of worship and our polity documents.[20] The report was not adopted in its entirety by the Conference and a significant moment of

---

[20] *Conference Agenda* 1995. See also Lenton, '"The Cry of the Beloved"'.

possibility was missed. This group became the Methodist Women's Forum, which continued to lobby the Church for change until it disbanded in the early 2000s.

The other group of women wanted to get together for mutual support. That group continues today as the Women Ministers Annual Gathering. There was a crossover between the two groups, but the Women's Forum focused on campaigning for the role of women in the Church, and went on to help set up the Gender Justice Committee in the Methodist Church, which has now been absorbed into our rather amorphous EDI work.[21]

Number crunching

Meanwhile the Church carried on being the Church, and so today in terms of women in leadership, seven of the Chairs of district, and there are thirty-three Chairs, are women, which is a vast improvement on ten years ago. It still means less than a third of district Chairs are women, when more than fifty percent of those entering training are women, as are almost fifty percent of ministers in the active work. We reached a peak of the number of women superintendents just before the Church adopted the Regrouping for Mission report. Since then we have lost ground. Women, some would argue, do not want to be superintendents of huge mega-circuits. Stereotypes of male and female styles of leadership come into play and are, of course, not necessarily true. In some cases, that where a number of circuits joined together and there were some women superintendents available, one of the men ended up being the ongoing superintendent and the women did not. There are still more women than men in part-time roles, in unpaid ministerial

---

[21] The Methodist Conference of 2020 has received a Council report and passed a number of Notices of Motion, which intend to enable a focused commitment to an inclusive church. EDI means 'equality, diversity, inclusion'.

roles, and in local appointment. This begs a question about how gender and leadership play out in the life of the Church.[22]

For a moment we might look not just at ordained women but consider the membership of the many committees that order our church life. There remain only two committees that have more than fifty percent women, and they are both pastoral committees. The ones to do with financial management, to do with strategy, ministers' stationing and so on, are still predominantly led by men.[23] The numbers skew easily, because some of our groups and committees are small, so if a woman resigns or ends her term of office and is replaced by a man, the statistics show a worsening situation. When looking at the picture as a whole, the trajectory towards better balance and inclusion is very slow. Numbers, quotas, and statistics matter because they offer a lens through which we see that the culture has not changed to the extent that we hoped in the heady days when the laughter changed sides.

Beyond the numbers

Cultural change has happened in some ways but not in others. On two occasions during my presidential year, I was in meetings talking to a male leader, and another male leader inserted himself physically between us to speak to that man as though I was not there. That is still happening, and I tell you I am no shrinking violet, and I was wearing my presidential cross at the time! You know if that is not 'the armour of righteousness' I do not know what is. The bad behaviour of particular individuals is one thing, but systemic and cultural issues remain a challenge for our Church. Eighteen months ago, a friend of mine posted on some closed Facebook groups about incidents of sexual harassment happening to women in the life of the Church. Within a fortnight 117 women contacted her about experiences they had had of either verbal or actual physical

---

[22] See also conclusion to chapter six.
[23] See for example *Minutes* (2019), pp. 75-9.

abuse from men within the life of the Church. These are challenges for all our leadership, male and female at the moment in the Church. We all need to ask questions. What is going on there? What kind of Church do we think we are? This is not the kind of Church I think I am part of and yet it is there, it is happening, and I wonder if there is something going on about the *zeitgeist*, about the world we are living in, where the impunity of world leaders to be able to say what they like without care, and to be known abusers and assaulters of women, and talk about it as a matter of pride, creates an atmosphere in which the whole of society gets caught up and tarnished.

My questions for all leaders in the Church, whether male or female are, how do we challenge that, how do we act against it, how do we speak against it? We might say, as we often do that 'we must start with ourselves'. Well I have been starting with myself for a very, very long time, and I would like others to do the same! We need to be alert, be aware, and be responsive. What we need to change culture is a leap of the imagination. It is that leap of pointing out what is ridiculous now; what is the nonsense now that deserves ridicule? We need to ask ourselves how do we enter into God's vision of what the Church and the world can be, as women, as men.

Global and local

Of course these questions are not only for Methodism in Britain. The General Secretary of the Methodist Church in Southern Africa is Charmaine Morgan. If you look at the leadership of Methodist churches around the world, there are very few that have women in the most senior positions. The Presiding Bishop in Southern Africa is male, but it is interesting how the General Secretary role tends to be the one with the hard power, not the soft power. The presidency in Britain is definitely a soft power, there are few actual powers, and you exercise them with great care and, if you are wise, with the advice of others. But the General Secretary or Secretary of Conference role is key within the life of most churches, it is where the hard power sits, and there are very few women across global Methodism who are in those roles.

I spent time in the church in Papua New Guinea, where women are ordained but are expected to fulfil limited roles. If they are not married, then they may be able to exercise some leadership in an academic way. In terms of the administration and the overall construction of the institution, there are no legislative barriers at all, but culturally it just is not going to happen. In a meal in the Bishop's house in one of the regions, the women sat on the floor to eat, whilst the men ate at the table. I learned quickly that if I did not go and help myself to food first, nobody else would as I was the guest of honour. I took my food and sat on the floor with the women, and caused enormous offence. I was a guest, so had to learn to play the guest game; to do so I, like Hatshepsut wearing the Pharaoh's beard, had to become an honorary man. I wonder what it is in our context a visitor might see that we do not?

Whilst in Papua New Guinea some young men in a training college asked me about the Methodist Church in Britain and human sexuality. We had a good conversation and they were really interested. I went on to say, 'I am interested in the role of women within your church and society'. They looked at me with a look that said, 'I do not know what you mean, it is not on the agenda, it is not an issue, this is the way the world is, and the way women are and the way men are.' It was possible to have a conversation about human sexuality because some of their friends are gay, so the leap of imagination had already been made, but you could not have a conversation about the role of women in leadership or any other role in the church, because it is not an issue, it is just not on the agenda, it is not recognized as being anything other than the way that the world was ordained to be.

I went on to the Solomon Islands and was hosted by the most extraordinary and capable woman superintendent. Marietta is the only woman superintendent in the Uniting Church of the Solomon Islands, which is made up of Methodists and others. My new friend was amazing, and she was getting on with the job of mission and ministry on the ground. I then spent twenty-four hours with the all-male bishops of the Solomon Islands, who were struggling with leadership matters. If Marietta had been present they would not have been having an argument, her compassionate and direct approach, which was not reliant on status would have cut right through the struggle. Within the wider culture of the community it was not possible. This is not to say, 'Gosh, aren't we good, and everybody else has a long way to go'. What I am wanting to get across is the idea of a leap of cultural imagination, that offers the ability to see that the most gifted person in the room for a particular moment is not necessarily the one you think is in charge. What was great about my friend in the Solomon Islands is that she was completely able to subvert the power and get things done, and it was fabulous to watch that happening.

The Methodist Church in Ecuador is about eighteen years old, and the women are very present, fulfilling roles of leadership; nobody even questions it, because there is something new emerging. They have not got an old way of doing it, they are discovering a new way. It is something again about a leap of imagination, a leap of the imagination it takes for an individual woman to think, 'God might be calling me to leadership'. We often have more personal baggage to put down than many men do, so need more imagination about the fact it is possible. As I write this in an academic context I am fighting with my personal impostor syndrome; that is a bit of baggage I need to put down. One of the things needed is to have the imagination to see ourselves not only in those positions, but also the imagination to say that the institution might change because we are there.

I live in Wembley, it is quite a busy place to live in, about fifteen minutes' walk to the stadium. My husband asked me last night, 'Where would women's football be if at the beginning of the twentieth century, the Football Association had not kicked them out?' I wonder where would Methodist ministry be, including women's ministry, if at the start of the twentieth century the dominant denominations had not decided to sacrifice women's vocations on the altar of becoming more respectable. We do not know; we could be in a better place; we could be in a worse place, but I doubt it.

The question for me going forward is: 'Where will we be in twenty years' time, and what leap of the imagination do we need to get us to that point?'

For the anniversary service at Wesley's Chapel for the fortieth anniversary of women's ordination, I wrote the hymn below. Nicola Morrison has written a tune, which is available on *Singing the Faith Plus*.[24] It is based on words within the liturgy for the Ordination of Presbyters.[25]

> Gracious God, you call your people
> to offer lives of love and care;
> serving, teaching, persevering,
> holding all your world in prayer.
>
> *We are worthy by your Spirit.*
> *We are worthy by your Son*
> *to proclaim your gospel story*
> *of a world in Christ made one.*
>
> Gracious God, you call your people
> to share the gospel of your grace;
> to declare that Christ's forgiveness
> is for all in every place.
>
> [and the chorus again, *'We are worthy . . .'*]
>
> Gracious God, you call your people

---

[24] M. Youngson, 'Gracious God, you call your people' (2014), https://www.methodist.org.uk/our-faith/worship/singing-the-faith-plus/posts/gracious-god-you-call-your-people-website-only/ (accessed 15 September 2020).

[25] See Methodist Church, *Methodist Worship Book* (London, 1999), pp. 297-312.

to your table, open, free;
drawing us to share together
in love's hospitality.

We are worthy by your Spirit.
We are worthy by your Son
to proclaim your gospel story
of a world in Christ made one.

I hope that, as a Church, we will take the leap of imagination to recognize all as worthy, by God's Spirit, to proclaim the gospel of grace.

Bibliography

Primary Sources: *Manuscripts and original images*

British Museum, London.

Print no 1906,0823.4.

Cornwall County Record Office.

Thorne, Mary O'Bryan, Ms Journal, X241/8.

Penzance Methodist Circuit, High Street Chapel, *Bible Christian Book of Services*, MR/PZ/125.

Duke University, David M. Rubenstein Rare Book and Manuscript Library, Frank Baker Collection of Wesleyana and British Methodism

Sarah Crosby Ms letter book, Bay 3356, Box 1.ts 1306-5-3:05.

Englesea Brook Museum, Englesea Brook, Cheshire.

Callin Papers, letter from R. W. Callin to E. Callin, 7 May 1918.

Circuit Plans Scrapbook no 36, November 1821 to January 1822.

Circuit Plans Scrapbook no 42, October 1824 to January 1825.

Mss Reports of Itinerant Preachers 1828, 80, 135, 153, 193.

Hereford Archive and Records Centre.

William Parlby's exercise book, BH 28/1/7.

Lambeth Palace Library, London.

Hickes letters, Lambeth Palace Library Ms 3171.

Methodist Archives at the John Rylands Library, University of Manchester.

Bible Christian Manuscript Journal 1824-52, Previous index reference MAW Ms 817; Calkin Reference GB 146.

Conference Ms Journal (Wesleyan).

Taft, Mary, Mss Letters, PLP 104/4.

Thomas, Diana, Letter to Mary Tooth 12 February 1816, Fl/7/3/4.

Tooth, R., Letter to M. Tooth, Fl/3/1/6, vol 3, Corr E-H.

Wesley, John letter to Ann Cutler, MA/2009/001/2.

Wesley, Charles, Hymns for Preachers Extraordinary, Ms MA 1977/583/8.

Wesley, Mehetabel, (Hetty) Ms Letter, MA DDWes 8/21.

Library of Birmingham, Wolfson Centre for Archival Research.

Autobiographical preaching diary of Mary Taft, Ms 977.

National Library of Wales, Aberystwyth (NLW).

Calvinistic Methodist Archive (CMA), Diaries of Howel Harris, 48, 18 August 1739; 72, 29 April 1741; 98, 31 March 1743.

CMA, Trevecka College/1 2945, p. 6, 3 February 1743; p. 50, 4 January 1744; p. 109, 16 July 1744; p. 143, 22 January 1745.

CMA, Trevecka Ms 213, Mary Giles to Howel Harris, 2 February 1740.
—, Ms 569, Elizabeth Thomas to Howel Harris, June 1742.
—, Ms 642, William Richard to Howel Harris, 12 September 1742.
—, Ms 817, Howel Harris to Marmaduke Gwynne, 12 March 1743.
—, Ms 823, Marmaduke Gwynne to Howel Harris, 21 March 1743.
—, Ms 856, Howel Harris to John Lewis, 18 April 1743.
—, Ms 940, Molly Williams to Howel Harris, 1 August 1743.
—, Ms 1197, William Jones and eleven others to Howel Harris, 25 June 1744.
—, Ms 1444, Ann Harry to John Belcher, 13 April 1746.
—, Ms 1388, 1780, Howel Davies to Howel Harris, 30 January 1748.
—, Ms 2013, Thomas William to Howel Harris, 19 October 1751.
—, Ms 2682, Jane Owens to Howel Harris, 27 June 1770.
—, Ms 2685, Mary Jones to Howel Harris, 10 August 1770.

CMA, Personal papers of Sarah Jane Rees ('Cranogwen'); 14182, Sermon on the Book of Proverbs 29:1; 14183, notebook containing lectures; HZ4/65.

NLW, Ms 18435B, p. 57. NLW, Ms 18435B, p. 17, 19 August 1741. NLW, Ms 20,516, 30 January 1757, 20 March 1757, 14 May 1757, 9 June 1757, 20 November 1757.

St Davids Probate SD/1770/220: Jenkin Lewis, Fareham, Hampshire (Blaen-porth), SD/1792/9: Morgan Hughes, Blaen-porth, (Cardigan, 1792).

Oxford Centre for Methodism and Church History, Oxford Brookes University, Wesley Historical Society Library.

Portrait of Mrs Mary Taft.

Christ Church, Oxford.

Wake Ms, 279. Visitation of Lincoln, 1712, Epworth entry.

Wake Letters 5 no 233, 20 November 1715.

Primary Sources: *Books, etc*

Adams, Douglas, *The Hitchhiker's Guide to the Galaxy* (London, 1980).

Anon., *An Account of Charity-schools Lately Erected in England, Wales, and Ireland* (London, 1706).

—, *Some Remarks on a Letter from the Reverend Mr. Whitefield to the Reverend Mr. Wesley, in a Letter from a Gentlewoman to her Friend* (London, 1741), [n.p.].

—, *Account of the Union Meeting for the Promotion of Scriptural Holiness held at Oxford, August 29th to September 7th, 1874* (London, 1874).

—, *Record of the Convention for the Promotion of Scriptural Holiness held at Brighton, May 29th to June 7th, 1875* (Brighton, 1875).

Antliff, William, *Woman: her position and mission* (London, 1856).

Arminian Magazine, later *Methodist Magazine*, later *Wesleyan Methodist Magazine*.

Arthur, William, *Tongue of Fire; or, the true power of Christianity* (London, 1856).

Astell, Mary, *A Serious Proposal to the Ladies, for the Advancement of their True and Greatest Interest* (London, 1697).

—, *Some Reflections upon Marriage* (London, 1700).

Banner of Holiness.

Bath Chronicle.

Bennett, John, *Strictures on Female Education, Chiefly as it Relates to the Culture of the Heart, in Four Essays, By a Clergyman of the Church of England* (London, 1787).

Bible Christian Magazine.

Bible Christian Minutes.

Bible Christian Minutes President's Circular.

Boardman, Mrs, *Who shall publish the glad tidings?* (Boston, 1873).

—, *Life and Labours of the Rev. W. E. Boardman, preface by the Rev. Mark Guy Pearse* (New York, 1887).

Boardman, William E., *The Higher Christian Life* (London, 1859, second edition 1871).

—, *'The Lord that Healeth Thee': (Jehovah-Rophi)* (London, 1881).

Bolton Chronicle.

Book of Services [Bible Christian] (London, 1897).

Booth, Catherine M., *Female Teaching: or, the Rev. A. A. Rees versus Mrs Palmer, being a reply to a pamphlet by the above gentleman on the Sunderland Revival* (London, 1861).

Booth-Tucker, Frederick St G. De L., *The Life of Catherine Booth* 2 vols (London, 1892).

Bourne, Frederick W., *The Bible Christians: their origin and history 1815–1907* (London, 1905).

Bowe, William, 'The Position of Woman in the Church', fourth paper, in *PM Quarterly Review*, vol 7, (1885).

Bray, Gerald (ed.), *Records of Convocation, vol 9 (1701-8), vol 10 (1710-13), vol 11 (1714-60), Canterbury* (Woodbridge, 2006).

Broad, John (ed.), *Bishop Wake's Summary of Visitation Returns for the Diocese of Lincoln 1706-15* 2 vols (Oxford, 2012).

Brown, John Holland, *Memoir of Charlotte Sophia Steigen Berger of Saffron Walden* (London, 1879).

Bryant, R., 'The Position of Woman in the Church', third paper, in *PM Quarterly Review*, vol 7, (1885).

Buchanan, James, *Plan of an English Grammar School Education* (London, 1770).

Butler, Josephine E. (ed.), *Woman's Work and Woman's Culture: a series of essays* (London, 1869).

Chilcote, Paul W., *Her Own Story: autobiographical portraits of early Methodist women* (Nashville, 2001).

—, *Early Methodist Spirituality: selected women's writings* (Nashville, 2007).

The Christian's Pathway to Power.

Christian Messenger.

Clarke, Adam, *Memoirs of the Wesley Family: collected principally from original documents* (London, 1823).

—, 2 vols (London, 1832).

Clowes, William, *The Journals of William Clowes* (London, 1844).

Coke, Thomas and Henry Moore, *The Life of the Rev John Wesley A.M.* (London, 1792).

Conder Nattrass, James, 'Great Yarmouth' in *PWHS*, vol 3, no 3, (1901), 73-7.

Curnock, Nehemiah (ed.), *The Journal of the Rev. John Wesley* (London, 1909-16).

Digest of the Rules, Regulations and Usages [of the Bible Christians] (London, 1892 and 1902).

Dunton, John, *The life and errors of John Dunton, late citizen of London, written by himself in solitude; with an idea of a new life, wherein is shewn how he'd think, speak, and act, might he live over his days again; intermix'd with the new discoveries the author has made in his travels abroad and in his private conversation at home* (London, 1705).

Dymond, George P., *Thomas Ruddle of Shebbear* (London, *c*.1913).

East London Observer.

Elaw, Zilpha, *Memoirs of the Life, Religious Experience, Ministerial Travels and Labours of Mrs. Zilpha Elaw, an American Female of Colour: together with some account of the great religious revivals in America* (London, 1846).

Eliot, George, [Mary Ann Evans pseud.] *Adam Bede* (Edinburgh, 1890).

Fletcher, John, *A Third Check to Antinomianism: in a letter to the author of* Pietas Oxoniensis (Bristol, 1772).

Freeman, Ann and Henry, *A Memoir of the Life and Ministry of Ann Freeman* (Exeter, NH, 1831).

Gilbert, Ann, 'Narrative' in *AM*, vol 18, (1795).

Gilbert, Henrietta F., *Memoirs of the late Mrs Mary Gilbert . . .* (London, 1817).

Gordon, Adoniram J., *The Ministry of Healing; or, miracles of cure in all ages* (London, 1882).

Greenfield, T., 'The Position of Woman in the Church', second paper, in *PM Quarterly Review,* vol 7, (1885).

Gregory, John, *A Father's Legacy to his Daughters; by the late Dr Gregory of Edinburgh* (Edinburgh, 1774).

Guide to Holiness.

Haley, John M. and Lesley J. Francis, *British Methodism: what circuit ministers really think* (Peterborough, 2006).

Herod, George, *Biographical Sketches of Some of those Preachers whose Labours Contributed to the Origination and Early Extension of the PM Connexion* (London, 1855, reprinted Stoke-on-Trent, 2002).

Hill, William, *Hill's Arrangement of Ministers and Probationers with Circuits* (London, 1819-1968).

Hughes, Garfield H. (ed.), *Gweithiau William Williams Pantycelyn, Cyfrol II: Rhyddiaith* (Cardiff, 1967).

Hughes, John, *Methodistiaeth Cymru, Cyfrol I* (Wrexham, 1851).

Jeffs, H. B., 'Our Women and the Centenary', in *PM Leader* (28 February 1907).

Kilner, John, *Remarks on Christian Women's Work in Heathendom* (London, 1874).

The King's Highway: a journal of scriptural holiness.

Lancashire Evening Post.

Lawson, William D., *Wesleyan Local Preachers* (Newcastle-upon-Tyne, 1874).

Locke, John, *Some Thoughts Concerning Education* (London, 1693).

Lloyd, Gareth, *The Fletcher-Tooth Papers* (Manchester, 1997-).

McGregor, John J., *Memoir of Miss Alice Cambridge* (Dublin, 1832).

Macpherson, J., 'The Position of Woman in the Church', first paper, in *PM Quarterly Review*, vol 7, (1885).

Maidstone Telegraph.

Mandeville, Bernard, 'An Essay on Charity and Charity Schools' in *The Fable of the Bees, or, Private Vices, Public Benefits* second edition (London, 1723).

Methodist Church of Great Britain, *Singing the Faith* (London, 2011).

Methodist New Connexion Minutes (Hanley, 1806).

Methodist Recorder.

Minutes of Conference (also *Minutes of Several Conversations at the . . . yearly conference of the people called Methodists . . .*) (London, with date). [Wesleyan to 1932. Methodist from 1932].

Moore, Henry, *The Life of Mrs Mary Fletcher Consort and Relict of the Rev John Fletcher . . .* (London, 1817).

Page, I. E., 'The Late Rev. Thornley Smith' in *The King's Highway*, vol 20, (1891), 357-8.

Palmer, Phoebe, *The Way of Holiness: with notes by the way: being a narrative of religious experience resulting from a determination to be a Bible Christian* (London, 1845).

—, *Faith and its Effects: or, fragments from my portfolio* (London, 1856).

—, *The Way of Holiness: with notes by the way: being a narrative of religious experience . . . First English edition, reprinted from the thirty-fourth American edition. With preface by the Rev. T. Collins* (London, 1856).

—, *Entire Devotion to God: a present to a Christian friend* (London, 1857).

—, *Incidental Illustrations of the Economy of Salvation: its doctrines and duties* (London, 1858).

—, *Promise of the Father: or, a neglected specialty of the Last Days. Addressed to the clergy and laity of all Christian communities* (New York, 1859).

—, *Four Years in the Old World: comprising the travels and evangelistic labours of Dr and Mrs Palmer in England, Scotland, Ireland and Wales* (New York, 1866).

— and Thomas C. Oden (ed.), *Phoebe Palmer: selected writings* (New York, 1988).

Parsons, T., 'The Position of Woman in the Church', fifth paper, in *PM Quarterly Review*, vol 7, (1885).

Patriot.

Pearce, E., Letter re 'Our Women and the Centenary' in *PM Leader* (7 March 1907).

Pearse, George, *Étude sur l'épître de saint Paul aux Romains* (Paris, 1875).

—, 'The Gift of the Holy Spirit' in *The King's Highway*, vol 5, (1876), 349-5.

— and Pearse, Jane B., *The Bible Women in France* (London, 1874).

Penuel.

Petty, John, *The History of the Primitive Methodist Connexion* (London, 1860).

Portsmouth Evening News.

Primitive Methodist Leader.

Primitive Methodist Magazine.

Primitive Methodist Minutes.

Primitive Methodist Quarterly Review and Christian Ambassador, NS 7 1885 Symposium: the position of women in the church, 223-45,423-42, 676-86.

Rand, Benjamin (ed.), *The Correspondence of John Locke and Edward Clarke* (London, 1927).

Rees, Arthur A., *Reasons for Not Co-operating in the Alleged 'Sunderland Revivals': in an address to his congregation* (Sunderland, 1859).

Report of the Wesleyan Methodist Thanksgiving Fund, 1878-1883 (London, 1883).

Ripley, Dorothy, *The Extraordinary Conversion and Religious Experience of Dorothy Ripley* (New York, 1810).

—, *The Bank of Faith and Works United* (New York, 1819).

Roberts, William, *Ffrewyll y Methodistiaid, neu Buttein-glwm Siencyn ac Ynfydog* (Shrewsbury, 1746).

Roche, John A., 'Mrs. Phoebe Palmer' in *The Ladies' Repository; a monthly periodical, devoted to literature, art and religion* (Cincinnati, 1866).

—, *The Life of Mrs Sarah A. Lankford Palmer: who for sixty years was the able teacher of entire holiness* (New York, 1898).

Rowley, Edith, *Fruits of Righteousness in the Life of Susanna Knapp* (Worcester, 1866).

Sankey, Ira D., *Sacred Songs and Solos* (London, 1878).

Sigston, James, *A Memoir of the Life and Ministry of Mr William Bramwell,* second edition (London, 1820).

Simmons, Jim, *Soapbox Evangelist* (Chichester, 1972).

Smith, Adam, *The Theory of Moral Sentiments; or, an essay towards an analysis of the principles by which men naturally judge concerning the conduct and character, first of their neighbours, and afterwards of themselves* . . . vol 2, sixth edition (London, 1790).

Smith, Thornley, *Memorials of Mrs Elizabeth Smith, wife of the Rev. Thornley Smith, including brief notices of the Wesleyan missions in South Africa and some occurrences connected with the recent war in that country* (London, 1848).

—, *Memoir of the Rev. Thomas Laidman Hodgson, Wesleyan missionary* . . . (London, 1854).

—, *The Earnest Missionary: a memoir of the Rev. Horatio Pearse, late General Superintendent of the Wesleyan Missions* (London, 1864).

—, *Walking in the Light: a memoir of Mrs Hannah Bairstow* (London, 1868).

—, *Won at Last: or, memoirs of Captain George and Mrs Hannah Smith* (London, 1870).

—, *Christian Theology; a selection of the most important passages in the writings of the Rev. John Wesley, A.M. arranged so as to form a complete body of divinity with a biographical sketch* (London, 1871).

—, *Memoirs of Rev. John Wesley Etheridge: including extracts from his writings, correspondence and poetry* (London, 1871).

—, *Expository Lectures on the First Epistle of St Peter* (London, 1878).

—, *Memoir of the Rev. John Whittle Appleyard, Wesleyan missionary in South Africa* . . . (London, 1881).

—, *A Christian Mother: memoirs of Mrs Thornley Smith with extracts from her letters* (London, 1885).

—, with John Holt Lord, *Memorials of* . . . *Emma Loutit, wife of* . . . *J[ames] Loutit* . . . (London, 1867).

Smith, Miss Thornley [Catherine Hannah Smith], 'Keeping God Waiting' in *Thy Healer and Faith Witness*, vol 6, (1889).

Stevenson, George J., *City Road Chapel London and its Associations, Historical, Biographical and Memorial* (London, 1872).

Taft, Mary, *Memoirs of the life of Mrs Mary Taft, formerly Miss Barritt written by herself* pts 1 and 2 (London, 1827), pt 3 (Shebbear, Devon, 1831).

Taft, Zechariah, *Original Letters Never Before Published, on Doctrinal, Experimental and Practical Religion* (Whitby, 1821).

—, *Biographical Studies of the Lives and Ministries of Various Holy Women* 2 vols (Leeds, 1825, 1828; reprinted Peterborough, 1992).

Telford, John (ed.), *John Wesley's Letters* 8 vols (London, 1931).

The Constitution.

Thorne, John, *A Memoir of James Thorne* (London, 1873).

Treffry, Richard jr, *Memoirs of Mrs Jane Treffry* (London, 1830).

Told, Silas, *An Account of the life, and dealings of God with Silas Told, late preacher of the Gospel: wherein is set forth the wonderful display of Divine Providence towards him when at sea, his many sufferings abroad . . .* (London, 1786).

United Methodist Magazine.

United Methodist Church Minutes of Conference.

Waddy, Adeline, *The Life of the Rev. Samuel D. Waddy* (London, 1878).

Waddy, Samuel D., *Ministerial Support. London Conference, 1860. The Substance of the Official Sermon and Ordination Charge [on Heb. 13 v17] of S.D.W.* (London, 1860).

Walford, John, *Memoirs of the Life and Labours of Hugh Bourne* (London, 1856; reprinted Stoke-on-Trent, 2002).

—, 'Remarks on the Ministry of Women' in William Antliff (ed.), *Memoirs of the Life and Labours of the late Venerable Hugh Bourne* (London, 1855).

Wallace, Charles jr (ed.), *Susanna Wesley: the complete writings* (Oxford, 1997).

—, *From a Mother's Pen: selections from the spiritual writings of Susanna Wesley* (London, 2019).

Watts, Isaac, *An Essay Towards the Encouragement of Charity Schools particularly those which are supported by Protestant Dissenters, for teaching the children of the poor to read and work* (London, 1728).

Wesley, John, *Minutes of Several Conversations* (London, 1779).

—, *A Collection of Hymns, for the Use of the People Called Methodists* (London, 1850).

—, 'A Female Course of Study' in *AM*, vol 3, (1780), 602-4.

—, 'An Account of the Disturbances in my Father's House' in *AM*, vol 7, (1784), 548-50, 606-8, 654-6.

—, ed. Baker, Frank et al., *The Works of John Wesley: bicentenary edition* (Oxford and Nashville, 1976-).

Wesleyan Reform Union Magazine.

Wheatley, Richard, *The Life and Letters of Mrs. Phoebe Palmer* (New York, 1884).

Who's Who in Methodism (London, 1933).

Wilkinson, John, *God Answers Prayer: some experiences in the life and labours of John Wilkinson* (London, 1902).

Wilkinson, Samuel H., *The Life of John Wilkinson, the Jewish Missionary* (London, 1908).

Secondary Sources

Aaron, Jane, *Nineteenth-century women's writing in Wales: nation, gender and identity* second edition (Cardiff, 2010).

Allchin, Arthur M., *Ann Griffiths: the furnace and the fountain* (Cardiff, 1976; pb. Cardiff, 1987).

Anon., *Wesley and His Successors: a centenary memorial of the death of John Wesley* (London, 1891).

—, 'Monod (Théodore)' in F. Lichtenberger (réd.), *Encyclopédie des sciences religieuses* (Paris, 1882), vol 13.

—, 'Monod, Théodore' in S. Macauley Jackson (ed.), *The New Schaff-Herzog Encyclopedia of Religious Knowledge* (London, 1910), vol 7, pp. 473-4.

Appleby, C. J., 'Ann Guard Carkeek' in *Journal of the Cornish Methodist Historical Association*, vol 9, no 3, (1999), 106.

Atkinson, Juliette, *Victorian Biography Reconsidered: a study of nineteenth-century 'hidden' lives* (Oxford, 2010).

Bailey, Joanne, *Parenting in England c.1760-1830: emotion, identity and generation* (Oxford, 2012).

Baker, Frank, *Charles Wesley As Revealed by His Letters*, The WHS lecture no 14 (London, 1948).

—, *John Wesley and the Church of England* (London, 1970).

—, 'Thomas Maxfield's First Sermon' in *PWHS*, vol 27, (1949-50), 7-15.

—, 'The People Called Methodists: Polity' in Davies, Rupert E., A. Raymond George and E. Gordon Rupp (eds), *History of Methodism in Great Britain*, vol 1, (London, 1965), pp. 213-55.

Barker-Benfield, G., *The Culture of Sensibility: sex and society in eighteenth-century* (London, 1992).

Barber, Jill, 'Hidden Voices: Hannah Maria Knowles, "A Mind of Unusual Strength"' in *The Ranters' Digest*, vol 18, (2018), 16-23.

—, 'More Hidden Voices: Ann Hirst and Emma Quarton' in *The Ranters' Digest*, vol 19, (2019), 20-4.

Bebbington, David, *Holiness in Nineteenth-Century England* (Carlisle, 2000).

Beard, Mary, *Women and Power: a manifesto* (London, 2017).

Beauvoir, Simone de, *The Second Sex*, trans. and ed. Howard M. Parshley, (London, 1953).

Beckerlegge, Oliver A., *United Methodist Ministers and their Circuits* (London, 1968).

Beers, Laura, *Red Ellen: the life of Ellen Wilkinson, socialist, feminist, internationalist* (London, 2016).

Bennett, Christi-An, 'Women's Work: The Role of Women in WM Overseas Mission in the Nineteenth Century' in *MH*, vol 32, no 44, (1994), 229-36.

Best, Gary M., *Charles Wesley: a biography* (Peterborough, 2006).

—, *John Cennick* (Bristol, 2016).

—, *Seven Sisters* (Weston-super-Mare, 2016).

—, *A Tragedy of Errors: the story of Grace Murray, the woman whom John Wesley loved and lost* (Bristol, 2016).

—, *The Cradle of Methodism 1739-2017* (Bristol, 2017).

Beynon, Tom (ed.), *Howell Harris, Reformer and Soldier (1714–1773)* (Caernarfon, 1958).

—(ed.), *Howell Harris's Visits to London* (Aberystwyth, 1960).

—(ed.), *Howell Harris's Visits to Pembrokeshire* (Aberystwyth, 1966).

—, 'Morfa Bach, Cydweli', *Cylchgrawn Cymdeithas Hanes y Methodistiaid Calfinaidd/Journal of the Historical Society of the Presbyterian Church of Wales*, 16 (1931).

Bowen, Ivor (ed.), *The Statutes of Wales* (London, 1908).

Bowen, James M., 'A Dream Fulfilled: The Life of Mary Ann Werry, Bible Christian, Preacher, Teacher and Evangelist' in *PWHS*, vol 61, no 6, (2018), 274-9.

Bowen, Marjorie, *Wrestling Jacob* (London, 1937).

Brailsford, Mabel R., *Susanna Wesley: the Mother of Methodism* (London, 1938).

Brown, Earl Kent, *Women of Mr Wesley's Methodism* (Metuchen, NJ, 1983).

Bundy, David, 'Keswick and the Experience of Evangelical Piety' in Edith L. W. Blumhofer and Randall H. Balmer (eds), *Modern Christian Revivals* (Urbana, IL, 1993), pp. 118-44.

—, 'Pauline Missions: The Wesleyan Holiness Vision' in Charles Yrigoyen jr (ed.), *The Global Impact of the Wesleyan Traditions and Their Related Movements*, Pietist and Wesleyan Studies, vol 14, (Lanham, MD, 2002), pp. 13-26.

—, 'Radical Holiness Becomes a World Christian Movement: the influence of Isabella Sarah Leonard in Great Britain, Australia and Singapore, 1881-1892' in William Kostlevy and

Wallace Thornton jr (eds), *The Radical Holiness Movement in the Christian Tradition: a festschrift for Larry D. Smith*, Studies in the History of World Christianities, vol 1, (Lexington, 2016), pp. 53-67.

—, 'Sophia Chambers, Founder of the Holiness Church: A Case Study of Victorian Entrepreneurial Religious Leadership' in *WMS*, vol 11, no 1, (2019), 24-9.

Burnham, C. Paul and Colin C. Short, 'Lillie Edwards (1863–1937): A Female Methodist Superintendent Minister from 1894 to 1911' in *PWHS*, vol 60, no 2, (2015), 64-73.

Burnham, Maureen B. and C. Paul, 'The Making of an Evangelical Minister: The Early Years of Frederick William Bourne (1830–1905)' in *PWHS*, vol 60, no 5, (2016), 199-213.

Burton, Vicki Tolar, *Spiritual Literacy in John Wesley's Methodism* (Waco, TX, 2008).

Butler, Melissa A., 'Early Liberal Roots of Feminism: John Locke's attack on patriarchy' in Nancy J. Hirschmann and Kirstie M. McClure (eds), *Feminist Interpretations of John Locke* (Pennsylvania, 2007).

Bygrave, Stephen, *Uses of Education: readings in enlightenment in England* (Lewisburg, 2009).

Calder, Sandy, *The Origins of Primitive Methodism* (Woodbridge, 2016).

Carwardine, Richard, *Trans-Atlantic Revivalism: popular evangelicalism in Britain and America, 1790-1865* (Westport, CT, 1978).

Chandler, Andrew, *Anglicanism, Methodism and Ecumenism: a history of the Queen's and Handsworth Colleges* (London, 2018).

— (ed.), *The Selected Writings of W. R. Ward* (Farnham, 2014).

Chilcote, Paul W., *John Wesley and the Women Preachers of Early Methodism* (Metuchen, NJ, 1991).

—, *She Offered them Christ: the legacy of women preachers in early Methodism* (Eugene, OR, 1993).

—, *The Methodist Defense of Women in Ministry: a documentary history* (Eugene, OR, 2017).

Church, Leslie F., *More about the Early Methodist People* (London, 1949).

Clarke, Eliza, *Susanna Wesley* (London, 1886).

Clarke, Simone and Michael Roberts (eds), *Women and Gender in Early Modern Wales* (Cardiff, 2000).

Cocks, W., 'Week St. Mary Circuit Celebrates 150 Years . . .' in *Old Cornwall*, vol 9, no 8, (1983), pp. 377-90.

Cooley, John K., *Baal, Christ and Mohammed: religion and revolution in North Africa* (London, 1963).

Cornwall, Robert D., *Visible and Apostolic: the constitution of the Church in High Church Anglican and non-juror thought* (Delaware, 1993).

Crisford, Carlos C., *A Golden Candlestick or Methodism in Eastbourne* (Eastbourne, 1913).

Curnow, Edwin A., *Bible Christian Methodists in South Australia 1850–1900: a biography of chapels and their people* (Black Forest, South Australia, 2015).

Currie, Robert, *Methodism Divided: a study in the sociology of ecumenicalism* (London, 1968).

Dallimore, Arnold A., *Susanna: the mother of John and Charles Wesley* (Darlington, 1992).

Davidoff, Leonore and Catherine Hall, *Family Fortunes: men and women of the English middle class, 1780–1950* (London, 1987).

Davies, Rupert E., A. Raymond George and E. Gordon Rupp (eds), *History of Methodism in Great Britain* 4 vols (London, 1965-82).

Davis, Justin A., *Schleiermacher and Palmer: the father and mother of the modern Protestant mindset* (Eugene, OR, 2019).

Daybell, James and Andrew Gordon, *Women and Epistolary Agency in Early Modern Culture, 1450–1690* (London, 2016).

Dews, D. Colin, 'Ann Carr (1783-1841) and the Female Revivalists of Leeds, a study in female preachers, secession and Primitive Methodism' in *From Mow Cop to Peake 1807-1932* (Leeds, 1982), pp. 15-31.

—, 'Ann Carr and the Female Revivalists of Leeds' in Malmgreen (ed.), *Religion in the Lives of English Women* (London and Bloomington, IN, 1986).

—, *Ranters, Revivalists, Radicals, Reformers and Revolutionaries: a celebration of Methodist local preaching in Yorkshire* (Leeds, 1996).

East, David, *My Dear Sally; the life of Sarah Mallet, one of John Wesley's preachers* (Loughborough, 2003).

Easton, David P., *A History of the Nonconformist Churches on the Isles of Scilly* (Isles of Scilly, 2009).

Evans, John, *Hanes Methodistiaeth rhan ddeheuol sir Aberteifi* (Dolgellau, 1904).

Field, Clive D., 'Adam and Eve: Gender in the English Free Church constituency' in *Journal of Ecclesiastical History*, vol 44, no 1, (1993), 63-79.

Field-Bibb, Jacqueline, *Women Towards Priesthood: ministerial politics and feminist praxis* (Cambridge, 1991).

—, 'The worst of heresies' in *Modern Churchman*, vol 33, no 4, (1992), 13-22.

Forsaith, Peter, 'The Curious Incident of Susanna Wesley's Rosebud Lips' in Virgoe, (ed.), *Angels and Impudent Women* (Loughborough, 2007), pp. 31-51.

—, *Image, Identity and John Wesley: a study in portraiture* (Abingdon, 2018).

Gardner, William B., 'George Hickes and the Origins of the Bangorian Controversy' in *Studies in Philology*, vol 39, no 1, (1942), 65-78.

Garlick, Kenneth B., *Garlick's Methodist Registry* (London, 1983).

George, A. Raymond, 'Ordination' in *DMBI*, p. 260.

Gibson, William, *The Church of England 1688-1832: unity and accord* (London, 2001).

—, '"None but Presbyterian Baptism": Samuel and Susanna Wesley, monarchy and marriage' in *PWHS*, vol 61, no 5, (2018), 179-86.

—, '*Strenæ Natalitiæ:* Ambivalence and Equivocation in Oxford in 1688' in *History of Universities,* vol 31, no 1, (2018).

—, *Samuel Wesley and the Crisis of Tory Piety, 1685-1720* (Oxford, 2021) forthcoming.

Gleave, Margaret, 'An Extraordinary Calling' in *The Ranters' Digest,* vol 15, (2017), 4-13.

Glen, Robert, 'An early Methodist Revival in the West Indies' in *WMS,* vol 9, no 1, (2017), 36-56.

Goodman, Joyce, 'Class and Religion' in James C. Albisetti (ed.) et al., *Girls' Secondary Education in the Western World* (New York, 2010).

Gordon, Eleanor and Gwyneth Nair, *Public Lives: women, family and society in Victorian Britain* (New Haven, 2003).

Graham, E. Dorothy, *Chosen by God: a list of the female travelling preachers of early Primitive Methodism* (Broxton, 1989).

—, 'Chosen by God: the Female Travelling Preachers of early Primitive Methodism', The WHS Lecture 1993 in *PWHS,* vol 49, (1993), pp. 77-95.

—, 'Women Local Preachers' in Geoffrey Milburn and Margaret Batty (eds), *Workaday Preachers: the story of Methodist local preaching* (Peterborough, 1995).

—, *Saved to Serve: the story of the Wesley Deaconess Order 1880-1978* (Peterborough, 2002).

—, 'Two Primitive Women Preachers' in *PWHS,* vol 56, (2007), 46-55.

—, *Chosen By God: a list of the female travelling preachers of early Primitive Methodism* second edition, enlarged (Evesham, 2010).

Graham, William T., *Wesley's Early Experiments in Education* (Ilkeston, 1990).

Gregory, Jeremy, 'Gender and the Clerical Profession 1660-1850' in R. N. Swanson (ed.), *Studies in Church History,* vol 34, (Bury St Edmunds, 1998).

Guy, John R., Kathryn Jenkins and Frances Knight (eds), *Journal of Welsh Religious History*, vol 7, 'Wales, Women and Religion in Historical Perspective', (1999).

Hammond, Geordan, *John Wesley in America: restoring primitive Christianity* (Oxford, 2014).

—, and Peter Forsaith (eds), *Religion, Gender and Industry: exploring church and Methodism in a local setting* (Eugene, OR, 2011).

Hardman, Keith J., *Charles Grandison Finney: revivalist and reformer* (Durham, 1987).

Harmon, Rebecca Lamar, *Susanna: mother of the Wesleys* (Nashville and New York, 1968).

Harrison, John F. C., *Late Victorian Britain 1875-1901* (London, 1990).

Hart, Elizabeth, 'Susanna Annesley Wesley—An Able Divine', in *Touchstone*, (May 1988), 4-12.

—, 'A Tinge of the Ideal: Trans-Atlantic Interpretation in Portraits of Susanna Wesley', in Neil Semple (ed.), *Canadian Methodist Historical Society Papers*, vol 8, 1991 (for 1988 and 1990), 137-57.

—, 'Susanna Wesley and her Editors' in *PWHS*, vol 48, no 6, (1992), 202-9, and vol 49, no 1, (1993), 1-10.

Hastling, Arthur H. L., *The History of Kingswood School: together with register of Kingswood School and Woodhouse Grove School, and a list of masters* (London, 1898).

Heath, Elaine A., *Naked Faith: the mystical theology of Phoebe Palmer* (Eugene, OR, 2009).

Heeney, Brian, 'The Beginnings of Church Feminism: Women and the Councils of the Church of England, 1897-1919' in Malmgreen (ed.), *Religion in the Lives of English Women 1760-1930* (London and Bloomington, IN, 1986), pp. 260-84.

Heitzenrater, Richard P., *Wesley and the People Called Methodists* (Nashville, 1995).

Hempton, David, *Methodism and Politics in British Society 1750-1850* (London, 1984).

—, *The Religion of the People: Methodism and popular religion* c.*1750-1900* (London, 1996).

—, *Methodism: empire of the Spirit* (New Haven, 2005).

Hill, Charles P., *British Economic and Social History 1700-1975* (London, 1977).

Hilton, Mary, *Women and the Shaping of the Nation's Young: education and public doctrine in Britain 1750-1850* (Aldershot, 2007).

Hindmarsh, D. Bruce, *The Evangelical Conversion Narrative* (Oxford, 2005).

Hirschmann, Nancy J., 'Intersectionality Before Intersectionality was Cool: the importance of class to feminist interpretations of Locke' in Hirschmann, *Feminist Interpretations of John Locke* (Pennsylvania, 2007).

Hodges, Herbert A., *Flame in the Mountains: Williams Pantycelyn, Ann Griffiths and the Welsh hymn*, ed. E. Wyn James (Tal-y-bont, 2017).

Hughes, Glyn T., 'Welsh-speaking Methodism' in Madden (ed.), *Methodism in Wales*, pp. 25-32.

Hurst, Terry, 'Biographies in Church Monuments: William Smith and Jane Vazeille of Newcastle upon Tyne' in David J. Hart and David J. Jeremy (eds), *Brands Plucked from the Burning: essays on Methodist memorialisation and remembering* (Evesham, 2013).

Ives, Arthur G. L., *Kingswood School in Wesley's Day and Since* (London, 1970).

James, E. Wyn, 'The Evolution of the Welsh Hymn' in Isabel Rivers and David L. Wykes (eds), *Dissenting Praise: religious dissent and the hymn in England and Wales* (Oxford, 2011).

Jenkins, Geraint H., '"An Old and Much Honoured Soldier": Griffith Jones, Llanddowror', *Welsh History Review*, vol 11, no 4, (1983), 449–68.

—, *The Foundations of Modern Wales: Wales 1642-1780* (Cardiff, 1987).

—, *Protestant Dissenters in Wales 1639–1689* (Cardiff, 1992).

—, Suggett, Richard, and White, Eryn M., 'The Welsh Language in Early Modern Wales' in Geraint H. Jenkins (ed.), *The Welsh Language before the Industrial Revolution* (Cardiff, 1997).

Jessop, William, *An Account of Methodism in Rossendale . . .* (Manchester, 1880).

Johnson, Dale A., 'Gender and the Construction of Models of Christian Activity: A Case Study in Church History' in *Studies in Christianity and Culture*, vol 73, no 3, (June 2004), pp. 247-72.

Jones, David Ceri, Boyd S. Schlenther, and Eryn M. White, *The Elect Methodists: Calvinistic Methodism in England and Wales 1735–1811* (Cardiff, 2012).

Jones, David G., *Cofiant Cranogwen* (Caernarfon, 1932).

Jones, Gerallt, *Cranogwen: Portread Newydd* (Llandysul, 1981).

Jones, Ieuan Gwynedd, *Explorations and Explanation: essays in the social history of Victorian Wales* (Llandysul, 1981).

Jones, Margaret P., 'From "The State of my Soul" to "Exalted Piety": women's voices in the Arminian/Methodist Magazine 1778-1821' in R. N. Swanson (ed.), *Gender and Christian Religion* (Bury St Edmunds, 1998).

—, '"Her Claim to Public Notice": reflections on the historiography of women in British Methodism' in Richard Sykes (ed.), *God's Own Story: some trends in Methodist historiography* (Oxford, 2003).

Jones, R. M., 'Ann Griffiths and the Norm', in Branwen Jarvis (ed.), *A Guide to Welsh Literature c. 1700–1800* (Cardiff, 2000).

Julian, John, *A Dictionary of Hymnology*, vol 2 (New York, 1907).

Kendall, H. B., *The Origin and History of the Primitive Methodist Church* 2 vols (London, 1905).

—, 'The Old Wells and the New' in *PM Leader* (24 January 1907).

Kaye, Elaine, Janet Lees and Kirsty Thorpe, *Daughters of Dissent* (London, 2004).

Kirk, John, *The Mother of the Wesleys: a biography* fourth edition (London, 1866).

Kimbrough, S. T. jr and Kenneth G. C. Newport (eds), *The Manuscript Journal of Charles Wesley MA* (Nashville, 2007).

Knighton, D. G., 'English-speaking Methodism' in Madden (ed.), *Methodism in Wales.*

Knights, Elspeth, 'A "Licensuous" Daughter: Mehetabel Wesley, 1697-1750' in *Women's Writing: the Elizabethan to Victorian period*, vol 4, no 1, (1997), 15-39.

Knights, Mark, *Devil in Disguise: deception, delusion, and fanaticism in the early English Enlightenment* (Oxford, 2011).

Kostlevy, William (ed.), *The A to Z of the Holiness Movement* (Lanham MD, 2020).

Laurence, Anne, *Women in England 1500-1760* (London, 1994).

Leary, William, *Ministers and Circuits in the PM Church: a directory* (Loughborough, 1990).

—, *Some Lincolnshire Methodists* (Loughborough, 1998).

Leetooze, Sher B., *The Damascus Road: short biographies of the preachers who served the Canadian Conference of the Bible Christians 1832-1884* (Bowmanville, ON, 2005).

Le Moignan, Christina, *Following the Lamb: a reading of Revelation for the new millennium* (Peterborough, 2000).

Lenton, John, *'My Sons in the Gospel': an analysis of Wesley's itinerant preachers*, The WHS Lecture 2000 (Loughborough, 2000).

—, *John Wesley's Preachers: a social and statistical analysis of the British and Irish preachers who entered the Methodist itinerancy before 1791* (Milton Keynes, 2009).

—, 'Labouring for the Lord: women preachers in Wesleyan Methodism 1802-1932—a revisionist view' in Richard Sykes (ed.), *Beyond the Boundaries: preaching in the Wesleyan tradition* (Oxford, 1998).

—, 'East Anglian Women Wesleyan Methodist Preachers in Wesleyan Methodism to 1910' in *East Anglian WHS Bulletin* (2008), 1-10.

—, 'Support Groups for Methodist Women preachers 1803-51' in Hammond and Forsaith (eds), *Religion, Gender and Industry: exploring church and Methodism in a local setting* (Eugene, OR, 2011), pp. 137-55.

—, 'Surviving Letters Received by Charles Wesley' in *Proceedings of the Charles Wesley Society* vol 19, (2015), pp. 43-58.

—, '"The Cry of the Beloved": Methodist Women Ministers 1973-1996' in *The Shropshire Wesley Historical Society Bulletin*, vol 28, (2018).

—, 'Mary Barritt Taft (1773-1851): A Successful Revivalist?' in *PWHS*, vol 62, no 1, (2019), 15-34.

Lloyd, Gareth, *Charles Wesley and the Struggle for Methodist Identity* (Oxford, 2007).

—, 'Sarah Perrin (1721-1787): Early Methodist Exhorter' in *MH*, vol 41, no 3, (2003), 79-88.

Lloyd, Jennifer M., *Women and the Shaping of British Methodism: persistent preachers 1807-1907* (Manchester, 2009).

—, 'Women Preachers in the Bible Christian Connexion' in *Albion*, vol 36, no 3, (2004), 451-81.

Lloyd-Morgan, Ceridwen, 'From temperance to suffrage?' in Angela V. John (ed.), *Our Mother's Land: chapters in Welsh women's history, 1830–1939* (Cardiff, 1991), pp. 135-58.

Lynch, Elizabeth Kurtz, 'John Wesley's Editorial Hand' in Jeremy Gregory (ed.), *John Wesley: tercentenary essays: proceedings of a conference held at the University of Manchester, June 2003*, Special Issue of the *Bulletin of the John Rylands University Library*, vol 85, (Manchester, 2005).

McEwen, Gilbert D., *The Oracle of the Coffee House: John Dunton's Athenian Mercury*, (San Marino, CA, 1972).

Mack, Phyllis, *Heart Religion in the British Enlightenment: gender and emotion in early Methodism* (Cambridge, 2008).

—, 'Religion, Feminism and the Problem of Agency: reflections on eighteenth century Quakerism' in *Signs: Journal of Women in Culture and Society*, vol 29, no 1, (2003).

Madden, Lionel (ed.), *Methodism in Wales: a short history of the Wesley tradition* (Llandudno, 2003).

Maddock, Ian J., 'The Whole World is now my parish' in Ian J. Maddock (ed.), *Wesley and Whitefield? Wesley versus Whitefield?* (Eugene, OR, 2019).

Maddox, Randy (ed.), *Aldersgate Reconsidered* (Nashville, 1990).

Malmgreen, Gail (ed.), *Religion in the Lives of English Women 1760-1930* (London and Bloomington, IN, 1986).

Mathers, Helen, 'The Evangelical Spirituality of a Victorian Feminist: Josephine Butler, 1828-1906' in *Journal of Ecclesiastical History*, vol 52, no 2, (2001), 282-312.

Megan, Siân, *Gwaith Ann Griffiths* (Llandybie, 1982).

Methodist Church, *Conference Agenda* (London or Peterborough).

—, *Hymns and Psalms* (Peterborough, 1983).

—, *Methodist Worship Book* (Peterborough, 1999).

Methodist Faith and Order Report on Inclusive Language and Imagery of God (Peterborough, 1992),

Milburn, Geoffrey, *Primitive Methodism* (Peterborough, 1992).

—, 'The Ranters in Hexhamshire' in *Hexham Historian*, vol 2, (1992).

—, and Margaret Batty (eds), *Workaday Preachers: the story of Methodist local preaching* (Peterborough, 1995).

Morgan, E. Athan, 'The Wesleys and Fonmon Castle, Glamorgan' in *Bathafarn: the Journal of the Historical Society of the Methodist Church in Wales*, vol 9, (1954), 38-41.

Morgan-Guy, John, '"Tinkers and other vermin": Methodists and the established church in Wales 1730–1800' in Dyfed W. Roberts (ed.), *Revival, Renewal and the Holy Spirit* (Milton Keynes, 2009), pp. 27-35.

Newton, John A., *Susanna Wesley and the Puritan Tradition in Methodism* (London, 1968).

Niebuhr, H. Richard, *Christ and Culture* (New York, 1951).

—, *The Meaning of Revelation* (New York, 1941; pb. 1960), pp. 44-5.

Norris, Clive Murray, *The Financing of John Wesley's Methodism c.1740-1800* (Oxford, 2017).

Noll, Mark, *The Rise of Evangelicalism* (Manchester, 2004).

Obelkevich, James, *Religion and Rural Society: South Lindsey, 1825–1875* (Oxford, 1976).

Overton, John H., *The Nonjurors, their Lives, Principles and Writings* (London, 1902).

Owen, Goronwy P. (ed.), *Atgofion John Evans Y Bala: Y Diwygiad Methodistaidd ym Meirionnydd a Môn* (Caernarfon, 1997).

Parlby, William, 'Diana Thomas of Kington: lay preacher in the Hereford Circuit 1759-1821', *PWHS*, vol 14, (1921), 110-1.

Patterson, William M., *Behind the Stars* (Queensland, 1974).

Paxman, David B., 'Imaging the Child: bad parents in the mid-eighteenth-century English novel' in *Journal of Eighteenth-Century Studies*, vol 38, no 1, (2015), 135-51.

Pelikan, Jaroslav, *The Christian Tradition: a history of the development of doctrine* (Chicago and London, 1971-91).

—, *The Vindication of Tradition* (New Haven, 1986).

Pestana, Carla G., 'Whitefield and Empire' in Geordan Hammond and David Ceri Jones (eds), *George Whitefield: life, context and legacy* (Oxford, 2016).

Picard, Liza, *Dr. Johnson's London: coffee-houses and climbing boys, medicine, toothpaste and gin, poverty and press-gangs, freakshows and female education* (London, 2000).

Pope-Levison, Priscilla, 'Pentecost in the Churches: Women in the Pentecostal League of Prayer' in *WMS*, vol 10, no 1, (2018), 46-65.

Porter, Roy, *England in the Eighteenth Century* (London, 1998).

Pryce, W., 'The Diffusion of the "Welch" Circulating Schools in Eighteenth-century Wales', *Welsh History Review*, vol 25, (2011), 486-519.

Quiller-Couch, Arthur, *Hetty Wesley* (New York and London, 1903).

Rack, Henry D., *Reasonable Enthusiast: John Wesley and the rise of Methodism* (London, 1989).

[The] Ranters Digest.

Raser, Harold, *Phoebe Palmer, Her Life and Thought* (New York, 1987).

—, '"Holding Tightly to the Promise of the Father": Phoebe Palmer and the legacy of the Fletchers in Mid-Nineteenth-Century Methodism' in Hammond and Forsaith (eds), *Religion, Gender and Industry: exploring church and Methodism in a local setting* (Eugene, OR, 2011), pp. 173-88.

Richey, Russell E., 'Methodism and Providence' in Keith Robbins (ed.), *Studies in Church History Subsidia 7: Protestant evangelicalism: Britain, Ireland, Germany and America c.1750 – c.1950* (Oxford, 1990).

Rivers, Isabel, *Vanity Fair and the Celestial City: Dissenting, Methodist, and evangelical literary culture in England 1720-1800* (Oxford, 2018).

Roberts, Gomer M., *Methodistiaeth Gynnar Gwaelod Sir Aberteifi*, Offprint of *Ceredigion, Journals of the Cardiganshire Antiquarian Society*, vol 5, no 1, (1964).

—, 'Y Llafurwyr Cynnar' in Gomer M. Roberts (ed.), *Hanes Methodistiaeth Galfinaidd Cymru: Cyfrol I: Y Deffroad Mawr* (Caernarfon, 1973).

—, 'O Nerth i Nerth' in Gomer M. Roberts (ed.), *Hanes Methodistiaeth Galfinaidd Cymru, Cyfrol II: Cynnydd y Corff* (Caernarfon, 1978).

Rose, Edward A., *Methodism in Cheshire to 1800* (Wilmslow, 1975).

—, 'Local Preachers and the Preaching Plan' in Geoffrey Milburn and Margaret Batty (eds), *Workaday Preachers: the story of Methodist local preaching* (Peterborough, 1995), pp. 143-64.

Rowden, Harold H., 'Waldegrave, Granville Augustus William, third Baron Radstock (1813-1913)' in *Oxford Dictionary of National Biography* (Oxford, 2004), vol 56, pp. 767-8.

Ryan, Linda A., *John Wesley and the Education of Children: gender, class and piety* (London, 2018).

—, 'John Wesley and the Teleology of Education' in William Gibson, D. O'Brien and M. Turda (eds), *Teleology and Modernity* (Abingdon, 2019), pp. 56-68.

Sackett, Alfred B., *John Jones: first after the Wesleys*, WHS Publication no 7, (Broxton, 1972).

Scotland, Nigel, *Apostles of the Spirit and Fire: American Revivalists and Victorian Britain*, Studies in Evangelical History and Thought, (Milton Keynes, 2009).

Shaw, Thomas, *The Bible Christians 1815-1907* (London, 1965).

—, and Short, Colin C., *Feet of Clay: the life and ministry of William O'Bryan, founder of the Bible Christians* (Porthleven, 2007).

Shercliff, Liz, *Preaching Women: gender, power and the pulpit* (London, 2019).

Shiman, Lillian Lewis, '"Changes are dangerous": Women and Temperance in Victorian England' in G. Malmgreen (ed.), *Religion in the Lives of English Women* (London and Bloomington, IN, 1986), pp. 193-215.

Shorney, David M., '"Women may preach but men must govern": Gender Roles in the Growth of the Development of the Bible Christian Denomination' in R. N. Swanson (ed.), *Gender and Christian Religion*, Studies in Church History 34 (Woodbridge, 1998), pp. 309-22.

Short, Colin C., *Durham Colliers and West Country Methodists* (Kidderminster, 1995).

—, *O'Bryan's Hymns* (Oxford, 2006).

Shrubb, Michael, *Feasting, Fowling and Feathers: a history of the exploitation of wild birds* (London, 2013).

Smith, Timothy L., *Revivalism and Social Reform: American Protestantism on the eve of the Civil War* (Nashville, 1957).

Snowden, Rita F., *Such a Woman: the story of Susanna Wesley* (London, 1963).

Spender, Dale, *Man Made Language* (London, 1980).

Stamp, William W., *The Orphan-house of Wesley, with notices of Early Methodism in Newcastle-upon-Tyne, and its vicinity* (London, 1863).

Stevenson, George J., *Memorials of the Wesley Family: including biographical and historical sketches of all the members of the family for two hundred and fifty years* (London, 1876).

Stott, Anne, 'Women and Religion' in Hannah Barker and Elaine Chalus (eds), *Women`s History: Britain 1700-1850: an introduction* (London, 2005).

Swift, Rowland C., *Lively People: Methodism in Nottingham 1740-1979* (Nottingham, 1982).

Swift, Wesley F., *The Romance of Banffshire Methodism* (Banff, 1927).

—, 'Women Itinerant Preachers of Early Methodism' in *PWHS*, vol 28, (1951-2), 89-94.

Sykes, Richard (ed.), *Beyond the Boundaries: preaching in the Wesleyan tradition* (Oxford, 1998).

Taves, Ann, *Fits, Trances and Visions: experiencing religion and explaining experience from Wesley to James* (Princeton, 1999).

Thompson, Edwin, '*This Remarkable Family*': a study of the Barritts of Foulridge 1750-1850, compiled from the memoirs and correspondence of the family* (Barnoldswick, 1981).

Tolley, Christopher, *Domestic Biography: the legacy of evangelicalism in four nineteenth-century families* (Oxford, 1997).

Tudur, Geraint, *Howell Harris: from conversion to separation 1735–1750* (Cardiff, 2000).

—, 'Papurau Howel Harris' in Geraint H. Jenkins (ed.), *Cof Cenedl XVI* (Llandysul, 2001), pp. 67-94.

Turner, John Munsey (ed.), *Methodism and Ministry: the ministry of women and men, unity and the future of Methodism. Articles by Rupert E. Davies* (Peterborough, 1993).

—, 'Methodism in England 1900-1932' in Davies, Rupert E., A. Raymond George and E. Gordon Rupp (eds), *History of Methodism in Great Britain*, vol 3, (London, 1983).

Tyerman, Luke, *The Life and Times of the Rev. Samuel Wesley MA, Rector of Epworth and Father of the Revs John and Charles Wesley* (London, 1866).

Valenze, Deborah, *Prophetic Sons and Daughters* (Princeton, 1985).

Vermes, Geza, *Jesus the Jew: a historian's reading of the Gospels* (Minneapolis, 1973).

Vickers, John (ed.), *A Dictionary of Methodism in Britain and Ireland* (Peterborough, 2000).

Vickery, Amanda, 'Golden Age to Separate Spheres? A Review of the Categories and Chronology of English Women's History' in *The Historical Journal*, vol 36, no 2, (1993), 383–414.

Virgoe, Norma (ed.), *Angels and Impudent Women: women in Methodism—papers given at the 2005 Conference of the Wesley Historical Society* (Loughborough, 2007).

Wallace, Charles jr, 'Charles Wesley and Susanna' in Kenneth G. C. Newport and Ted A. Campbell (eds), *Charles Wesley: life, literature and legacy* (Peterborough, 2007).

Walmsley, Robert, 'John Wesley's Parents: Quarrel and Reconciliation' in *PWHS*, vol 29, no 3, (1953-4), 50-7.

Walsh, John, 'Origins of the Evangelical Revival' in Gareth V. Bennett and John Walsh (eds), *Essays in Modern Church History in Memory of Norman Sykes* (London, 1966).

—, 'Religious Societies; Methodist and Evangelical' in W. J. Shiels and D. Wood (eds), *Voluntary Religion* (Oxford, 1986), pp. 279-302.

Ward, W. Reginald, *Religion and Society in England 1790-1850* (London, 1972).

—, 'The legacy of John Wesley: the pastoral office in Britain and America' in Anne Whiteman, J. S. Bromley and P. G. M. Dickson (eds), *Statesmen, Scholars and Merchants: essays in eighteenth-century history presented to Dame Lucy Sutherland* (Oxford, 1973), reprinted in Andrew Chandler (ed.), *The Selected Writings of W. R. Ward* (Farnham, 2014).

Warner, Laceye C., *Saving Women: retrieving evangelistic theory and practice* (Waco, TX, 2007).

Watson, Pauline, *'Two Scrubby Travellers': a psychoanalytic view of flourishing and constraint in religion through the lives of John and Charles Wesley* (Abingdon, 2018).

Wearmouth, Robert F., *Methodism and the Common People of the Eighteenth Century* (London, 1945).

Weatherhead, Leslie D., *The Christian Agnostic* (London, 1965).

Webb, Pauline, *World-Wide Webb: journeys in faith and hope* (Norwich, 2006).

Werner, Julia S., *The Primitive Methodist Connexion: its background and early history* (Wisconsin, 1984).

White, Charles E., *The Beauty of Holiness: Phoebe Palmer as theologian, revivalist, feminist, and humanitarian* (Grand Rapids, 1986).

White, Eryn M., *The Welsh Bible* (Stroud, 2007).

—, *The Welsh Methodist Society: the early societies in south-west Wales 1737–1750* (Cardiff, 2020).

—, 'Popular Schooling and the Welsh Language 1650–1800' in Geraint H. Jenkins (ed.), *The Welsh Language before the Industrial Revolution* (Cardiff, 1997), pp. 324-37.

—, 'The Established Church, Dissent and the Welsh Language' in Jenkins (ed.), *The Welsh Language before the Industrial Revolution* (Cardiff, 1997), pp. 235-87.

—, 'Women in the Early Methodist Societies in Wales', *Journal of Welsh Religious History*, 7 (1999), 95-108.

—, 'Women, Religion and Education' in S. Clarke and M. Roberts (eds), *Women and Gender in Early Modern Wales* (Cardiff, 2000), pp. 210-33.

—, 'Whitefield, Wesley and Wales' in *PWHS*, vol 58, no 3, (2011), 136-50.

Williams, Glanmor, *Welsh Reformation Essays* (Cardiff, 1967).

—, *The Welsh and their Religion: historical essays* (Cardiff, 1991).

—, William Jacob, Nigel Yates and Frances Knight, *The Welsh Church from Reformation to Disestablishment, 1603–1920* (Cardiff, 2007).

Williams, Siân R., 'The true "Cymraes": Images of women in women's nineteenth century Welsh periodicals' in Angela V. John (ed.), *Our Mother's Land: chapters in Welsh women's history, 1830–1939* (Cardiff, 1991), pp. 69-91.

Wilson, David R., *Church and Chapel in Industrializing Society: Anglican ministry and Methodism in Shropshire, 1760-1785* (New York, 2017).

—, '"Thou shal[t] walk with me in white": Afterlife and Vocation in the Ministry of Mary Bosanquet Fletcher' in *WMS*, vol 1, (2009), 71-85.

Wilson, Linda, *Constrained by Zeal: female spirituality amongst Nonconformists, 1825–1875*, Studies in Evangelical History and Thought (Milton Keynes, 2000).

Wood, Laurence W., *The Meaning of Pentecost in Early Methodism: rediscovering John Fletcher as John Wesley's vindicator and designated successor* (Lanham, MD, 2002).

Woodley, S., '"Oh Miserable and Most Ruinous Measure": the debate between private and public education in Britain, 1760-1800' in Mary Hilton and Jill Shefrin (eds), *Educating the Child in Enlightenment Britain: beliefs, cultures, practices* (Farnham, 2009), pp. 21-40.

Yates, Kelly D., 'Jeffrey the Jacobite Poltergeist: the politics of the ghost that haunted the Epworth rectory in 1716-17' in *Wesleyan Theological Journal*, (2015), pp. 68-79.

Youngson, Michaela, *The Weaver, the Word and Wisdom: worshipping the triune God* (Werrington, 2007).

Theses and unpublished material

Batty, Margaret, 'The contribution of local preachers to the life of the Wesleyan Methodist Church until 1932, and to the Methodist Church after 1932, in England', University of Leeds PhD thesis, 1969.

Everson, Elisa A., '"A Little Labour of Love": The Extraordinary Career of Dorothy Ripley, Female Evangelist in Early America', Georgia State University PhD thesis, 2007.

Graham, E. Dorothy, 'Chosen by God: the female itinerants of early Primitive Methodism', PhD thesis (Birmingham, 1986).

Johnson, Melvin, 'The National Politics and Politicians of Primitive Methodism: 1886-1922', University of Hull PhD thesis, 2016.

Potter, Claire, 'The Influence of Danish Missionaries to India on Susanna Wesley's Methods of Education and Inspiration, and the Subsequent Influence on John Wesley', unpublished paper given at the Oxford Institute of Methodist Theological Studies, (August 2013).

Yould, Guy M., 'The origins and transformation of the Non-juror schism, 1670-1715: illustrated by special reference to the career, writings and activities of Dr. George Hickes, 1642-1715', University of Hull PhD thesis, (1979).

On-line sources

Aletha's Journal (30 July 2019) quoting Susanna Wesley: http://www.cometothefire.org/alethasjournal/2019/7/30/the-fruit-of-one-mothers-prayers. Accessed 10 July 2020.

Batchelor, Jenny, 'Mary Astell'; *The Literary Encyclopedia* https://www.litencyc.com/php/speople.php?UID=168&rec=true. Accessed 29 August 2020.

Beddoe, Deirdre, 'Rees, Sarah Jane [pseud. Cranogwen] (1839–1916), sailor, schoolmistress, and poet', *Oxford Dictionary of National Biography* (2007). https://www.oxforddnb.com/view/10.1093/ref:odnb/978019861

4128.001.0001/odnb-9780198614128-e-48648. Accessed 5 August 2020.

Dolman, Robert, 'Rough Informal Energy: The Story of Primitive Methodism', a talk given at Castle Street Methodist Church, Cambridge (31 May 2007). https://www.castlestreet.org.uk/rough-informal-energy-the-story-of-primitive-methodism/. Accessed 20 June 2020.

Graham, E. Dorothy, 'Female itinerants of early Primitive Methodism, with special reference to those stationed in missionary situations' (2005). http://www.methodistheritage.org.uk/missionary-history-graham-female-itinerants-2005.pdf. Accessed 10 June 2020.

—, 'The Wesley Deaconess Order 1890-1978', https://www.primitivemethodistwomen.org/the-wesley-deaconess-order/ Accessed 2 September 2020.

—, 'Women in Methodism and other topics', https://www.primitivemethodistwomen.org/ Accessed 2 September 2020.

Johnson, Melvin, 'The National Politics and Politicians of Primitive Methodism: 1886-1922', University of PhD thesis, 2016, https://hydra.hull.ac.uk/assets/hull:15456a/content. Accessed 11 June 2020.

Lepore, Jill, 'How to write a paper for this class' (2009) https://scholar.harvard.edu/files/jlepore/files/lepore_how_to_write_a_paper_2009_0_1.pdf Accessed 2 September 2020.

Lightfoot, John, *The Power of Faith and Prayer exemplified in the Life and Labours of Mary Porteus* (London, 1862). https://www.myprimitivemethodists.org.uk/content/people-2/primitive_methodist ministers/p/mary_porteous_nee_thompson. Accessed 20 June 2020.

The Methodist Church, The history of the Methodist Diaconal Order, Wesleyan Deaconesses. https://www.methodist.org.uk/about-us/the-methodist-church/the-diaconal-order/the-history of-the-methodist-diaconal-order/. Accessed 25 April 2020.

The Methodist Church, (17 June 2014) Methodist Church celebrates 40 years of women's ordination.

https://www.methodist.org.uk/about-us/news/latest-news/all-news/methodist-church-celebrates-40-years-of-women-s-ordination/. Accessed 11 June 2020.

Mills, Joan, *What are our thoughts on Women Preachers? The female itinerant preachers of the Bible Christian Church.* Access https://dcx0k27cd6yp9.cloudfront.net/wp-content/uploads/2015/04/The-Female-Itinerant-Preachers-of-the-Bible-Christian-Church.pdf. Accessed 2 September 2020.

My Primitive Methodists, 'William Antliff', https://www.myprimitivemethodists.org.uk/content/people2/primitive_methodist_ministers/a-2/william_antliff_dd. Accessed 13 June 2020.

My Primitive Methodists, 'Elizabeth Elliot', https://www.myprimitivemethodists.org.uk/content/people-2/lay-people/surnames-beginning-with-e/elizabeth_elliot_1810-25_of_oswestry. Accessed 11 June 2020.

My Primitive Methodists, 'Ethel Snowden', https://www.myprimitivemethodists.org.uk/content/people-2/lay-people/surnames-beginning-with-s/snowden-ethel-nee-annakin-1881-1951. Accessed 12 June 2020.

My Primitive Methodists, 'John Swales', https://www.myprimitivemethodists.org.uk/content/people2/primitive_methodist_ministers/s-2/john-swales. Accessed 12 June 2020.

Oxford Centre for Methodism and Church History at Oxford Brookes University YouTube channel, https://www.youtube.com/channel/UCplXKBopIZBtsrj02WUSZJw/videos (accessed 8 November 2020).

Palmer, Phoebe, digital image: Image available via digital collections https://digitalcollections.nypl.org/items/79c1ff9c-c2a5-9f57-e040-e00a18061f18. Accessed 20 July 2020.

Patmore, Coventry, 'Angel in the House' (1854) https://en.wikipedia.org/wiki/The_Angel_in_the_House#The_poem. Accessed 11 June 2020.

Personalpedia.wordpress, 'Dorothy Ripley (1767-1832) Believe it or Not', https://personalpedia.wordpress.com/2008/06/10/dorothy-ripley-1767-1832-believe-it-or-not/. Accessed 10 June 2020.

Vickers, John (ed.), *A Dictionary of Methodism in Britain and Ireland* (Peterborough, 2000). http://dmbi.online/#:~:text=Welcome,holders%2C%20the%20Methodist%20Publishing%20House. Accessed 10 August 2020 et al.

Watts, Isaac, 'O for a strong, a lasting faith' https://hymnary.org/text/o_for_a_strong_a_lasting_faith. Accessed 30 October 2019.

Westbrook, Robert, book review dated 8 April 2019 in *The Christian Century*, vol 24, (2019), https://www.christiancentury.org/review/books/jill-lepore-s-book-civics-course-americans-need/. Accessed 2 October 2020.

Youngson, Michaela, 'Gracious God, you call your people' (2014) https://www.methodist.org.uk/our-faith/worship/singing-the-faith-plus/posts/gracious-god-you-call-your-people-website-only/. Accessed 15 September 2020.

Biblical References

Exodus 2:4-10	316n.
Exodus 15:26	229n.
Exodus 20:5	237n.
Numbers 11:29	240n.
Numbers 19:7-22	319
Numbers 20:1-2	319
1 Samuel 3:18	83n.
Nehemiah 6:7	239
Proverbs 29:1	123n.
Isaiah 45:2	132
Isaiah 58:1	129n.
Joel 2:28-9	255, 258
Matthew 18:20	195n.
Mark 16:15	240n.
Luke 4:13	129n.
John 4:5-42	302
John 11:28	178n.
Acts 2	247
Acts 2:1-14	189n.
Acts 2:17	273
Acts 2:18	255n.
Romans 10:9-10	245
Romans 12:1	247
1 Corinthians 1:27	273
1 Corinthians 9:16	176n., 190n.
1 Corinthians 14:34-5	90n., 180, 273
2 Corinthians 6:16-7:1	244
Galatians 3:28	288n.
1 Timothy 2:11-13	90n.
2 Timothy 1:6	182n.
1 Peter	227
1 Peter 4:8	146n.

Index

Aberystwyth, Cardigan. 118, 137
Abraham, Charles 171
activism, of women 95, 111, 223, 228
agency, individual 16, 24, 27, 95, 127, 172
Aitken, Robert 223
Aitken, William 223, 231
Aldersgate Street, London 244
Allen, Elizabeth 154, 160-1
Alnwick, Northumb. 142
Altrincham, Ches. 242
America 23, 25-6, 79-80, 93-4, 123, 133n, 162, 166, 238, 253, 261n, 276-7, 280-1,
    see also Declaration of Independence; Revolution, American
American evangelists 210, 211, 229, 250, 255, 277
American Historical Association 15
American Methodist Episcopal Church 94, 238
American Society of Church History 15
Annakin, Ethel 279
    see also Snowden, Mrs Philip
Anne, Queen 37
Annesley, Samuel [Susanna Wesley's brother] 46-7

Annesley, Samuel [father] 33, 44n, 45n, 57
Annesley, Susanna 24, 33, 46
    see also Wesley, Susanna
Ansdell, Jane 165-6
    see also Suddard(s), Jane
Antigua 134, 139
Antliff, William 269-70
Arminian Magazine 6, 46, 59, 65, 72
Arminian Methodists 156, 274
Arminian theology 23, 76 151
Armstrong, George 284
Arthur, William 221, 231
Ashford, Kent 204
Association [Calvinistic Methodist] 101-7, 111, 119
Astell, Mary 40, 42, 54, 65
Atkinson, Juliette 216
Atkinson, Robert 160
Attwood, Mrs 302
Australia 193
authority 8, 27, 30, 53, 259
    of the church 44
    in marriage/family 32, 40-1, 52-3, 60
    of men 40, 52, 211
    of ministers and preachers 87, 99, 146-7, 153, 211-12, 259, 281
    see also patriarchal society

Printed in Poland
by Amazon Fulfillment
Poland Sp. z o.o., Wrocław
07 October 2021

375d9cf3-c0a4-42b3-99e3-a95a0fd54810R01